ENGLISH FI

A Dictionary

ENGLISH FIELD-NAMES
A Dictionary

John Field

ALAN SUTTON
1989

ALAN SUTTON PUBLISHING
BRUNSWICK ROAD · GLOUCESTER · UK

ALAN SUTTON PUBLISHING INC
WOLFEBORO · NEW HAMPSHIRE · USA

First published 1972

British Library Cataloguing in Publication Data

Field, John, *1921–*
English field names.
1. England. Fields. Names
I. Title
914.2′0014

ISBN 0-86299-591-4

Cover photograph: Trevor Rowley

Printed in Great Britain by
The Guernsey Press Company Limited,
Guernsey, Channel Islands.

CONTENTS

INTRODUCTION

Scope of the work

Field-names may be defined as the names of all pieces of land forming part of the agrarian economy of a town or village. The term thus excludes the names of streets, industrial sites, mineral workings, mountains, forests, and similar areas, the names of which are studied elsewhere, though agricultural land adjoining such features may be named from them. Many town-dwellers are surprised to learn that every piece of land under cultivation bears a name of its own. Although the casual visitor to the countryside seldom hears these names, they are in constant use by those who (in any sense) live by the land. The names are more frequently used in speech than in writing, and, compared with records containing major place-names, there are fewer documents to provide convenient sources for the field-name collector. This also partly accounts for field-names being less permanent than major place-names—a complicating factor in the pursuit of the early forms necessary for a firmly based interpretation of any place-name. Other difficulties result from the many boundary changes and rearrangements brought about by the enclosure of open fields, and by random and sometimes inexplicable renaming of individual pieces of land.

Major place-names (ie the names of counties, towns, villages, etc) have been objects of scholarly interest for a very long time, but field-names received little attention until about forty years ago. The inclusion of lists of field-names in *The Place-Names of Northamptonshire* (1933) was regarded as a remarkable innovation. Subsequent volumes published by the English Place-Name Society have included longer and longer lists, and the seven or eight hundred field-names cited for Northamptonshire are now seen to be a very small beginning indeed when placed against those in recent volumes of the Society. In the Cheshire volumes, for instance, lists amounting to several hundreds of names are by no means unusual for individual parishes.

This growing attention is not entirely accounted for by the progress of place-name studies. Place-name specialists have an interest (primarily linguistic) in the names for their own sake, or for the sake of conclusions that can be drawn from them regarding the language of those who first used the names;[1] but both they and other scholars will look beyond the structure and meaning of the words to the external significance of the field-names. Agricultural historians will find in many names indications of the agrarian past of the locality—the layout of former open fields, crops grown centuries ago, changes in the use of land, and so on. Genealogists and students of local history will find, embodied in some names, the names of families formerly owning or occupying particular pieces of land. For the archaeologist field-names provide clues to ancient earthworks and tumuli and to buildings of long ago, the only other evidence of which lies buried beneath the soil.

On a more mundane level, field-names provide a supply of ready-made street names when the land is built on, and this very fact has provided a starting point for many ordinary people who are interested in the history of their own neighbourhood. Other people collect the names out of the fascination that the picturesqueness of many examples holds for them. But, whatever may be the reason for the interest, sooner or later comes the enquiry: 'What does this name mean?' The aim of the present work is to go some way towards supplying an answer. It can hardly be expected, for reasons set out below, that every possible field-name should be listed here, but at least some general guidance may be found in interpreting those that are not included. It cannot be too often repeated that modern forms of names are not a reliable basis for explanation; early forms must be hunted out. Quite often the meaning of these will not be hard to find, though training and experience are required to arrive at the interpretation of a good many names.

Most of the examples included in this book are nineteenth-century or current names, a major source of information being the many Tithe Apportionment documents of the first half of last century. Earlier names have been recovered from a great variety of private and public records, most, of course, relating to land transactions. When it is realised that in 1871 there were more than 23 million acres of arable and pasture land in England, the possibility of a complete enumeration of field-names will be seen to be remote. It is obvious that only a small proportion can be studied in a single volume, and the making of a representative selection has been one of the principal problems in the compilation of this book.

In the making of the selection, certain principles have been followed. An attempt has been made to include a substantial number of examples in every category of field-name. Details of the classification will be found in Appendix 2. Rare names, especially those for which no plausible explanation could be offered, have normally been excluded; 'ownership' names (such as Brown's Meadow or Jackson's Close) have been omitted on account of sheer weight of numbers, as explained below on p xviii. All forms known to the author have been recorded of names selected for inclusion, as well as the names of all townships where these forms occur.

Fields, furlongs, and closes

The meaning of the word *field* itself has changed during the twelve hundred years of its recorded existence in English. The term was first used to distinguish the areas cleared of trees from the tracts of forest found by the earliest settlers in Britain. In this sense of 'open country' the word is an element in certain major place-names, such as Hatfield, Sheffield, and Enfield. The cultivation of the land by the settlers brought about the transfer of the name to 'unenclosed land used for agriculture', and in those parts of the country where the system was practised, each of the main divisions of the common arable land (the 'great fields') was designated by this term, preceded by a distinguishing epithet. The great fields often received such obvious names as North Field or Near Field, or were related to some adjacent feature and called Wood Field, Mill Field, or Brook Field, or were located with reference to an adjoining parish. A survey of Carnanton, Cornwall, in 1606, names North Field, West Field, South Field, and Churchway Field.[2] Goldington in Bedfordshire had Church Field, River Field and Windmill Field;[3] in Laxton, Nottinghamshire, there were West Field, Mill Field and South Field (with an earlier fourth field, East Field, enclosed in the seventeenth century). Breedon in Leicestershire had four great fields before complete enclosure in 1758: Great Field, Wood Field, Nether Field and Dam Field.

The great fields were divided into smaller areas, known as 'furlongs' or 'shots', and these were subdivided into the strips or plots held by individual tenants. Each furlong had its own name but it is perhaps worth recording that the strip subdivisions did not, being referred to when necessary simply as the holding of a particular man within a named furlong. Furlong-names also come within the scope of the field-name student; many survive to this day as the names of modern enclosed fields.

The hedged, walled or fenced closes, the areas of land that we loosely term 'fields' today, are completely different from either the medieval open fields or their constituent furlongs. The modern unit is normally much smaller than one of the great fields, or even one of the furlongs, though in some places the recent removal of hedges to facilitate mechanised cultivation has produced tracts of land comparable in size to the medieval units. The process of enclosure, which brought about the pattern we now see in the countryside, was more gradual than is sometimes supposed. Consolidation of holdings within the open fields took place piecemeal from the fourteenth century onwards, and the transformation of entire parishes from the open-field system to the present arrangement of enclosed farms occasionally occurred well before the eighteenth century.[4] Breedon on the Hill was already partly enclosed when a map was drawn in the mid-eighteenth century. The boundaries of the closes on the north and west edges of Wood Field were left undisturbed in the enclosure of that time. In some parts of England, moreover, enclosed agriculture seems to have been practised from very early times. These considerations are relevant to field-name study, and the enclosure history of a particular place has a bearing on the origin and descent of current field-names.

The term *field-name* may thus be applied to any of three different entities—a common field under the open-field system, one of the furlongs composing an open field, or an enclosed piece of land. Although many current names arose when enclosure took place, or even more recently, a large number can be traced back through six or seven centuries to field or furlong appellations that may have been assigned before the Norman Conquest. On the other hand, hundreds of names recorded in medieval documents have now gone out of use (or, technically, have been 'lost'), but the problem of their interpretation and even their location still remains, and adds immeasurably to the interest and pleasure of field-name study.

But whether field-names are of proven antiquity or of post-enclosure origin, it will be found that the method of designating plots of land remains essentially the same now as it was in the Middle Ages. Modern fields, for instance, are often named in terms of their size, and examples of Great Close, Little Field, Big Meadow and similar names abound throughout the country. Names of the same type were used of medieval furlongs. In Shangton, Leicestershire, *Muclecroft* ('big croft') and *Smalesike* ('small streamside meadow') occur in a fourteenth-century document; and a deed of 1327 relating to Norton, Derbyshire, mentions *Le Mikelmedu* ('great meadow').

In the modern names Michael Meadow (Lowdham, Notts) and Michael Heath (St Michaels, Herts), the process known as 'popular etymology' has wrought its transforming work, substituting for a term that is no longer current (*micel*, 'great') a word that is more familiar or is regarded as more appropriate. Little 'Un, a modern name found at Hoby in Leicestershire, is probably a development of *Litil Eng*, recorded in a fourteenth-century terrier preserved in the Henry Huntington Library in California; though it retains the idea of smallness, the modern name misses the force of the second component (*eng*, 'meadow'). In another current Hoby name, Austrian Meadow, which was *Oustreng* ('eastern meadow') in the fourteenth century, both elements of the older form have been transmuted, and the etymologically superfluous word *Meadow* added. Doubtless many modern (and even earlier) names arrived at their recorded form through the influence of popular etymology, though the results are not always so picturesque as those just quoted.

Another large class of modern names comprises those referring to the ownership of the land. Names like Bennet's Close, Great Clarke's Bush, Gorman Close, and Grant's Leys commemorate some of the landowners and occupiers in Stoughton, Leicestershire, and are all to be found in the Tithe Award which was drawn up in 1845. The bearers of the surnames may well have been living when the Tithe Commissioners were at work, but a similar name in the Peterborough Enclosure Award of 1811—Hammond's Meadow—was even then several centuries old, being traceable to *Hamondesmedwe* of 1380. Sometimes an archaic form of surname indicates a medieval origin, eg Tom o' th' Hall Piece, in the Tithe Award for Edale, Derbyshire.

The form of field-names

The form of field-names, particularly of modern ones, differs from that of most major place-names in at least one important respect: whereas most major names (eg London, York, Manchester, Durham) consist of only a single word, field-names are usually two-word phrases, the single-word exceptions being far rarer than major names consisting of two or more words. Bakehouse Field, Bell Rough, Causeway Croft, Great Delight, Marl Piece, Pinfold Field, Bares Orchard, Little Rough and Wichhouse Field—all these occur in the Tithe Award for Austerson, Cheshire; in the published list,[5] thirty-one of the names consist of two or three words, and only seven are single-word names.

Apart from Great Delight, which is a special case of a name of the fanciful type, the second word in each name cited above is a generic term that occurs very frequently in every list of field-names; having been once defined, this second element, which for ease of reference may be called the *denominative* component, can be left aside when a name is being interpreted. It so happens that the first words in the list above—the *qualifiers*—bear more or less obvious meanings, though this is not to say that the interpretation of the names presents no difficulties.

Definitions and explanations in the dictionary section of this work are, therefore, normally restricted to the qualifiers; in any one entry, examples of names may be given in which the same or a related qualifier occurs, with numerous denominatives, in a wide range of places. For this reason, the definition is usually worded '... ... land', or 'piece of land which . . .', and so on, so that separate explanations of Close, Furlong, Field, Leasow, Sike, etc, are not required within any single entry, but are listed and defined in Appendix 1.

Many denominatives are, in fact, 'significant words', ie in addition to their use as proper names they are employed in other linguistic contexts as common nouns; though, in some field-names, the denominatives have undergone some modification, there has not been the same general development of these components as there has of great numbers of qualifiers. *Croft* is one of the few notable exceptions to this rule, being found in numerous interesting guises.

It is this transmutation of names that requires to be systematically explained by place-name scholars. Interpretation is not the intuitive understanding of a name, but a disciplined analysis of possible meanings, based on established principles. The first prerequisite in the elucidation of a field-name, as of any other place-name, is the tracing of early forms of the name, a process that is often more disappointing in field-name research, however, than in the study of major names. Not only are most place-names longer-lived than many field-names, but the latter tend to be mentioned less in documents than the former. A well-documented sequence of names can often be adduced to support a place-name interpretation; such a sequence is unusual for field-names, though there are some impressive exceptions.

The longevity of field-names

The idea that all field-names enjoy but a short life must be resisted, and the following examples show that survival through seven or even eight centuries is by no means impossible:

Bambrick (Warton, Lancs): *Baunebrec* c 1230 ('bean hill')
Clay Furlong, (Everdon, Northants): *Claifurlong* 1240
Dead Hills Field (Ely, Cambs): *Dedhil* c 1195
Great Lands (Crosby Ravensworth, Westmorland): *Gretelandes* c 1210
Home Field (East Barnet, Herts): *Le Homfeld* 1267
Long Crote (Harpenden, Herts): *Langecroft* 1220
Longlands (Lowther, Westmorland): *Langelandes* c 1240
Mill Field (Lea, Lancs): *Mulnefeld* c 1265
The Moor (Whaddon, Cambs): *Le Mor* 1309

Norcroft (Eakring, Notts): *Northcroft* c 1200
Rough Mead (Calne, Wilts): *Rouwemede* 1232
Rubborough Meadow (Farnborough, Warwickshire): *Rouburgh* 1246 ('rough hill')
Sowerbutts (Winmarleigh, Lancs): *Le Sourbut* c 1220

Forms as early as those quoted can be traced for many names in every county, and modern names can be found in some counties in direct succession from names recorded in Saxon land charters.

At the other end of the time-scale, Gas Close is the name of a piece of land adjoining the Kibworth gas works in Leicestershire; Navigation Close is found in several places as the name of a field beside a canal. Pylons, recorded in Dorset at Whitchurch Canonicorum and Lytchett Minster, registers the impact of further technological progress. Similarly, alongside names commemorating famous events of military history such as Blenheim, Maida, and Waterloo (for which see the appropriate entries in the Dictionary) can be placed field-names recalling a more recent conflict, eg Bomb Crater at Corfe Castle in Dorset, and Bomb Holes at Buckland Ripers in the same county.[6]

Names celebrating historical events are only a small proportion of the total. They will, indeed, have only a limited interest for those seeking early forms, since these names are obviously of no greater antiquity than the events they commemorate. Such names, however, contribute to the present-day picture, and are as worthy of collection and study as those in any other class.

Classification of field-names

A tentative classification of field-names, with a few examples of each type, is tabulated in Appendix 2. It may be appropriate here to say something about the categories in the classification. The basis of the division is the significance of the names, and so the qualifier normally determines the class to which a name is assigned.

The first classes comprise names related directly to such measurable quantities as size and distance; very common names, such as Five Acres, belong here, as do North Field and First Close. Even of these, questions can be asked. How big are the fields called Great Close? Are there variations from county to county? Do acreage names declare the exact areas of the fields?

Only fragmentary conclusions can be drawn from select lists, but in the alphabetical entries of the Dictionary a good sample of references is provided for all the recorded acreages, from Half Acre to Twenty Acres and above. The ironic use of some large numbers is duly noted, but the literal reference of Four Hundred Down and Thirteen Hundred Down (both in Westbury, Wilts) is also worthy of remark.[7]

Transferred names for remote and other fields often attract considerable notice. Not only America and Newfoundland, China and Dunkirk, Scotland and the Isle of Elba, but also Jerusalem, Canaan, and Babylon are evoked to suggest the tedium of the labourer's journey to land on the very edge of the parish or farm. The numerous examples of Bunker's Hill are well known. The editors of *Place-Names of Hertfordshire* expressed doubt about its connexion with the place in Massachusetts where General Howe defeated the colonial forces in 1775. Bunkers Farm in Abbots Langley, the editors argued, was to be associated with a family referred to in fifteenth-century documents.[8] This may be so, but the different denominative (*Farm* rather than *Hill*) may be very significant, and it is noteworthy that no examples of Bunker's Hill have been found earlier in date than the battle, so that it is probable that the usual explanation is the right one.[9]

Fanciful names also occur in other categories; among the names relating to soil, for example, are to be found Featherbed and Pudding Bag, alluding respectively to soft and to sticky soil. Among the names referring to fertility and profitability fanciful examples are even more numerous. Bare Arse, Isle of Want, Dreadful, and Mountain of Poverty are but a few instances of the pejorative kind of name. On the credit side are Land of Promise, Have a Good Heart, and Paradise. The last name may be occasionally ironical, in which case it means the same as Purgatory, Hell Hole, Gomorrah, or Cain's Piece.

Other categories refer more specifically to agricultural processes and crops. Among names of these types are those relating to the state of cultivation (eg Ploughed Close, Meadow Close or Grass Leasow) and including less obvious names such as Beaten Flat, Push Ploughed Field and Gascoignes. Crops alluded to include familiar cereals (though occasionally under scarcely recognisable names) and vegetables. Fruit trees also lend their names to fields, and an interesting number of names point to a once widespread cultivation of grapes in England.

Wild plants of various kinds are also, not surprisingly, referred to in field-names; there are numerous allusions to gorse and fern in medieval furlong-names, and many other wild shrubs and herbs supplied names, either because they were troublesome, or on account of conspicuous beauty (to which it must not be supposed that rustic eyes of any period were blind) or their usefulness as herbal remedies.

References to buildings on, or adjoining, the fields include the frequent Hall Close and House Close, and what may turn out to be the most common field-name of all, Barn Close. Workhouse Field, in Croydon, Surrey, might be plausibly interpreted at its face value, but a form dated 1493 points to a different origin: the medieval name, *Workeoste*, indicates that the building was a kiln or oast.

Names of domestic and farm animals make up a large class. Among early names, Goose Acres is fairly common in the Midlands, and A. H. Smith noted the numerous instances in Westmorland of Bull Copy; it occurs no fewer than twenty-seven times in that county. The denominative signifies a small piece of woodland or scrubland, and names in other counties (Bull Piece, Bull Gores, etc) confirm Smith's observation: 'According to Caxton . . . "a great bole is suffisid with right litil pasture", and after the enclosures this seems to have been the view of the local farmers'.[10] Probably the most picturesque names in this class will be found grouped with *Goodins Ox* in the Dictionary section.

Very many modern (and not a few earlier) field-names embody personal names. These have been excluded, in general, from the alphabetical entries in this work, for several reasons. First, a complete interpretation of such names depends on the identifying of the individual or family whose name the land bears. This is not always an impossible task, but it is essentially one for the local scholar. When a field-name survey of a district or parish is undertaken, reference should be made to baptismal and other registers, wills, marriage settlements and similar documents, in an attempt to relate the piece of land to a particular family. A second and even more cogent reason for omitting 'ownership' names is their very numbers. In some parishes, the tithe lists show four-fifths of the names as belonging to this type. There is clearly scope for a detailed study of these names, but this should be accompanied by a wide range of local investigations of the kind already mentioned.

References to owners or occupiers other than by their names direct our attention to Old Woman's Close, Four Men's Field, Maiden Acre and Keeper's Close. The beneficiary of the income from land is alluded to in names in a separate category, which includes Hospital Meadow, The Prebend, and Poors Close. Ecclesiastical endowments of various kinds figure in a number of names. In addition to chantries, there are references to the maintenance of bell-ropes, church lamps and the fabric of the church building, as well as to various dignitaries whose income was provided from the rent of land.

In another category are found field-names relating to the physical elevation of the land, the gradient of slopes, or geographical features such as brooks, hillocks and waterfalls. Names alluding to roads and bridges are placed in a separate class. Shape is referred to in a number of different ways, not uncommonly by means of fanciful names such as Shoulder of Mutton.

Names which are possibly of archaeological significance will be of interest to those who are looking for signs of early settlements: Rampart Close, Five Fools Mead and Blacklands are examples of this type of name. References to the supernatural, such as Fairy Land, Goodman's Acre and Boggart Hole, occur sporadically. Possible references to pagan rites are to be detected in some names, and associated with these are allusions to traditional ceremonies.[11]

There are yet other names which seem entirely arbitrary. There is, of course, an arbitrary element in the bestowing of any name whatsoever. It was probably a matter of personal taste whether a remote field was called New York or New Zealand, but at least a notional connexion can be found between the name and the fact of the remoteness of the land. But in names commemorating historical events, no such connexion is evident, and entirely external reasons of date or mere whim account for such an appellation as Maida Hill or Waterloo Close. A group of names in Elwick Hall in Co. Durham demonstrates a pattern of commemorative naming. The names are unusual in that they have no denominatives: Duke, Blucher, Wellington, Nelson and Waterloo obviously all refer to the Napoleonic War. A similar mode of naming is found at Dalston and at Alston in the adjoining county of Cumberland.

The arbitrary name-bestower *par excellence*, however, was Thomas Hollis who in the eighteenth century named about a hundred pieces of land in Halstock, Dorset. Hollis's special interest—amounting, indeed, to something like an obsession—was the Great Rebellion. People, events and ideas that were duly celebrated included not only those connected directly with the Puritan revolution but also many from classical times. Tribute is paid to Hollis's activity by listing the names in Appendix 3.

Names alluding to boundary land (as distinct from remote fields) represent a separate category, and include No Man's Land, Ball Close and Mear Oak Close. The Rogationtide ceremonies provide a good selection of names within this class, eg Amen Corner, Luke Stone and Epistle Field. Names referring to tenure and to other legal aspects of land ownership constitute a separate category and include Proxies, Copyhold Carr and Encroachment. Perposture Field in Frensham, Surrey, and Purpresture Meadow in Haslemere, are also names of this class; these have their origin in the term *purpresture*, which means an illegal enclosure or encroachment.

Land used for industrial purposes is generally excluded from attention here, but many fields adjoining or containing mineral workings or furnaces were named from them, and so Cinder Croft, Coal Pit Close and Kill Close are typical of names given to cultivated land adjoining industrial sites. Other land had a double use: grazing land might also serve occasionally as a place for the drying of dyed or finished cloth; Dyer Lands, Frame Close, Quisters Hey and Rack Close are a few examples in this category. Land used for recreational purposes was likewise never solely so employed. When games were played on a piece of grassland, the land would be put to this use only a few times each year, so names like Football Butts should not suggest weekly fixtures from August to May. Names of the Plaistow type may refer to assemblies for serious purposes, including courts of various kinds, as well as to recreational gatherings.

Linguistic aspects of field-names

The citation of early forms and the reference to place-name

elements embodied in the field-names listed in the Dictionary will serve as a constant reminder of the linguistic basis of name studies. The Survey of English Place-Names has already demonstrated the contribution name studies have to make to information about the English language, particularly with regard to the history of its vocabulary and dialectal variations.

It is not too much to claim that the developing study of field-names will make its own special contribution to this body of knowledge. An important factor to be reckoned with in studying the early forms of major names, as H. C. Wyld pointed out long ago,[12] was the 'tendency of official scribes to spell names according to the conventional London manner', which obscured local features and regional characteristics. Documentary sources of field-names do not, for the most part, suffer this disadvantage. Estate deeds and terriers were usually written in the locality. Local compilation prevailed even to the period of the operation of the Tithe Commutation Act of 1836, when the apportionments were drawn up by commissioners resident in the area.

Field-name studies also offer the linguist a further advantage: within any one document there are likely to be a number of separate items exhibiting a peculiarity of form or spelling, in contrast with the single example offered by a major place-name. In an early terrier the name of a township will obviously occur, but in the enumeration of pieces of land held by the tenant not only will various denominatives be repeated, such as *furlong*, *shot*, *flat*, *or wong*, but a large number of different qualifiers may appear that will be of interest to the investigator.

Before the linguist can apply his own special methods to the names, the early forms must obviously be collected; in the course of general collection, particular names can be specially marked and a distribution map prepared. Variant forms of *croft*, for instance, were first noted in Surrey and Hertfordshire; subsequent surveys produced examples, and indeed additional variants, in other counties. Similarly, *pingle* seems to replace *pightle* in some areas, but in other places both are found within a single parish.[13] It would also be interesting to discover whether there is a regional pattern in the many variations of *Conery*, *Coneygree*, and *Conygar*. Even the distribution of terms like *close* and *leasow* has yet to be studied.

Many topics involving linguistic problems in connexion with

field-names would no doubt require the attention of other specialists, but the methods of the linguist could be used to assemble and assess the evidence before calling in the expert knowledge of agriculturists or agrarian historians.

Practical work in field-name studies

The names included in this book represent but a small fraction of those currently in use in England. An attempt has been made to trace examples from all parts of the country, but inevitably some counties are better represented than others. This study is still in its early years; as it advances, collections of names will doubtless become available for many areas at present unsurveyed. Some readers of this work may consult it for guidance on the meaning of a single name they may have encountered. An interpretation may be suggested for similar or analogous forms, but only the collection of early forms of the name concerned can confirm such an interpretation.

Collecting and mapping the field-names within a parish or district is an interesting and valuable activity, and if the material is assembled carefully, useful conclusions may be drawn from it. A sound basis for a collection may be established by taking the names from a parish Tithe Apportionment—sometimes in local custody, but usually to be found in the appropriate county record office.

Nineteenth-century handwriting presents few problems in transcription, but a certain self-discipline is required to ensure scrupulously accurate copies of the lists in the document. The exact spellings should be carefully adhered to, however unusual or 'wrong' they may appear to be. Moreover, all names should be collected; a judgement that particular names (eg Six Acres or Brown's Close) are too commonplace to deserve attention is a heresy into which beginners often fall. If one thing is to be learnt from this study it is that things are often not what they seem, and even if such names bear the self-evident interpretation expected, they are still not without interest. Reasons for recording commonplace names are their use in locating other pieces of land—no piece of a jigsaw puzzle is less important than another—and in establishing the variations in naming patterns between one place and another.

Tithe and similar documents are normally related to an

accompanying map, and names and other information should be, if possible, plotted on a similar map. A glance at p xxv will enable the reader to understand much more about some of the names than would be conveyed by the most detailed comments added to a list. It will be observed, for instance, that Triangle is no longer three-cornered, and the numbering suggests that the reason for this is the removal of a hedge. Similarly, the locations of Front Piece, Summerhouse Field, and Pigeonhouse Field with reference to Preston Montford Hall can also be readily seen.

Estate deeds, rent records, and estate agents' particulars of sale (which often contain detailed maps) are also valuable sources of names, supplementing or even replacing tithe documents in the compilation of basic lists.

The open-field pattern of a parish may often be ascertained from the enclosure award, though these documents are sometimes disappointingly defective in information about the names and locations of furlongs. Earlier forms of field and furlong names may be found in quantity in such records as glebe terriers (which are preserved in series, sometimes beginning in the sixteenth century, but almost always including several seventeenth-century documents) or estate deeds. Terriers are documents listing the holdings of an individual landowner or tenant, particularly necessary in the days of open-field farming: glebe terriers list the pieces of land belonging to the parish living.

Deeds referring to individual pieces of land may name furlongs (usually with the name of the great field in which they are located) possibly from the early Middle Ages onwards. Such documents may still be found in private hands but public record offices, both in the county towns and in London, hold vast stores of them. The deciphering of early handwritings requires some instruction and patient practice, but it is an attainable skill and not a mysterious gift bestowed on only a chosen few.

A good collection of names would be one in which a clear succession of forms can be found for a substantial number of modern names. Many parish series fall short of this, but may still be valuable in themselves. Although interpretation calls for training and experience, the assembling of early forms is clearly an essential prerequisite—so that the labours of enthusiastic amateur collectors are just as important as the etymological expertise of the specialist. Extra-linguistic evidence must be taken into account in the explanation of any place name,[14] and for the field-name student this implies that knowledge of the topography, history, and agrarian practices of the area is fundamental. Those who are able to investigate not only names but also the fields themselves are in the happy position of being able to contradict or confirm many tentative interpretations—a privilege often denied to the study-bound scholar.

Local collections and studies may be carried out by individuals or (perhaps better) by groups. Current field-names may be obtained by direct enquiry of owners or workers on the land. Lists compiled by this method should be laid beside similar ones derived from documents, inserting early forms when they, too, have been collected. The result of such surveys might be to produce a complete list of the names in the area, or to establish the former open-field layout, the mapping of which may call for further field work.

A study of this kind would be a useful project for an archaeological society, Women's Institute, or local history society. Adult classes in schools and colleges, and students in colleges of education, might use such studies as a basis for various kinds of inter-disciplinary work. In some counties, between the wars, valuable investigations were undertaken by children in village schools, the results being published in the county volumes of the English Place-Name Society. Despite the changes in school organisation that have taken place since 1945, there must be many places today where similar field-work could still be incorporated in the curriculum. It would make its own contribution both to the educational enlargement of those taking part and to a most interesting and valuable body of knowledge.

NOTES

1. Thus Wainwright concludes from the field-names in a document of 1322 relating to Hoby, Leicestershire, that the people there 'were still speaking a language that had much in common with the language of the Danes who had settled in the area four and a half centuries before' (*Archaeology and Place-Names and History*, 88). This section in a regrettably brief book contains a most readable discussion of fundamental points in field-name study.
2. Cf H. L. Gray, *English Field Systems*, 263.

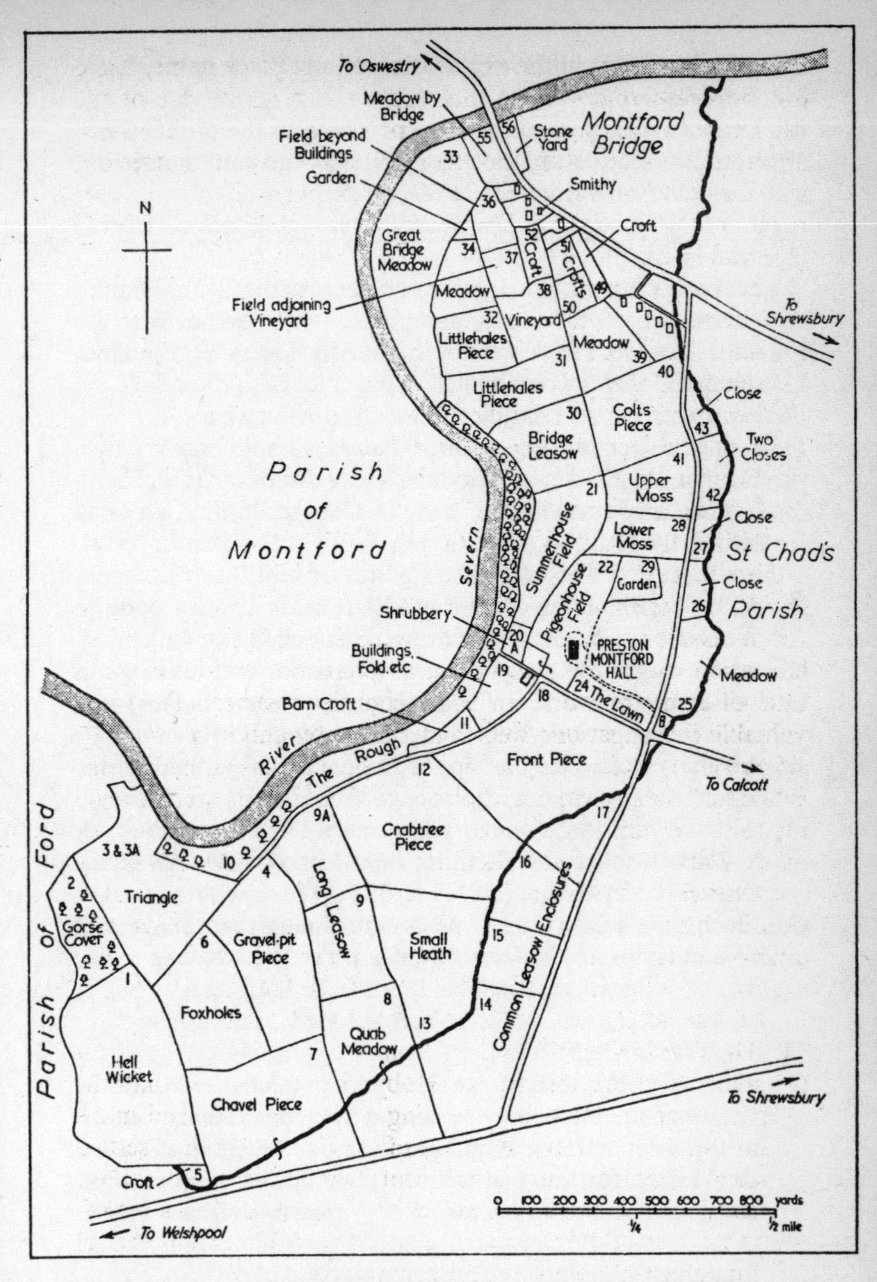

A typical enclosed township: the field pattern of the Tithe Map of Preston Montford, Shropshire

3. See the map in F. G. Emmison, *Some Types of Common-Field Parish*, 12–13.
4. For a concise summary of recent views on the progress and nature of enclosure, see Joan Thirsk, 'The common fields', *Past and Present*, No 29 (1964), 3–25.
5. J. McN. Dodgson, *The Place-Names of Cheshire* (EPNS XLVI), iii, 131.
6. Barbara Kerr ('Dorset fields and their names', 254–5) cites these and other names associated with World War II; Austerity Drove (Wareham St Martin, Dorset) dates from the peace that succeeded it.
7. For other names relating to size, see p xiii above.
8. J. E. B. Gover and others, *Place-Names of Hertfordshire*, 76–7.
9. George R. Stewart, *American Place-Names*, OUP, 1970, traces the Massachusetts name to George Bunker, an early settler. It should be noted that the form of the name in USA, where it occurs several times, is Bunker Hill.
10. A. H. Smith, *Place-Names of Westmorland*, i, 30, quoting W. Caxton, *The Game and Playe of Chesse*, 1474, 112.
11. Archaeological and supernatural references tend to merge in folk etymologies. Five Fools Mead (Shepreth, Cambs) was earlier *le fyfhowes* 13c, 'five burial mounds' [ON *haugr*]. Popular stories often attempt to account for the modern forms of such names without reference to their documented history.
12. H. C. Wyld, 'Place-names and English linguistic studies', in A. Mawer and F. M. Stenton, *Introduction to the Survey of English Place-Names*, (EPNS I), 1924, 135.
13. Among the relatively few places containing both *pingle* and *pightle* names are Hayton, Notts and the West Riding townships of Wentworth, Bradfield (*Pighehulle* 1442, *Pingles* 1433), Ecclesfield (*Pyghill* 1416, *le Pynghill* 1565), South Hiendley, and Worsborough.
14. Some consequences of ignoring topographical evidence in particular are alluded to by Wainwright, who rightly insists on the utter irrelevance of proposing a 'linguistically possible' interpretation that is known from other sources to be wrong. See *Archaeology and Place-Names and History*, 42–3.

ARRANGEMENT OF THE DICTIONARY

The dictionary entries interpret and explain the names listed. The head-words in bold type are modern names, usually from Tithe Awards (of c 1840) or later documents. Details of sources are not given, but can usually be traced from the county surveys of the English Place-Name Society. Early names (ie names believed to be no longer in use), or early forms of modern names, are printed in italics and dated.

Reference to places where the field-names are to be found is important, and the names of relevant parishes are listed immediately after the field-name. These lists are in the following order: first, alphabetically by counties, so that Devon names precede Dorset ones, and so on; then, within the county groups, parishes are also enumerated alphabetically. All county names are abbreviated in accordance with EPNS convention. An early form recorded in one of the parishes is printed in brackets after the name concerned, with the date of the document in which it occurs. Occasionally, an early form is used as a head-word; in this case it is printed in italics (and not in bold type as other head-words are) and is followed by the parish name and county abbreviation, with the date last. If a date occurs within a list of parishes following a modern name, it is to be understood that the name occurs in that form in pre-enclosure documents, but is not known to have survived to the present time.

The meaning of a name or group of related names follows the list of forms and locations. As mentioned above, the interpretation ignores the significance of particular denominatives. Thus Cleave Down, Cleave Orchard, Cleeve Acre, Cleeve Tining, Cleeves, Cleve, and Cleves are grouped together after The Cleave, and all are interpreted as 'land on a slope or bank', without the addition of separate meanings of the denominatives, for which reference may be made to Appendix 1.

Place-name elements occurring in field-names are generally inserted in square brackets after the meaning. So placed, the elements normally refer to the main qualifier of the entry. Occasionally they may be cited within the list of forms, and then they refer to particular denominatives, serving to confirm an origin suggested in Appendix 1.

ABBREVIATIONS

AN	Anglo-Norman
Angl	Anglian (dialect of Old English)
Bd	Bedfordshire
Bk	Buckinghamshire
Brk	Berkshire
c	*circa*, 'about' (c 1250, 'about 1250')
c	century (12c, 'twelfth century')
C	Cambridgeshire
Ch	Cheshire
Co	Cornwall
Cu	Cumberland
D	Devon
Dan	Danish
dat	dative case
Db	Derbyshire
dial.	dialect(al)
Do	Dorset
Du	Durham
EMidl	East Midland(s)
EMnE	Early Modern English
EPNS	English Place-Name Society
ERY	East Riding of Yorkshire
Ess	Essex
ESax	East Saxon (dialect of Old English)
Gl	Gloucestershire
GL	Greater London
Ha	Hampshire
He	Herefordshire
Hrt	Hertfordshire
Hu	Huntingdonshire
K	Kent
L	Lincolnshire
La	Lancashire
Lei	Leicestershire
ME	Middle English
Midl	Midland(s)
MnE	Modern English
Mx	Middlesex
Nb	Northumberland
NED	*A New English Dictionary* ('Oxford English Dictionary') Oxford 1933
Nf	Norfolk

NRY	North Riding of Yorkshire
Nt	Nottinghamshire
Nth	Northamptonshire
O	Oxfordshire
OE	Old English
OF	Old French
ON	Old Norse
OW	Old Welsh
OWSc	Old West Scandinavian
PN	Place-name(s); volumes of the English Place-Name Society (eg PNCh, ii, 234: '*The Place-Names of Cheshire*, volume ii, page 234'. See Bibliography, pp 282–5)
R	Rutland
Sa	Shropshire
Sc	Scandinavian
Sf	Suffolk
So	Somerset
Sr	Surrey
St	Staffordshire
Sx	Sussex
t.	tempore (t. Ed 4, 'in the time of Edward IV')
W	Wiltshire
Wa	Warwickshire
We	Westmorland
WMidl	West Midland(s)
WSax	West Saxon (dialect of Old English)
Wo	Worcestershire
WRY	West Riding of Yorkshire
Wt	Isle of Wight
*	a postulated form, ie a word found as a place-name element but lacking other exemplification

Note Counties to which parishes etc are assigned in this Dictionary are normally those of the EPNS volume(s) concerned. Changes brought about by boundary revisions since 1888 are generally ignored.

A

Abbats Hay, Elton Ch [OE *(ge)hæg*] (1); **High & Low Abbot,** Hoff We; **Abbot Bottom,** Asby We [OE *botm*] (2); **Abbot Flat,** Staveley Db [ON *flat*]; **Abbot Yard,** Pilsley Db; **Abbots Acre,** Frodsham Lordship Ch (3); **Abbots Brook,** Egham Sr (4); **Abbots Close,** Litlington C (5); **Abbots Clough,** Marley Ch [OE *clōh*] (6); **Abbots Croft,** Byley cum Yatehouse Ch (7); **Abbots Flatt,** Stublach Ch (8); **The Abbots Ground,** Oxford O; **Abbots Hay,** Prestbury Ch (9); **Abbots Hill Meadow,** Beaford D; **Abbots Mead,** Aldenham Hrt (10); **Abbots Park,** Wessington Db (11); **Abbots Pleck,** Alvechurch Wo [ME *plek*]; **Abbotts Laughton,** Hampden in Arden Wa [OE *lēac-tūn*] (12): 'land whose income contributed to the support of an abbot' [ME *abbat*]. A few examples are, however, 'land owned or occupied by a man named Abbot'. The abbots known to be referred to are (1) Chester, (2) Shap, (3) Vale Royal, (4) Egham, (5) Wymondley, (6) Chester, (7) Dieulacres, (8) Chester, (9) Chester, (10) Westminster, (11) Darley, (12) Kenilworth.

Abbey Close, Minchinhampton Gl (1); **Abbey Croft,** Warburton Ch (2); **Abbey Farm,** Histon C (3), Ickleton C (4), Wolvey Wa (5); **Abbey Hay,** Stockham Ch [OE *(ge)hæg*] (6); **Abbey Hill Nook,** Allestree Db (7); **Abbey Lands,** Chelmorton Db, Knossington Lei (8), Wroxton O (9); **Abbey Mead,** Middlezoy So; **Abbey Meadow,** Leicester Lei (10); **Abbey Moor,** Axminster D: 'land belonging to an abbey of monks or nuns' [ME *abbeye*]. The abbeys concerned, where known, were (1) Trinitarian Nuns of Caen, (2) Cockersand, (3) Eynsham, (4) Calder, (5) Combe, (6) Norton Priory, (7) Darley, (8) Owston, (9) Wroxton Priory, (10) Leicester.

Abbots Hall, Great Wigborough Ess (*Salcote Abbesse* 1291, *Abbas Hall* 1577), 'land endowed for the support of an abbess', the abbess of Barking being the one referred to.

Above Dikes, Firbank We; **Above Farm,** Blackawton D; **Above Gate,** Grasmere We; **Above Park,** Whitwell We; **Above Street Field,** Kirton Smeaton WRY [OE *strǣt*, 'Roman road, paved road']; **Above Town,** Billesdon Lei [OE *tūn*, 'village']: 'land on the higher side (of the named feature)' [OE *bufan*]. See Buff Town Close.

Acorn Beck, Burton We [ON *bekkr*]; **Acorn Close,** West Hall Db; **Acorn Field,** Marton Ch, Codnor & Loscoe Db; **Acorn Tree Close,** Ilkeston Db; **Acorn Yard,** Spurstow Ch: self-explanatory.

(The) Acre(s), Aston by Sutton Ch, Blackden Ch, Blakenhall Ch, Capesthorne Ch, Hatton Ch, Hockenhull Ch, Keckwick Ch, Walgherton Ch, Ashover Db, Callow Db, Ible Db, Holwell Do, Barwell Lei, Odstone Lei; **Acre Bit,** Horsley Db; **Acre Cleave,** Wellow So [OE *clīf*]; **Acre Fen,** Chatteris C (*Le Acreffenne* 1682); **Acre Field,** Southwick W (*Acrefeild* t. Jas 1), Dillicar We; **Acrelands,** Bottesford Lei; **Acre Marsh,** Beaford D: 'strip(s) of arable land' or 'piece(s) of land having an area of one acre' [OE *æcer*].

Adder Field, Hale Ch, Sutton Ch; **Adderhill,** Pauntley Gl; **Far & Near Adder Mead,** Sandbach Ch: 'land on which vipers abounded' [OE *nǣddre*].

Adfield, Moulton Ch; **Adland,** Sywell Nth: 'headland, land at the edge of an arable strip on which the plough was turned' [OE *hêafod-land*].

Ainholmes, Grassington Cu, 'detached piece of land' [ON *afnám*].

Akerleys, King's Norton Lei; **Akermans Meadow,** Woodeaton O (*Akermanmede* 1366): 'land assigned to the (manorial) ploughman' [OE *æcer-man*].

Alage, Woodford Nth, 'remote, lonely'. The field is near the parish boundary [ME *alange*].

Alburys, Batcombe So, possibly 'old earthworks' [OE *eald, burh*].

Alcove, Mortimer Brk; **Alcove Meadow,** Stretton Db: 'secluded hollow of land'.

Alder Bungs, Astley Abbots Sa [ME *banke*]; **Alder Car Fen,** Earls Colne Ess (*Aldercarre* 1454) [ON *kjarr*]; **Alder Carr,** Hildersham C, Alderwasley Db, Hope Db, Rufford Nt; **Alder Close,** Great Longstone Db; **Alder Field,** Charlesworth Db; **Alder Gully,** North Stoneham Ha [ME *golet*]; **Alder Gutter,** Tottenham Mx; **Alder Ham,** Seagry W [OE *hamm*]; **Alderlands,** Baughurst Ha; **Alder Leasow,** Dawley Magna Sa [OE *lǣs*]; **Alderley,** Kelsall Ch

[OE *lēah*]; **Alder Mead,** Reading Brk; **Alder Meadow,** Nether Alderley Ch, Longford Db, Groby Lei; **Alder Moor,** Beaulieu Ha, Durley Ha, Eversley Ha, Fordingbridge Ha, Heckfield Ha, Ringwood Ha, Romsey Ha; **Aldergo Meadow,** Brailsford Db [OE *gāra*]; **(The) Alders,** Boxford Brk (*Sutholre* 1277), Burghfield Brk, Clifton & Compton Db, Holwell Do, Newent Gl, Alverstoke Ha, Bedworth Wa, Coventry Wa, Underbarrow We; **Alders Holt,** Crookham Ha [OE *holt*]: 'land on which alder trees grew' [OE *alor*]. The alder (*Alnus glutinosa*) favours a moist and even marshy habitat, where its brushwood builds up a bed known as a carr, alluded to in some field-names. The timber was much used for clog-making in the past, as well as for the production of charcoal. See also Aller Bed, Oldery Field, The Owlers.

Ale Bottle Clump, Worksop Nt, alludes to the shape of a plantation of trees.

All Stones, Stanmore Mx, is probably a derogatory name for a very stony field.

Allam Field, Moss WRY; **Allum Bank,** Mansergh We (*Allebanc* 13c); **Allum Field,** Banstead Sr (*Allen Field* 1570); **Allum Meadow,** Church Hulme Ch; **Allumn Piece,** Piddington O; **Allums,** North Elmsall WRY; **Alum Field,** Wincle Ch: some, though perhaps not all, of these names may refer to the presence of alum in the soil.

Allas, Pilton So, '(land with) alder trees' [OE *alor*].

Alldicks, Hemel Hempstead Hrt (*Aldwicke* 1623); **Alwix,** Berkhamsted Hrt (*Aldewykes* 1309): 'old dairy farm' [OE *ald*, *wīc*].

Allebones Spinney, Turvey Bd, 'white poplar copse'. The timber of the abele (*Populus alba*) is light in weight and was formerly used in the construction of carts; the twigs from coppiced trees provided material for rough baskets.

Allege, Islip Nth; **Allenge,** Lowick Nth: 'remote, lonely' [ME *alange*].

Aller Bed, Ilsington D; **Aller Park,** Ashreigney D; **Allers Meadow,** Sutton Down Ch, Beaford D: 'land on or near which alder trees grew' [OE *alor*].

Allotment, Beer D, Ault Hucknall Db, Smalley Db, Weston Underwood Db; **Allotment Field,** Long Critchell Do: 'land assigned to an individual'. When used alone in modern names, the term normally refers to small vegetable gardens rented by residents otherwise without land of their own. In enclosure documents the term is usually combined with the name of the person to whom the land was allocated.

Alma, Dronfield Db, Selston Nt: a name for remote land; it commemorates the battle (1854) during the Crimean War and probably carries the suggestion of harsh climate and bitter toil, as well as the great distance of the field from the village.

Almond Field, Arrow Wa, 'land by, or containing, almond trees'.

Alms Close, Ullesthorpe Lei; **Almshouse Close,** Rawcliffe WRY; **Almshouse Meadow,** Henhull Ch; **Alms Land,** Mortimer Brk: 'land providing funds for almshouses'.

Ambuscade, Acton Scott Sa, 'land covered in undergrowth, suitable for an ambush'.

Amen Corner, Marple Ch, Babworth Nt, Edwinstowe Nt, Rufford Nt, Chitterne W, Crudwell W, Upton Lovell W; **Amen Pingle,** Spondon Db: during the Rogation-tide ceremony of beating the bounds of the parish, the procession halted at specified places for particular parts of the ceremony, and land nearby was occasionally named with reference to the words of the service. Cf Epistle Field, The Gospel.

America, Sawston C, Sutton C, Handforth cum Bosden Ch, East Anstey D; **America Close,** Long Stanton C; **America Farm,** Holt Lei, Darlton Nt; **America Field,** Ewelme O; **America Plantation,** Kirkbampton Cu; **American Meadow,** Brimington Db: transferred name alluding to remote pieces of land.

Amsterdam, Carrington Ch, transferred name alluding to high dykes alongside the river Mersey.

Anchor Croft, Dodcott cum Wilkesley Ch. See Ankerage.

Ancient Homestead, Buckminster Lei; **Ancient Land,** Arclid Ch; **Old Ancient Field,** Cranage Ch: 'land formerly used otherwise than at present'. *Ancient* implies no greater antiquity than (say) fifty or sixty years; *land* probably has the special meaning 'strip of arable ground'.

The Angle, Chadlington O; **Angle Close,** Market Bosworth Lei; **Angles,** Hillfield Do; **Upper Angles,** Ecchinswell Ha: 'L-shaped field' or 'land in the bend of a river' [ME *angle*].

The Anglings, Gaddesby Lei, probably 'land from which a stream may be fished'.

Aniseed, Little Longstone Db, 'land on which anise was grown'. Anise (*Pimpinella anisum*) is a native of the Near East, but has been cultivated in small quantities in England since the sixteenth century; the seed has both culinary and pharmaceutical uses.

Ankerage, Tortworth Gl; **Ankersholm,** Doveridge Db: 'land occupied by a hermit' [ME *ancre*].

Ant Bank, Arnesby Lei; **Anthill,** Upper Slaughter Gl; **Anthills (Great & Little),** Watlington O; **Antifield,** Shawell Lei; **Ants Hill Field,** South Stoneham Ha: 'land infested with ants'. Antifield is probably adapted from Anthill Field [OE *æmette*, *hyll*].

Antigua, Alpraham Ch, transferred name for a remote piece of land.

Apley, Dronfield Woodhouse Db; **Appelwraye,** Torpenhow Cu (*Appelwra* 1296) [ON *vrá*]; **Apple Croft,** Bovingdon Hrt; **Apple Croud,** Sandhurst Brk [OE *croft*]; **Appledore,** Somerton So; **Appledores,** North Bradley W (*Apuldurmede* 1362); **Apple Field,** Dutton Ch, Lymm Ch, Rugby Wa (*Appletrestub* t. Ed 3); **Apple French,** Newbold Astbury Ch [surname *French*]; **Apple Garth,** Barton We, Calverley WRY [ON *apaldrs-garðr*]; **Apple Haugh,** Croydon Sr (*Appley Hawe* 1543) [OE *haga*]; **Appleton,** Aldershot Ha [OE *tūn*]; **Appletree Close,** Axminster D, Bakewell Db, Sturston Db, Knossington Lei, Thurlaston Lei; **Appletree Field,** Pownall Fee Ch, Hatton Db, High Easter Ess (*Appeltonefelde* 1411), Wheathampstead Hrt (*Apildorecroft* 1346); **Appletree Fields & Shaw,** Lamberhurst K [OE *sceaga*]; **Appletree Flatt,** Purston Jaglin WRY; **Apple Tree Furlong,** Hope Db, Ufton Wa; **Appletree Garth,** Rawcliffe WRY [ON *apaldrs-garðr*]; **Appletree Ground,** Kintbury Brk, Mortimer Brk, Manston Do; **Appletree Lands,** Hutton Roof We; **Appletree Vere,** Alton Ha; **West Apple**

Tree, Desborough Nth (*Westapeltre* 1207); **Appletrees,** Great Waltham Ess: 'land on which apples were grown, or land adjoining an apple-orchard' [OE *æppel, æppel-trēow, æppel-tūn*, ON *apaldr* ('apple-tree'), OE *apuldor*].

Apple Dumpling Butts, Kingham O; **Applepie Corner,** Burford O; **Applepie Ground,** St Mary Bourne Ha; **Applepie Piddle,** Nuffield O; **Apple Pie Piece,** Milford Ha; **Applepie Pightle,** Mapledurham O [ME *pightel*]: 'land on which willow-herb grew'. The great hairy willow-herb (*Epilobium hirsuta*) is given these picturesque names in some parts of the south of England.

Apron, Hulse Heath Ch, 'patch of ground almost entirely within the boundaries of a larger field'.

Apse Field, Redbourn Hrt; **Apshanger,** Kingsclere Ha (*Asphanger* 17c) [OE *hangra*]: 'land on which aspen trees grew'. The aspen (*Populus tremula*) is native to Britain; its wood, apart from other uses to which all poplar timber is put, is much employed in the match industry [OE *æpse*].

Apsleys, Almondsbury Gl (*Abbotisley* 1540), 'abbot's clearing or grassland' [ME *abbat*, OE *lēah*].

Aqueduct Meadow, Shackerstone Lei, self-explanatory.

Arbour (Lower & Upper), Shorthampton O; **Arbour Pightle,** Burghfield Brk: possibly 'land near or containing an earthwork' [OE *eorð-burh*].

Ardic, Ware Hrt (*Aldewyke Mede* 15c), 'old dairy-farm' [OE *ald, wīc*].

Aristogyton, Halstock Do; **Aristotle,** Halstock Do: arbitrary names bestowed by Thomas Hollis in the eighteenth century to commemorate people, events, and virtues that he admired. Aristogiton (*sic*) was executed in 514 BC for his part in a plot to kill the Pisistratid tyrants, Hippias and Hipparchus, then ruling in Athens. Aristotle, the Greek philosopher, was doubtless honoured by Hollis for his political writings.

The Arles, Taynton Gl, '(land with) alder trees' [OE *alor*].

Armitage, Hallaton Lei, Swannington Lei, Great Haseley O; **Armitty,** North Duffield ERY (*Le Hermitage* 1280): 'hermitage' [ME *ermitage*].

Arras, Market Weighton ERY (*Herges* 1156), 'shielings, upland pastures used in summer' [ON *erg*].

Ash, Harlestone Nth (*Assfurlong* c 1320); **Ash Acre,** Beer D, Ashmore Do, South Stoneham Ha; **Ash Balk,** Clayworth Nt; **Ash Close,** Burghfield Brk, Edlaston Db, Carlton Curlieu Lei, Evington Lei, Huncote Lei, Swinebrook O, Wroxton O; **Ash Copse,** Newington O; **Ash Crate,** Sandhurst Brk (*Asshe Crofte* 1549) [OE *croft*]; **Ash Croat,** Standon Hrt [OE *croft*]; **Ash Croft,** Chilveley Brk, Lower Withington Ch, Chinley Db, Harlow Ess, White Colne Ess, Cirencester Gl, Blendworth Ha, King's Walden Hrt (*Assecroft* 1300), Keresley Wa (*Aschecroft* 1411), Packwood Wa (*Asshincroft* 1591), Beetham We; Purston Jaglin WRY; **Ash Dikes,** Bruntingthorpe Lei; **Ash Field,** Aston iuxta Mondrum Ch, Calveley Ch, Debden Ess, Gestingthorpe Ess (*Little Ashfeld* 1338), Little Horkesley Ess, Thaxted Ess, St Peters Hrt (*Asshefelde* t. Ed 4), Evington Lei, Hinstock Sa, Caterham Sr; **Ash Furlong(s),** Kingsley Ch, Fifehead Neville Do, Hursley Ha, Illston Lei (*Aschforlong* 1382), Lillington Wa; **Ash Furlong Close,** Merton O; **Ash Ground,** Wardington O; **Ash Grove,** Avening Gl; **Ash Hayes,** Wellow So [OE *(ge)hæg*]; **Ash Hedge Close,** Medbourne Lei (*Ashgate* 1298); **Ash Hill,** Sherington Bk, Sancton ERY, Withcote Lei, Swerford O, Radford Semele Wa; **Ashill Field,** Chobham Sr (*Eysshele* 1446) [OE *lēah*], Aldershot Ha; **Ash Holt,** Stoughton Lei, Darlton Nt, Fledborough Nt, Hayton Nt; **Asholt Ing,** Methley WRY [ON *eng*]; **Ash Land,** Durley Ha; **Ash Lease,** Wickwar Gl; **Ash Leaze,** Horton Gl, Thornbury Gl, Trowbridge W [OE *lǣs*]; **Ashley,** North Stoke So; **Ashley Field,** Balsham C (*Ayssele* 1251), Colerne W; **Ashleys,** Lacock W (*Asseleye* 1232); **Ash Meadow,** West Anstey D, Carlton Curlieu Lei, Shangton Lei; **Ash Piece,** Bicester O: **Ash Plank Meadow,** Charlton on Otmoor O [ME *planke*]; **Ash Plantation,** Stretton Parva Lei; **Ash Plants Field,** Beaford D; **Ash Rein,** Ferry Ryston WRY [ON *reinn*]; **Ashridge,** Chute W; **Ash Spinney,** Goadby Lei; **Ash Tree Close,** Bakewell Db, Coleorton Lei, Beal WRY; **Ash Tree Ground,** Kintbury Brk, Hinton St Mary Do; **Ash Verlon,** Amesbury W [OE *furlang*]; **Ashen Close,** Burghfield Brk; **Ashen Croft,** Knowle Wa (*Asshincroft* 1591); **Ashen Flatt,** Bosley Ch [ON *flat*]; **Ashen Hill,** Steventon Ha; **(The) Ashes,** Holwell Do, Braunston R; **Ashy Moor,** Buerton Ch: 'land near or containing ash trees' [OE *æsc*]. The ash (*Fraxinus excelsior*) is a native tree and flourishes throughout Britain, contributing to the beauty of many different types of scenery. Its timber is still used for tool handles and sports equipment, being particularly resistant to shock and strain. It is also used in the building of large vehicles.

Asker Meadow, Bosley Ch, 'land on which lizards were found' [MnE dial. *asker*].

Aspage, Belchamp St Pauls Ess (*Le Haspeheg* 1181); **Hostage Wood,** Blatherwycke Nth (*Haspehege* 1227): 'hedged enclosure secured with a lock' [OE *hæpse, hecg*].

Aspen Butts, Hathersage Db [ME *butte*]; **Aspen Close,** Hazelwood Db; **Aspenny,** Hullavington W (*Apshanger* c 1300) [OE *hangra*]; **Aspers Close,** Willaston Ch (*Asphale* 1260) [OE *halh*]; **Aspin Croft,** Eaton Ch; **Aspin Hurst,** Adlington Ch; **Aspland Hill,** Dufton We; **Asps,** Adlington Ch: 'land on or near which aspen trees grew'. See also Apse Field [OE *æpse*].

(The) Assart(s), Mansfield Woodhouse Nt, Hartwell Nth, Handborough O; **Assart Close,** Mansfield Nt; **Assart Land,** Clipstone Nt; **Great & Little Sarch,** Puttenham Sr; **Prestgrave Sart,** Prestgrave Lei: 'land taken into cultivation by clearing a section of forest land' [ME *assart*].

The Assocs, Norton Lindsay Wa, '(land covered in) tufts of coarse grass' [OE *hassuc*].

Auberry Hill, Aspenden Hrt (*Aldebere* 13c), Feckenham Wo; **Aubrey,** Little Compton Wa; **The Aubreys,** Redbourn Hrt (*3 Crofts Called Auldeburys* 1529): 'old earthworks' [OE *ald, burh*].

August, Enbourne Brk; **August Leaze,** Alveston Gl; **August Meadow,** Bray Brk: 'land used as pasture during August'. Cf Lammas Close.

Australian Farm, Wilburton C, transferred name for remote land. Possibly there is also a suggestion in this name that work there was comparable to a sentence in the penal settlement in Australia. See also Botany Bay.

Austrian, Hoby Lei (*Oustreng* 14c), 'eastern pasture' [ON *austr, eng*].

Avenham Field, Carleton La, Preesall La: 'land newly taken into cultivation' [ON *afnám*].

Averhill, Kelham Nt (*Averlandes* 13c), 'land on which oats were grown' [ON *hafri*].

Awkward Croft, Stoke upon Tern Sa; **Awkward Meadow,** Scarcliffe Db; **Awkward Roods,** Oxton Nt: derogatory name for land that is unreliable or difficult to cultivate.

Ayca, Casterton We, 'oak mound or hill' [ON *eik*, *haugr*].

Aynam, Skelsmergh We, 'land newly taken into cultivation' [ON *afnám*].

The Aytes, St Stephens Hrt, 'islands'—alluding to low-lying land beside the river, subject to flooding [OE *iggoð*].

B

Babylon, Boreham Ess (*Babelond* 1399), neither a biblical allusion nor a remoteness name, but probably 'Babba's arable land' [OE *land*].

Babylon, Ely C, transferred name for remote land beyond the river, the term doubtless carrying with it all the derogatory suggestions of the biblical allusions to Babylon.

Bacchus Close, Ripley Db, 'land by a bakery'. See Backhouse.

Bache, Alvechurch Wo; **Bage,** Alderwasley Db; **Batch Close,** Enstone O (*Bacheden* c 1260); **Batch Field,** Painswick Gl; **Batch Ground,** Baltonsborough So; **Batch Paddock,** Batcombe So; **Batch Wood,** Pilton So; **Beach Piece,** Aston Wa: 'land by a stream' [OE *bæce*].

Back Field, Torkington Ch, Walworth Du; **Backguards,** Burton We [ON *garðr*]; **Back of Burn,** Longsleddale We; **Back o' th' Barn,** Edale Db, Halstead Lei; **Back o' th' Barn Meadow,** Bosley Ch; **Back o' th' House,** Aston Db; **Back Piece,** Eyam Woodlands Db; **Backside,** Aston Grange Ch, Tarvin Ch, Walgherton Ch, Chinley Db, Eyam Db; **Backside Close,** Buckminster Lei; **Backside Meadow,** Illston Lei, Odstone Lei: 'land behind a house, field, or other named feature'.

Backhouse, Heversham We; **Backhouse Brow,** Chinley Db; **Backhouse Wood,** Essendon Hrt (*Bachouscroft* 1375): '(land by) bakery'.

Bacon, Halstock Do, arbitrary name honouring Francis Bacon, Lord Verulam.

Bacon and Beans Meadow, Waterpury O, a complimentary name alluding to the luxurious diet to be expected from the profits derived from the field.

Bacon Close, Ferry Friston WRY; **Bacon Croft,** Hope Db; **Bacons Meadow,** Feering Ess: probably embodying the surname Bacon.

Bacon Field, Epping Ess (*Le Bekyn* 1386); **Bacon Furlong,** Milcombe O: 'land by a beacon' [OE *bēacen*].

Bad Field, Timperley Ch; **Bad Mead,** Hinton Parva Do; **Bad Meadow,** Durrington W: probably the literal expression of a regrettable fact.

Badger Close, Middle Aston O, Kendal We; **Badger Fen,** Dersingham Nf; **Badger Oaks,** Elland WRY; **Badger Wood,** Westbury on Trym Gl; **Badgers Leasow,** Alvechurch Wo; **Bagbeare Down,** Billesdon Lei [OE *bearu*]: 'land on which badgers were found'. Other possible origins for some of these names are the surname Badger and ME *baggere*, 'hawker'.

Bailey Brow, Pownall Fee Ch; **Bailey Close,** Kendal We; **Bailey Croft**, Pownall Fee Ch, Hutton Roof We; **Bailey Field**, North Bierley WRY (*Bayliffe Field* 1689); **Bailiffs Close,** Aston Wa; **Bailiwick Acre,** Berkhamsted Hrt: 'land assigned to the bailiff of the manor or borough' [OF *baillie*].

(The) Bake, Boyton W, Sutton Veny W; **Bake Barn,** Fonthill Bishops W; **Bake Field,** Burcombe W; **Bake Land(s),** Brown Condover Ha, Chilton Condover Ha, Crawley Ha, Hurstbourne Priors Ha, Kings Worthy Ha, Orcheston St George W; **The Bakes,** Tisbury W; **Bakeums,** Milford Ha [OE *hamm*]: 'pared and burnt land'. See also Burnbacked Meadow.

Balambs, Mortimer Brk; **(The) Balance,** Bray Brk, Hognaston Db; **Balance Close,** Wallington Hrt; **Long Balance,** Little

Downham C; **Top, Middle, Far, Bottom Balance,** Ashby Folville Lei; *Balland Hill,* King's Norton Lei 1638; **Ballands,** Haselbech Nth, Headley Sr, Limpsfield Sr; **Ballands Field,** Elstead Sr; **Little Ballands,** Limpsfield Sr; **Ballards,** Ashby St Ledgers Nth: 'land on which beans were grown' [OE *bēan, land*].

Bald Ham, Ringwood Ha, 'bare enclosure' [OE *hamm*].

(The) Balk, Hathersage Db, Chilwell Nt, Darlton Nt; **Broad Balk,** Harpenden Hrt; **Balk Close,** East Retford Nt, Edwinstowe Nt, Eggborough WRY; **Balkey Field,** Newbottle Du: 'unploughed boundary land'. [OE *balca*]. See also The Baulk.

The Ball, Toot Baldon O, Chiddingfold Sr; **Ball Close,** Alvechurch Wo (cf. *Balleforlonge* 1299); **Ball Coppice**, Ashmore Do; **Ball Croft,** Barwell Lei; **Ball Field,** Lower Whitley Ch; **Balls Acre,** Ashton-under-Wychwood O; **Balls Croft,** Alverstoke Ha; **Balls Hill,** Crowhurst Sr (*Balleshill* 1418); **Balshay,** Wrington So [OE *sceaga*]: 'land by a boundary mound' [ME *balle*].

Balsam, Widecombe in the Moor D, Tetsworth O; **Balsam Ground,** Inkpen Brk; **Balsom Low,** Somerford Booths Ch: 'land on which touch-me-not grew'. The balsam (*Impatiens noli-tangere*) is an uncommon but conspicuous plant occasionally found on arable land. It is not, of course, the source of pharmaceutical balsam; this is the exotic *Myroxylon toluifera.*

Banafurlong, Great Longstone Db [OE *bēan*, ON *haugr*]; **Ban(n)-croft,** Runcorn Ch, Brimpsfield Gl, Toddington Gl, Yelvertoft Nth (*Bancroft* 1116), Brandon Wa, Sheldon Wa, Thornton WRY; **Bancroft Field,** Tytherington Ch; **Bancroft Meadow,** Inkpen Brk; **Band Furlong,** Great Haseley O; **Bandland(s),** Repton Db, Foxton Lei, Glen Magna Lei, Husbands Bosworth Lei, Brackley Nth (*Benlond* 1259), Brigstock Nth (*Banlond* 1480), Chadlington O; **Bandleys,** Bobbingworth Ess (*Benlee* 1307); **Bandonhill,** Beddington Sr [OE *dūn*]; **Bangland,** Whichford Wa; **Banland(s),** Hendon Mx, Brington Nth, Lenchwick Wo; **Bann Close,** Foston Lei: 'land on which beans were grown' [OE *bēan*].

(The) Bank, Hough Ch, Rope Ch, Wistaston Ch, Castleton Db, Derwent Db, Fooloe Db (*Le Bank* 1296), Billesdon Lei, Stockerston Lei; **Bank Dale,** Haltwhistle Nb; **Bank Field,** Clotton Hoofield Ch, Eaton Ch, Walgherton Ch, Bere Alston D, Horley

Sa; **Bank Flat,** Out Rawcliffe La [ON *flat*]; **Bank Hall,** Chelmorton Db [OE *halh*]; **Bank Hay,** Charlesworth Db [OE (*ge*)*hæg*]; **Bank Head Close,** Abney Db; **Bankey Close,** Wardley R; **Bankey Ground,** Shawell Lei; **Bankey Meadow,** Carlton Curlieu Lei; **Banks,** Elwick Hall Du, Blaston St Michael Lei; **Banks Down,** Longparish Ha; **Banky Field,** Tytherington Ch, Hurstpierpoint Sx; **Banky Leasow,** Frodesley Sa, Minsterley Sa; **Banky Piece,** Alderbury Sa: 'land on or by a slope or embankment' [ME *banke*].

Bank Croft, Little Dunmow Ess (*Bancroft* 1315), 'bean enclosure' [OE *bēan*, *croft*].

Bannet Tree Hay, Thornbury Gl; **Bannot Orchard,** Hawkesbury Gl; **Bannut Tree Yard,** Cound Sa; **Bannutt Tree Bank,** Marley Wo; **Bonnut Tree Leaze,** Wickwar Gl: 'land by or containing walnut trees' [MnE dial. *bannut*].

Banquetting Field, Henley O, 'land used for refreshments'—not necessarily lavish alfresco meals, but probably the snacks taken by workers at midday.

Barass, Ashley Ch; **Barlass Meadow,** Moreton Corbet Sa; **Big Barrass** (also **Bosom, Briary, Little, Severn Barass**), Cressage Sa: 'land by a barrier or flood defencework' [ME *barres*].

Barbadoes, Crich Db, Sandiacre Db, Kentmere We; **Barbados,** Berrington Sa: a transferred name for remote land.

Barbary Field, Whitwell We, probably 'land on which barberry grew', alluding to the shrub *Berberis vulgaris*.

Barcelona, Minchinhampton Gl, a transferred name for a remote field, possibly bestowed at the time of the Peninsular War.

Barcroft, Painswick Gl; **Bare Acre,** Preesall La; **Bare Bottoms,** Outseats Db [OE *botm*]; **Bare Field,** Elton Ch, Wimbolds Trafford Ch, Alton Pancras Do; **Bare Flat,** Swannington Lei; **Bare Hill,** Glooston Lei, Longden Sa: 'land on which hard barley is grown' [OE *bere*]. This type of barley, also known as *bere*, is the four- or six-rowed variety now grown mainly in the north of England and in Scotland (*Hordeum vulgare tetrastichon*/*hexastichon*). The more commonly grown type is *Hordeum distichon*, with only two longitudinal rows of fertile spikelets.

Bare Arse, Butley Ch, Worldham Ha, Nateby La, Woodplumpton La, Hallaton Lei; *Bare Arse Furlong*, Claybrook Lei 1674; **Bare Bones,** Kintbury Brk, St Stephens Hrt, Stanwell Mx, High Ham So, Worplesdon Sr, Mere & Zeals W, Calbourn Wt; **Barefoot Close,** South Leigh O; **Bare Knuckles,** Great Eccleston La; **Bareleg(g)(s),** Buriton Ha, Long Sutton So, Melksham W: derogatory names for unproductive land.

Bare Gains, Oxenhall Gl, a derogatory name for unprofitable land. Cf Never Gains, Small Gains.

Bargain Meadow, Church Coppenhall Ch; **Bargains,** Milford Ha; **Bargans Field,** Blakenhall Ch: 'land acquired by purchase or exchange' is the most likely interpretation, through 'land in dispute' seems also possible [ME *bargaine*].

Barhill, Ashton Nth (*Berehul* 14c), 'barley hill' [OE *bere*, *hyll*].

Bark Mill, Thorne WRY; **Bark Mill Brow,** Sutton Ch; **Bark Pits,** Heckmondwike WRY; **Barker Ing,** Crigglestone WRY; **Barkers Close,** Blaston St Giles Lei; **Barkers Moor,** Alvanley Ch; **Barkhouse Close,** Kendal We, Rydal We; **Barkhouse Ing,** Cleckheaton WRY: 'land by or containing a tannery'. Oak-bark was the regular source of tannin for the preparation of hides, and the trades of tanner and barker were closely related, some tradesmen following both.

Barkers Field, Garton ERY (*Barkerie* 12c), 'sheepfold' [ME **barkarie*].

Barley Arrish, Ilsington D; **Barley Ash,** Newdigate Sr [OE *ersc*]; **Barley Bank,** Alkmonton Db; **Barley Close,** Abney Db, Kington Magna Do, Billesdon Lei, Breedon on the Hill Lei, Elsfield O; **Barley Combe,** Priors Dean Ha, Wellow So [OE *cumb*]; **Barley Crate,** Erlestoke W [OE *croft*]; **Barley Croft,** Bollington Ch, Lyme Handley Ch, South Normanton Db, Binstead Ha, Aspenden Hrt; **Barley Field,** Burton Ch, Pownall Fee Ch, Hardwick with Tusmore O, Little Ness Sa; **Barley Furlong,** Laughton Lei; **Barley Garth,** Darrington WRY [ON *garðr*]; **Barley Graves,** Frodsham Ch [OE *grǣfe*]; **Barley Green,** Wychwood O; **Barley Hill,** Minchinhampton Gl, Mottisfont Ha, Hallaton Lei, Cosgrove Nth (*Barlichull* 1364); **Barley Iron,** Buxton Db [OE *hyrne*]; **Barley Land Ings,** Cridling Stubbs WRY; **Barley Lands,** Great

Burstead Ess; **Barley Leasow,** Harley Sa; **Barley Leys Meadow,** Windsor Brk; **Barley Meadow,** Longford Db, Osbaston Lei; **Barley Mire,** Barton We; **Barley Orchard,** Inkpen Brk; **Barley Piece,** Mollington O; **Barley Pingle,** Green Fairfield Db; **Barley Shanks,** Moston Ch [OE *scanca*, 'leg, long narrow field']; **Barley Slait,** North Cerney Gl; **Barley Tongue,** Manley Ch: 'land on which barley was grown' [OE *bǣrlic*].

Barn Close, very common; **Barn Croft,** Chelford Ch, Aston Wa; **Barn Field,** Enbourne Brk, Dutton Ch, East Barnet Hrt, Lilley Hrt, Lamberhurst K, Coulsdon Sr (*Bernefeld* 1431), Croydon Sr (*Bernefeld* 1296), Headley Sr (*Le Bernehawe* 1342); Berkswell Wa, Stoneleigh Wa; **Barn Flat(t),** Runcorn Ch, Abney Db, Castleton Db, Hylton Du, Cabus La, Carleton La, Fishwick La, Thornton La [ON *flat*]; **Barn Ground,** Kington Magna Do, Hardwick with Tusmore O, Idbury O; **Barn Heath,** Church Lawford Wa; **Barn Leasow,** Frodesley Sa, Cold Norton St; **Barn Mead,** Holwell Do; **Barn Meadow,** Alresford Ha, Frodesley Sa, Fillongley Wa; **Barn Park,** West Alvington D; **Barn Tyning,** Bratton W [OE *tyning*]: 'land by, or containing, a barn' [OE *bere-ærn*].

Barnacle, Dodcott cum Wilkesley Ch (*Banacre* 1547), 'bean land' [OE *bēan*, *æcer*].

Barrack Field, Stebbing Ess (*Berewykfelde* 1384), Odiham Ha; **Great Barracks,** Great Clacton Ess (*Berewyke* 1438); **Barrick Copse,** Kilmerton Ha; **Barwicks,** Ugley Ess (*Le Berewykefeld* 1240): 'barley farm' [OE *berewīc*].

Barrell Hill, Pillerton Wa (*Berehull* 1340); **Barrel Piece,** Hankerton W (*Berewelle* c 1300): 'land on which barley was grown', the early forms alluding respectively to a hill and a spring; the word *Hill* in the Pillerton name is therefore redundant, as is not uncommonly found when an element becomes unintelligible by erosion or by the replacement of a term [OE *bere*, *hyll*, *wella*].

Barren Close, Abney Db, Buckhorn Weston Do; **Barren Field,** Lamberhurst K; **Barren Ground,** Fifield O: 'infertile land'.

Barrow Field, Laverstoke Ha, Forncett St Peter Nf; **Barrow Fields,** North Burton ERY (*Suthberges* 1299); **Barrow Holme,** Weeton with Preece La; **Barrow Meadow,** Poulton La; **Barrows,** Out Rawcliffe La: 'land with a tumulus' [OE *beorg*].

Barrow Ground, Naunton Gl (*Bearuwe* 716–43), 'land by a wood' [OE *bearu*].

Barwicks, Ugley Ess, see Barrack Field.

Bastwood, Beetham We, '(land by) lime wood'. *Bast* is specifically used of the outer bark of the lime tree (*Tilia cordata*); from this fibrous material, gardener's bass is prepared.

Bath Close, Cotesbach Lei; **Bath Meadow,** Dadlington Lei; **First & Second Bath Piece,** Dadlington Lei; **Bath Spinney,** Galby Lei: 'land by a pond' [OE *bæð*].

Batterdock, Parwich Db; **Batterdock Field,** Rainow Ch; **Batterdocks,** Green Fairfield Db: 'land on which butterburs grew', referring to the plant, *Petasites vulgaris.*

Battle Bank, Sproston Ch; **Battle Butts,** Crook We; **Battle Field,** Alvechurch Wo; **Battle Flatt,** Frolesworth Lei; **Battle Sale,** North Weald Basset Ess; **Battles Piece,** Bishops Sutton Ha: 'land on which juridical battles took place'. Trial by battle went out of general use after the introduction of the jury system; incredibly, the last juridical battle was in 1819.

Baulk Hazlebadge Db, Ratley Wa; **Baulk Field,** Lilley Hrt; **Baulk Furlong,** Treswell Nt: '(land by) unploughed boundary strip' [OE *balca*].

Bawdy Croft, Hazelwood Db, a derogatory name for infertile land.

Be Quick, Highnam Gl, either a whimsical formation of uncertain meaning (perhaps a reference to a very small field) or an eroded form of Bee Croft or the like.

Beach Piece, Aston Wa, see Batch Close.

Beacon Bunny, Hordle Ha [MnE dial. *bunny*, 'ravine in cliffs']; **Beacon Field,** Thorpe Bulmer Du; **Beacon Hill,** Eling Ha, Billesdon Lei; **Beaken Field,** Sarisbury Ha: 'land on which signal fires were lighted' [OE *bēacon*].

The Beak(e), Piddington O, Chitterne W, Compton Chamberlayne W, Melksham W; **Beak Field,** Micklehurst Ch; **Lower & Upper Beake** Ground, Elmley Castle Wo; **Beak Land,** Tufton Ha; **Beak Meadow,** Wootton St Lawrence Ha: 'land reclaimed for ploughing by paring and burning of turf'. The term here used, together with Burnbake, appears to be limited to southern English counties and those of the south-west Midlands; it may be that the Cheshire example does not belong here, especially as in that county the process is usually referred to in names such as Push Ploughed Field. See also Burnbacked Meadow.

Bean Acre, Woodchester Gl, Lacock W; **Bean Beatings,** Hope Db; **Bean Close(s),** Stanton Db, Buckhorn Weston Do, Holwell Do, Kington Magna Do, Manston Do, Burrough Hill Lei, Hanwell Mx, Snaith WRY; **Bean Clough,** Bosley Ch [OE *clōh*]; **Bean Croft,** Marston Mortaine Bd (*Benhull* 1232), Sandhurst Brk, Lyme Handley Ch, East Horndon Ess, Horton Gl; **Beanfare,** Dillicar We [OE *fær*]; **Bean Field,** Helsby Ch, Thorpe Thewles Du, Bushey Hrt (*Benecroft* 1425), Kirkby Mallory Lei, Kenley Sa; **Bean Flatt,** Adlington Ch; **Bean Furlong,** Merton O; **Bean Half Acre,** Milford Db; **Bean Hay,** Lee W [OE (*ge*)*hæg*]; **Bean Headland,** Ramsden O; **Bean Hill,** Comberton C, Castleton Db (*Benehill* 1457), Daglingworth Gl, Barlestone Lei, Purton W, West Ashton W (*Benhulle* 1341), Beoley Wo; **Bean Hills,** Lamport Nth (*Banehill* 1503); **Bean Lands,** Eyam Db, Kempsford Gl, Eversley Ha, Hursley Ha, Minety W, Stanton Fitzwarren W (*Le Benelonde* 1347), Calverley WRY; **Bean Leaze,** Hullavington W [OE *lǣs*]; **Bean Marsh,** Dersingham Nf; **Bean Moor,** Cricklade W; **Bean Pightle,** Forncett St Peter Nf [ME *pightel*]; **Bean Shots,** Sherborne St John Ha [OE *scēat*]; **Bean Stalk,** Davenport Ch: 'land on which beans were grown' [OE *bēan*].

Bear Close, Witney O; **Bear Croft,** Church Minshull Ch, Fifehead Neville Do, Hinstock Sa; **Bear Field,** Churcham Gl; **Bear Furlong,** Milton under Wychwood O; **Bear Hay & Lands,** Crowell O; **Bear Piece,** Hungerford Brk: 'land on which hard barley was grown'. See also Barcroft [OE *bere*].

Bear Park, Witton cum Twambrook Ch, possibly 'land on which bear-baiting took place'.

Bear Shoulder, Askham Nt, ie 'bare shoulder', a derogatory name.

Beaten Flat, Great Longstone Db; **Beaten Ridding,** Stockport Etchells Ch; **Beatlands,** Ilsington D: possibly 'pared and burnt land'. See The Beak(e).

Beck Allans, Grasmere We [MnE dial. *allan*, 'streamside strip']; **Beck Close,** Kilnwick ERY (*Atte Bec* 1333), Coston Lei, Shangton Lei (*Hengebek* 14c), Hockerton Nt, Tuxford Nt, Walton WRY; **Beck Field,** Woodplumpton La; **Beck Holme,** Hugill We [ON *holmr*]; **Beck Meadow,** Elswick La; **Becking Close,** Darlton Nt [ON *eng*]: 'land by a brook' [ON *bekkr*].

Beckon Field, Crofton Ha, 'land on which a beacon was sited' [OE *bēacen*].

Bedlam, Manea C, Horsley Gl, Wrington So; **Bedlam Bottom,** Farleigh Wallop Ha [OE *bytme*]; **Bedlam Meadow,** North Lopham Nf; **Bedlam Pasture,** Welford on Avon Gl; **Bedlams,** Meesden Hrt; **Bedlams Holme,** Staffield Cu [ON *holmr*]; **Bedlams Nook,** Shenton Lei: a derogatory name, alluding to the Royal Bethlem Hospital in London, an old-established institution for the insane. The term was also used of discharged patients; they were licensed to beg, and possibly some of these fields were their stations or even dwelling places (cf Beggar Bank).

Bee Croft, Marple Ch, Curbar Db; **Bee Garth,** Long Marton We [ON *garðr*]; **Bee Hole Meadow,** Chapel en le Frith Db: 'land on which bees were hived, or where bees were abundant' [OE *bēo*].

Beech Acre, Pishill O; **Beech Field,** Watford Hrt, West Horsley Sr; **Beech Tree Field,** Bampton D; **Beechen Clump,** Middleton Stoney O: 'land near or containing beech trees'. The beech (*Fagus sylvatica*) is a native tree [OE *bece*]. It is occasionally used in a heavily clipped form as a hedging shrub. The nuts, or beech-mast, were formerly widely used for the feeding of pigs.

Beer Furlong, Milton under Wychwood O; **Beerleigh,** Hinton St Mary Do; **Beers Plot**, Holwell Do: 'land on which hard barley was grown' [OE *bere*]. See also Bear Close.

Beggar Bank, Sowerby WRY; **Beggar Bush,** Ashchurch Gl, Wickwar Gl, Wardington O; **Beggar Croft,** Eyam Db, Abbots Langley Hrt; **Beggar Ground,** Shifford O; *Beggar Hades*, King's Norton Lei 1638 [OE *hēafod*(*land*)]; **Beggar Hill,** Wroxton O; **Beggar Moor,** Buxton Db; **Beggar Place,** Bradwell Db; **Beggars Bank,** Frodesley Sa; **Beggar's Bush,** Henbury Gl, Hexton Hrt, Over Seal Lei, Charlbury O, Sutton Coldfield W; **Beggars Bush**

Furlong, Wroxton O; **Beggar's Copse,** Kirdford Sx; **Beggar's Corner,** Odiham Ha; **Beggar's Croft,** Minshull Vernon Ch, Shavington cum Gresty Ch, St Mary Bourne Ha; **Beggars Dean,** King's Walden Hrt [OE *denu*]; **Beggar's Field,** Dodcott cum Wilkesley Ch, Newhall Ch; **Beggars Garden,** Basing Ha; **Beggars Hole,** Fordingbridge Ha; **Beggars Land,** Houghton Ha; **Beggars Lane Close,** Enderby Lei; **Beggars Lot,** Andover Ha; **Beggars Meadow,** Headley Ha; **Beggars Patch,** Bramhill W; **Beggars Shaw,** Cookham Brk (*Beggers Croft* 1615); **Beggars Tyning,** West Kinton W; **Beggar's Well,** Alderwasley Db; **Beggary,** Eaton Socon Bd (*La Beggerie* 1227), Market Bosworth Lei; **Beggary Close,** Carlton Lei; **Beggary Intake,** Marston Montgomery Db; **Beggary Kitchen,** Whitwick Lei; **Beggary Pingle,** Ashleyhay Db: 'haunt of, or dwelling place of, beggars; worthless land'.

Bell Acre(s), Cookham Brk, Duffield Db, Osmaston Db, Langford W; **Bell Butts,** Dorchester O; **Bell Close,** Bolsover Db, Great Gaddesden Hrt (*Bellcrofte* 1494), Marlborough W; **Bell Croft,** Smisby Db; **Bell Field,** Burghfield Brk, Minshull Vernon Ch, Plumley Ch, Hampstead Mx, Bletchingley Sr (*Belacre* 1229), Croydon Sr, Adwick le Street WRY, Gomershal WRY; **Bell Ground,** Lockerley Ha; **Bell Leasow,** Stirchley Sa; **Bell Leaze,** Chippenham W [OE *lǣs*]; **Bell Mead,** Hungerford Brk, Sawbrdgeworth Hrt; **Bell Meadow,** Feering Ess, North Lopham Nf, Windlesham Sr; **Bell Piece,** Crowmarsh O, Salford O; **Bellringers Close,** Cubbington Wa; **Bell Rope Close,** Scarscliffe Db; **Bell Rope Field,** Stondon Massey Ess, Mansfield Nt, Reigate Sr; **Bell Rope Leys,** Histon C; **Bell Rope Piece,** Melbourne Db; **Bell Ropes,** Great Henny Ess (*Bellrope* 1600), Michelmersh Ha, Clipston Nth, Cranford Nth, Gayton Nth, Grafton Underwood Nth, Harlestone Nth (*Belleropes* 1320): 'endowed land for the provision and maintenance of church bells and ropes, or for the payment of bellringers'.

Bellandes Furlong, Barkestone Lei 1579; **The Bellands,** Alderbury Sa: possibly as Bell Acre(s) (qv).

Bellandy Bit, Alderwasley Db; **Bellandy Piece,** Walton Db; **Bellond Field,** Hathersage Db: 'land poisoned by powdered lead ore' [MnE dial. *belland*].

Benbank, Murton We (*Bentbank* 1718); **Bennett Hill,** Holwell Do; **Bennety Coppice,** Ashmore Do; **Bennety Meadow,** Enbourne Brk; **Bent,** Monks Coppenhall Ch; **Far & Near Bent,** Eaton Ch; **Great & Little Bent,** Crewe Ch (*The Bent* 1580); **Bent Acre,** Castleford WRY; **Bent Field,** Allostock Ch, Aldershot Ha; **Bent Hill,** Grimsargh La, Lambrigg We; **Bent Nook,** Woodplumpton La; **Benty Leasow,** Frodesley Sa: 'land on which bent grass grew' [OE *beonet*]. The bents are a group of grasses belonging to the *Agrostis* genus; they are not good grazing.

Bendons, Ampney Crucis Gl (*Myddulbenyndone* 1388, 'middle beany hill') [OE *bēanen, dūn*]; **Ben Field,** Birtles Ch, Horley Sr (*Benffeld* 1355); **Ben Hill & Stiles,** Painswick Gl; **Benleigh,** Hinton St Mary Do; **Bennel,** Great Bardfield Ess (*Benehale* 1321) [OE *halh*]; **Benverland,** Henstridge So [OE *furlang*]: 'land on which beans were grown' [OE *bēan*].

Bere Lands, Petersfield Ha, 'strips on which hard barley was grown' [OE *bere*]. See also Barcroft.

Berill, Burton Overy Lei; **Berrel,** Woodford Halse Nth; **Berril Hedge,** Tysoe Wa (*Berihul* 1284); **Berrill,** Lydbury North Sa; **Beryl,** Maidford Nth: 'hard barley hill' [OE *bere*].

Bermuda, Chilvers Coton Wa, a transferred name for a remote piece of land.

Best Close, Burton Overy Lei, Stretton Parva Lei, Eye & Dunsden O; **Best Field,** Westbury Sa; **Best Lands Hill,** Bushby Lei; **Best Leasow,** Worthen Sa [OE *lǣs*]: a complimentary name for very fertile land.

Bethlehem Hill, Alveston Gl, may be a transferred name for distant land, or a name of the same type as Bedlam (qv).

Better and Worse End, Sowerby WRY, indicates land of varying quality.

Betterest, Brough & Shotton Db, ie 'best', of which it is a dialect form. See Best Close.

Betthams, Hillfield Do, '(land at) valley bottoms' [OE *bytme*].

Betuynzegatis, Illston Lei 1364 [ON *gata*]; **Between the Rivers,** Boxford Brk; **Between Towns,** Donington Lei, Galby Lei [OE *tūn*, 'village']; **Betweenways Furlong,** Chadlington O; **Beyond the Brook,** Newbold & Dunston Db: self-explanatory names compounded with prepositions [OE *begēondan, betwēonan*].

Bickerage (Upper & Lower), Hinstock Sa; **Bickers Court,** Tanworth Wa; **Bickerstone** or **Biggearsden,** Wychwood O (*Bykeresden'* 1300): 'land used by a bee-keeper' [OE *beocere*].

Big Acres, Orton on the Hill Lei [OE *æcer*]; **Big Butts,** Bradwall Ch; **Big Close,** Alderwasley Db, Offcote & Underwood Db, Frisby Lei; **Big Field,** Belstone D, East Anstey D, Leebotwood Sa; **Big Ground,** Prescote O; **Big Hopes,** Poynton Ch [ME *hop*]; **Big Leasow,** Alderbury Sa, Harley Sa, Stirchley Sa; **Big Mead,** East Anstey D; **Big Meadow,** Hulland Db, Risley Db, Dadlington Lei, Kibworth Beauchamp Lei, Habberley Sa, Minsterley Sa, Stapleton Sa: self-explanatory.

Bigg Lands, Meathop We; **Bigham,** Barbon We: 'land on which barley was grown' [ON *bygg, holmr*, OE *land*].

Big Price, Sherington Bk (*Rysc* 1300, *Upper Price* 1580): '(big piece of) rushy land' [OE *rysc*]. *Price* was probably formed by misdivision of *Upper Rice* (or perhaps of *Up Rice*).

Birchanger, Ilsington D [OE *hangra*]; **Birch Close,** Boxford Brk, Welford Brk, Desford Lei; **Birch Croft,** Bovingdon Hrt; **Birch Dale,** Cold Norton St; **Birch Field,** Bosley Ch, Greenford Mx, Worplesdon Sr, Allesley Wa; **Birch Frith,** Wichkam Ha [OE (*ge*)*fyhrð*]; **Birch Grove,** Epping Ess (*Birchesgrove* 1414); **Birch Hill,** Newstead Nt (*Byrkhill* 1350), Ford Sa; **Birch Ley Wood,** Gestingthorpe Ess (*Burcheley* 1538); **Birch Leys,** Hemel Hempstead Hrt [OE *lēah*]; **Birch Moss,** Over Alderley Ch; **Birch Nook,** Congleton Ch; **Birch Tree Close,** Bradley Db; **Birchen Bye,** North Rode Ch [OE *byge*, 'bend']; **Birchen Field,** Mobberley Ch (*Le Birchenfeld* 1334), Newbold Astbury Ch; **Birchen Flatt,** Moston Ch [ON *flat*]; **Birchet Field,** Charlwood Sr; **Birchett Copse,** Horley Sr [OE *-et*, 'copse']; **Birching Ing,** Crigglestone WRY [OE *-ing*, ON *eng*]; **Birchy Field,** Kenley Sa, Pontesbury Sa, Alvechurch Wo: 'land on which birch trees grew' [OE *birce*]. The birch tree (*Betula alba*) grows abundantly all over England. Its bare twigs are still used in the making of garden brooms, but, except in turnery, its timber finds few industrial applications.

Birdhope, Elsdon Nb, 'bird valley' [OE *bridd, hop*].

Birk Field, Skipwith NRY; **Birket Hill,** Warcop We; **Birkhill,** Elsdon Nb; **Birk Rigg,** Bardon We [ON *hryggr*]; **Birkill Field,** Sutton Ch [OE *hyll*]; **Birks,** Hoff We, Morland We; **Burks,** Brougham We: 'land with birch trees' [ON *birki*].

Bishop Field, Scrooby Nt; **Bishop's Field,** Albury Hrt; **Bishops Mead,** Broxbourne Hrt; **Bishops Meadow,** Burghfield Brk, Bolton We: 'land owned by a bishop' [OE *biscop*].

Bishop's Field, King's Walden Hrt (*Busshopp Fyeld* 16c); **Bishops Leys,** Great Henny Ess (*Busshieleaze alias Bishoppes* 1600): 'bushy enclosure (in marshland)' [OE *busc, hop*].

Bismereforlong, Kintbury Brk c1250, 'furlong of disgrace', alluding to an unpleasant situation or, more probably, to the site of a medieval crime [OE *bismer,* 'scandal, infamy', *furlang*].

(The) Bit(t), Ashby Folville Lei, Evington Lei, Crook We, Skelsmergh We: 'very small piece of land' [OE *bita*].

Bitter Bit, Rosliston Db; **Bitter Nails,** Millington Ch; **Bitterum Field,** Sawston C (*Bitterholm* 1235) [ON *holmr*]: possibly 'land with sour soil', though the reference may be to a harsh climate.

Bittersweet, Acton Scott Sa, 'land on which woody nightshade grew'. This plant (*Solanum dulcamara*) owes both its popular name and the botanical specific term to the taste of its poisonous berries—first bitter and then sweet.

Black Acre, Betchton Ch, Alphamstone Ess, Lindsell Ess (*Blakeacre* 1426), Froxfield Ha; **Black Breach,** South Cerney Gl [OE *bræc*]; **Black Bush,** Aldbrough ERY, Ridge Hrt; **Black Bush Bottom,** Lambourne Brk; **Black Bush Furlong,** Milton under Wychwood O; **Black Bush Quarter,** Swinbrook O; **Black Butts,** Cookham Brk, Inkpen Brk, Bollington Ch, Elswick La, Out Rawcliffe La, Shenton Lei, Elmley Castle Wo; **Black Cleugh,** Kirkhaugh Nb [OE *cloh*]; **Black Close,** Welford Brk, Litton Db, Watlington O; **Black Croft,** Over Alderley Ch, Tabley Superior Ch, Buckhorn Weston Do, Hadlow K, Berkswell Wa, Maxstoke Wa(*Blakelonde* t. Hy 7); **Black Dale,** Haltwhistle Nb; **Black Earth,** Bollington Ch, Buxton Db; **Blackeyer,** Bredbury Ch [EMnE *ear,* 'arable land']; **Black Field,** Calveley Ch, Coulsdon Sr (*Blakefeld*

1548), Woking Sr (*Blackpre* t.Ed 6 [ME *pre*]); **Black Flatt(s),** Alpraham Ch, Alston La; **Black Furlong,** Burghfield Brk; **Black Garden,** Chinnor O; **Black Ground,** Kingsley Ch [OE *grund*]; **Black Halves,** Windley Db; **Black Ham,** Shifford O [OE *hamm*]; **Black Hill,** Haltwhistle Nb; **Black Iron,** Wykin Lei [OE *hyrne*]; **Blackland(s),** Duxford C (*Le Blakelond* 1296), Aylesbeare D, Eckington Db, Hinton St Mary Do, Great Waltham Ess, Hatfield Broad Oak Ess (*Blakelond* 1439), Hatfield Peverel Ess, Fareham Ha, Greenford Mx (*Blacklond* 1537), Kelham Nt (*Blakeland* 13c), Horspath O, Swalcliffe O, Tetsworth O (*La Nither Blachelande* 1197), Mickleham Sr, Mitcham Sr, Slimfold Sx (*Blakelond* 1338); **Black Leaze,** Mere & Zeals W; **Black Leys,** East Hatley C; **Black Mead,** Hermitage Do, Wickwar Gl; **Black Meadow,** Bollington Ch, Narborough Lei; **Blackmire(s),** Eckington Db, Shackerstone Lei; **Black Moor,** Wellow So; **Black Moore Hole,** Kilburn Db; **Black Moss,** Tarvin Ch [OE *mos*]; **Black Orchard,** Hillfield Do; **Black Park,** Ilsington D; **Black Patch,** Shavington cum Gresty Ch; **Black Piece,** Morley Db; **Black Pit Close,** Baddesley Clinton Wa; **Blackamore,** Staverton Nth (*Blakemore* t.Ric 2): 'black land, ie land with dark soil or vegetation' [OE *blæc*]. Soil may be blackened by fire, surface water, or coal. The destruction of earlier habitations by fire may sometimes give rise to the name, but it is unreasonable to see in every instance of *Blacklands* evidence of an archaeological site. *Black Bush* names may refer to the blackthorn (*Prunus spinosa*) or may signify land darkened by bushes of any kind.

Blacksmith's Close, Galby Lei, Stretton R; **Blacksmith's Croft,** Risley Db: 'land by a smith's forge'.

Blackthorn, Yateley Ha; **Blackthorn Bottom,** Arnesby Lei: 'land near or on which sloe trees grew'. The sloe (*Prunus spinosa*) has conspicuously black branches and bears black fruit; its blossoms, however, are snow-white. The alternative common names, blackthorn and whitethorn, are therefore not so paradoxical as they appear to be [OE **blæcþorn*].

Blake Bank, Kendal We; **Blake Field,** Ashton on Mersey Ch, Tabley Superior Ch, Tarporley Ch (*Le Blackfield* 1417); **Blake Flatt,** Birches Ch; **Blake Hay,** Butley Ch [OE *(ge)hæg*]; **Blakelands,** Snarestone Lei, Southwell Nt (*Blakelandes* 14c); **Blakemile**

Close, Mickleover Db [OE **mylde*]; **Blakemoor,** Mackworth Db, Long Lawford Wa (*Longblakemora* c 1150); **Blakethwaite,** Whitwell Wo [ON *þveit*]: 'black, or bleak, land' [OE *blæc*, ON *bleikr*].

Bleach Field, Haltwhistle Nb; **Bleach Yard,** Matlock Bath Db; **Bleaching Croft,** Hulme Wakefield Ch; **Bleaching Ground Meadow,** Reading Brk; **Bleachry Field,** Plumley Ch: 'land on which cloth was bleached'.

Bleak Down Field, Gatcombe Wt; **Bleak Field,** Somerford Booths Ch, Waddington Sr; **Bleak Hill,** Scraptoft Lei; **Bleaklands,** Foxton Lei; **Bleak Moor,** Hartington Nether Quarter Db: 'cold, exposed land' [OE *blāc*, ON *bleikr*].

Blenheim, Alverstoke Ha, Bulwell Nt; **Blenheim Homestead,** Northmoor O: transferred name (not necessarily suggesting remoteness) commemorating Marlborough's victory in 1704.

Bloody Meadow, High Legh Ch, Tewkesbury Gl: possibly 'land near the site of a battle'. The second example is indeed close to such a place, where the battle of Tewkesbury was fought in 1471.

Blucher, Elwick Hall Du, see Duke.

Bluebell Close, Calver Db, 'land on which bluebells grew'. The bluebell (*Scilla nutans*) is a widely distributed flower of open woodland country.

Blue Button, Yetminster Do; **Blue Button Field,** Cheadle Ch, Nether Alderley Ch, Odd Rode Ch: 'land on which devil's bit scabious grew'. This plant is *Scabiosa succisa*; its purplish-blue flowers are to be seen on grassland from July to October.

Blue Cap, Casterton We, Clayton WRY: 'land haunted by blue tits'; the blue tit (*Parus caeruleus*) has a blue cap, not a black one like other tits.

Boar Close, Green Fairfield Db; **Boar Garth,** Rawcliffe WRY; **Boar Lands,** Ecchinswell Ha; **Boars Butts,** Stony Stretton Sa: 'land on which a male pig was kept' [OE *bār*].

(The) Bog, Sutton Ch, Bakewell Db, Redlynch W; **Bog Close,** Bushby Lei, Stainmore We, Rawcliffe WRY; **Bog Furlong,** Milton under Wychwood O; **Bog Meadow,** Congleton Ch, Bushby Lei, Longden Sa; **Bog Moor,** Fairford Gl; **Bog Piece,**

Cromford Db, Beal WRY; **Bog Rough Field,** Hatton Ch; **Boggy Close,** Aston Flamville Lei; **Boggy Field,** Houghton on the Hill Lei; **Boggy Ground,** Adderbury O; **Boggy Meadow,** Wykin Lei, Alvechurch Wo; **Boggy Nuke,** East Murton Du [ME *nōk*]; **(The) Bogs,** Dutton Ch, Harley Sa, Solihull Wa: 'waterlogged land' [ME *bog*].

Bogard Hall Close, North Bierley WRY; **Boggard Hole,** Greetland WRY; **Boggart Field,** Sale Ch; **Boggart Hole,** Newsham La: 'land haunted by a goblin' [MnE dial. *boggart*]. The name was applied to land which was heavily shaded, secluded, pot-holed etc.

Bohemia, Redlynch W, a transferred name applied to remote land.

Bold Field, Butley Ch, 'land near or containing a building' [OE *bold*].

Bomb Crater, Corfe Castle Do; **Bomb Holes,** Buckland Riper Do: self-explanatory names dating from World War II.

Bone Dust Bit, Anstey Hrt; **Bone Dust Field,** Snelson Ch, Stoke Ch; **Bone Dusted Field,** Green Fairfield Db; **Bonefield,** Beeston Ch; **Bone Field Hill,** Strickland Roger We; **Bonewaste,** Pickmere Ch; **Bonewaste Field,** Monks Coppenhall Ch: 'land dressed with bone dust'. The grinding of bones as manure began in the neighbourhood of Sheffield in the late eighteenth century; it is said that the discovery of their value resulted from some observant person's noticing the good growth of crops on land where bones had been stored for manufacturing into knife-handles.

Bong Acre, Bramhall Ch; **Bongs,** Acton Grange Ch, Halton Ch (*Le Litelbankfeld* 1283), Walton Inferior Ch, Weston Ch, Bonsall Db; **Bongs Field,** Appleton Ch: 'land on or near an embankment' [ME *banke*].

Boos(e)y Pasture, Alpraham Ch, Nantwich Ch; **Boozey Moor,** Moore Ch; **Boozy Field,** Chorley Ch; **Boozy Pasture,** Cound Sa, Smethcott Sa; **Bowsey Field,** Goostrey cum Barnshaw Ch; **Bowsing Ground,** Dowdeswell Gl: 'land with or near cowstalls' [OE *bōsig*]. In some areas the name also denoted land on which an outgoing tenant could continue to graze his animals for a limited period after the expiry of his lease.

Boot Close, Ilkeston Db; **Boot Foot and Leg,** Offcote & Underwood Db: 'land shaped like a boot'.

Border Close, Arlington D; **Border Piece,** Kintbury Brk: self-explanatory.

Borough Field, Pilling La; **Borough Piece,** Overton Ha (*Ruh Beorh* 909); **Borough Wong,** Knossington Lei: 'land on a hill' [OE *beorh*].

Borrens, Barbon We; **Borrums,** Casterton We; **Borwens,** Hutton Roof We; **Green Burwains,** Lupton We: '(land marked by) cairns' [OE *burgǣsn*].

Borrow Bread, Bleasby Nt, perhaps 'broad piece of land by a hill' [OE *beorg, brǣdu*].

Bosom Holme, Goosnargh La, possibly 'land by cowstalls' [OE **bōs*, dative plural *bōsum*].

Botany Bay, March C, Handforth cum Bosden Ch, Loughton Ess, Aston Hrt, St Stephens Hrt, Ware Hrt, Atterton Lei, Babworth Nt, Teversall Nt, Checkendon O, Eye & Dunsden O, Lewknor O, Atchen Sa, Dawley Magna Sa, Farlow Sa, Ford Sa, Hordley Sa, Leighton Sa, Neen Sollars Sa, Pontesbury Sa, Selattyn Sa, Wrockwardine Sa, Chiddingfold Sr, Castle Eaton W, Sutton Verny W, Monks Kirkby Wa; **Botany Bay Close,** Billesdon Lei; **Botanybay Wood,** Tabley Inferior Ch; **Bottany Bay,** Lambrigg We: transferred name for a remote piece of land. Coupled with the idea of distance may well be that of the hard labour associated with the penal settlement in New South Wales.

Bothhill, Hinton St Mary Do; **Bottle Hill,** Hannington Ha; **Bottle Meadow,** Norbury Ch; **Bottle Park,** Codnor & Loscoe Db: 'land near or containing a building' [OE *bōðl, bōtl*].

Bottom, Chelmorton Db; **Bottom Acre,** East Anstey D; **Bottom Close,** Boxford Brk, Alderwasley Db, Norton Db, Billesdon Lei, Galby Lei, Harston Lei, Muston Lei, Thurnby Lei, East Dereham Nf; **Bottom Field,** Kintbury Brk, Kingsley Ch, Over Alderley Ch, Houghton on the Hill Lei, Ash Sr, Crigglestone WRY; **Bottom Hill Close,** Kirk Langley Db; **Bottom Meadow(s),** Frisby Lei, Illston Lei, Lubbenham Lei, Scraptoft Lei, Stoughton Lei, Martinsthorpe R; **Bottom Moss,** Tarvin Ch; **Bottoms,** Alvarley

Ch, Barrow Ch, Burton Ch, Crich Db, Pleasley Db: 'land at the lowest point' [OE *botm*].

Bound Close, Galby Lei; **Boundary Field,** Tytherington Ch; **Boundary Piece,** Clifton & Compton Db; **Bounds,** Great Warley Ess; **Bounds Piddle,** Mortimer Brk [ME *pightel*]: 'land on a border'.

Bove Town, Bere Alston D, Easton Grey W: 'land above the village' [OE *bufan, tūn*].

Bow Close, Kintbury Brk; **Bow Croft,** Painswick Gl; **Bow Furlong,** Bloxham O; **Bowhay,** Beaford D: 'land with a curving boundary' [OE *boga*].

Bowlaway, Mortimer Brk; **Bowling Alley,** Sandbach Ch, Alderwasley Db, Dore Db, Eastleach Martin Gl, Baschurch Sa; **Bowling Alley Furlong,** South Weston O; **Bowling Close,** Bishop's Sutton Ha; **Bowling Green,** Handforth Ch, Little Leigh Ch, Over Alderley Ch, Ashmore Do, Holwell Do, Kington Magna Do, Hylton Du, Welham Lei, Meathop We; **Bowling Leys,** Barwell Lei: 'land level enough for, or actually used for, the game of bowls'.

Brackenber, Great Strickland We [ON *berg*]; **Brackendale,** Fraisthorpe ERY; **Bracken Hill,** Garton ERY (*Brackenill* 12c); **Brackenrigg,** Casterton We, New Hutton We; **Brackeny Close,** Wingerworth Db: 'land on which bracken grew' [ON *brakni*].

Bramble Croft, Nazeing Ess (*Brambilfeld* 1475), Abbots Langley Hrt, Lamberhurst K; **Bramble Down Park,** Ilsington D; **Bramble Field,** Bures Ess, Aldershot Ha; **Bramble Furlong,** Mere & Zeals W; **Bramble Park,** Blackawton D; **Brambletye,** Effingham Sr [OE *tēag*]; **Bramble Wood,** Hassingham Nf; **Bramblets,** Thursley Sr; **Bramlands,** Battersea Sr now GL (*Brembellond* 1445): 'land on which blackberries grew' [OE *bremel*].

Brand, Knossington Lei; **Brand Hill,** Ferry Fryston WRY; **Brandalls Croft,** Allesley Wa (*Brondhull* t.Ed 1) [OE *hyll*]; **Brandles,** Dawley Magna Sa [OE *hyll*]: 'site of burning' [OE *brand*].

Bran Iron Piece, Ilsington D; **Brandarts Bank,** Smethcott Sa; **Branderland,** Milburn We; **Brandert,** Westbury Sa; **Brandier(s),**

Minety W, Purton W; **Brandies,** Holwell Do; **Brandis Park,** Widecombe D; **Brandish Marsh,** Somerton So; **Brandit,** Spurstow Ch: 'field shaped like a trivet'. The names seem to be peculiar to the SW and WMidl counties, for which reason the Westmorland example is doubtful [MnE dial. *brandis*].

Brandy Bottle, Great Longstone Db, 'bottle-shaped land'.

Brant Bank, Beetham We; **Brant Dalt,** Kentmere We [MnE dial. *dalt*, 'share of common field']; **Brant Field,** New Hutton We; **Brant Healds,** Whinfell We; **Branthill,** Arnesby Lei; **Branthill Close,** Tur Langton Lei; **Brant Pasture,** Preston Patrick We: 'steep land' [ON *brant*].

Bratch Ground, Idbury O; **Bratch Two Acres,** Ashmore Do; **(The) Breach,** Bucklebury Brk, Mortimer Brk, Cholmondeston Ch, Heage Db (*Le Breche* 13c), Hinton Martell Do, Witham Ess, Hawkesbury Gl, Medstead Ha, Burrough on the Hill Lei, Knossington Lei, Bourton O (*Brechfurlong* 1323), Monkton Combe So, Brinkworth W, Draycot Cerne W, Long Newnton W, Malmesbury W (*Le Nether Breche* 13c), Sherston W (*Le Breche* 13c), Hartlebury Wo; **Breach Close,** Hugglescote Lei, Norton juxta Twycross Lei; **Breach Field,** Popham Ha, Godalming Sr; **Breach Furlong,** Knossington Lei; **Breach Gate,** Weston So; **Breach Mead,** Send Sr; **Breach Meadow,** Stratton St Margaret W; **Breach Piece,** Pirton Hrt (*Lytelbrache* 1409); **The Breaches,** Burghfield Brk, Garsington O (*La Breche* 13c); **Breaches Fan,** Byfleet Sr [OE *fenn*]; **Breeches,** Ashdon Ess (*Brach* 1387), Leamington Hastings Wa (*Le Breech* t.Ed 3); **Breeches Meadow,** Barnton Ch, Crowley Ch (*Le Breche* 1487); **Bretch,** Croughton Nth, Eydon Nth (*La Brech* c 1200), Weedon Lois Nth; **The Britches Hay,** Grappenhall Ch: 'land (newly) broken' [OE *brēc*].

Bread and Cheese Lands, Paddington Mx; **Bread and Cheese Meadow,** Huncote Lei: either a fancifully complimentary name or 'land on which refreshment was taken'.

Breadcroft, King's Walden Hrt (*Bradecroft* 1597), Ackworth WRY; **Bread Crofts,** Bletchington O (*Bradecroft* 1139, *Bredecroft* c 1130); **Bread Doles,** Hathersage Db; **Bread Meadow,** Elstead Sr (*Bryde Meade* 1577); **Bread Piece,** Witherley Lei; **The Breeds,** Bartlow C: 'land among, or consisting of, broad strips' [OE *brǣdu*].

Break Back, Stanton by Bridge Db, Chaceley Gl, Marshchapel L 1598; **Break Back Meadow,** Middleton & Smerril Db; **Break-heart,** West Pennard So, Potterne W; **Broken Back,** Wroxton O (*Break Back Furlong* 1768): derogatory names for intractable land.

Breast, Kirkby Lonsdale We, Patterdale We; **Breast Lands,** Castleton Db, Nursling Ha; *Breest*, Great Bowden Lei 1679 (*Le Brest* 1343); **Breastfield,** Nether Staveley We: 'convex piece of land, rounded like a breast' [OE *brēost*].

Breast of Veal, Henhull Ch; **Breast of Veal Field,** Edleston Ch: probably refer to the shape of the field.

Breck Close, Eaton Nt; **Breck Field,** Poulton La, East Markham Nt; **Breckridge,** Gawsworth Ch [OE *hrycg*]; **Brecks,** Perlethorpe Nt, Dewsbury WRY: 'land on a slope' [ON *brekka*].

Brewery Close, Derby Db; **Brewhouse Field,** Hunsdon Hrt; **Brewhouse Mead,** Bennington Hrt, Ewhurst Sr; **Brewhouse Meadow,** Albury Sr: 'land by, or containing, a brewery'.

Briar Croft, Stirchley Sa; **Briar Furlong,** Alvechurch Gl, Bampton O, Lower Heyford O, Swerford O; **Briar Hill,** Sulgrave Nth (*Brerehull* c 1200); **Briar Land,** Steeple Barton O (*Brerfurlong* c 1200); **Briar Lands,** Painswick Gl; **Briary Close,** Mortimer Brk; **Briary Croft,** Bosley Ch, Pownall Fee Ch; **Briary Field,** Adlington Ch, Butley Ch; **Briary Flat,** Carleton La, Poulton La; **Brier Close,** Walkeringham Nt (*Brerebusk* t.Hy 6); **Brier Hill,** Foxton Lei 1755; **Brier Leaze,** Iron Acton WRY; **Briery Close,** Kendal We, Crigglestone WRY; **Briery Field,** Kings Langley Hrt, Pontesbury Sa; **Briery Flat,** Eaton Ch; **Briery Hay,** Sutton Ch; **Briery Knowl,** Hope Db; **Briery Loons,** Weston Ch [OE *land*]: 'land on which eglantine grew'. The sweet briar (*Rosa rubiginosa*) is now regarded as a separate species from other wild roses, but in earlier times *briar* was used of any of the species.

Brick Close, Cookham Brk, Kintbury Brk, Snaith WRY; **Brick Field,** Clewer Brk, Pownall Fee Ch, Hornchurch Ess; **Brick Garth,** Newbottle Du, Rawcliffe WRY; **Brickhill,** Cropredy O; **Brickhill Butts,** Southwell Nt; **Brickiln Bottom,** Itchen Stoke Ha; **Brickkiln Close,** Alderwasley Db, Baggrave Lei, Billesdon Lei, Measham Lei, Forncett St Peter Nf, Ashwell R; **Brick Kiln Croft,**

Treales La; **Brickkiln Field,** Eaton Ch, High Legh Ch, Walworth Du, Bishop's Stortford Hrt, Alston La, Brierley Hill St; **Brickkiln Ground,** Adderbury O; **Brick Kiln Hill,** Hampton Lucy Wa; **Brickkiln Hoppet,** Magdalen Laver Ess; **Brickkiln Leasow,** Church Pulverbatch Sa, Dawley Magna Sa, Frodesley Sa, Stirchley Sa, Alvechurch Wo; **Brickkiln Piece,** Enbourne Brk, Mortimer Brk; **Brickkilns,** Bayford Hrt; **Brick Yard,** Mappowder Do; **(The) Brickle,** Shephall Hrt, Hampton Lucy Wa: 'land on which bricks were made'. Clay was dug as near the building site as possible and kilns were to be found in many places; the *Brickhill* names may well be from an earlier *Brick-kil(n)* form [OF *brique*, OE *cyln*].

Brides Hall, Ardeley Hrt (*Breggehyll* 1474) [OE *hyll*]; **Bridge Close,** Buckhorn Weston Do, Burton Lazars Lei, Dadlington Lei, Shackerstone Lei; **Bridge Croft,** Nether Peover Ch; **Bridge End,** Bakewell Db, Bamford Db, Haltwhistle Nb; **Bridge End Field,** Ashford Db; **Bridge Field,** Wheelock Ch, Peldon Ess (*Breggefeld* 1558), Kings Norton Lei; **Bridge Holme,** Derwent Db, Barnacre La, Goosnargh La, Haighton La, Whittingham La; **Bridge Ing Croft,** Froggatt Db; **Bridge Leasow,** Kenley Sa, Preston Montford Sa; **Bridge Mead,** Burghfield Brk, Woking Sr; **Bridge Meadow,** Clewer Brk, Eyam Woodlands Db, Elstead Sr; **Bridge Orchard,** Blackawton D; **Bridge Park,** Alphington D; **Bridge Pightel,** Reading Brk, Edmonton Mx [ME *pightel*]: 'land by a bridge' [OE *brycg*].

Brigg Close, Hook WRY; **Brigg Meadow,** Poulton La; **Brighills,** Morland We; **Briglands,** Bampton We; **Stone Brig Carr,** Newton with Scales La: 'land by a bridge'. These names embody the Scandinavianised form *brygg* of OE *brycg*.

Brittany, Stainmore We, a transferred name for remote land.

Broad Acre, Warburton Ch; **Broad Arse Piece,** Fenny Bentley Db; **Broad Balk,** Harpenden Hrt; **Broadbalk Furlong,** Kintlington O; **Broad Butts,** Whifell We; **Broad Carr,** Everton Nt [ON *kjarr*]; **Broad Close,** Boxford Brk, Chievely Brk, Reading Brk, Alderwasley Db, Fleckney Lei 1684; **Broad Coomb,** Croydon Sr (*Brodecombe* 1493) [OE *cumb*]; **Broad Corner,** Ilsington D; **Broad Croft,** Gumley Lei 1610, Coulston W; **Broad Dole,** Belchamp St Paul's Ess (*Brodedole* 1404), North Bierley WRY; **Broad**

Field, Burghfield Brk, Chorley Ch, Norton Ch, Pott Shrigley Ch, Wingwall Ch, Abbots Langley Hrt (*Le Brodefeld* 1382), Kings Langley Hrt, Banstead Sr, Chiddingfold Sr, Preston Richard We, Leigh Wo, Rawcliffe WRY; **Broad Flat(s),** Eaton Ch, Abney Db; **Broad Furrows,** Glooston Lei; **Broad Garth,** Pontefract WRY; **Broad Grove,** Wimbolds Trafford Ch; **Broad Ham,** Swinford O; **Broadham Field,** Lympsham So; **Broad Heath,** Wallerscote Ch; **Broad Hey,** Hockenhull Ch, Keckwick Ch; **Broad Holme,** Whitwell We; **Broad Ing(s),** Kendal We, Normanton WRY; **Broad Lands,** Alresford Ha; **Broad Leasow,** Dawley Magna Sa, Yockleton Sa; **Broad Leaze,** Manston D, Lechlade Gl; **Broad Lees,** Horsell Sr; **Broad Leza,** Stretton under Fosse Wa [OE *lǣs*]; **Broad Marsh,** Wettenhall Ch, Chapel en le Frith Db (*Brademersc* t.Hy 3); **Broad Mead,** Cirencester Gl, Berkhamsted Hrt (*Le Brodemede* 1300), Bratton W (*Brodemede* 1249); **Broad Meadow,** Wimpole C, Mottram St Andrew Ch, Kibworth Harcourt Lei; **Broadmoor,** Weston So; **Broad Moss,** Winnington Ch; **Broad Park,** Ashburton D, Bere Alston D, East Allington D; **Broad Piece,** Enbourne Brk; **Broad Royd,** Methley WRY; **Broad Shord,** Ditcheat So [OE *sceard*]; **Broad Shutt,** Bakewell Db; *Broad Wong*, Tur Langton Lei 1638 [ON *vangr*]: 'wide piece of land' [OE *brād*].

Broadspear, Highclere Ha, 'tapering field with curved sides'.

Brock Hill, Mortimer Brk (*Brokehill* 1552), Brigstock Nth (*Brokehill* 1480): 'hilly land by a stream' [OE *brōc*, *hyll*].

Brock Hill, Woking Sr; **Brock Hole(s),** Gawsworth Ch, Gretton Nth, North Elmsall WRY (*Brockhold* 1563), Beetham We; **Brockholes Carr,** Hardhorn La; **Brockholes Field,** Headington O; **Brockholes Hey,** Newton with Scales La; **Brockholes Ing,** Sowerby WRY; **Brockle(s),** Bures Ess (*Brochole* 14c), Woodmansterne Sr (*Brochole* 1360); **Brockles Row,** Worplesdon Sr; **Big & Little Brockless,** Newton Ch (*Brocholas* 1486); **Brock Pits,** Settrington ERY (*Brocpittes* 13c); **Brocoli,** Laxton Nt (*Brockeley Syke* 1626); **Brogdell,** Harpenden Hrt (*Brokdelfeld* 1487); **Brook Field,** Little Totham Ess (*Le Brokholefeld* 1340); **Brookwell Hill,** Thames Ditton Sr (*Brokholehill* 1548): 'land by badger setts' [OE *brocc-hol*].

Brook Close, Houghton on the Hill Lei, Lubenham Lei; **Brook Croft,** Birtles Ch, Cheadle Ch, Alderwasley Db; **Brook Field,** Cranage Ch, Elton Ch, Buckhorn Weston Do, Carlton Curlieu Lei; **Brook Flatt,** Minshull Vernon Ch, Newbold Astbury Ch; **Brook Furlands,** Ilmington Wa (*Brocforlong* t.Hy 3); **Brook Furlong,** Rosliston Db (*Brokforlong* 1365), Alresford Ha, Berkhamsted Hrt, King's Norton Lei 1638; **Brook Ground,** Galby Lei; **Brook Hays,** Preston on the Hill Ch; **Brook Inhams,** Burghfield Brk; **Brook Land,** Old Warden Bd (*Le Brooke* 1422); **Brook Leasow,** Habberley Sa, Kenley Sa; **Brook Meadow,** Billesdon Lei, Noseley Lei, Stoughton Lei, Ashford Mx (*Le Brok* t.Ric 2), Shiplake O, Yaxley Sf; **Brook Verland,** Holwell Do (OE *furlang*): 'land beside a stream' [OE *brōc*].

Brook Field, pre-enclosure great field name in Salford Bd, Rampton C, Stretham C, Arnesby Lei, Cosby Lei, Lockington Lei, North Kilworth Lei, Orton on the Hill Lei, Stonton Wyville Lei.

Broom Bank, Whinfell We; **Broom Butts,** Eakring Nt; **Broom Close,** Bucklebury Brk, Chieveley Brk, Mortimer Brk, Belstone D, Alderwasley Db, Longbridge Deverell W, Old Hutton We, Owston WRY; **Broom Closes,** West Anstey D, Eggborough WRY; **Broom Field,** Reading Brk, Holmesfield Db, Kelvedon Ess (*Bromfeld* 1294), Farnham Sr, Pirbright Sr; **Broom Hay,** Over Alderley Ch [OE *(ge)hæg*]; **Broom Hill,** Ashreigney D, Elwick Hall Du, Coleorton Lei, Kettering Nth (*Bromhill* 1400); **Broom Hills,** Mappowder Do, Bedfont Mx; **Broom Park,** Beaford D, Ilsington D; **Long Brooms,** Eastleigh Ha; **Broomy Bank,** Washington Du, Haltwhistle Nb; **Broomy Knoll,** Pownall Fee Ch; **Broomy Leasow,** Walgherton Ch, Alderbury Sa, Pontesbury Sa, Alvechurch Wo: 'land on which broom grew'. Broom (*Cytisus scoparius*) is abundant all over England [OE *brōm*].

Buckthorn, Hursley Ha; **Buckthorn Meadow,** Ashford Db: 'land on which buckthorn grew'. The thorny shrub (*Rhamnus catharticus*) was used for the production of charcoal and a green dye, as well as being the source of a purgative.

Buff Town Close, Market Bosworth Lei, Misterton Lei 1639; **Bufton,** Chilbolton Ha, Deene Nth (*Bovetown Field*

t. Eliz 1); **Buftons,** Tufton Ha, Tugford Sa: 'land above the village' [OE *bufan, tūn*].

Bull Acre, Tabley Superior Ch (*Bulehalith* 13c), Oddington Gl; **Bull Banks,** Broughton Astley Lei; **Bull Carr,** Hope Db [ON *kjarr*]; **Bull Close,** Alderwasley Db, Great Milton O, Handborough O, Stadhampton O, Yaxley Sf, Hatfield WRY; **Bull Copy,** Casterton We and 26 other places in We; **Bull Crates,** North Poorton Do [OE *croft*]; **Bull Croft,** Ovenden WRY; **Bull Dole,** Everton Nt; **Bull Dyke,** Hallerton Lei; **Bull Field,** Tytherington Ch, East Allington D; **Bull Flat,** Peover Superior Ch; **Bull Folly,** Watlington O; *Bull Gores,* King's Norton Lei 1638; **Bull Hams,** Holwell Do [OE *hamm*]; **Bull Hern,** Reading Brk (*Bulherne* t.Ed 6) [OE *hyrne*]; **Bull Hill,** Eyam Woodlands Db, Pilsley Db; **Bull Leas,** North Newington O [OE *lǣs*]; **Bull Lee,** Bamford Db; **Bull Marsh,** Middleton Stoney O; **Bull Mead,** Hungerford Brk, Hardenhuish W, Yatton Keynell W; **Bull Meadow,** Marston Ch, Barking Ess, Sandford St Martin O, Hartlebury Wo; **Bull Park,** Sutton Downes Ch, Peckleton Lei; **Bull Parlour,** Cadeby Lei; **Bull Piece,** Belgrave Lei, Hugglescote Lei, Piddington O, Thorpe Audlin WRY; **Bull Slack,** Kentmore We [OWSc *slakki*]; **Bull Yard,** Over Alderley Ch; **Bulley Closes,** Duston Nth (*Bulehou* 13c) [OE *hōh*]; **Bullham Corner,** Charlbury O; **Bullpricks,** Weston La [ON *brekka*]; **Bulls Field,** Berrynarbor D; **Bulls Head Nook,** Twycross Lei; **Bulls Meadow,** Ashreigney D; **Bulls Nook,** Carlton Lei, Twycross Lei; **Bulls Piece,** Cookham Brk, Godington O; **Bulls Tail,** Donington Lei, Milton under Wychwood O; **Bulwardine,** Feckenham Wo [OE *worðign*]: 'land on which a bull was kept' [OE **bula*]. Cf Introduction, p xviii.

Bullace Tree Close, Rawcliffe WRY, self-explanatory.

Bungalow Field, Axminster D, self-explanatory name of recent origin.

Bunker's Hill, Girton C, Wisbech C, Walgherton Ch, Duffield Db, Aldbury Hrt, Bovingdon Hrt, Little Berkhamsted Hrt, Elkesley Nt, Norton Nt, Worksop Nt, Shalford Sr, Dunchurch Wa, Offchurch Wa; **Bunker's Hill Farm,** Lubenham Lei; **Bunkus Hill,** Clayworth Nt: transferred name commemorating the battle in Massachusetts in 1775, at which General Howe defeated the colonial forces but suffered very great losses himself. See Introduction, p xvii.

Burn Crooks, Eldon Nb; **Burn Field,** Haltwhistle Nb: 'land by a stream' [OE *burna*].

Burnbacked Meadow, Romsey Ha; **Burnbake,** Ashmore Do, Kington Magna Do, Hordle Ha, Northmoor O, Downton W, Ebbesborne Wake W, Fovant W, Marin W, Mere & Zeals W, Winterbourne Dauntsey W; **Burn Baked Piece,** Kintbury Brk; **Burn Beak,** Melbury Abbas Do; **Burn Brake,** Fifehead Magdalen Do; **Burnt Bit,** Winterbourne Came Do: 'land prepared by paring and burning' [EMnE *bake, beak*]. This process begins with the removal of turf and weeds by means of a mattock or a push plough; the herbage is then piled into beehive-like structures, and the ash produced by the slow combustion of these heaps is ploughed in without delay. The practice is sometimes said to date from the time of the Napoleonic wars, but it is fully described in Edward Lisle's *Observations in Husbandry* (1757), this account being based on the author's own experiences and on material from an unnamed work by a M Duhamel. Cf Push Ploughed Field, Paring Field.

Burnt Acre, Pickmere Ch; **Burnt Ash,** Coleorton Lei [OE *ersc*]; **Burnt Balls,** Ashley Walk Ha; **Burnt Bridge Pightle,** Burghfield Brk; **Burnt Close,** Billesdon Lei; **Burnt Croft,** Ecchinswell Ha; **Burnt Earth,** Over Alderley Ch; **Burnt Ground,** Tichborne Ha; **Burnt Hill,** Sherington Bk (*Le Brendeho* c 1300) [OE *hōh*], Twycross Lei, Chastleton O, Thornton WRY; **Burnt Ing(s),** Styrrup Nt, Owston WRY; **Burnt Knoll,** Gawsworth Ch [OE *cnoll*]; **Burnt Lands,** Broadwas Wo; **Burnt Leys,** Hayton Nt; **Burnt Piece,** Upton Lei; **Burnt Ridding,** Wheatley Nt [OE **ryd-ing*]: 'land cleared by burning' or 'land on which a fire has taken place'.

Burrow Field(s), Hungerford Brk (*Barrowfield* 1548), Alphington D, Priors Dean Ha, West Bridgford Nt; **Burry,** Highcliffe Ha: 'land by or on a mound' [OE *beorg, burh*].

Burtree Bank, Underbarrow We; **Burtyberry,** Thornton La: 'land on which elder trees grew' [OE *burtre*].

Burwandes, Newby We (*Borghanes* 1279); **Burwens,** Musgrave We: 'cairns', such heaps of stones being used occasionally to mark boundaries [OE *burgǣsn*].

Bury Close, Walkern Hrt (*Aldebery* 1381); **Bury Field,** Hitching Hrt; **Bury Fields Meadow,** Artington Sr (*Le Bury* 1397); **Bury Mead,** Weston Hrt; **Bury Meadow,** Hemel Hempstead Hrt: 'land by or with a fortification or fortified manor house'. At Walkern there was once a castle, and the remains of the moat are still visible, though elsewhere it is probable that nothing more secure than a manor house is alluded to [OE *burh*].

Burying Ground Mead, Beaminster Do, 'cemetery'. This is a piece of land on which the Nonconformist James Daniel 'erected a chapel, in the vicinity of which his family's graves can still be seen' by way of thanksgiving for his escape from Royalists in 1658 (cf B. Kerr 'Dorset fields and their names', 234).

Bush Close, Bushby Lei; **Bush Field,** Kintbury Brk, Marden He, Bovingdon Hrt; **Bushel Leaze Meadow,** Mortimer Brk (*The Busshie Leaze* 1564); **Bushy Close,** Buckhorn Weston Do, Stanwell Mx, Yaxley Sf; **Bushy Hope,** Chingford Ess [OE *hop*]; **Bushy Pightle,** Burghfield Brk: 'land covered with bushes' [OE *busc*].

Butt Close, Galby Lei, Hassingham Nf. Warminster W; **Butt Field,** Berkhamsted Hrt, Stoughton Lei, Long Ditton Sr; **Butt Furlong,** North Newington O, Watlington O; **Butt Hill,** Ferry Fryston WRY; **Butt Hills,** Bridlington ERY (*Keldebuttes* 13c); **Butt Piece,** Long Sutton Ha: **Butt Shot,** Mortlake Sr (*The Buttys* 15c); **(The) Butts,** West Alvington D, Sheldon Db (*Buttes* 1617), Sewerby ERY, Lechlade Gl (*Les Buttes* 1448), Holmer He, Breedon on the Hill Lei, Kirtlington O (*Butforland* c 1220): generally 'land formerly irregularly shaped end-pieces of the common field', though a few may be 'land used for archery' [ME *butte*].

Butterbers, Mallerstang We; **Butter Bush,** Pyrton O: 'land on which butter burs grew'; the leaves of this plant (*Petasites fragrans*) were used as butter wrapping.

Buttercake, Urkington Ch; **Butter Close,** Hillfield Do; **Butter Croft,** Curbridge O; **Butter Field,** Barrow Ch, Great Hucklow

Db, Isleworth Mx, Bix O; **Butter Hays,** Hermitage Do; **Butter Hill,** Throcking Hrt (*Boterwelfeld* 1422); **Butter Hole,** North Bierley WRY; **Buttericks,** Hendon Mx (*Boterwyk* c 1322); **Butterlands,** Wincle Ch (*Botirlond* 1286); **Butter Meadow,** Boxford Brk; **Butter Pasture,** Belper Db; **Butter Steep,** Sandhurst Brk, Winkfield Brk: 'good land, producing rich butter' [OE *butere*].

Butter Dish, Crosby Garret We, a complimentary name for good land.

Buttermilk Field, Peover Superior Ch; **Buttermilk Meadow,** Brailsford Db: either complimentary names or a reference to the colour of the soil.

Buttock (Great), Compton Ha; **Buttocks Corner,** Cherhill W: names alluding to the conformation of the land.

C

Cabbage Close, Tissington Db, Swepstone Lei; **Cabbage Ground,** Lyme Handley Ch, Bruern O; **Cabbage Piece,** Hungry Bentley Db, Frolesworth Lei: self-explanatory.

Cacklemackle, Great Longstone Db, '(land on which was found) the poorest sort of lead ore' [MnE dial. *cacklemackle*].

Cae Hyn, Weston Ch, 'older field' [W *cae*, 'field'; *hŷn*, comparative of *hên*, 'old'].

Caile Field, Fifehead Magdalen Do, 'land on which kale was grown'.

Cain and Abel Field, St Paul's Walden Hrt, 'land by a representation of Cain and Abel'; it is said that a piece of sculpture was sited here.

Cains Ground, Heddington W, Market Lavington W; **Cains Mead,** Hillfield Do; **Cain's Meadow,** Bovingdon Hrt; **Cain's Moor,** Soberton Ha; **Cain's Piece,** Tottenham Mx; **Cane Lands,** Pamber Ha: fanciful names for infertile land. Cain's punishment was to be a fugitive and a wanderer, with the assurance that whatever land he ploughed, it would not yield a harvest (*Gen* 4).

Calais, Nuffield O, a transferred name for a distant field.

Calamini Close, Cromford Db, possibly 'land on which zinc ore occurred'. Calamine is carbonate of zinc.

Calf Acre, Enbourne Brk; **Calf Close,** Alkmonton Db, Great Hucklow Db, Cassop Du, Heworth Du, Burrough on the Hill Lei, Coston Lei, Isley Walton Lei, Scalford Lei, Preston Richard We, North Elmsall WRY; **Calf Croft,** Capesthorne Ch, Eaton Ch, Mere Ch, Southowran WRY; **Calf Field,** Haltwhistle Nb; **Calf Garth,** Preston Du, Durrington WRY; **Calf Hull Hill,** Whitwell We [OE *hulu*, 'shed']; **Calf Lears,** Witley Sr [OE *lǣs*]; **Calf Meadow,** Blaston St Giles Lei; **Calf Parrock,** Mansergh We; **Calf Yard,** Abney Db; **Calver Croft,** Alderwasley Db; *Calvers Close*, Medbourne Lei 1626 (*Le Calver Breche* 13c); **Calves Close,** Windsor Brk, East Allington D, Breedon Lei, Tooley Park Lei; **Calves Croft,** Torkington Ch, Sandon Hrt (*Chalcroft* 1222), Harley Sa; **Calves Lease,** Burghfield Brk [OE *lǣs*]; **Calves Leaze,** Boxford Brk, Itchen Abbas Ha; **Calves Meadow,** Drayton O; **Calves Pasture,** Alphamstone Ess; **Calves Pightle,** Steeple Morden C, Yaxley Sf: 'land on which calves were kept' [OE *cealf*].

Cambridge Close, Withybrook Wa, 'land owned by a college of Cambridge University', in this instance Trinity College.

Cammack Field, Horndon on the Hill Ess; **Cammick Hay,** Kington Magna Do; **Cammick Hill,** Buckhorn Weston Do; **Cammuck Redding,** Waltham Holy Cross Ess: 'land on which rest-harrow grew'. No authority can be found for A. H. Smith's interpretation of this plant-name as 'kex, cow-parsley' (*Elements*, i 79); the fifteenth-century *Breviarium Bartolomaei* gives 'Cam̄oc, Resta bovis, retinens boves in aratro', which would appear to allude to *Ononis spinosa* [OE *cammoc*].

Camomile Close, Brackenfield Db, Stretton Db: 'land on which corn chamomile grew', alluding to *Anthemis arvensis*, a weed of cultivated fields.

Camp Close, Newbury Brk (*Campden* 1376) [OE *denu*], Belgrave Lei; **Camp Corner,** Chippenham W; **Camp Croft,** Andover Ha; **Camp Field,** Thorpe Thewles Du, Feckenham Wo; **Camp Ground,** Great Barrington Gl; **Great & Little Camps,** Stondon Massey Ess: probably 'enclosed land' [OE *camp*].

Camping Close, Girton C, Histon C, Little Thetford C, Sawston C, Wentworth C: 'field used for camp-ball' [ME *camping*]. This early form of football seems to have been played without many rules but with an indefinite number of players in each team.

Canaan Farm, Rempstone Nt, transferred biblical name for remote land.

(The) **Canada,** Kingsterndale Db, Stretton R, Avebury W; **Canada Allotments,** Ashley C: transferred names for distant pieces of land.

Canal Close, Glen Parva Lei; **Canal Field,** Catterall La, Claughton La, Woodplumpton La; **Canal Meadow,** Ingol & Cottam La, Brooksby Lei: self-explanatory.

Canalls, Dunchurch Wa (*Kaluenhul* t.Ed 3), despite its modern form (which still bears a recognisable relationship to the medieval one) is 'bare hill' [OE *calu*, *hyll*].

Candle Ground, Bibury Gl; **Candle Hill,** Winston Gl: possibly land endowed for the provision of candles in the parish church.

Candlemas Croft, Bisley Gl, possibly 'enclosure endowed to provide candles on the feast of the Purification'. The feast of the Purification of the Blessed Virgin was the occasion for a blessing and distribution of candles, purchased with funds sometimes provided by income from land. Cf Bell Acres.

Candlestick Hill, Alveston Gl; **Candlesticks,** Widecombe D: probably an endowment (cf Bellropes Field and Candle Ground), but there may be an allusion to the plant, Herb Robert, locally known as 'candlesticks'.

(The) **Cangle,** Langley Ess, Much Hadham Hrt; **Cangle Farm,** Halstead Rural Ess; **Cangles,** Barley Hrt, St Peters Hrt; **Long Cangles,** Henham Ess; **Cangley,** Gosfield Ess, Great Easton Ess: 'fenced enclosure' [ME *cangel*].

Cannery, Knossington Lei, 'rabbit warren' [ME *coningre*].

Canonhams, Banstead Sr; **Cannonheath,** Kinsclere Ha: 'land formerly owned by canons'. The *hammas* at Banstead were granted to the canons of St Mary Overy in 1170; the Kingsclere name alludes to the canons of Rouen, early holders of the manor.

Caper Croft, Over Alderley Ch, refers either to the caper spurge (*Euphorbia lathyris*), the seeds of which were used for pickling, or to the nasturtium, locally known as Capucine capers.

Caper Meadow, Shipton under Wychwood O (*Capronemede* 1391): 'land on which caprons were grown'; the capron was a kind of strawberry.

Caravan Field, Berrynarbor D, a modern self-explanatory name.

Carbut Whins, Washington Du, 'gorse bushes on broad triangular patch of land' [ME *gār-brēde,* ON **hvin*].

Carfax Field, Ockham Sr, is near a crossroads [OF *carrefors*].

Carr, Alderwasley Db (*Le Kerr* 1415); **Carr Banks,** Cassop Du; **Carr Close,** Belmont Du, Darlton Nt, Eastoft WRY; **Carr Croft,** Bosley Ch; **Carr Doles,** Tuxford Nt; **Carr Field,** Houghton le Spring Du; **Car(r) Meadow,** Rostherne Ch, Cantley Nf, Brigstock Nth (*Le Carr* 1480); *Carrs,* Kibworth Beauchamp Lei 1652: 'boggy land' [ON *kjarr*].

Carr Field, a pre-enclosure great field name in Bruntingthorpe Lei, Myton on Swale NRY, and Marton cum Grafton WRY.

Carraway, East Stour Do, alludes to *Carum carvi,* the essential ingredient of seedcake and kümmel. This umbelliferous plant was once extensively cultivated in England.

Carrot Bank Field, Adderley Sa; **Carrot Ground,** Pownall Fee Ch; **Carrot Pightle,** Burghfield Brk: self-explanatory.

Carry Nothing, Newbold Astbury Ch, a derogatory name.

The Carsie, Shephall Hrt; **Causeway Butts,** Bryning La; **Causeway Close,** Kingston Magna Do, Halstead Lei, Hinckley Lei; **Causeway Field,** Acton Ch, Edleston Ch, Henhull Ch, Bilsborrow La, Goosnargh La, Preston La; **Causeway Hey,** Hardhorn La [OE *(ge)hæg*]; **Causeway Mead,** Mortimer Brk; **Causeway Meadow,** Woodcott Ch, Solihull Wa; **Causeway Piece,** Langley & Ruckley Sa; **Causey Close,** Whitgift WRY; **Causey Croft,** Mere Ch; **Causey Meadow,** Larbreck La: 'land by a raised road across marshy ground' [NF *caucie*].

Carvers Meadow, Shepreth C (*Caldberwe* 1280, *Calwverfeld* 1458), 'meadow on the cold hill' [OE *cald, beorg*].

Casshaw Croft, Newbold Astbury Ch, 'cat's wood' [OE *cat(t)*, *sceaga*].

Castle Field, Macclesfield Ch (Buckingham Place or Macclesfield Castle), Hazelwood Db (*Castlefeld* 1415—Duffield Castle), Thornton La, Stirchley Sa; **Castle Garths,** Cornsay Du (Rowley Castle); **Castle Hill,** Cookham Brk, Berrynarbor D, Elwick Hall Du; **Castle Holme,** Aislaby Du; **Castle How,** Old Hutton We: names alluding to named castles or to prehistoric fortifications. Castle How suggests a place of archaeological interest. [OE *castel*, ON *haugr*, 'mound'].

Catbrain, Ludford Sa; **Catbrainhill,** Bourton O; **Catsbrain(s)** Hinton St Mary Do, Loughton Ess, Churcham Gl (*Le Cattsbrayn* 1544), Hawkesbury Gl, Rockhampton Gl, South Cerney Gl, Pirton Hrt, Maidford Nth (*Kattesbreyn* 13c), Barford St John O, Churchill O, Enstone O, Wardington O, Woodeaton O, Banstead Sr, Bratton W, Highworth W; **Cat's Brain Coppice,** Cuddesdon O; **Catsbrain Field,** Uckington Gl; **Catsbrain Furlong,** South Weston O, Wroxton O, Whitchurch Wa; **Cats Brain Ground,** Shirburn O; **Catsbrain Hill,** Great Barrington Gl, Beddington Sr: 'land with soil consisting of rough clay mixed with pebbles' [ME **cattes-braȝen*]. The examples are limited to south and central England.

Cat Furlong, Appleby Lei; **Cat Hill,** Everton Nt; **Cat Holes,** Hallerton Lei; **Catgreaves,** Moston Ch [OE *grǣfe*, 'grove']: names indicating land which, for one reason or another, was haunted by cats.

Catch Cow, Walton upon Trent Db, a puzzling, but probably uncomplimentary, name.

Catch Crop Field, Thorpe Thewles Du, land on which the main crop is intersown with a fast-growing one.

Catstail, Napton Wa (*Le Cattestailles* c 1500); **Cats Tail Marsh,** Cantley Nf; **Cats Tail Furlong,** Milton under Wychwood O; **Cats Tail Meadow,** Little Coggeshall Ess (*Cattistaylesmede* t.Ed 1); **Cattail Field,** Pownall Fee Ch; **Cat Tails,** Orton We: 'land on which timothy grass grew'; each of the densely tufted grasses of the genus *Phleum* bears the name cat's tail, qualified by a specific term, but *Phleum pratense*, the flower panicles of which can be as much as a foot long, justifiably enjoys the name without qualification. It is an important fodder plant.

Cattle Park, Beaford D: self-explanatory [ME *catel*].

Caudle Meadow, Welham Lei, Abberton Wo; **Caudle's,** Staverton Nth (*Caldewellehul* 1320); **Caudwell Head,** Farmington Gl; **The Cawdell,** Carlton Curlieu Lei; **Cawdwell Meadow,** Inkberrow Wo: 'land by cold well or spring' [OE(Angl) *cald, wella*].

Causeway Butts, see The Carsie.

Chalice Field, Hurstbourne Tarrant Ha; **Chalice Pightle,** Heckfield Ha: 'land endowed for the provision of altar wine' [ME *chalice*, 'cup'].

Chalk Close, Crowmarsh O, Whitchurch O; **Chalk Dale,** Wigginton Hrt (*Le Chalke Delle* 1556); **Chalk Dell,** Willian Hrt (*Chalkedell* 13c); **Chalk Dell Close,** St Paul's Walden Hrt, Stevenage Hrt (*Chalkdellefeld* t.Ric 2); **Chalk Dell Field,** Odiham Ha, Bramfield Hrt (*Chalkdellefelde* 1403), Essendon Hrt; **Chalk Dell Wood,** Tewin Hrt (*Chalkdellefeld* 1413); **Chalk Furlong,** Ispden O; **Chalk Ground,** Bucklebury Brk, Lambourn Brk, Mortimer Brk, Alton Pancras Do; **Chalk Hill,** Thaxted Ess; **Chalk Hill Field,** West Clandon Sr; **Chalk Leaze,** Box W; **Chalk Pit Close,** Chieveley Brk, Lambourn Brk, Chinnor O, Rotherfield Greys O; **Chalk Pit Field,** Hinton Parva Do, Saffron Walden Ess; **Chalk Pit Ground,** Shirburn O; **Chalk Pits,** Ashby St Ledgers Nth: 'land from which chalk was obtained' or 'land on which chalk was used'. The practice of improving clayey soils by the addition of chalk, brought occasionally from quite distant quarries, was established before the eighteenth century. The term *dell* is used particularly, but not exclusively, of chalk pits in Hertfordshire [OE *calc, dell*].

Challenge Moor, Churchill O, 'land in disputed ownership' [OF *calenge*].

Chance, Cuckney Nt, a derogatory name, suggestive of seclusion and unreliability.

Chancel Pightle, Cantley Nf, 'land by the east end of a church'.

Changeables, Elkstone Gl, 'land with soil of various colours and kinds'.

Chanters Mead, Mappowder Do, 'land providing for a precentor'.

Chantry Barn, Durrington Sx (*Chaunt'ylond* 1492); **Chantry Boggs,** Pittington Du; **Chantry Close,** Melbourne Db, Norton Db, Tisbury W, Crigglestone WRY; **Chantry Mead,** Hungerford Brk (*Chauntre Mede* 1552); **Chauntry Piece,** Alton Ha: 'land forming part of the endowment of a chantry'. A chantry was a fund for the maintenance of a priest whose sole duty was to say mass daily for the souls of the founder and his family [ME *chaunterie*].

Chapel Acre, Hillfield Do; **Chapel Acres,** Hook WRY; **Chapel Close,** Chieveley Brk, Winterborne St Martin Do, Hitchin Hrt (*Chapell Felde* 15c), Market Bosworth Lei, Nettlebed O, Wardley R, Kendal We; **Chapel Field,** Eaton Ch, Pickmere Ch, West Alvington D, Helion Bumpstead Ess (*Chapelfelde* 15c), Berkhamsted Hrt, Yockleton Sa, Hambledon Sr, Morland We; *Chappel Garth*, Hurworth Du 1717; **Chapel Green,** Burghfield Brk; **Chapel Leys,** Upton Lei; **Chapel Meadow,** Langley & Ruckley Sa; **Chapel Orchard,** Holwell Do: 'land by or with, or forming the endowment of, a chapel' [ME *chapel*].

Char Coal Field, Whatcroft Ch, 'land on which charcoal was burnt'.

Charity Close, Rotherby Lei, Bushwood Wa; **Charity Pastures,** Burghfield Brk: names indicating that the rent of the land provided funds for a charitable purpose. The Tithe Award for Rotherby gives the owners of Charity Close as 'Overseers of the Poor'.

Charl Down, Overton Ha, 'chalk hill'. Cf *Cealcrithe* in a charter of 909, 'chalk stream' [OE *cealc, rið, dūn*].

Charles Croft, Meesden Hrt, (*Chalfcroftmade* t.Ed 3), 'calf croft' [OE *cealf, croft*].

Charmer, Warcop We; **Charming Field,** Elton Ch: complimentary names for easily managed land.

Chart Field & Shaw, Oxted Sr; **Chart Four Acres,** Albury Sr; **Chart Shaw,** Bletchingley Sr: names alluding to rough, sandy, infertile land; a shaw is a copse or small wood [OE *ceart, sceaga*].

Charterville Allotments, Minster Lovell O, alludes to a land experiment conducted by Feargus O'Connor between 1845 and 1848. This Chartist scheme had the laudable aim of providing four acres of land for every bona-fide applicant.

Chatter Holt, Eynsham O (*Charterhold* 1650), refers to the tenure of land by charter, in earlier times a less secure method than by fine, since a copy of the latter would always be preserved among official documents [ME *chartre*].

Cheap Lands, Cuckney Nt, 'lands obtained by purchase' [OE *cēap*].

Cheat Meadow, Blackawton D; **Cheat Piece,** Hallow Wo: possibly land which *escheated*, ie reverted to the crown or another owner on the termination of an entail. See also Chesscroft.

Checker Meadow, Ashleyhay Db; **Checkers,** Ibstock Lei; **Checkers Mead,** Alresford Ha; **The Chequer,** Sale Ch; **Chequer Close,** Hillingdon Mx, Rawcliffe WRY; **Chequer Field,** Altofts WRY (*Chakborde* 1323), Pontefract WRY (*The Chekers* 1526); **Chequer Leys,** Eakring Nt; **Chequers Meadow,** Hatfield Hrt, Lamberhurst K: 'land with variegated soil'. Alternate patches of light and darker soil gave the bare earth the appearance of a chess board [ME *cheker*].

Cheesecake, Kemble Gl, Coston Lei; **Cheesecake Butts,** Kingham O; **Cheesecake Close,** Enderby Lei, Frolesworth Lei, Greetham R; **Cheesecake Furlong,** Shipton under Wychwood O; **Cheesecake Meadow,** Hoby Lei; **Cheesecake Piece,** Hallaton Lei 1707, Newton Harcourt Lei 1796, Wymondham Lei, Kings Newnham Wa; *Cheiskake Peece*, Houghton on the Hill Lei 1681; *Chiskoke Meadowe*, Glooston Lei 1634: these names appear to refer to the shape, or other conformation, of the field. In some Leicestershire documents of the seventeenth century, the term 'a cheesecake piece' is used as a common noun, implying some readily recognisable characteristic of the land concerned. Dr M. Gelling has noted that the term is also used of the fruit of the common mallow (*Malva sylvestris*). See PNO 376.

Chemistry, North Rode Ch, probably 'land on which artificial fertilisers were used'. The name may well be the wry or derogatory comment of old-time agriculturists.

Cherry Breck, Babworth Nt [OE *bræc*]; **Cherry Close & Common,** Piddington O; **Cherry Croft,** Laleham Mx; **Cherry Crote Field,** Mucking Ess [OE *croft*]; **Cherry Garden,** Bere Alston D, Wix Ess; **Cherry Orchard,** Chipping Campden Gl, Wormington Gl, Loughborough Lei; **Cherry Tree Wick,** Wigginton Hrt [OE *wīc*]: self-explanatory. Like *pease* and *coppice*, OF *cherise* was regarded as a plural in ME, and a singular form ME *chiri* or *cheri(e)* was devised from it, giving the modern word.

Cheshire Acre, Wirswall Ch, 'piece of land having an area of 10,240 square yards'. It is worth noting that this township was in the parish of Whitchurch, Shropshire, this anomaly being perhaps the reason for emphasising the name of the neighbouring county.

Chesil Pits, Clifton Hampden O; **Chisley Field,** Albury Hrt (*Cheslefelde* t. Hy 6); **Chissel Acre,** Bleadon So; **Chissel Field,** North Wootton So; **Great & Little Chissels,** Bathampton So; **Chissil Green,** Peover Superior Ch: 'land from which gravel was got' [OE *ceosol*].

Chestnut Heys, Mobberley Ch (*Chesworth Hey Meadow* 1693), an alteration of the local family name de Chesworth, on record from 1440.

Chesnutt Tree, Milcombe O; **Chestnut Field,** Reading Brk: self-explanatory. The wood of the sweet chestnut (*Castanea sativa*) is of considerable utility, especially for such things as fencing, hurdles, gate posts, and props and poles for supporting fruit trees.

Chesscroft, Checkendon O, alludes to rye bromegrass (*Bromus secalinus*) formerly a common weed in wheatfields. An alternative popular name is *cheat*, which may be an element in names like Cheat Meadow (qv).

Chicken Field & Graves, Brindley Ch [OE *grǣfe*]; **Chickens Croft,** Inkpen Brk: self-explanatory.

Chicory Field, East Anstey D, alludes to *Cichorium intybus*, either in its wild form or planted as a fodder or salad crop, or for use as a coffee additive (for which purpose the roots are dried, roasted, and ground).

Childermas Hill, Dutton Ch, alludes to Holy Innocents' Day (28 December), but for a reason that remains obscure; such references often relate to a change of tenancy or of use.

Childs Land, Goring O (*Childeslond* 1366), 'land of a young nobleman' [OE *cild*].

Chilwell Meadow, Dedham Ess (*Cheldewelle* 1241, *Chyldwyll* 1392), 'meadow by the cold spring' [OE *ceald*, *wella*].

Chimney Close, Mortimer Brk; **Chimney Piece,** Cound Sa; **Great Chimney Piece,** Laverstoke Ha: fanciful names for long, narrow fields.

China Field, Alvechurch Wo; **China Lands,** Curbridge O; **China Leasow,** Childs Ercall Sa; **China Pasture,** Ashford Db: names alluding to the remoteness of these fields.

Chintz Pattern, Meathop We, probably land whose soil presents a variegated appearance.

Chipping Furlong, Guilden Morden C, was probably the site of an annual fair [OE *ceping*, 'market'].

Chop(p)ing Knife, Beighton Db, Aislaby Du: a triangular field, shaped like a cook's chopping knife.

Christ Croft, Hillbeck We, probably a church endowment.

Christmas Hill, Bilton Wa (*Christemerehul* t.Ed 3), 'hill on which stood a crucifix as a boundary mark' [OE *cristel-mǣl*, *(ge)mǣre*].

Church Acre(s), Blackawton D, Fairford Gl, Church Oakley Ha, Sutton Venny W; **Church Balk,** Hayton Nt; **Church Bank,** Wybunbury Ch; **Church Close,** Bucklebury Brk, Burghfield Brk, Mortimer Brk, Evington Lei, Goadby Lei, Illston Lei, Thorne WRY; **Church Croft,** Great Longstone Db, Holwell Do; **Church Field,** Goldington Bd, Gawsworth Ch, Nether Peover Ch (*Chyrchefeld* t.Hy 3), Mellor Db, Alverstoke Ha, Lamberhurst K, Cowley O, Ash Sr, Eartham Sx, Iron Acton WRY; **Church Flatt,** Treswell Nt; **Church Furlong,** Baggrave Lei, Spelsbury O; **Church Hill,** Catesby Nth (*Kirkehill* 1272); **(The) Church Land,** Inkpen

Brk, Adderbury O (*Le Chirchelonde* 1381); **Church Meadow,** Long Critchell Do, Billesdon Lei, Isley Walton Lei, Aston Wa; **Church Park,** Belstone D; **Church Pasture,** Slawston Lei; **Church Piece,** Stretton Magna Lei: 'land beside, or belonging to, a church' [OE *cirice*].

Church Field, pre-enclosure great field name in Hinxton C, Swepstone Lei, Thornton Lei, Bladon O, Terrington NRY, Eartham Sx, Hurstpierpoint Sx, Bilton WRY, Marston WRY, Moor Monkton WRY, Swillington WRY, Wickersley WRY.

Church Leys, Hankelow Ch (*Chircheleges* 13c), 'clearing by a mound or barrow' [OW *cruc*, OE *lēah*]. This meaning is suggested in view of the topography, and because of the absence of any church in the neighbourhood. See PNCh, iii, 90.

Church Way Field, Holmer He, 'land on the road to the church'.

Cinder Croft, Mottram St Andrew Ch, Wickwar Gl; **Cinder Field,** Torkington Ch, Horley Sr; **Cinder Hill,** Chorley Ch, Marton Ch, Nether Alderley Ch, Stayley Ch, Tabley Superior Ch (*Le Sindurhul* c 1300), Wilboarclough Ch; **Cinder Hills,** Lower Withington Ch (*Le Sinderhulles* 1337), Godstone Sr, Gomersal WRY; **Cinderlands,** Bradford WRY; **Cinder Leaze,** Melksham W; **Cinder Meadow,** Pontesbury Sa: probably 'land on which cinders or slag are spread or heaped', though at least one (Melksham) is possibly 'separate land' [OE *sinder*, *sundor*].

Cinqe Foin Piece, Beechamwell Nf; **Cinque Foil Field,** Steeple Morden C; **Cinquefoil Ground,** Leafield O; **Cinque Foin Close,** Tadlow C; **Cinque Foin Field,** Whaddon C: possibly 'land on which potentilla grew', though 'land on which sainfoin was grown' is more probable in that sainfoin is agriculturally more significant (see Sainfoin Close). If the most common of the cinquefoils is alluded to, this is *Potentilla repens*—creeping cinquefoil. The uncertainty arises because Sainfoin and Cinquefoil sound almost identical to English ears.

Clam Park, Staveley Db; **Clemhunger,** Over Ch; **(The) Clemley,** Over Ch, Wisterston Ch, Acton Burnell Sa; **Cleml(e)y Park,** Crowton Ch, Little Longstone Db, Yockleton Sa: 'damp, infertile, clayey land' [OE **clǣme*]. For a full discussion, see PNCh, iii, 47.

Clapper, Pilton So; **Clapper Field,** Freefolk Ha, Alfold Sr; **Clapperhangs,** Wharton Ch; **Clapper Mead,** Amport Ha; **Clapperpits,** Pyrton O, Shirburn O; **Clapper Wood Hill,** Henley O (*The Clapurs* 1479): 'land with rabbit burrows' [ME *clapere*].

Claw (Great & Little), Ashreigney D, 'land in the fork of a river' [OE *clā*].

Clay Acre, Pownall Fee Ch, Twemlow Ch, Yeardsley Ch; **Clay Assarts,** Leafield O; **Clay Bank,** Hook Norton O; **Clay Bank Close,** Everton Nt; **Clay Cliff,** North Elmsall WRY; **Clay Close,** Sherington Bk, Bucklebury Brk, Newbury Brk (*Cleypyttys* 1453); **Claycotts,** Abbotsham D [OE *cot*]; **Clay Croft,** Dewsbury WRY, Eggborough WRY; **Clay Field,** Chorley Ch, Dodcott Ch, Rushden Hrt, Headington O (*Cley Close* 1605); **Clay Flat,** Eaton Ch, Little Marton La; **Clay Furlong,** Halstead Lei, Everdon Nth, Welton Nth; **Clay Garson,** Weston Birt Gl [OE *gærs-tūn*]; **Clay Hill,** Westoning Bd (*Clayhull* 1460), Enbourne Brk, Hethe O, Leigh Sr; **Clay Hill Field,** Watlington O (*Clayhull* 1300); **Clay Ings,** Everton Nt [ON *eng*]; **Claylands,** Worksop Nt, Spelsbury O; **Clay Lease,** Bray Brk [OE *lǣs*]; **Clay Pasture,** Newbottle Du; **Clay Piece,** Miserden Gl; **Clay Pit Close,** Croxton Nf, Ellingham Nf; **Clay Pit Field,** Speen Brk, Much Cowarne He, Broadfield Hrt (*Claypet* 1346); **Clay Pit Ground,** Windsor Brk; **Claypit Shot,** Wandsworth Sr now GL (*Claiputte* 1177): **Clay Pits,** Widdington Ess, Quennington Gl, Illston Lei, Deddington O (*Le Cleyputtes* 1306); **Clay Shord,** Potterne W [OE *sceard*]; **Clayshot(t)(s),** Harpenden Hrt (*Clayhel* 1390), Wheathampstead Hrt (*Clayfeld* 1380); **Clayett Mead,** Grittleton W (*Cleyate* 940) [OE *gēat*]; **Clays,** Esher Sr: 'land with clayey soil' or 'land from which clay was dug' [OE *clǣg*].

Clay Field, pre-enclosure great field name in Goadby Marwood Lei, Hoby Lei.

Clear Gains, Sherfield English Ha, complimentary name for a productive field.

The Cleave, Arlington D; **Cleave Down,** Arlington D; **Cleave Orchard,** Billesdon Lei; **The Cleeve,** Corston So; **Cleeve Acre,** Hope Mansel He; **Cleeve Meadow,** Inkberrow Wo; **Cleeve Tining,** Corston So; **Cleeves,** East Anstey D; **Cleve,** Manston

Do; **Cleves,** North Wootton So, Shepton Mallet So, Bremhill W (*Le Clif* 937): 'land on a slope or bank' [OE *clif*].

Cleaver Close, Upton Gray Ha; **Cleaver Furlong,** Milton under Wychwood O: 'land infested with goose grass' [OE *clife*]. This plant (*Galium aparine*) is characterised by its habit of adhering to passing objects by means of reflexed hooks on its stems and leaves; the fruit is also hooked.

Cleehill, Oundle Nth (*Claihil* 13c), 'clay hill' [OE *clæg, hyll*].

Cliff Field, Abbotsham D; **Cliff Moss,** Wharton Ch; **Cliff Slade,** Markfield Lei [OE *slæd*]; **Clift Field,** Shalford Ess (*Clyffeld* 1503); **Clift Hay,** Pitminster So [OE (*ge*)*hæg*]: 'land on a slope' [OE *clif*].

Clip and Go, Broad Town W; **Clip Yard,** Bruntingthorpe Lei: 'land on which sheep were sheared'. Cf Shear and Go.

Clod, Rainow Ch, Preesal with Hackinsall La (*Littleclod, Muckleclod* 1265); **Clod Hut,** Dutton Ch; **Clod Leys,** Billesdon Lei: 'land with lumpy soil' [ME *clod*].

The Close, Wirswall Ch, self-explanatory.

Cloud (Lower & Upper), Wellow So; **Cloud Field,** Ebrington Gl; **Cloud Hills,** Quenington Gl, Goadby Lei; **Cloud Leasow,** Berrington Sa; **Clouds,** Stainmore We; **East Clouds,** Houghton le Spring Du; **Clouds Wood,** Little Hadham Hrt (*Clude* 1277); **Cloudy Field,** Lyme Handley Ch: 'land with rocky outcrops' [OE *clūd*].

(**The**) **Clough,** Congleton Ch, Hulme Walfield Ch, Chapel en le Frith Db, Whittingham La (*Le Cloch* c 1220); **Clough Close,** Eggborough WRY; **Clough Croft & Field,** Alcumlow Ch, Moreton Cu; **Clough Field,** Fallibroome Ch; **Clough Meadow,** Gawsworth Ch, Charlesworth Db; **Clow Close,** Smisby Db; *Clow Field*, Stillingfleet NRY c 1750: 'land in a deep valley' [OE **clōh*].

Clover Balk Close, South Elmsall WRY [OE *balca*]; **Clover Close,** Alkmonton Db, Blackwell Db, Kingston Magna Do, Heworth Du, Aston Flamville Lei, Bushby Lei, Hinckley Lei, Hoby Lei, Narborough Lei, Stretton Magna Lei, Upton Lei; **Clover Croft,** Henbury Ch; **Clover Flat,** Carleton La [ON *flat*]; **Clover Inhams,**

Holwell Do [OE *innām]; **Clover Lands,** Holwell Do; **Clover Leasow,** Acton Burnell Sa, Kenley Sa; **Clover Ley,** Wolstaston Sa; **Clover Sitch,** Hope Woodlands Db [OE *sīc*]: 'land on which clover grew'. As a cultivated crop, clover was an essential element of the Agrarian Revolution; its utilisation owed much to the work of Sir Richard Weston in the mid-seventeenth century (see Ernle, *English Farming Past and Present*, 107–8) [OE *clǣfre*].

Coach Croft, Minshull Vernon Ch; **Coach Nook,** Keckwick Ch: 'land infested with couch-grass' [OE *cwice*].

Coal Pit Close, Beighton Db, Stanton by Bridge Db, Billesdon Lei, Coleorton Lei, Crigglestone WRY, Liversedge WRY; **Coal Pit Field,** Pott Shrigley Ch, Leebotwood Sa, Pontesbury Sa, South Elmsall WRY; **Coal Pit Hill,** Minety W; **Coal Pit Ground,** Lenchwick Wo [OE *grund*]; **Coal Pit Leasow,** Stapleton Sa: 'land by a colliery'.

Coal Will, Croscombe So, Shepton Mallet So; **Colwell,** Batcombe So: '(land by) cool spring or well' [OE *cōl*, *wella*].

Cobra or **Cogboro,** East Farndon Nth (*Calkberwe* 1285), 'limestone hill' [OE (Angl) *calc*, *berg*].

Cockadine, Harley Sa [OE *worðign*]; **Cockborow,** Brigstock Nth (*Cockesbarowe* 1469) [OE *bearu*, 'wood']; **Cock Crow,** Stalbridge Do; **Cockerhead,** Brigstock Nth (*Cokerode* 1469); **Cockroad,** Holwell Do, Hook Do; **Cockroad Close,** Sherfield English Ha; **Cockroad Coppice,** Mappowder Do; **Cockroad Hill,** Burley Ha: 'woodcock territory' [OE *cocc*, *cocc-rodu*]. The woodcock (*Scolopax rusticola*) is a haunter of oak woods, particularly those containing marshy places; the bird habitually circles its territory at dusk, this flight being called 'roding'. The form dated 1469 is of interest in that it takes back the history of the word nearly two hundred years further than the earliest NED citation.

Cockaigne Close, Winster Db; **Cockaynes,** Alresford Ess (*Cockayne* 1279); **Cockaynes Croft,** Tarporley Ch; **Cockeneys Croft,** Urkington Ch: 'land of idleness', a somewhat enigmatic transfer of the name of the imaginary country of medieval legend [OF *Coquaigne*].

Cockbill, Southam Wa (*Coccebyle* 998), Stretton on Dunsmore Wa (*Cockebile* 1199); **Cockbillock,** Priors Hardwick Wa;

Cogbill, Avon Dassett Wa: 'sharply projecting land on a boundary' [OE **cocc-bill*].

Cock Field, Priors Dean Ha; **Cock Hill,** Doddenham Wo; **Cockhill Pits,** Liversedge WRY; **Cocklate,** Lambrigg We [ON *leikr*, 'playing place']; **Cock Leys,** Hayton Nt [OE *lēah*]; **Cockmire,** Shap Rural We; **Cockmoor Hill Furlong,** Boxford Brk; **Cock Stone,** Abney Db; **Cockup,** Oxenhope WRY [OE *hop*]; **Cockwood,** Stainmore We; **Cocks Crowed,** Wormingford Ess [OE *croft*]; **Cocks Greave,** Beetham We [ON *grǣfe*]: probably all names referring to woodcock, the habits of which have been closely studied by country people for centuries. Field-names and minor names record the clearings where it could be seen in its twilight roding (cf Cockerhead, Cockroad etc above), and was there often netted; this activity, and its erratic flight when flushed among trees, doubtless gave rise to such names as Cocklates. See also Cockadine.

Cocked Hat, Durnford W, Almondbury WRY; **Cock'd Hat & Pinch,** Kinnerley Sa; **Cocked Hat Plantation,** Elkesley Nt; **Cockthat,** Bradwell Db: 'land shaped like a tricorne hat'.

Cockin Hitches & Meadow, Bosley Ch; **Cockins,** Elmstead Ess: 'land containing cock-fighting pens' [EMnE *cocking*].

Cockle Close, Burton Lazars Lei; **Cockle Furlong,** Drayton St Leonard O: 'land on which corn-cockle grew', this plant being *Lychnis githago*, a handsome weed of cornfields [OE *coccul*].

Cockpit, Charlbury O, Little Ness Sa; **Cock Pit Field,** Witton cum Twambrook Ch; **Cockpit Pasture,** Burghfield Brk; **Cockpitts,** Avening Gl; **Cockspits,** Dedham Ess: 'land on which cock fights were held'.

Cockroad, see Cockadine.

Cockshead, Dowdeswell Gl, Breedon on the Hill Lei; **Cockshead Field,** Macclesfield Ch (Le *Cocsude* 13c, *Le Cockshete* 1301); **Cockshed,** Twyning Gl; **Cockshoot(s),** Bisley Gl, Chadworth Gl, Painswick Gl, Liversedge WRY; **Cock Shoot Corner,** Aston Rowant O; *Cockshoot Furlong*, Kibworth Lei 1780; **Cockshoot Hill,** Minster Lovell O; **Cockshoot Leaze,** Almondsbury Gl; **Cockshot,** Shenley Hrt, Merrow Sr; **Cockshot Copse,** Kirtlington

O (*Cokkeshot* 1422); **Cockshot Field,** Reading Brk; **Cockshot Hill,** Horton Gl, North Claines Wo; **Cockshot Wood,** Bowness We, Balne WRY, Farsley WRY; **Cockshots,** Burghfield Brk, Knebworth Hrt; *Cockshott,* Heworth Du 1770; **Cockshut,** North Rode Ch; **Cockshut Meadow,** Pott Shrigley Ch; **Cockshutt,** Brierley Hill St, Corley Wa, Elmdon Wa, Beetham We; **Cockshutts,** Odd Rode Ch; **Coxet Field,** Baddiley Ch: 'glade through which woodcock dart, and where they can be hunted' [OE **cocc-scȳte*].

Cock Walk Field, Weston Ch (*The Cocke Walke* 1670), 'land on which game-cocks were reared'.

Codling Orchard, Martley Wo, alludes to hard apples, suitable only for cooking [ME *codling*].

Cold Bakers, Loughton Ess (*Cowle Bakers* 1675),'(land used by) charcoal burners' [OE *col*].

Cold Bit, Upton Lei; **Cold Castle Tyning,** Upton Scudamore W [OE *castel*]; **Cold Chair Leasow,** Hodnet Sa [ME *chere*, 'cheer']; **Cold Comfort,** Churcham Gl, Tetbury Gl; **Cold Comfort Farm,** Heythrop O; **Cold Crate,** North Wraxall W [OE *croft*]; **Cold Halfacres,** Tideswell Db: 'bleak, cheerless land'.

Coldharbour, Sherington Bk, Winterbourne Gl, Herriard Ha, South Muskham Nt, Sutton Bonington Nt, Berrow So, Corston So, Pilton So, Shepton Mallet So, West Pennard So, Capel Sr, Box W, Stratford upon Avon Wa, Underbarrow We; **Coldharbour Farm,** Knapwell C, Bletchingley Sr; **Coldharbour Field,** Basingstoke Ha, Nursling Ha, St Stephens Hrt, Lamberhurst K; **Coldharbour Ground,** Sysonby Lei; **Coldharbour Wood,** East Allington D: 'sheltered place in the open' [OE *cald, here-beorg*].

Cold Kitchen, Shere Sr; **Cold Roast,** Merstham Sr; **Cold Tale,** Underbarrow We [MnE dial. *tale*, 'pottage']: derogatory names for bleak land, uninviting as cold kitchens or cold food.

The College, Bunbury Ch (1); **Great & Little College,** Cookham Brk (2); **College Close,** Whitgift WRY (3); **College Croft,** Market Bosworth Lei; **College Farm,** Wootton Wawen Wa; **College Field(s),** Alston La (4), Buerton Ch (5); **College Hall,** Enbourne

Brk [OE *halh*]; **College Lane,** High Legh Ch (6); **College Meadow,** Thorpe Sr (7): 'land owned by a college'. The institutions concerned are: (1) Chantry of St Boniface, Bunbury; (2) Eton College; (3) Catharine Hall, Cambridge; (4) St John's, Cambridge; (5) Priory of St Thomas, Stafford; (6) Christ Church, Oxford; (7) St Stephen's, Westminster.

Colt Hill, Odiham Ha; **Colts Close,** Thurlaston Lei, Harwick with Tusmore O; **Colts Craught,** Alveston Gl [OE *croft*]; **Colts Field,** West Anstey D; **Colts Nook,** Cadeby Lei; **Colts Piece,** Preston Montford Sa: 'land on which young horses were kept' [OE *colt*].

Comb Close, Cherington Gl; **Comb Hill,** Haltwhistle Nb; **Combe Park,** Berrynarbor D; **Combes Hill,** Staverton Nth (*Cumbes* t.Ric 2); **Combs,** Great Oakley Ess (*Cumba* 1218); **Coomb,** North Wootton So; **Great Coombe,** Deddington O (*Coumbefurlong* 1422) **Higher & Lower Coombe,** Abbotsham D; **The Coombs,** Carlton Curlieu Lei: 'land in a narrow valley' [OE *cumb*].

Come By Chance, Brampton Cu: fanciful name for a small field, remote and hard to find.

Common Close, Barwell Lei; **Common Down,** Long Critchell Do; **Common Field,** Kingsclere Ha, Overton Ha, Tichborne Ha, Ardeley Hrt (*Le Comon Falofeild* 1559); **Common Field & Meadow,** Enbourne Brk; **Common Leasow,** Smethcott Sa; **The Common Marsh,** Boxford Brk: either 'land held by the community' or 'land enclosed from common land'.

Compass, Cowley O (*Compass Field* 1778), 'compost', referring to land that was either heavily manured or was the site of a dung heap.

Conduit Close, Shangton Lei; **Conduit Field,** Baggrave Lei; **Cundy Close,** Normanton Db (*Conduth Leys* 1450): 'land with a channel, water pipe, or aqueduct' [ME *cundite*].

Conegar, Hungerford Brk; **Conegree,** Sherston W; **(The) Conery,** Scraptoft, Lei, Snarestone Lei, Cound Sa, Bulkington Wa, Rowington Wa, Solihull Wa; **Nether Conery,** Broughton Astley Lei; **Conery Close,** Melbourne Db; **Conery Garden,** Loughborough Lei; **Conery Hill,** Blaston St Giles Lei; **Conery Nook,** Linby Nt; **Coneygar Mead,** Nursling Ha; **Coney Grays,** Shipbrook Ch; **Coneygre,** Painswick Gl, Fledborough Nt, Broughton

Poggs O, Garsdon W; **Coneygre Mead,** Hinton Martell Do; **(The) Coneygree,** Notgrove Gl, Crudwell W, Exhall Wa; **Coneygree Meadow,** Offchurch Wa; **Coney Gree Plantation,** Great & Little Houghton Nth; **Coney Green,** Saintbury Gl (*Le Connyger* 1539), Tachbrook Wa, Kempsey Wo; **Coneygres,** Charlton W; **Coney Grey Flatts,** Calveley Ch; **Conger Hill,** Toddington Bd (*Cungar, Cunniger* 1597); **Conigre,** Speen Brk, Horsley Gl (*Cunyngerfeld* 1595); **Conigree Close,** Laxton Nt, Foleshill Wa; **Connigarr Close,** Hungerford Brk (*Conagecroft* 1365); **Conygar,** Alton Pancras Do, Boyton W; **Great Conygars,** Manston Do; **Conygre,** Priston So: 'rabbit warren' [ME *coni(n)ger*]. The rabbit was probably introduced into England by the Normans, and has been valued as food ever since. *Conigers* or rabbit warrens were deliberately established in sandy parts of estates, and a good many of the names probably allude to these, though some may well refer to places to which the animal had spread without human aid. Stamp (*Man and the Land*, 212) considers that the original warren rabbits may have been of a domestic breed, since black skins were much sought after.

Coney Burrow(s), Chingford Ess, Wethersfield Ess (*Le Connyngreth* 1489), Lamberhurst K; **Coney Burrow Field,** Bocking Ess (*Le Conyngere* 1417); **Coney Bury,** Rowington Wa [ME *borow*]; **Coney Close,** Saffron Waldon Ess (*Connyclose* 1605), Chelsea Mx, Aldborough Nf; **Coney Corner,** Chinnor O, Hampton Lucy Wa; **Coney Croft,** Capesthorne Ch; **Coney Dell,** Berkhamsted Hrt; **Coney Fare,** Bures Ess (*Conyngere* 1488), Stebbing Ess (*Le Conyngerhegge* 1412); **Coney Farrow,** Lamarsh Ess (*Conyngeryslond* 1399) [OE *fær*]; **Coney Furlong,** Twickenham Mx; **Coney Greave,** Marton Ch; **Coney Greeves,** Pinnock & Hyde Gl [OE *grǣfe*]; **Coney Grove,** Marton Ch, Hitchin Hrt (*Conynger* 1381); **Coney Hole Field,** Tandridge Sr (*Conyholes* t.Ed 3); **Coney Wall,** Chertsey Sr; **Coney Yards,** Pittington Du; **Coneys Acre,** North Poorton Do: 'land on which rabbits were found'. The early forms of some of these names suggest that they are merely adaptations of ME *coninger*, but others may be independent formations from ME *coni* with an appropriate denominative. The word *cony* (still current in legal and furriery contexts) was originally the normal name for the animal, *rabbit* being applied only to the young.

Congellons, Durley Ha; **Congous Grove,** Plessey Ess: 'goblin-haunted land' [ME *kongon*].

Constable Dole, Everton Nt; **Constable Piece,** Boyleston Db; **Constable's Bank,** North Newington O; **Cunstable Baulk,** Treswell Nt: 'land assigned for the use of the parish constable'; in at least one place the land was reserved for the bull and the boar of the village.

Coppice Castle, Hook Do; **Coppice Close,** Chieveley Brk, Mortimer Brk, Hillfield Do; **Coppice Field,** Bray Brk, Clewer Brk; **Coppice Leasow,** Frodesley Sa, Kenley Sa; **Coppice Loons,** Leftwich Ch [OE *land*]; **Coppice Meadow,** Knossington Lei; **Copse Close,** Hook Do; **Copse Field,** Windsor Brk; **Copse Piece,** Chieveley Brk; **Cop(p)y,** Peover Superior Ch, Blaston St Giles Lei; **Copy Field,** Hough Ch; **Copy Leasow,** Wolstaston Sa: 'land by or containing a thicket'. These names allude to the practice of inducing new growth by cutting down mature trees to ground level. The form *copy* arose through the term *copis* being regarded as a plural [ME *copis*].

Copyhold, Burghfield Brk; **Copyhold Carr,** Hope Db; **Copyhold Close,** Hope Db, Benson O: 'land held at the will of the lord of the manor', such a tenure being authenticated by a copy of the court roll.

Corn Close, Alkmonton Db, Alton Pancras Do, Elwick Hall Du, Cotesbach Lei, Stoughton Lei; **Corn Furlong,** Fifehead Neville Do; **Corn Ground,** Holwell Do; **Corn Hay,** Hillfield Do; **Corn Hill,** Shipbrook Ch, Weston on the Green O (*Cornhulle* 1220), Bleadon So, Longsleddale We; **Corn Mead,** South Cerney Gl; **Corn Pasture,** Alderwasley Db; **Corn Piece,** North Newington O; *Hither and Far Cornefield,* Woodham Du 1717: 'land on or beside which corn was grown' [OE *corn*].

Corner Acre, Ashmore Do; **Corner Bit,** Disley-Stanley Ch, Eaton Ch; **Corner Close,** Donington Lei, Shawell Lei, Eggborough WRY; **Corner Field,** Bucklebury Brk, Berrynarbor D, Great Hucklow Db; **Corner Flats,** Houghton le Spring Du; **Corner Ground,** Burghfield Brk; **Corner Marsh,** Manston Do; **Corner Piece,** Alderwasley Db, Welham Lei, Leebotwood Sa: 'land in a corner of the fields, or by a road junction'.

Corner Green Inclosure, Calveley Ch, 'rabbit warren' [ME *coniger*].

Cornwall, Highworth W; **Corsica,** Dalston Cu: transferred names for remote fields.

Cort Field, Gestingthorpe Ess (*Cotefeild* 1538); **Cote Field,** Ollerton Ch, Peover Superior Ch; **Cote Hill,** Husbands Bosworth Lei; **Cote Leasow,** Church Pulverbatch Sa, Frodesley Sa, Yockleton Sa; **Cote Leys,** Alkmonton Db; **Cote Meadow,** Langley & Ruckley Sa; **Court Close,** Houghton le Spring Du, Charlton on Otmoor O; **Court Field,** Peover Superior Ch; **Court Leasow,** Alderbury Sa; **Courts Hill,** Whaddon C (*Le Cotes* 1398): 'land with, or near, a cottage or cottages' [OE *cot*].

Cottage Close, Lowesby Lei, Muston Lei, Stoughton Lei; **Cottage Field,** Abbotsham D; **Cottage Ground,** Welham Lei; **Cottage Holt,** Illston Lei; **Cottage Meadow,** Mortimer Brk, Berrynarbor D; **Cottage Piece,** Peckleton Lei: self-explanatory.

Cottagers Close, Coston Lei, Laughton Lei; **Cottagers Lotts,** Sibford Gower O: 'land set aside for tenants of cottages', implying a right associated with the occupation of particular cottages.

Cottney Furlong, Southam Wa (*Cotmanfurlong* 1336), 'furlong allocated to the cottars' [OE *cot, man*]. Other examples are found among medieval names, eg *Cotmannedole*, Sharnbrook Bd 13c, *Cotmannemed*, Chertsey Sr 1313, and *Cotmanfeld*, Lambeth Sr now GL 1546.

Couch Croft, Aston by Budworth Ch; **Couch Field,** Hartlebury Wo: 'land infested with couch grass' [OE *cwice*]. See also Twitch Common.

Cow Close, Offerton Db, Hook Do, Aston Flamville Lei, Breedon on the Hill Lei, Hallaton Lei, Narborough Lei, Scraptoft Lei; **Cow Craught,** Alveston Gl [OE *croft*]; **Cow Croft,** Tring Hrt; **Cow Down(s),** Bibury Gl, Coln St Aldwyn Gl [OE *dūn*]; **Cow Fair Close,** Newbury Brk [OE *fær*]; **Cow Field,** Aylesbeare D; **Cow Garston,** South Stoke So [OE *gærs-tūn*]; **Cow Hay,** Runcorn Ch, Charlesworth Db [OE *(ge)hæg*]; **Cow Head,** Dunham Massey Ch [OE *heafod*]; **Cow Hey,** Chapel en le Frith Db, Derwent

Db; **Cow Holm**(e), Docker We, Thorne WRY; **Cowick,** Walkern Hrt (*Cowyk* 1341); **Cow Lane,** Mere Ch, Brightwell Baldwin O; **Cow Leasow**(s), Dumbleton Gl, Adderley Sa, Frodesley Sa, Cold Norton St, Alvechurch Wo; **Cow Leaze,** Bucklebury Brk, Chieveley Brk, Speen Brk, Fifehead Neville Do, Hook Do, Horton Gl, South Cerney Gl, Thorley Wt; **Cow Leys,** Green Fairfield Db, Loughton Ess; **Cow Marsh,** Cantley Nf; **Cow Moss,** Stanthorne Ch; **Cow Park,** East Allington D; **Cow Pasture**(s), Hayfield Db, Hope Db, Little Hucklow Db, Stony Middleton Db, Cornsay Du, Frodesley Sa; **Cow Redding,** Brough We [OE **ryding*]; **Cow Ridding,** Minshull Vernon Ch; **Cow Rigg,** Brough We [ON *hryggr*]; **Cowsitch,** Castleton Db (*Cowsick* 1625) [OE *sīc*]: 'land on which cows were kept' [OE *cū*].

Crab Close, Lambourne Brk; **Crab Croft,** Downham Ess; **Crab Dells,** St Paul's Walden Hrt (*Crabden* 1426); **Crab Wood,** Farley Sr (*Crabbefeld* 1334); **Crabtree**(s), Chieveley Brk, Lamport Nth (*Crabtre Pece* 1465); **Crabtree Acre,** Beetham We; **Crabtree Butt,** Derwent Db; **Crabtree Close,** Enbourne Brk, Alderwasley Db, Ash Db, Barwell Lei, Norton juxta Twycross Lei, Scraptoft Lei, North Elmsall WRY; **Crabtree Corner,** Bloxham O; **Crabtree Field,** Eaton Ch, Hinton St Mary Do, Raby Du, Barking Ess, Peldon Ess (*Crabtrefeld* 1440), Codicote Hrt (*Le Crabbetrowefeld* t.Ed 2), Rickmansworth Hrt, North Lopham Nf, Henley O, Kirtlington O; **Crabtree Flatt,** Cheadle Ch, Purston Jaglin WRY; **Crabtree Ground,** Burghfield Brk, Barcheston Wa; **Crabtree Lands,** Morland We; **Crabtree Leasow,** Harley Sa, Langley & Ruckley Sa, Cold Norton St; **Crabtree Leys,** Halstead Lei; **Crabtree Piece,** Hathersage Db, Preston Montford Sa, Brierley Hill St; **Crab Tree Pightle,** Cantley Nf; **Crabtree Wong,** East Markham Nt, Wellow Nt: 'land near, or containing, crab-apple trees' [ME *crabbe*].

(The) Crate, Lambourn Brk, Fifehead Neville Do, Crondall Ha, Henstridge So, North Stoke So, Shepton Mallet So, North Newnton W; **Cratt Close,** Tisbury W; **The Craught,** Abenhall Gl; **The Crawts,** Newent Gl; **Crowds,** Long Sutton So: 'small enclosure(s)' [OE *croft*].

Crazy Croft, Andover Ha, probably 'land with an irregular boundary', though there may be an allusion to cracks in the soil.

Crouch Acre, Hursley Ha; **Crouch Bottom,** Kensworth Hrt; **Crouch Field,** Long Sutton Ha (*Crouchfield* 1690); **Crouch Hill,** Holwell Do, Laxton Nt (*Cruchewelle* 1232) [OE *wella*]; **Crouch Mead,** Birchanger Ess (*Cruchemede* 1301), Little Hallingbury Ess: 'land by a cross' [OE *crūc*].

Crowbarrow, Longsleddale We; **Crow Bottom,** Bosley Ch; **Crow Burrow,** Hulme Walfield Ch [OE *burh*]; **Crow Close,** Alderwasley Db; **Crow Down,** Abbots Anne Ha; **Crow Furlong,** Hitchin Hrt; **Crow Hill,** Medbourne Lei; **Crow Meadow,** Enbourne Brk, Inkpen Brk (*Crawemed* t.Hy 3); **Crow Nest,** Burghfield Brk, Sutton Ch, Berrynarbor D, Odstone Lei: 'land frequented by crows' [OE *crāwe*].

Cuckle Pool, Minsterworth Gl; **Cuckold Corner,** Rushbury Sa; **Cuckolds Bush,** South Warnborough Ha; **Cuckolds Corner,** Bisley Gl: 'secluded piece of land favoured for illicit love-making'.

Cuckoo Alter, Redmarley D'Abitot Gl; **Cuckoo Bush,** Gotham Nt; **Cuckoo Close,** Blaby Lei, Wanlip Lei, Heptenstall WRY; **Cuckoo Field,** Walworth Du; **Cuckoo Hill,** Alvechurch Wo, **Cuckoo Meadow,** Habberley Sa; **Cuckoo Nest,** Winkfield Brk; **Cuckoo Nook,** Swannington Lei; **Cuckoo Oak,** Cranage Ch; **Cuckoo Park,** Burnaston Db, Melbourne Db, Skellow WRY; **Cuckoo Pen(s),** Ampney Crucis Gl, Avening Gl, Cromhall Gl, Didmorton Gl, Lechlade Gl, Painswick Gl, Staverton Gl, Exbury Ha, Lamberhurst K, Beckley O, Broadwell O, Kirtlington O, Sydenham O; **Cuckoo Thorn,** Gawsworth Ch, Hursley Ha; **Cuckow Butts,** Offerton Db: all alluding in some way to the cuckoo (*Cuculus canorus*), but the connexion is not always clear. Occasionally there may be a literal reference to woods regularly visited by cuckoos. Cuckoo Bush alludes to the exploit of the 'wise men' of Gotham, who attempted to confine the bird by linking their hands around a thorn bush. The many examples of Cuckoo Pen are often taken to refer to this, or a similar, legend; but it is equally likely that the story may represent a popular interpretation of the name, and these hill-top clumps of trees may have been pagan holy places (cf Cuckoo Alter).

Cuckstool Field, Carleton La, Little Marton La; **Cuckstool Meadow,** Little Marton La; **Cuckstone Meadow,** Ashton La: 'land near or containing a ducking-stool'. Scolds and fraudulent shopkeepers were formerly submerged as a punishment for disorderly behaviour.

Culver Butts, Fencot & Murcot O; **Culver Close,** Bramley Ha; **Culver Copse,** Elvetham Ha; **Culver Croft,** Wheathampstead Hrt (*Culvermad* 1510); **Culver Down,** Timsbury Ha; **Culver Field,** Banstead Sr; **Culver Haw,** Littleton C, Walton on the Hill Sr; **Culver Hay,** Cricklade W; **Culver Hill,** Wrington So; **Culver House Close,** Oxford O; **Culver House Mead,** St Stephens Hrt; **Culver House Tyning,** South Stoke So; **Culver Lands,** Mappowder Do; **Culver Mead,** Wellow So: 'land on which doves abounded, or on which there was a dovehouse' [OE *culfre*, *hūs*].

Culverton, Hatfield Hrt (*Culverhouseclose* 1468), Bleadon So, Henstridge So: 'land containing a dove house' [OE *culfre*].

Cumberland Meadow, Bingham Nt, either a transferred place-name referring to remote land, or a name commemorating the military exploits of the eighteenth-century Duke of Cumberland.

Cundell Field, Datchworth Hrt (*Cundell* 1363), 'cows' valley' [OE *cū*, genitive plural *cūna*, *dell*].

Cuningar, Kington Magna Do, **Cuninger**, Littleton Ha; **The Cunnacre,** Adlington Ch; **Cunnery,** Castleton Db, Peckleton Lei, Polesworth Wa; **Cunnery Meadow,** Foston Lei; **Cunniger Field,** Bishopstoke Ha; **Cunning Flat,** Crosby Garrett We; **Cunning Garth,** Millom Cu; **Cunninger,** Bibury Gl, Popham Ha; **Cunnygar,** Iron Acton Gl (*Conigere* 1377); **Cunnygaw Hill,** Welford Brk; **Cunry,** Newstead Nt; **Cunygre,** Garsden W: 'rabbit warren'. See also Conegar [ME *coninger*].

Cup and Saucer Field, Cropredy O, alludes to the remnants of Cropredy Cross; the shaft is fragmentary and the base is hollowed.

Cupboard Hill, Warborough O; **Cupboards,** Lewknor O: complimentary names for productive land.

Cupid's Close, Stanton by Bridge Db. See Coal Pit Field.

Cupola, Ashover Db, Bradwell Db; **Cupola Field,** Eyam Db: 'land by a cupola-furnace'. These small blast-furnaces were used in this area, for lead-smelting, from early in the eighteenth century,

Cursed Oxgong, Weaverham cum Milton Ch 1334, derogatory name for intractable land; an oxgang was a measure of land, one-eighth of a ploughland, about twenty acres.

Cushy Bank, Bosley Ch; **Custard Mead,** Dorchester O; **Custard Meadow,** Barton Stacey Ha; **Custard Stiles,** Lillington Do [OE *stīgel*, 'steep ascent']: 'land frequented by wood pigeons' [OE *cūscote*].

Cut Field, Beckley & Stowood O; **Cutlinch,** Buckhorn Weston Do; **Cutts Meadow,** Mobberley Ch: 'land drained by deep furrows' [ME **cut*].

Cut Throat, Alverstoke Ha; **Cut Throat Coppice,** Solihull Wa; **The Cut Throats,** Tanworth Wa: 'land on which a murder took place'.

Cutting Knife, Smallwood Ch; **Cutting Knife Close,** Hartshorne Db: 'land from which whetstones were obtained'.

D

Daffydown Field, Fareham Ha; **Daffydowndilly Clump,** Middle Aston O: 'land on which daffodils grew'.

Daft Field, Adlington Ch, possibly a complimentary name, since the original sense of the word was 'mild, gentle' [OE *gedæfte*].

Dagtail Piece, Pawler O, 'endowed land for the provision of gripping-pieces for bell-ropes'.

Dairy Close, Billesdon Lei, Shawell Lei; **Dairy Ground,** Catthorpe Lei, Helmdon Nth (*Le Deyfurlonge* c 1420), Bloxham O, Kirtlington O, Middle Aston O, Pyrton O; **Dairy House Leasow,** Church Pulverbatch Sa; **Dairy Meadow,** Billesdon Lei: self-explanatory [ME **dey*]

Daisey Bank, Bosley Ch, Cold Norton St; **Daisy Close,** Wirksworth Db; **Daisy Common,** Corscombe Do; **Daisy Croft,** Clayton WRY; **Daisy Field,** Berrynarbor D; **Daisy Ground,** Holwell Do; **Daisy Leasow,** Alderbury Sa; **Daisy Piece,** Belper Db; **Dazie Croft,** Beauchief Db: 'land on which daisies grew'.

Dam Acres, Oakham R; **Dam Brow,** King's Meaburn We; **Dam Close,** Eyam Db (*del Domm* 1354), North & South Wheatley

Nt; **Dam Croft,** Tabley Superior Ch; **Dam Furlong,** Boughton Nth (*Damfurlong* 1394); **Dam Meadow,** Breedon Lei, Forncett St Peter Nf; **Dams,** Washington Du, Galby Lei, Stoughton Lei: '(land by) an obstruction in a river, or a pool formed by means of a bank across a watercourse' [ME *damme*].

Damas Acres, Norton Ch; **Damas Grove,** Middlezoy So; **Damask Cross,** Tring Hrt; **Damaskfield Copse,** Hampstead Norris Brk; **Damask Green,** Weston Hrt; **Damask Lays,** Finstock O; **Damask Lye,** Monkton Combe So [OE *lēah*]; **Damasks Piece,** Northmoor O: possibly 'land marked with a pattern resembling damask', the markings, in relief, being often provided by the ridge and furrow of medieval cultivation. *Damask* is derived from *Damascus*, the patterned materials originally having come from that city. The early forms of Damask Green, *Damehawes* t.Ric 2, *Damehawsegrene* t.Hy 8, and *Dame Hause Grene* 1533, point to an interpretation 'green by the lady's enclosure', though other evidence is required to establish whether an endowment dedicated to the Blessed Virgin, or a noble lady's property, or a convent of nuns, is concerned here.

Damson Field, Hugglescote Lei, 'field with damson trees'. This type of plum (*Prunus domestica* var. *Damascena*) also originated in Damascus.

Dancers Meadow, Sherborne St John Ha; **Dancing Plain,** Alresford Ha: 'land on which dancing took place'.

Dane Croft, Harpenden Hrt (*Danefeilde* 1598), Hitchin Hrt (*Danfeld* 1409); **Dane Field,** Redbourn Hrt (*Denefield* 1540); **Danes,** Hopesay Sa; **Dankard,** Kimpton Hrt (*Dan Croft* c 1840): '(land in a) deep wooded valley' [OE *denu*].

Dane Meadow, Stanthorne Ch, 'meadow beside the river Dane'. The river-name, according to Ekwall (ERN 112–3), means 'slow-moving stream', but Dodgson suggests that the description is ironic (PNCh i 20).

Danes Blood, Stevenage Hrt, 'plant which sprang up where Danish blood was spilt'. This plant, the Danewort (*Sambucus ebulus*), is now very rare in Hertfordshire, the effect of the slaughter of Scandinavians having evidently worn off.

Dangerous Acre, Dunham Massey Ch; **Dangerous Meadow,** Myddle Sa: an uncomplimentary name, suggesting special hazards to life or solvency.

Dark Flatt, Elwick Hall Du, possibly indicates soil of a colour markedly contrasting with that of adjacent land. Dark may, however, represent Daywork, as in Two Dark (qv).

Darling, Milburn We, a designation of approval.

Day Close, Ashreigney D; **Day Croft,** Sutton Downes Ch; **Day Loont,** Partington Ch [OE *land*]: 'land allocated to the dairy-man, or containing the dairy' [ME *dey*].

Day Math, Crewe Ch, Eaton Ch, Hulse Heath Ch; Norbury Ch; **Day's Mo(w)th,** Widecombe D; **Demath,** Bollington Ch: 'one day's mowing', a customary unit for measuring meadowland [OE **dæg-mæð*].

Day(s) Work, Barthomley Ch, 'one day's work', a unit of area used of arable land [OE *dæg-weorc*]. J. McN. Dodgson (*Notes & Queries*, April 1968, 123) explains the name as alluding 'to service rendered to the lord of the manor by the customary tenant'.

Dead Acres, Almondsbury Gl; **Dead Close,** Basing Ha; **Dead Furlong,** Boddington Gl; **Deadhill Mead,** Bisley Sr; **Deadlands,** Bourton on the Water Gl, Charlbury O, Hullavington W; **Dead Leys,** Barley Hrt; **Deadmore,** Frisby Lei 1638, Ashby St Ledgers Nth (*Dedemore* 1366); **Dead Whong,** Kneesall Nt; *Dedewong*, Sall Nf 1354 [ON *vangr*]: 'disused, worn-out land' [OE *dēad*].

Dead Charl Field, Abbots Anne Ha; **Dead Shells,** Welton Nth (*Dedchurl* 13c): 'land on which a peasant died' [OE *dēad, ceorl*].

Deadlake, Widecombe D, '(land by a) dead stream'; this land adjoins a valley through which a small stream flows in wet weather only.

Deadman, Ampney Crucis Gl, Glen Magna Lei; **Deadmans,** Wickwar Gl; **Deadmans Bottom,** Burghclere Ha, Crowell O; **Deadmans Bush Furlong,** Benson O; **Deadmans Close,** Carlton Curlieu Lei; **Deadmans Clough,** Fernilee Db; **Deadmans Field,** Acton Ch; **Deadmans Furlong,** Dorchester O; **Deadmans Grave,**

Hallaton Lei, Ealing Mx, Peterborough Nth (*Dedmanslond* 1380), Warmington Nth; **Deadmans Holme,** Cleveley La; **Deadmans Moor,** Munstead Ha; **Deadmans Slade,** Barton on the Heath Wa; **Dedman,** Great Gaddesden Hrt (*Apud le Dedeman* 1494); **Dead Woman Lane Close,** Shapwick Do; **Dead Womans Field,** St Stephens Hrt, Fetcham Sr: 'place where a man or woman died, or where a dead body was found'. The field in Acton is 'the burial place of the fifty men killed in a Civil-War skirmish, January 1644' (PNCh, iii, 127).

Dean, Sherington Bk, Chieveley Brk, Kintbury Brk, Elwick Hall Du, Compton Sr; **Dean Bottom,** Hinton Martell Do; **Dean Close,** Welford Brk (*The Den Close* 1552); **Dean Croft,** Hemel Hempstead Hrt; **Dean Field,** Arrington Ch, Froxfield Ha, Bovingdon Hrt (*Deanfeild* 1623), Albury Sr (*Denelonde* 1492); **Dean Flash,** Alderwasley Db [ME *flasshe*, 'swamp']; **Dean Land,** Newdigate Sr; **(The) Dean Meadow,** Staines Mx (*Le Dene* t.Ric 2), Compton Bassett W (*Denefurlong* 1304): '(land in a) valley' [OE *denu*].

Dear Bolt, Clifton Ch; **Dear Bought,** Chorley Ch, Mobberley Ch, Pownall Fee Ch, Mitcheldean Gl, Barnacre La, Cleveley La, Nateby La, Warton La; *Dereboght*, Sall Nf 13c; *Derebouth*, Chatteris C 1240: derogatory name for land regarded as a poor bargain.

Debdale, Ashby Folville Lei, Burrough on the Hill Lei, Evington Lei, Muston Lei, Shawell Lei, West Langton Lei, Islip Nth (*Debbedale* 1223), Welton Nth (*Depedale* 1365), West Haddown Nth (*Depedale* 1200); **Debdhill Farm,** Misterton Nt (*Depedale* 1286); **Deepdale,** Kirby Underdale ERY, Kirkburn ERY (*Depedale* c 1200), Knossington Lei, Sutton in Ashfield Nt (*Depedalesyde* 1315), Harlestone Nth: '(land in a) deep valley' [OE *dēop*, *dæl*].

Deer Acre, Broadwas Wo; **Deer Cote Hey,** Halton Ch [OE *cot*, (*ge*) *hæg*]; **Deer Dale Wood,** Rufford Nt; **Deer Garths,** Witherslack We [ON *garðr*]; **Deer Meadow,** Melbourne Db (*Le Deresmedowe* 1482), Cantley Nf; **Deer Park,** Elsdon Nb [ME *park*]; **Deer Pleck,** Hermitage Do [ME *plek*]; 'land on or near which deer were seen' [OE *dēor*].

Delfs, East Murton Du; **Delft,** Crook & Willington Du; **The Delph,** Feltwell Nf; **Delph Field,** Brighouse WRY; **Delph**

Meadow, Church Laughton Ch; **Delve(s) Close,** Alderwasley Db, Newbottle Du: 'land by a quarry' [OE (*ge*) *delf*].

(The) Dell, Kimpton Hrt, Odstone Lei; **Dell Close,** Basing Ha, Cheriton Ha; **Dell Crate,** Ellisfield Ha [OE *croft*]; **Dell Croft,** Redbourn Hrt; **Dell Field,** Alton Ha, Froxfield Ha, Hambledon Ha, Great Gaddesden Hrt (*Dellecroft* 1434), Hemel Hempstead Hrt; **Dell Mead,** Hatfield Hrt; **Dell Orchard,** King's Warden Hrt (*Dellcroft* 1597); **The Dells,** Braughing Hrt: 'valley, chalk-pit' [OE *dell*].

Demesne, Temple Sowerby We; **Big & Little Demesne,** Clifton Ch; **Demesne Land(s),** Bonsall Db, Snydale WRY: 'land occupied by the lord of the manor' [AN *demesne*].

Dencher Field, Merstham Sr (*Denshire Field* 1791); **Denshers Meadow,** Aston Flamville Lei; **Denshire Field,** Hadlow K; **Devonshire Banks,** Betchton Ch: 'land which has been pared and burnt'. This process was described in the mid-seventeenth century by Sir Richard Weston in *Discours of the Husbandrie used in Brabant & Flanders.* He referred to the practice 'which wee call Devonshiring' (cf Ernle, *English Farming Past and Present*, 107). See also Burnbacked Meadow.

Devils Acre, Hadlow K; **Devils Bed,** Calne W; **Devils Bush Field,** Staines Mx; **Devil's Dell,** Alton Ha; **Devils Den,** Chart Sutton K; **Devils Dole,** Enfield Mx; **Devil's Own,** Norton Lindsey Wa: derogatory names for unproductive or difficult land.

Devils Bit, Stoke Lyne O, 'land on which scabious grew', alluding to devil's bit scabious (*Scabiosa succisa*).

Devil's Neck, Harpenden Hrt; **Devil's Nick,** Lamberhurst K: 'long, narrow fields'.

Dial(s) Close(s), Ault Hucknall Db, Titchfield Ha, Graveley Hrt, Wilford Nt, Sandford St Martin O; **Dial Field,** Stretton Ch, Kimpton Hrt, Pirton Hrt, Ridge Hrt, Friern Barnet Mx, Thornton WRY; **Dial Hill,** Aldsworth Gl; **Dial Mead,** Ridge Hrt; **Dial Parrock,** Kirby Lonsdale We; **Dial Piece,** Swyncombe O; **Dial Row,** Kintbury Brk; **Dyal Croft,** Sproston Ch; **The Dyall Garth,** Hetton le Hole Du; **Dyle Yard,** Hodsock Nt: 'land near or containing a sun-dial, or having a dial cut in the turf'.

Diamond, Cressage Sa, alludes to the shape of the field.

Dibdel, Littleton Ha, Sparsholt Ha; **Dibdens,** Ringwood Ha; **Dip Acre,** Shipton under Wychwood O; **Dip Dell,** North Mimms Hrt (*Depdell* 1467); **Dip Moor,** Bradwall Ch: 'deep land' [OE *dēop*].

Dig Butts, Little Marton La; **Dig Field,** Nether Peover Ch; **Dig Hole(s),** Antrobus Ch, Goosnargh La, Rawcliffe with Tarnacre La; **Dig Lake,** Antrobus Ch, Lymm Ch, Thelwall Ch [OE *lacu*, '*stream*']; **Dig Mire,** Barnacre La: 'land on which ducks were kept' [MnE dial. *dig*].

The Dingle, Twemlow Ch; **Dingle Dongle,** Great Ness Sa; **Dingle Field,** Hatton Ch; **Dingle Piece,** Alvechurch Wo: 'land by a deep hollow' [ME *dingle*].

Dirtbroad Butt, Ashton on Mersey Ch; **Dirt Croft,** Buckhorn Weston Do; **Dirt Hole,** Green Fairfield Db; **Dirt Meadow,** High Legh Ch; **Dirt Reins,** Newby We [ON *reinn*]; **Dirty Bottom,** Pyrton O; **Dirty Close,** Toot Baldon O; **Dirty Field,** Macclesfield Forest Ch; **Dirty Ing,** Brough We [ON *eng*]; **Dirty Lane Close,** Great Hucklow Db; **Dirty Meadow,** Altrincham Ch, Sutton Downes Ch, Kirkby Mallory Lei; **Dirty Piece,** Longford Db: 'muddy land'.

Dirty Shanks, Pilling La, a derogatory name implying that all the land is good for is to soil the legs of those working on it.

Discovery, Thelwall Ch, a name for a remote, secluded field.

Dish Potts, Houghton le Spring Du, '(land covered in) shallow holes'.

Dismal Brow, Longsleddale We [OE *brū*]; **Dismals,** Bentworth Ha; **Long Dismals,** Cookham Brk (*Dismarke* 1502): 'gloomy or unlucky land', though the Cookham name probably embodies the surname of John Dismers, named in local records in 1322 [OF *dis mal*, Lat *dies mali* 'evil days'].

Distants, Great Hucklow Db, self-explanatory.

Ditch Croft, Peover Superior Ch; **Ditch End,** Alderwasley Db; **Ditch End Close,** Burton Overy Lei; **Ditch Field,** Mere Ch, Great Amwell Hrt (*Dichfeld* 1374); **Ditch Furlong,** Twickenham

Mx (*Dichfurlong* 1343): 'land with, or near, a drainage channel' [OE *dīc*].

Dobbin Croft, Partington Ch, possibly 'small enclosure for an old horse' [MnE dial. *dobbin*].

Dock Close, Blaston St Giles Lei, Warborough O; **Dock Field,** Aston Hrt (*Dockcroft* 1638); **Dock Furlong,** Sibford Ferns O; **Dockham,** Winstone Gl; **Dockhams,** Houghton Ha [OE *hamm*]; **Dock Leasow,** Cold Norton St; **Dock Mead,** Furneux Pelham Hrt (*Dockemeade* 1556); **Dockey Field,** Lostock Graham Ch (*Dokkefeld* 1494), East Anstey D; **Dockey Whong,** Hoveringham Nt (*Dokewonge* 1548) [ON *vangr*]; **Docky Close,** Thurlaston Lei; **Docky Leasow,** Frodesley Sa: names alluding to the dock (*Rumex* spp), a troublesome weed [OE *docce*].

Dockeray Meadow, Charlesworth Db [ON *vrá*, 'nook']; **Docker Bank,** Underbarrow We: 'land in a valley' [ON *dokk*].

Doctor's Close, Holt Lei; **Doctor's Down,** East Allington D; **Doctor's Field,** Alphington D: 'land allocated to the doctor'.

Doe Croft, Binstead & Neatham Ha, Odiham Ha; **Doe Field,** Brereton cum Smethwick Ch; **Doe Lands,** Barton We; **Doe Meadow,** Heage Db (*Daweacre* 1415); **Does Hill,** Highclere Ha; **Doe's Piddle,** Mortimer Brk: these names possibly all refer to the female fallow deer, but the meaning of MnE dialect *doe*, 'to fatten (cattle)' cannot be ruled out (cf PNCh ii 277).

Dog Croft, Bennington Hrt (*Dockcroft* 1638); **Dog Flatt,** Askham We; **Dog Furlong,** Pucklechurch Gl (*Dockfurlong* 1571); **Dog Holt,** West Alvington D; **Dog Lane,** Alkmonton Db: the two early forms cited indicate that none of these names can be treated as self-explanatory, and it may well be argued that 'land on which dock was abundant' makes better sense in almost every instance.

Dog Kennel, Windsor Brk, Piddington O; **Dog Kennel Close,** Bucklebury Brk, Church Gresley Db, Herriard Ha, Evington Lei; **Dog Kennel Field,** Marton Ch, Aldershot Ha, Chiddingfold Sr; **Dog Kennel Ground,** Mortimer Brk; **Dogs Kennel,** Holwell Do: 'land on which dogs were kennelled', some names possibly alluding to the hounds belonging to a hunt.

Dog Kennel Farm, Offley Hrt, a derogatory name.

Dog Tails, Hylton Du; **Dogtails Copse,** Odiham Ha: 'land on which dog's-tail grass grew'. Crested dog's-tail grass (*Cynosurus cristatus*) is common throughout England, particularly on old grasslands.

Dole Croft, Sale Ch; **Dole Field,** Earls Colne Ess; **Dole Mead,** Stoke Park Ha, Broxbourne Hrt (*Dolemade* 1391); **Dole Meadow** Keckwick Ch; Wappenham Nth (cf. *Smaledole* 1200); **Dolings,** Hassingham Nf; **Doul Field,** Lindsell Ess (cf. *Broddole* 1466), Great Mapleshead Ess: 'common land divided into shares' [OE *dāl*].

Donation Land, Sherborne St John Ha, a charitable endowment.

Dora's Field, Rydal We, 'land owned by Dora'. William Wordsworth gave this land to his daughter.

Doubtful Piece, Calne W, derogatory name for unreliable land.

Dove Bank, Hulme Walfield Ch; **Dove Close,** Enbourne Brk; **Dove Field and Mead,** Bray Brk; **Dove Field Close,** Abney Db; **Dove Hole Close,** Burrough on the Hill Lei; **Dove Lands,** Barbon We; **Dove Moor Close,** Melbourne Db; **Dove Royd,** Gomersal WRY [OE **rodu*]; **Dove Slack,** Firbank We (*Duuesclake* 1201): 'land frequented by doves' [OE *dufe*].

Dove Coat, Upper Rawcliffe La; **Dove Coat Garth,** Ferry Fryston WRY; **Dove Coat Meadow,** Great Eccleston La; **Little Dovecoat Field,** Elwick Hall Du; **Dove Cote Close,** Aston Flamville Lei, Breedon on the Hill Lei, Illston Lei, Lockington Lei, Twycross Lei; **Dove Cote Garth,** North Elmsall WRY [ON *garðr*]; **Dove Cote Hey,** Thistleton La; **Dovecot Holt,** Babworth Nt; **Dove Cote Leys,** Stretton Parva Lei; **Dovehouse Close,** Whaddon C, Appleton Ch, Croxall Db, Welford on Avon Gl, Ashwell Hrt, Pirton Hrt, Shangton Lei, Stretton Parva Lei, Adderbury O, Bicester O, Churchill O, Claydon O, Hook Norton O, Shorthampton O (*Dufcote Close* 1551), Wolvercote O, Yaxley Sf; **Dove House Croft,** Lamash Ess; **Dovehouse Field,** Ardleigh Ess, Earls Colne Ess, Feering Ess, Layer Marney Ess (*Dufhousefeld* 1331), Stansted Mountfitchet Ess (*Dowffehousecroft* 1516), North Mimms Hrt; **Dovehouse Furlong,** Wroxton O; **Dovehouse**

Home Close, Prescote O; **Dovehouse Mead,** Romford Ess, Stapleford Tawney Ess; **Dovehouse Meadow,** Pattiswick Ess (*Dufhowse Crofte* 1465): 'land containing, or adjoining, a dovecote'. The dovecote (or culverhouse, or pigeonhouse) was an important feature of the rural economy from the thirteenth century onwards; it was often a substantial building, and so would be the kind of landmark that would provide an obvious designation for crofts and closes.

Dreadful, Dunham Massey Ch, a derogatory name (cf Terrible).

Drift (Great), Edmondthorpe Lei; **Drift Close,** Harston Lei; **Drift Piece,** Ashleyhay Db; **Driftway,** Alton Ha, Froyle Ha; **Drove Close,** Kibworth Lei; **Drove Piece,** Mortimer Brk; **Drove Road,** Croxton Nf: 'land adjoining road along which cattle were driven' [ME *drift*, OE *drāf*].

Dripping Pan, Haughton Nt, 'land in a shallow depression'.

Drum Field, Over Wallop Ha, 'land on which recruiting took place'.

Drumble, Andlem Ch, Somerford Booths Ch; **Drumble Field,** Hatherton Ch, Snelston Ch; **Upper Lower, Little Drumbles,** Lanley & Ruckley Sa; **Drumble Plantation,** Blakenhall Ch; **Dumbello Meadow,** Minshull Vernon Ch [OE *hol*]; **The Dumbles,** Annesley Nt, Hucknall under Huthwaite Nt: 'land in a hollow or shady dell' [OE **dumbel*].

Drunkards Bush Close, Beechamwell Nf, a derogatory name for rough, unproductive land.

Drunken Field, Alton Ha, 'water-logged land'.

Dry Banks, Sherington Bk; **Dry Brook,** Denton O (*On Drygean Broc* 956); **Dry Close,** Cookham Brk, Abbotsham D, Hillfield Do, Holwell Do, North Lopham Nf; **Dry Docking,** Forncett St Peter Nf [OE *docce*, ON *eng*]; **Dry Field,** Twemlow Ch, Woodford Ch, Chinley Db; **Dry Ground,** Hungerford Brk, Bruern O, Crawley O; **Dry Hills,** Bakewell Db; **Dry Leaze,** Burghfield Brk, Bagendon Gl; **Dry Leys,** Tadlow C [OE *lǣs*]; **Dry Mead,** Mortimer Brk, Manston Do; **Dry Meadow,** Berrynarbor D, West Anstey D; **Dry Piece,** Bampton D; **Dry Pits,** Shipbrook Ch: self-explanatory names [OE *drȳge*].

Dub Close, Shap We; **Dub Gils,** Crackenthorpe We [ON *gil*]; **Dub Side,** Docker We: 'land beside, or containing, a pool' [OE **dubb*].

Dublin Acre, Shap Rural We, a transferred name for a remote field.

Duck Field, Bucklebury Brk; **Ducklands,** Holme We; **Duck Mead,** Hendon Mx; **Duck Meadow,** Sheet Ha, Evington Lei, Shalford Sr; **Duck Poodle,** Waterpury O; **Duck Puddle,** Forest Hill with Shotover O, Grafton & Radcot O: 'land containing a duckpond'.

Ducket, Dalston Cu; **Duffers,** Furneux Pelham Hrt, North Lopham Nf, Shenington O; **Duffers Close,** Eltisley C; **Duffers Field,** Ware Hrt (*Dovehouse Field* 1674); *Duffous Yeard*, East Dereham Nf 1628 (*Duffowseyard* 1474): 'land containing a dovecote or dove-house'. See also Dove Coat.

Ducking Stool, Nether Peover Ch, 'land adjoining place of punishment for scolds'.

Duck's Acre, Rushall W, land named in honour of Stephen Duck (1705–56). The Duke of Wellington gave the land to endow an annual dinner for local threshers in memory of Duck, the thresher poet, who was born in Rushall.

Duffers, see Ducket.

Duke, Elwick Hall Du, an arbitrary name commemorating the Duke of Wellington; adjoining fields are named Nelson and Oxford, and not far away are Blucher, Donkin, Wellington and Waterloo. Elsewhere in the parish are St David and St Peter.

The Dumples, Norton juxta Twycross Lei, Eakring Nt; **Dumpole Close,** Hatfield WRY: 'land in a depression' [OE **dumpel*].

Dundee, Markfield Lei, probably indicates a remote piece of land.

Dung Croft, Reading Brk (*Dongecrofte* t.Ed 6), Lechlade Gl; **Dung Field,** Byley Ch; **Dung Lands,** Stevenage Hrt (*Dongedelond* t.Ric 2); **Dungy Leaze,** Almondsbury Gl; **Dungy Mead,** Wickwar Gl: 'land to which manure was applied' [OE *dung*].

Dungmix Field, Haslemere Sr, 'land containing manure heap' [OE *mixen*].

Dunkirk, Little Downham C, Bakewell Db, Hawkesbury Gl, Holwell Lei, Strickland Roger We; **Dunkirk Wood,** Newton Ch: commemorative names, probably alluding to the Duke of York's unsuccessful siege of Dunkirk in 1793, with overtones of remoteness and difficult management.

Dunnocks (Great & Little), East Dereham Nf; **Dunnocks Bank,** Sutton Downes Ch; **Dunnocks Fold,** Alsager Ch: 'land on which dunnocks were seen'. The dunnock is the hedge sparrow (*Prunella modularis*) [OE *dunnoc*].

Dust Furlong, Gilmorton Lei; **Dust Hill,** Easton Neston Nth: self-explanatory names [OE *dūst*].

Dutch Elm Walk Yard, Shirburn O, alludes to land by an avenue of elm trees, *Dutch* being a general term for any variety other than the most familiar one.

Dyehouse Lot, Pilling La; **Dye House Meadow,** Kettleshulme Ch; **Dyehouses Yard,** Hurdsfield Ch; **Dyer Lands,** Kirkoswald Cu: 'land adjoining, or containing, a dye-works'.

E

Eaning Close, Badby Nth, 'land on which lambing ewes were kept' [OE *geēane*, 'yeaning'].

Earthquake Plantation, Birdsall ERY, alludes to a landslide.

Eastbach Meend, West Dean Gl [OE *bece*, OW *minid*]; **East Close,** Ford Du, Billesdon Lei, Greetham R, Hambleton R; **East Croft,** Bucklebury Brk (*East Crat* 1674); **East Demesne,** Hylton Du; **East Down,** Alwington D, Ashreigney D; **East Field,** Littleport C, Sherston W; **East Hill,** Kintbury Brk, Billesdon Lei, Carshalton Sr (*Le Esthelde* 1548); **East Mead,** Hillfield Do; **East Nook,** Bakewell Db; **East Rift,** Hylton Du [ME *rift*, 'cleft, chasm']: 'land on the east side' [OE *ēast*].

East Field, pre-enclosure great field name in (among many others): Easington ERY, Harpham ERY, Hornsea ERY, Sproatley ERY, Turnstall ERY, Welwick ERY, Belchamp St Paul's Ess, Broadfield Hrt, Asfordby Lei, Frisby on the Wreake Lei,

Harston Lei, Hungerton Lei, Peatling Parva Lei, Thrussington Lei, Bulmer NRY, Elvington NRY, Flaxton NRY, Marske NRY, Banstead Sr, Askham Richard WRY, Ledsham WRY, Thryborgh WRY.

Easter Barton, Berrynarbor D [OE *beretūn*]; **Easter Chalk Paddock,** Reading Brk; **Easter Close,** Ashreigney D; **Easter Field,** South Kirby WRY, Wilsden WRY; **Easter Greaves,** Helsby Ch; **Easter Hill,** East Anstey D; **Easter Meadow,** Aston Subedge Gl, Aston Wa; **Easter Piece,** Middleton & Smerrill Db: either 'eastern piece of land' or 'land by a sheepfold' [OE *ēasterra, ēowestre*].

Easy Close, Newton Unthank Lei; **Easy Furlong,** Chadlington O: complimentary names for good land.

Eating House Meadow, Checkley Ch, Nantwich Ch (*Heatyng House Yorde* 1545): 'land adjoining a building in which brine was evaporated'. Such buildings were also known as wich-houses. See Wich Field.

Ed Field, Shipbrook Ch, 'land enclosed from furlong headland' [OE **hēafodland*].

Edenbro, Frampton Cotterell Gl (*Enedebergh* 1290), 'duck hill' [OE *ened*, 'duck'; *beorg*].

Edinburgh Farm, Day Drayton C, transferred name for a remote piece of land, to the south of which is Scotland Farm.

Egg Croft, Bosley Ch; **Egg Holme,** Strickland Ketel We; **Egg Moor,** Longden Sa: possibly 'land on which snowberries were found'; the snowberry (*Symphoricarpus racemosus*) is a shrub of the elder family which bears large white berries [MnE dial. *egg*].

Egypt, Wheatenhurst Gl, Weston Hrt; **Egypt Farm,** Rivenhall Ess: transferred name for a remote piece of land.

(The) Eight Acres, Norton Ch, Blackwell Db, Eaton & Alsop Db, Eckington Db, Osmaston Db, Alton Pancras Do, Fifehead Neville Do, Hermitage Do, Holwell Do, Mappowder Do, Houghton le Spring Du, Newbottle Du, Barnsley Gl, Billesdon Lei, Bushby Lei, Foston Lei, Frolesworth Lei, Hoby Lei, Knossington Lei, Peckleton Lei, Ratby Lei, Shawell Lei, Welham Lei, Stretton

R, Westbury Sa; **Eight Acre Close,** Billesdon Lei; **Eight Acre Pildash,** Odstone Lei [OE **pilede æsc*, 'peeled ash tree']: 'land having an area of eight acres or thereabouts' [OE *æcer*].

Eight Butts, Agden Ch, Acton Burnell Sa; **Eight Day Math,** Betchton Ch, Haslington Ch, Monks Coppenhall Ch, Tetton Ch, Warmingham Ch; **Eight Day(s) Work,** Marton Ch; **The Eight Land,** Armley WRY: 'land with an area of eight units'. See Day Math, Day Work.

Eightman Mead, Little Milton O; **Eight Men's Intake,** Mansfield Nt: 'land worked or owned by eight men'.

The Eight Pounds Close, Walworth Du; **Eight Shilling Meadow,** Chorley Ch: 'land valued at the stated sum of money'.

Eighteen Acres, Alton Pancras Do, Hillfield Do, Holwell Do, Foston Lei, Foxton Lei; **Eighteen Acre Close,** West Langton Lei: 'land with an area of approximately eighteen acres' [OE *æcer*].

Eighteen Pennyworth, Altrincham Ch; **Eighteen Pounds Close,** Huntwick WRY: 'land valued at the stated sums of money'.

Eighteen Swaths, Bamford Db, 'meadow land having a breadth of eighteen scythe-cuts' [OE *swæð*].

Eighteens Furlong, Isley Walton Lei, probably a former division of the common field comprising eighteen lands [OE *furlang*].

Elbow, Eggborough WRY, Sowerby WRY; **Elbow Acre,** Boddington Gl; **Elbow Close,** Great Longstone Db, Green Fairfield Db, Matlock Bath Db, Beal WRY; **Elbow Corner,** Offley Hrt; **Elbow Field,** Byley Ch; **Elbow Furlong,** Warborough O; **Elbow Hempnay,** Beer D; **Elbow Leys,** Great Bowden Lei; **Elbow Meadow,** Odd Rode Ch, Welham Lei; **Elbow Paddock,** Wellow So; **(The) Elbows,** Lyme Handley Ch, Ringwood Ha: 'land with sharp turn(s) in its boundaries, especially adjacent to a stream' [OE *elnboga*].

Elbrows, Shudy Camps C (*Eldebery* 1303), 'old fortification' [OE *ēald, burh*].

Elder Beds, Hartington Middle Quarter Db; **Elder Field,** Flaunden Hrt; **Elder Holme,** Burrough on the Hill Lei; **Elderland,** Ashmore Do; **Eldermore,** Shepton Mallet So; *Elderstobes*,

Saddington Lei 1638; *Elderstubb*, Smeeton Westerby Lei 1652; **Elder Stubbs,** Forest Hill with Shotover O, Banstead Sr; **Elder Stump,** Sherington Bk, Kislinbury Nth (*Elderstobbe* 14c); **Elder Wells,** Bremhill W (*Ellenwell* 1592); **Eldern Stub,** Dunchurch Wa: 'land on which elder trees grew, or which contained stumps of elder trees' [OE *ellern, stubb*].

Eleven Acres, Beer D, Duffield Db, Alton Pancras Do, Hillfield Do, Mappowder Do, Evington Lei, Pontesbury Sa; **Eleven Acre Riddance,** Silchester Ha [OE **ryding*]: 'land having an area of eleven acres'.

Eleven Day Math, Austerson Ch, see Day Math.

Elf Lands, Eakring Nt (*Elflandes* 13c); **Elfa Hills,** Hutton in the Forest Cu (*Elfhow* 1488) [ON *haugr*]; **Elve Field,** Garsington O; **Elves Tyning,** Castle Combe W [OE *tȳning*]; **Elwell Field,** Garsington O (*Elfwelle* 1240) [OE *wella*]: 'land haunted by a fairy or by fairies' [OE *elf*].

The Ell, Tetton Ch; **(The) Long Ell(s),** Bexhampton Ha, Witherley Lei; **Low East & Low West Ell,** Newbottle Du; **Ell Batch Copse,** Broadwas Wo [OE *bæce*]; **Ell Close,** Alderwasley Db, Eyam Db, Christchurch Ha, Billesdon Lei, Broughton Astley Lei, Over Seal Lei, Purston Jaglin WRY; **Ell Field,** Sutton Downes Ch, Widecombe D; **Ell Furlong,** Osmaston Db; **Ell Ground,** Buckhorn Weston Do, Henbury Gl, Old Sodbury Gl, Melksham W; **Ell Paddock,** Bishop's Waltham Ha; **Ell Pightle,** Sandhurst Brk: 'L-shaped piece of land'.

Ellands (High & Low), Thorne WRY (*Yelande*, *Elande* 1546), 'arable strips beside water' [OE *ēa-land*].

Ellen Hole, Mapleton Db; **Ellen Holme,** Scallthwaiterigg We (*Ellinholme* 1714); **Ellenhurst,** Thelwall Ch; **Ellen Tree,** Treswell Nt, Crigglestone WRY (*Ellyntree Shutt* t.Jas 1); **Ellentrees,** Altofts WRY: 'land with elder trees' [OE *ellern, ellen*].

Ellerbeck, Barbon We [ON *bekkr*]; **Eller Flatt,** Docker We [ON *flat*]; **Eller Greaves,** Helsby Ch [OE *grǣfe*]; **Ellerholme Farm,** Hatfield WRY; *Ellerschawe*, Beetham We 12c [OE *sceaga*]: 'land with alder trees' [ON *elri*].

Elm Close, Beal WRY, Sharlston WRY; **Elm(s) Field,** Much Cowarne He, Lockington Lei; **Elm Ground,** Holwell Do; **Elm Hayes,** Westwood W; **Elm Hill,** Tilstone Fearnall Ch; **Elm Ing,** Casterton We; **Elm Intake,** Wilsen WRY; **Elm Leys,** Burrough on the Hill Lei; **Elm Piece,** Kintbury Brk: 'land by elm trees' [OE *elm*].

Elve Acre, Hatfield WRY (*Alevenacre* 1483), 'piece of land eleven acres in area'.

Elve Field, Garsington O, see Elf Lands.

Em Furlong, Stanton Db, 'land shaped like the letter M'.

Emmett Hill, Ockham Sr, 'hill infested with ants' [OE *ǣmette*].

Emmy Downs, High Easter Ess (*Le Ympetoun* 1329); **Empty Common,** Cambridge C (*Le Impeye* 1432); **Empty Field,** Woodditton C (*Impheyfeld* 1338): 'sapling enclosure, nursery for young trees' [OE *impe*, *(ge)hæg*]. See also Imp Copse.

Empole, Old Nth (*Enedepol* 13c), '(land by) duck pond' [OE *ened*, *pōl*].

Empty Purse, Boxwell Gl, Hawkesbury Gl: derogatory name for unprofitable land.

Enam (High), Great Singleton La; **Long Enam,** Stalmine La; **Enams,** Blencogo Cu; **Enholmes,** Patrington ERY (*Ingholmes* 1828): 'piece of land taken in for cultivation'; the term was applied to land habitually cultivated when the remainder of the great field was left fallow [ON *afnam*].

Encroachment, Duffield Db, 'common land taken into private tenure'.

Engine Close, Codnor & Loscoe Db, Great Longstone Db, Wensley & Snitterton Db; **Engine Field,** Bollington Ch, Edale Db, Newbottle Du, Pontesbury Sa; **Engine Meadow,** Sandhurst Brk; **Near & Far Engine Piece,** Coleorton Lei: 'land on which agricultural or other machines were sited'.

England, Sherington Bk 1580; **Old England,** Welham Lei; **England Meadow,** Welham Lei; **England Shot,** Kilmeston Ha [OE *scēat*]; **Englands,** Fingringhoe Ess, Arnesby Lei, Horley

Sr; **Englands Pen,** Little Somerford W: 'land cultivated for the owner's use and not let to a tenant' [ME *inland*].

Ennox, Monkton Combe So, South Stoke So; **Enochs,** Westerleigh Gl; **Enoch's Barn,** Horsley Gl (*Innocke* 1595, *Innox* 1639); **Enocks,** Stalbridge Do; **Enox,** Avening Gl, Corston So; **Enox Piece,** Kingston St Michael W (*Northynnokes* 1428): 'land temporarily enclosed for cultivation'. See also Inake [ME *inhōke*].

Envy Hall, Harpenden Hrt, a derogatory name for poor land.

Epistle Field, Bishop's Castle Sa, 'land on which the epistle is read during Rogationtide processions'. See also The Gospel, Luke Stone, The Psalms.

Everlasting, West Alvington D, Cardeston Sa: 'land requiring interminable labour'.

Everybody's Mead, West Parley Do, 'grassland common to all, not divided into lots'.

Every Years Land, Kingham O, Warborough O: 'fertile land that does not require to be left fallow'.

Ewe Close, Burton Lazars Lei; **Ewe Field,** Holwell Lei; **Ewe Lays,** Gatcombe Wt; **Ewe Leaze,** Alton Pancras Do, Holwell Do [OE *lǣs*]; **Ewe Lee,** Eyam Woodlands Db; **Ewe Yean Ground,** Aldsworth Gl: 'land reserved for ewes' [OE *eowu*].

Ewe Down, Collingbourne Kingston W (*Iudon* 1241); **Ewetree Green,** Lamberhurst K: 'land adjoining or containing yew trees' [OE *īw*].

Ewster Ham, Harwick O, 'land with a sheepfold' [OE *ēowestre, hamm*].

Experiment Field, Adderbury O, probably alludes to agricultural improvement. As early as 1757, observes Lord Ernle, 'Francis Home had insisted on the dependence of agriculture on "Chymistry". Without a knowledge of that science, he said, agriculture could not be reduced to principles'. (*English Farming Past and Present*, 216). After Humphrey Davy's pioneer work in agricultural chemistry, and Coke's wide-ranging improvements, tests and trials became as much a part of the agrarian way of life as ploughing, hedging and ditching.

F

Factory Close, Crich Db; **Factory Holm,** Claughton La; **Factory Meadow,** Rispham with Norbreck La: 'land adjoining a factory'.

Fag Acre, Muston Lei; **Fag End,** Cookham Brk; **Fag Leasow,** Pontesbury Sa: 'last and poorest lands to be allotted', but the Pontesbury name may be a variant of Feg(g) (qv).

Fair Ground, Northmoor O; **Fair Holme,** Claughton La [ON *holmr*]; **Fair Place Piece,** Cardiston Sa: either 'land on which an annual fair was held', or 'fine piece of land' [OE *fæger*].

Fairley, Cheshunt Hrt (*Foley* 1278, *Fouley*, *Foulley* 1549), 'pleasant clearing', deliberately altered from 'filthy clearing', which the early forms clearly mean [OE *fæger*, *fūl*, *leah*].

Fairy Croft, Halstead Rural Ess; **Fairy Field,** Marton Ch; **Fairy Ground,** Combe O; **Fairy Holes,** Newby We; **Fairy Land,** West Felton Sa; **Fairy Pit,** North Stoke So: 'land said to be haunted by fairies'.

Fallow Close, Dadlington Lei, Illston Lei; **Fallow Field,** Wharton Ch, Hope Db, Nettlebed O; **Fallow Gores,** Hope Woodlands Db; **Fallowing Close,** Liversedge WRY: 'arable land', evidently in the neighbourhood of pieces of land otherwise cultivated—probably grassland [OE *falh*, *fælging*].

Famish Acre, Marksbury So; **Famish Beggar,** Corsham W; **Famish Croft,** Sutton Sa; **Famish Leys,** Monkhopton Sa; **Famish Park,** Stanton Lacy Sa: derogatory names for unproductive land.

Fan Damons, Kemerton Gl, ie Van Diemen's (Land), a transferred name for remote fields. See Van Dieman's Land.

Fan Field, Great Waltham Ess (*La Fanne* 1402), Ware Hrt (*Fanfeld* 15c); **Fan Mead,** Ashwell Hrt: 'marshy land' [OE (ESax) *fænn*].

Fan Hall, Hadlow K (*Farnhale* 1447), 'fern nook' [OE *fearn*, *halh*].

Far Close, Alderwasley Db, Barwell Lei, Willoughby Waterless Lei; **Far Field,** Hope Woodlands Db, Houghton le Spring Du, Twycross Lei, Haltwhistle Nb, Stretton R; **Fargrass,** Ashwell R; **Far Meadow,** Carlton Curlieu Lei, Evington Lei, Goadby Lei,

Knossington Lei, Loughborough Lei, Ashwell R; **Far Pasture,** Newton Unthank Lei; **Far Piece,** North Rode Ch, Spelsbury O; **Farther Slade,** Hatherton Ch: 'land a great(er) distance from the village' [OE *feor*].

Far Islam, Ashton on Mersey Ch, a picturesque name for a remote piece of land.

Fardel, Wrington So; **The Fardol,** Upper Heyford O; **Fardol Green,** Upper Heyford O; **Farundell Furlong,** Stanton Gl: 'fourth part' [OE *feorða(n)*, *dǣl*, 'share'].

Farn Breck, Stalmine La [ON *brekka*]; **Farne Fields,** Hornsey Mx (*Fernefeld* 1 489); **Farnham Field,** Braughing Hrt (*Farndunehille* 13c): 'fern-covered land' [OE *fearn*].

Farthing, Bourton O, Feckenham Wo; **Farthing Acre,** Green Fairfield Db; **Farthing Clay,** Brindley Ch; **Farthing Croft,** Amport Ha; **Farthing Field,** Great Horkesley Ess (*fferdyngs* 1505), Monxton Ha, Charlbury O; **Farthing Flatt,** Over Alderley Ch; **Farthing Grove,** Broadwas Wo; **Farthing Hill,** Hendon Mx; **Farthing Lands,** Aldershot Ha; **Farthing Meadow,** Faddiley Ch, Hope Db; **Farthing Piece,** Rowington Wa; **Farthing Pightle,** Bucklebury Brk (*Farthinges* c 1590); **Farthinghams Meadow,** Sherborne St John Ha [OE *hamm*]; **(The) Farthings,** Kingsley Ch, Chingford Ess, Little Sampford Ess (*ffarthinge* t.Eliz 1), Great Gaddesden Hrt (*Netherferthing* 1369), South Croxton Lei, Shipton under Wychwood O (*Le Fardynge* 1551), Hambledon Sr: 'fourth part'; in a few instances the name may allude (possibly ironically) to the value of the land, and it is possible that some may embody the surname Farthing [OE *feorðung*].

Fat Close, Abney Db, Pittington Du; **Fat Field,** Lewknor O; **Fatland Field,** Lamberhurst K; **Fatlands,** Baggrave Lei, Rotherby Lei; **Fat Pasture,** Bruen Stapelford Ch, Minshull Vernon Ch: 'rich land'.

Featherbed, Maidford Nth; **Feather Bed Field,** Dunham Massey Ch, Rudheath Ch; **Feather Bed Ground,** Ecchinswell Ha; **Feather Field,** Ashmansworth Ha: 'land with soft soil'.

Fegg (Further, Little, Lower, Near, Upper), Cardiston Sa; **Feggy Leasow,** Bulthy Sa; **Far, Long, Near, Short Feggy Leasow,** Cold Norton St; **Feggy Meadow,** Bulthy Sa: 'marshy land'.

Fennel Pleck, Isley Walton Lei, 'land on which fennel grew'. [OE *fenul*, ME *plek*]. This herb (*Fœniculum vulgare*) was formerly widely cultivated; it was (and is) used pharmaceutically as well as in sauces served with fish.

Fern Close, Cookham Brk; **Fern Cote,** Bucklebury Brk (*Fern Croft* 1791) [OE *croft*]; **Fernel,** Weedon Lois Nth (*Fernehill* 1593); **Fern Field,** Eyam Woodlands Db; **Fern Furlong,** Burford O; **Fernhill,** Tytherington Ch, Fifehead Neville Do, Scraptoft Lei, Salford O, Martley Wo; **Fernhill Furlong,** Ramsden O; **Ferney Bank,** Whitegate Ch; **Ferny Field,** East Tisted Ha, Chiddingfold Sr; **Ferny Furlong,** Horspath O; **Ferny Hay,** Brough & Shatton Db [OE (*ge*)*hæg*]; **Fernyhough Close,** Biggin Db (*Le Fernyhalghe* 1376) [OE *halh*]: 'land covered in fern' [OE *fearn*, *fearnig*].

Fifteen Acre Close, Donington Lei; **(The) Fifteen Acres,** Matlock Bath Db, Alton Pancras Do, Holwell Do, Hallaton Lei: 'piece of land fifteen acres in area' [OE *æcer*].

Fifteen Butts, Mooresbarrow Ch, 'close taking in fifteen short strips of an open field' [ME *butte*].

The Fifteens, Upton O, possibly land held in trust for the purpose of payment of the tax known as *fifteenths* (cf PNO, 332).

Fill Barns, Medbourne Lei, a complimentary name for fertile land.

Fingerpost Close, Dadlington Lei, Frolesworth Lei; **Fingerpost Field,** Dodcott cum Wilkisley Ch, Hough Ch, Newhall Ch, Peover Superior Ch, Arnesby Lei; **Fingerpost Leasow,** Acton Burnell Sa, Pitchford Sa: 'land near a signpost'.

Fir Close, Sall Nf; **Fir Demesne,** Hylton Du; **Fir Orchard,** Kintbourne Brk; **Fir Tree Close,** Ashleyhay Db, Clifton & Compton Db; **Fir Tree Meadow,** Pontesbury Sa; **Fir Tree Piece,** Enbourne Brk: 'land near, or containing, fir trees'.

Firebeacon, Beaford D, the site of a signal fire [OE *bēacen*].

Firmity, Evenley Nth; **Furmenty Slade,** Bradfield Nth [OE *slæd*]: 'land on which *frumenty* was grown', alluding to a type of wheat; alternatively, the reference may be to a kind of wheaten porridge, in which case the name may indicate spongy soil.

First Close, Tansley Db, Oadby Lei; **First Field,** Bere Alston D; **First Hill,** Blackawton D; **First Lount,** Oadby Lei [ON *lundr*]; **First Meadow,** Rotherby Lei, Willoughby Waterless Lei; **First Wong,** Muston Lei [ON *vangr*]: 'the nearest section of a divided close'.

Fish Croft, Buckhorn Weston Do; **Fish Fields,** Moston Ch; **Upper & Lower Fish Pits,** Brierley Hill St; **Fishpond Close,** Kniveton Db, Wirksworth Db, Barton in the Beans Lei, Beechamwell Nf, Ashwell R; **Fishpond Leasow,** Wattlesborough Sa; **Fish Ponds,** Thorpe Thewles Du; **Fish Still,** St Mary Bourne Ha [OE (WSax) *stiell*, 'fishing place']; **Fishery Meadow,** Cookham Brk: 'land adjoining a stream or pond, from which fish can be got'.

Fitch Field, Hulse Ch, Tetton Ch, Wharton Ch: 'land on which vetches were grown', referring to the fodder crop, *Vicia sativa.*

Five Acre Field, Newbottle Du; **Five Acre Mead,** Hermitage Do; **Five Acre Meadow,** Evington Lei; **Five Acres,** Sherington Bk, Bollin Fee Ch, Arlington D, Berrynarbor D, Alderwasley Db, Codnor & Loscoe Db, Matlock Bath Db, Wirksworth Db, Holwell Do, North Poorton Do, Newbottle Du, Stoughton Lei, Hinstock Sa, Ansley W, Cubbington Wa (*Fiveacres* 1200), and many other places; **Five Acres Close,** Hulland Db, Goadby Lei: 'land five acres in area, or adjoining such a piece of land' [OE *æcer*].

Five and Four Acres, Berrynarbor D; **Five and Fowkes,** Hadlow K (*Five and four acres* 1835): 'land combining two closes of the stated areas'.

Five Ash Bank, Idbury O; **Five Bushes,** Itchen Stoke Ha; **Five Bushes Furlong,** Churchill O; **Five Oak Copse,** Wychwood O; **Five Oaks,** Newton Purcell O, Habberley Sa; **Five Tree Hill,** Shepshed Lei: 'land containing a clump of five trees or bushes, or adjoining such a clump'.

Five Butts, Ashton on Mersey Ch, Bradwell Ch, Helsby Ch; **Five Cornered Field,** Onston Ch; **Five Lands,** Holbrook Db, Blackfordby Lei; **Five Lees,** Darley Db [OE *lēah*]; **Fivelin Nook,** Nunkeeling ERY (*Five Ley Nook* 1786); **Five Quarters,** Thelwall Ch; **The Five Roods,** Belper Db, Flagg Db; **Five Yards,** Wellow So: names alluding to area, measured in various ways.

Five Cornered Close, Atterton Lei; **Five Cornered Field,** Onston Ch: self-explanatory.

Five Day(s) Math, Chorley Ch, Minshull Vernon Ch, Rope Ch, Sound Ch, Tetton Ch; **Five Day(s) Work,** Marton Ch, Staffield Cu, Edale Db, Crook & Willington Du: 'areas of land representing five days' ploughing or mowing for a single labourer'. J. Dodgson, in *Notes and Queries*, NS 15 (1968), 123–4, suggests that the names relate to land worked for the lord of the manor, this customary service being reckoned in days.

Five Penny, Little Longstone Db; **Fivepenny Slack,** West Heslerton ERY (*Fivepeniland* 13c); **Five Pennyworth,** Smallwood Ch; **The Five Pound Piece,** Shavington cum Gresty Ch, Rotherfield Greys O; **Five Shilling Meadow,** Evington Lei; **Five Shillings,** Basford Ch, Crewe Ch, Shavington cum Gresty Ch; **Five Shillingsworth,** Blakenhall Ch: names alluding to the value of the land.

Flacks Field, Taksley Ess (*Flexmere* 1378), 'land on which flax was grown' [OE *fleax*, ME *mire*].

Flag Ditch Slad, Milton under Wychwood O; **Flag Holm,** Everton Nt; **Flaggwire Croft,** Gawsworth Ch; **Flaggy Doles,** Desford Lei; **Flaggy Mead,** Kintbury Brk: 'land on which marsh plants grew'; the iris may be alluded to, but some of the names, especially Flagwire Croft, may point to reeds or rushes, the coarse stalks of which are called *wire* in some dialects.

Flaishet, Holwell Do; **(The) Flash,** North Rode Ch, Claughton La, Enfield Mx, Eakring Nt, Cound Sa, Godalming Sr; **Flash Croft,** Manley Ch, Upper Rawcliffe La, Hayton Nt; **Flash Dales,** Carnaby ERY (*Flaiskedaile* 1306) [ON *deill*]; **Flash Field,** North Rode Ch, Weaverham cum Milton Ch, Woodford Ch, Goosnargh La; **Flash Meadow,** Marthall cum Warford Ch, Bradley Db, Woodplumpton La; **Flash Wood Meadow,** Chinley Db; **Flashett,** Ewhurst Sr: 'swampy or waterlogged land' [ODan *flask*, ME *flasshe*].

Flake Pits, Rainow Ch, 'flax holes', probably the same as gig-holes, in which fire was kindled to dry the flax laid on hurdles across the surface of the ground.

(The) Flat Close, Mortimer Brk, Buckhorn Weston Do, Evington Lei, Glooston Lei, Illston Lei; **Flat Field,** Harley Wa; **Flat**

Furlong, Bamford Db; **Flat Leasow,** Leebotwood Sa, Alvechurch Wo; **Flat Meadow,** Charlesworth Db, Hinton Parva Do; **Flat Shutt,** Alveston Db [OE *scēat*]: either 'level piece of ground' or 'land enclosed from a division of the common field' [ON *flat*].

Flax Butts, Eaton Ch, Eyam Db, Bryning La, Inkberrow Wo; **Flax Close,** Clifton & Compton Db, Goadby Lei, West Langton Lei; **Flax Croft,** Elston La; **Flax Field,** Darley Db; **Flaxhill,** Hook Norton O (*Flexhulle* 1260); **Flaxland(s),** Everdon Nth, Grafton Underwood Nth, Hook Norton O (*Flexlond* 1240), Aston Wa, Broadwas Wo (*Flexlond* 1240); **Flax Mead,** South Newington O; **Flax Piece,** Kingsterndale Db, Northington Ha; **Flaxsitch,** Duffield Db [OE *sīc*]; **Flaxen Hill,** Tichborne Ha; **Flaxen Mead,** Hambledon Ha: 'land on which flax was grown' [OE *flēax*]. This crop was widely cultivated in England in the seventeenth and eighteenth centuries, but declined considerably just before the beginning of the nineteenth century.

Flimborough, Winwick Nth (*Flinteboru* t.Hy 3) [OE *beorg*]; **Flint Close,** Holwell Do, Donnington Lei; **Flinty Cliffs,** Aston upon Trent Db (*Flinticlif* c 1235): 'land with flinty soil' [OE *flint*].

Flit Furlong, Toot Baldon O (*Fletefurlong* 1212); **Flit Mead,** Toot Baldon O: 'land beside a stream' [OE *flēot*].

Flitland(s), Rowland Db, Heather Lei, Ibstock Lei, Braybrook Nth (*Flithul* 1250) [OE *hyll*], Yelvertoft Nth (*Flyhtlond* 1390); **Flittam,** Bryning with Kellamergh La (*Flitteholm* 1230) [ON *holmr*]: 'land in dispute' [OE (*ge*)*flit*, 'dispute']. It will be found that the fields are on parish boundaries.

Flood Acre, Alresford Ha; **Floodgate Close,** Dadlington Lei; **Floodgate Meadow,** Broughton Astley Lei; **Floodlands Field,** Gatcombe Wt; **Flude Piece,** Glenfield Lei: 'land subject to flooding'. [OE *flōd*].

Foal Garth, North Elmsall WRY; **Foal House Close,** Heather Lei; **Foldcatts,** Medbourne Lei (*Folcotes* 1344) [OE *cot*]: 'land used for young horses' [OE *fola*].

(The) Folly, Dry Drayton C, Higher Whitley Ch, Durham Du, Bibury Gl, Wheathampstead Hrt, Cleveley La, Upton Lei,

West Langton Lei, Besthorpe Nt, Bradford on Avon W, Chippenham W, Latton W, Long Newnton W, Lyneham W, Netheravon W, Roundway W, Yatton Keynell W, Bishops Itchington Wa, Halford Wa, Napton on the Hill Wa, Skelsmergh We; **Great & Little Folly,** Prittlewell Ess; **Folly Bank,** Peakirk Nth; **Folly Bottom,** Amesbury W; **Folly Close,** Ashleyhay Do, Great Bowden Lei, Peckleton Lei, Treswell Nt, Marksbury So; **Folly Clump,** Burcombe W; **Folly Copse,** Stitchcombe W, Hartlebury Wo; **Folly Dyke,** Lound Nt; **Folly Farm,** Albury Hrt, Aldbury Hrt, Totteridge Hrt, Tring Hrt, Box W, Corsham W; **Folly Field,** Lambourn Brk, Aldenham Hrt, Steeple Aston O; **Folly Green,** Stisted Ess; **Folly Grove,** Great Amwell Hrt; **Folly Hill,** Itchen Stoke Ha, Staunton in the Vale Nt, Dorchester O; **Folly Orchard,** Welham Lei; **Folly Paddock,** Alton Ha; **Folly Plantation,** Owthorpe Nt; **Folly Wood,** Hothersall La, Great Cheverell W, Warminster W; **Lower & Upper Follys Ground,** Kiddington O; **Foolish Coppice,** Hinton Martell Do: 'land near or containing an eccentric or extravagant building'. This group of names is ripe for further research; previous investigators have established that most of the names allude to buildings erected for the sake of caprice rather than utility, and that a connexion with French *feuillée,* in the sense of 'shelter made of foliage', is extremely doubtful. The frequent application of the name to copses and clumps of trees is, however, noteworthy.

Football Butts, Todenham Gl; **Football Close,** Crich Db, Snarestone Lei; **Football Field,** Bamford Db; **Football Garth,** Calverley WRY; **Football Ground,** North Newington O: 'land on which the game of football was played'.

Footpath Field, Berrynarbor D, East Anstey D; **Footroad Close,** Broughton Astley Lei; **Footroad Field,** Sandbach Ch; **Footroad Meadow,** Barlestone Lei; **Footway Field,** Sandbach Ch, Habberley Sa; **Footway Leasow,** Frodesley Sa, Kenley Sa: 'land adjoining a footpath'.

Ford Mead, Purton W; **Ford Meadow,** Bushby Lei, Stockerston Lei; **Ford Piece,** Shenton Lei: 'land by a ford' [OE *ford*].

Fore Down, East Allington D [OE *dūn*]; **Fore Field,** Hook Do, Haltwhistle Nb; **Forlands,** Hutton Roof We; **Forehead,** Barnsley

Gl (*Foreyardesmede* 1488) [OE *geard*]; **Foreword,** Eakring Nt (*Forewodebec* 13c) [OE *wudu*]: 'land in front' [OE *fore*].

Foreshooter, Dorchester O; *Forthshetere*, Hook Norton O 1270: 'land projecting across, or within the boundaries of, another piece' [OE *forð-scēotere*].

Forest Breck, Hodsock Nt [OE *bræc*]; **Forest Close,** Glenfield Lei, Leighfield R; **Forest Flat,** Owston WRY; **Forest Meadow,** East Allington D; **Foresters Close,** Somerby Lei: 'land adjoining a forest'.

Forge Field(s), Sandbach Ch, Mellor Db, Lamberhurst K; **Forge Leasow,** Harley Sa; **Forge Meadow,** Tetton Ch, Harley Sa; **Forge Piece,** Harley Sa: 'land adjoining a smithy' [ME *forge*].

Forked Close, Ashmansworth Ha; **Forked Piece,** Windsor Brk: 'bifurcated field'.

(The) Forty, Oldbury upon Severn Gl (*Forthey* 1497), Hendon Mx, Crowmarsh O, Harpsden O; **Forty Field,** Chigwell Ess, Little Compton Wa; **Forty Furlong,** Horspath O; **Little Forties,** Highclere Ha: 'peninsula of higher ground projecting into a marshy area' [OE *forð*, *ēg*, 'island'].

(The) Forty Acre(s), Alpraham Ch, Ashton Ch, Bramhall Ch, Calveley Ch, Clotton Hoofield Ch, Siddington Ch, Ashreigney D, Turnditch Db, Fifehead Magdalen Do, North Poorton Do, Bibury Gl, Great Stretton Lei, Stockerston Lei, Wymondham Lei; Stretton R; **North & South Forty Acres,** Peatling Parva Lei: 'land of about forty acres in area'. In the absence of evidence to the contrary, a literal interpretation of the name is proposed for these examples. But cf The Forty.

Forty Acres, Widecombe D (1), Snareston Lei (2); **Forty Acres Close,** Lubenham Lei (3); **Little Forty Acre,** Stretton Parva Lei (4): ironic names for very small fields; the actual areas being (1) 18 perches, (2) less than 1½ acres, (3) about a quarter of an acre, and (4) 1 acre 21 perches. See also Hundred Acres.

Forty Shilling Close, Rowington Wa, alludes to the value of the land.

Foulmere Pit, Croxton Nf [ON *marr*]; **Foul Quab,** Mickleton Gl [OE *cwabba*]; **Foul Sitch,** Tansley Db [OE *sīc*]; **Foul Sloe,** Alton

Ha; **Foul Slough,** Aldham Ess, Hatfield Hrt (*Foweleslowe* 14c); **Foulslough Field,** North Lopham Nf [OE *slōh*]; **Foul Syke,** Ingol & Cottam La (*Fulesiche* 1230) [OE *sīc*]: 'boggy land, especially land contaminated by sewage' [OE *fūl*].

Foundry Piece, Kintbury Brk, self-explanatory.

(The) Four Acres, Lower Whitley Ch, Blackawton D, Alderwasley Db, Codnor & Loscoe Db, Tissington Db, Holwell Do, Boxwell Gl, Shenton Lei, Cressage Sa (and many other places); **Four Acre Close,** Duffield Db; **Four Acre Field,** Newbottle Du; **Four and a Half Acres,** Hillfield Do: 'land with the stated acreage'.

Four Ashes, Bradford WRY; **Four Oaks,** Dadlington Lei, Berkswell Wa: 'land containing a clump of trees of the named species'.

Four Butts, Aston juxta Mondrum Ch, Leese Ch; **Four Closes,** Kibworth Lei; **Four Ends,** Evington Lei; **Four Land End Close,** Alderwasley Db; **Four Lands,** Outseats Db; **Four Lees,** Wilsen WRY; **Four Leys,** Muston Lei; **Four Nook,** Nateby La; **Four Riggs,** Eldon Nb [ON *hryggr*]; **Four Square,** Barton in the Beans Lei: names alluding to the composition or shape of the field in various ways.

Four Day(s) Math, Tetton Ch, Edale Db, Dowdeswell Gl, Berkswell Wa; **Four Day(s) Work,** Adlington Ch, Blackden Ch, Bosley Ch, Buglawton Ch, Eaton Ch, Bradley Db, Edale Db, Hope Db, Feckenham Wo: 'land measured in daymath or daywork units'. See Five Day Math.

Four Shillings Croft, Sutton Hoofield Ch, alludes to the value of the land.

Fourteen Acre(s), Beer D, Codnor & Loscoe Db, Alton Pancras Do, Hillfield Do, Hinton Martell Do, Hinton St Mary Do, Holwell Do, Barrons Park Lei, Evington Lei, Illston Lei, Ratby Lei, Stockerston Lei; **Fourteen Acre Close,** Baggrave Lei; **Fourteen Acres Field,** Walworth Du: 'land with an area of fourteen acres'.

Fourteen Day Math, Ridley Ch, see Five Day Math.

Foxborough Close, Foxton Lei; **Fox Burgh,** Brooksby Lei [OE *beorg*]; **Fox Close,** Beechamwell Nf, Bix O; **Foxcover,** Elwick

Hall Du, Coston Lei; **Foxcover Close,** Scraptoft Lei; **Fox Covert,** Billesdon Lei, Kings Norton Lei, Peatling Magna Lei; **Fox Croft,** Kings Clere Ha; **Fox Dell,** Church Oakley Ha; **Fox Dells Field,** Bishops Stortford Hrt; **Foxdenhill,** Upper Slaughter Gl; **Fox Down,** Steventon Ha; **Fox Field,** Alderwasley Db, Nazeing Ess; **Foxgrove,** Wellow So; **Foxhedges,** Nazeing Ess; **Fox Hill,** Barwell Lei, Weedon Lois Nth, Austrey Wa (*Foxholes* 1213); **Foxhole(s),** Steeple Morden C (*Foxhole* 13c), Halton Ch, Manston Do, Stapleton Gl, Dorchester O, Preston Montford Sa, Pilton So, Church Lawford Wa (*Foxholes* 12c); **Foxhole Bank,** Adderbury O; **Foxhole Field,** Newbottle Du; **Foxhole Furlong,** Benson O; **Foxleaze Park,** Lyndhurst Ha; **Fox Lezzers,** Alveston Wa [OE *lǣs*]; **Foxmoor,** South Stoke So: 'land frequented by foxes' [OE *fox*].

Frame Close, Binstead & Neatham Ha; **Frame Field,** Hinton Ampner Ha, Titchfield Ha; **Frame Hay,** Weston Ch: 'land containing cloth-stretching frames'.

France, Buglawton Ch, Ropley Ha; **France Field,** Barton Stacey Ha: transferred name for remote fields.

Franchise Croft, Alderwasley Db; **Franchise Field,** Owston WRY: 'land conferring suffrage rights (under the unreformed electoral system), or providing sanctuary' [ME *franchise*].

The Freeboard, Carburton Nt, Ardley O, Headington O, Kiddington O; **Free Border,** Knossington Lei: 'uncultivated edge of an arable field, serving as a right of way'.

Freehold Close, Houghton le Spring Du; **Freeholders Wood,** Minsterley Sa: 'land held or used by virtue of free tenure'.

Freeths, Shepton Mallet So, 'woodland' [OE *fyhrð*].

French Bank, Skelsmergh We; **French Field,** Bostock Ch, Newbold Astbury Ch, Tilstone Fearnall Ch, Worplesdon Sr; **French Flat,** Dalston Cu; **French Ground,** South Stoke So, Wellow So; **French Mead,** Brockenhurst Ha: ambiguous names, possibly originating in the surname French, or in the names of various crops reputedly of French origin, or (in at least one instance—Dalston Cu) in commemoration of the Napoleonic wars.

French Grass, Chetnole Do, Evershot Do, Kingston Magna Do; **French Grass Field,** Long Critchell Do, Bradford on Avon W; **French Wheat Field,** Ollerton Ch, Rostherne Ch: 'land on which was grown either sainfoin (*French grass*) or Bordeaux wheat (*French wheat*)'.

Friars Crofts, Reading Brk; **Friars Field,** Grendon Wa; **Friars Mead,** Oxford O: 'land owned by, or held in trust for, communities of friars'; the term *friar* was occasionally used of orders other than those of mendicants [ME *frere*].

Friday Close, Stretton Db; **Friday Field,** Essendon Hrt (*Frydayefeld* 1421), Baddesley Ensor Wa; **Friday Flatt,** Marthall cum Warford Ch, Crofton WRY; **Friday Grove Field,** North Mimms Hrt (*Fridayesgrove* 1419); **(The) Fridays,** Poole Ch, Hempstead Ess, Writtle Ess (*Frydayes* 1419); **Fridays Close,** Easton Neston Nth; **Fridays Gate,** South Cerney Gl; **Fridays Hill,** Tandridge Sr; **Fridays Mead,** Hawkesbury Gl, Reigate Sr; *Fridaieslake*, Wharton Ch c 1230: possibly 'land on which manorial service was performed on Fridays' [OE *Frīgedæg*]. Some examples may well allude to the unlucky implications of the sixth day of the week. The surname Friday is another possible origin.

Fright Field, Dunsfold Sr (*Frythecrosse* t.Ed 6); **Frith Meadow,** Romsey Ha; Mansfield Nt: 'woodland' [OE *fyrhð*].

Frith and Brith, Kintbury Brk, possibly 'sanctuary'; the name may be a conflation of *Frith and Grith* (both terms implying 'peace, safety') and OE *friðborh*, 'peace pledge'.

Frog Hall, East Dereham Nf, Hatfield WRY; **Frog Hole(s),** Repton Db, Fifehead Magdalen Do, Manston Do; **Frog Marsh,** Abbotsham D; **Frog Mead,** Holwell Do, Croydon Sr; **Frog More,** East Pennard So; **Frog Park,** Calow Db; **Frog Sick,** Crich Db: 'land haunted by frogs'; the reference in some names may be ironic (of poor land with boggy soil etc) rather than literal [OE *frogga*].

Front Piece, Preston Montford Sa, 'land in front of a (great) house'.

Full Belly Dale, Gildersome WRY, complimentary name for productive land.

Fulling Mill Field, Steep Ha, 'land adjoining a cloth-finishing works'.

(The) **Furlong,** Alton Pancras Do, Frodesley Sa; **Furlong Close,** Aston Db: 'close consisting of one of the divisions of the former common field' [OE *furlang*].

Furnace Close, Repton Db; **Furnace Field,** Hunsworth WRY: 'land near a smelting furnace' [ME *forneis*].

Furry Close, Kings Norton Lei; **Furzebal(l),** East Allington D, West Alvington D [OE **ball*]; **Furze Brake,** Fifehead Neville Do; **Furze Close,** Chieveley Brk, Carnanton Co, Belstone D, Ilsington D, Arnesby Lei, Noseley Lei, Ellingham Nf; **Furze Down(s),** Alphington D, North Cerney Gl; **Furze Field,** Reading Brk, Leigh Sr, Worplesdon Sr; **Furze Ground,** East Dereham Nf; **Great Furze Ground,** Hermitage Do; **Furze Hill,** Cold Overton Lei, Croxton Nf; **Furze Hill Hoppett,** Welham Lei [OE **hoppet*]; **Furze Park,** Beaford D, West Alvington D; **Furze Piddle,** Upton Grey Ha [ME *pightel*]; **Furzen Hill,** Speen Brk; **Furzey Close,** North Poorton Do; **Furzey Common,** Mappowder Do; **Furzey Furlong,** Alton Pancras Do; **Furz(e)y Ground,** Hillfield Do, Toot Baldon O; **Furzey Lands,** Hook Do; **Furzy Field,** Itchen Stoke Ha, Croydon Sr (*Lez Firsen* 1543); **Furzy Green Field,** Holwell Do; **The Fuzzens,** Prescote O; **Fuzzy Ground,** North Newington O: 'land on which gorse grew'. [OE *fyrs, fyrsen*]. Numerous other field names allude to this plant (*Ulex europaeus*) under the synonyms *gorse* and *whin.*

G

Gall, Knossington Lei; **Gallands,** Priors Dean Ha; **Gallant,** Hillfield Do; **Gallant Furlong,** Astley Abbots Sa; **Gall Close,** Burghclere Ha; **Gall Park,** Belstone D; **The Gauls Meadow,** Gaddesby Lei; **The Gaw,** Allostock Ch: 'barren, wet land' [OE *galla*].

Gallantree Field, Adderley Sa; **Gallantry Bank,** Walton Superior Ch: **Gallas Field,** Crigglestone WRY; **Galley Acres,** Bakewell Db (*Gallowacre* 1598); **Galley Field,** Gestingthorpe Ess (*Galwefeld* 1370); **Galley Hill,** Stopsley Bd (*Galowehil* 1504); **Galley Nap,** Broadwell Gl; **Galleys Croft,** Meesden Hrt (*Gallowecroft* 1511); **Galleys Field,** Great Leighs Ess (*Galeffeld* 1329); **Gallow Close,**

Lubenham Lei; **Gallow Field,** Castle Hedingham Ess (*Galewefeld* 1390), Stebbing Ess (*Le Galwis* 1429); **Gallow Leys,** Wellow Nt; **Gallow Meadow,** Lubenham Lei; **Gallow Tree Close,** Lockington Lei; **Gallows Close,** Hempstead Ess, Handborough O, Old Hutton We; **Gallows Corner,** Ampney Crucis Gl; **Gallows Field,** Berkhamsted Hrt (*Galeweieshill* 1357); **Gallows Ground,** Reading Brk, Barnsley Gl; **Gallows Hill,** Steeple Morden C, Kempley Gl, Appleby Lei; **Gallows Meadow,** Enbourne Brk; **Gallows Piece,** Melbourne Db; **The Gaultry** Cossington Lei: 'site of a gallows'. It was not unusual for a manor to have its own gallows for the execution of thieves and other criminals [OE *galga, galg-trēow*].

Galloping Field, Shephall Hrt, said to be so called because a former owner of the manor house kept horses here for steeplechasing.

Gaol Meadow, Duffield Db, 'land near a prison'.

Garbage Furlong, Newbury Brk; **Garbits,** Crosby Ravensworth We; **Garborough,** Scalthwaiterigg We; *Garbrades,* Irthington Cu 1205; *Garbred,* Lambrigg We 1205; **Garbridge Close,** Murton We; **Garbridge Top,** Crosby Garrett We; **Garbroad Close,** Foxton Lei; **Garbroods,** Castleton Db; **Garbutts,** Desborough Nt (*Gorbrodefurlong* 1207); **Gardbroad,** Gumley Lei: 'land in the gore of the common arable field'; strips in the gore were broad rather than long, in order to produce worthwhile allotments of land in these wedge-shaped areas [ME *garbrede*].

Garden Close, Newbury Brk, Billesdon Lei, Stretton Magna Lei; **Garden Field,** Eaton Ch, Norton Ch, Crich Db, Arnesby Lei; **Garden Hill,** Brough We; **Garden Meadow,** Enbourne Brk, Chorley Ch; **Garden Pightle,** Forncett St Peter Nf [ME *pightel*]: 'land used for horticulture' [NF *gardin*].

Garlands, Therfield Hrt (*Garlondes* t.Hy 8), Barlestone Lei: 'strips in the gore of the common field' [OE *gāra, land*].

Garlic Field, Hatfield Hrt (*Garlykesmere* 1487); **Garlic Lands,** Farnham Sr; **Garlick Close,** Ashford Db; **Garlick Copse,** Kings Somborne Ha; **Garlick Hill,** Banstead Sr: 'land in or near which garlic was grown' [OE *gār-lēac*]. Garlic is found as a wild plant in England, but the plant (*Allium sativum*) was also formerly cultivated not only for its culinary value but also for pharmaceutical use, being a specific in the treatment of leprosy.

Garskin Bottom, Mickleham Sr; **(The) Garson,** Binstead & Neatham Ha, Horsell Sr; **Garson Meadow,** Bix O (*Rughgarston* 1399); **Garsons,** Idbury O, Seale Sr; **Garston,** Long Sutton So, Middlezoy So, Wellow So; **Garston Close,** Bentworth Sr; **Garston Pound Ground,** Burghfield Brk; **Garstones,** Orcheston St Mary W (*Le Garston* 1422); **Gascoignes,** Stourton W; **Gascons,** Windsor Brk (*Garstoneshull* 1267); **Gascons Meadow,** Egham Sr (*Upgarston* 1336); **Gascowing Meadow,** Weybridge Sr (*Gaston* 1548); **Gascoyne(s),** Charminster Do, Stoke Dabernon Sr; **Great Gaskin,** Chobham Sr; **Gaskin(g)s,** Bradley Ha, Hatfield WRY; **Gassons,** Hawkesbury Gl, Brize Norton O, Woking Sr, Hullavington W; **Gaston(s),** Worplesddon Sr (*Garston* 1351), Latton W, Malmesbury W; **Gaston's Field,** Hambledon Ha; **Gastons Ground,** Bibury Gl (*Garsintune* 1327); **Gawson,** Avebury W: 'grass enclosure, paddock' [OE *gærs-tūn*].

(The) Garth, Washington Du, Cuckney Nt, Ashwell R, Dillicar We: 'enclosure' [ON *garðr*].

Gastfield, Dumock Gl, 'land infested with gorse' [OE *gorst*].

Gate Close, East Dereham Nf (*Gathemedewys* 1474); **Gate Field,** Goosnargh La, Pilling La, Westby La; **Gate Leasow,** Kenley Sa; **Gate Moss,** Goosnargh La: 'land by a road' [ON *gata*].

Gate Saddles, South Elmsall WRY; **Gate Settleings,** Kendal We [ON *eng*]; **Gate Shackles,** Walton WRY: '(land at) a crossroads' [ME *gate-shadel*].

Gaudy Ground, Pontesbury Sa, 'land on which weld was grown'. Weld, or dyer's greenweed (*Reseda luteola*), was the source of a bright yellow or yellow-green dye [OF *gaude*].

Gawtree Thorn, Castleton Db (*Le Galtrethorne* 1455); **Gawtry,** Bradwell Db: 'site of a gallows' [OE *galg-trēow*].

Gazebo Piece, Egham Sr, 'land containing a garden-house or pavilion' [MnE *gazebo*].

Georgia Spinney, Osbaston Lei, a transferred name for remote land.

Geranium Field & Meadow, Hyde Ch, 'land on which cranesbill flourished'. Although few species of this genus are referred to popularly as 'geranium', the similarity of the leaves of most of them to those of the garden pelargonium, which is commonly so called, no doubt accounts for the name.

Gibbet Copse, Chawton Ha; **Gibbet Hill,** Weston Hrt (*Le Gybet, Gybethul* t.Ric 2); **Gibbets Field,** Brierley Hill St: 'land on which a gallows stood'. Although commonly regarded as synonyms, *gibbet* and *gallows* were not convertible terms at all periods, the former being used from the sixteenth century onwards for the single post with a jib from which the dead bodies of certain criminals were hung in chains [ME *gibet*].

Gibraltar, Rainow Ch, Fledborough Nt; **Gibraltar Close & Wood,** Cookham Brk; **Gibraltar Mill,** Werneth Ch; **Gibraltar Pasture,** Hollingwath Ch; **Gibraltar Wood,** Denton La: a transferred name alluding to land that was not only remote but possibly also rock-like.

Gig Field, Norton Ch; **Gig Hole,** North Rode Ch; **Gig Hole Field,** Ashley Ch: 'land containing pools in which flax was retted' [ME *gigge*].

Gil Closes, Rydal We; **Gill Holme,** Treales La; **Gill Meadow,** Freckleton La: 'land in, near, or containing a deep narrow valley' [ON *gil*].

Gilead Farm, Feltwell Nf, not, apparently, a transferred biblical name, but an altered form of a surname. Walter de Geylode is named in a rental, t.Ed 1.

Gin House Bank, Byley Ch, refers to the building containing an engine or agricultural machine of some kind.

Ginger Bread Close, Tideswell Db, Pyrton O; **Gingerbread Hill,** Bix O; **Gingerbread Well,** Beetham We: names possibly alluding to elaborately shaped pieces of land.

Gipsey's Close, Duffield Db; **Gipsey Plot,** Alton Pancras Do; **Gipsy Bottom,** Durweston Do: 'land used by gypsies'.

Gist Head & Foot, Musgrave We (*The Ieast* 1660), 'rented pasture' [ME *agist*].

Glade Shade, Heptonstall WRY (*Gledshaye* 1574, *The Gleid Shade* 1796); **Glead Marsh,** Battersea Sr now GL (*Glydemarshe* 1474); **Glead Wing,** Kentmere We: names alluding to the kite (*Milvus milvus*), which was a breeding species almost throughout Britain until the end of the nineteenth century. In Glade Shade, the second component seems to be a rhyming replacement of *shay*, a dialect variant of *shaw* [OE *sceaga*, 'wood']. Glead Wing may allude to the shape of the field [OE(Angl) *gleoda*, 'kite'].

Glebe Close, Long Critchell Do, Alexton Lei; **Glebe Land,** Alexton Lei, Chipping Norton O; **Glebe Mead,** Mappowder Do; **Glebe Meadow,** Swepstone Lei: 'land assigned to a clergyman as part of his benefice'.

Goal Meadow, Galby Lei; **Goaly Mead,** Ditcheat So: 'barren, wet land' [OE *galla*].

The Goar, Steventon Ha; **Gore Acre,** Bullington Ha; **Gore Corner,** Treswell Nt; **Gore Field,** Minshull Vernon Ch (*La Gore* 1220), Ashmore Do, Hornchurch Ess (*Gorfeld* 1240), Takeley Ess (*Gorefeld* 1403), Andover Ha, Hursley Ha, Anstey Hrt; **Gore Hill,** Southrop Gl; **Gore Mead,** Kingsbury Mx; **Gore Park,** Widecombe D; **Gore Pleck,** Ashmore Do; **Gore Tyning,** Nettleton W; **The Gores,** Merrow Sr, Worplesdon Sr: 'land in the triangular remnant of the field after a rectangular pattern of furlongs had been drawn up' [OE *gāra*].

Goarbroade, Oundle Nth (*Garebrode* 1261); **Gorbet Dole,** Bole Nt; **Short Gorbroad,** Iffley O; **Gorbutts,** Tideswell Db: 'land in the gore of the field'. See also Garbage Furlong [ME *garbrede*].

Gods Knowl, Over Alderley Ch (*The Gorst Knowes* 1654), 'gorse-covered hillocks' [OE *gorst*, *cnoll*].

Gold Close, Wensley Db; **Gold Field,** Buxton Db, Heptonstall WRY; **Gold Ham,** Ringwood Ha [OE *hamm*]; **Gold Hay,** Daresbury Ch; **Gold Hill,** Cowley Gl; *Goldhulle*, Hampton Gay O 1185; **Gold Meadow,** Aldershot Ha; **Gold Oak Copse,** Pamber Ha; **Gold Rings,** Romsey Ha; **Golden,** Acton Scott Sa; **Golden Acre,** Matlock Db, Painswick Gl; **The Golden Dress,** Clive & Sansaw Sa; **Golden End,** Sherrington O; **Golden Field,** Bulmer Ess; **Golden Furlong,** Crowell O; **Golden Garth,** Hatfield WRY; **Golden Hill,** Frampton Cotterell Gl, Longsleddale We; **Golden**

Holme, Rampton Nt: 'land characterised by a golden colour'. The colour may come from an abundance of yellow flowers, but occasionally (particularly with names like Gold Rings) the reference may be to 'fairy rings'—circular patches of yellowish grass, discoloured by fungal growth.

Goldfinder, Little Stretton Lei, complimentary name for a profitable field.

Gold Hord, Chiddingfold Sr; **Goldings Field,** Colne Engaine Ess (*Le Goldhord* 1390): 'land on which treasure has been found' [OE *gold-hord*].

Golgotha, Barfreston K, either an uncomplimentary reference or an allusion to topography, this is the Hebrew name for Calvary, and means 'place of the skull'.

Goltry Close, Groby Lei, 'site of a gallows' [OE *galg-trēow*].

Gomorrah Close, Snaith WRY, a biblical name transferred to express unambiguous disapproval of an infertile field, as unproductive as the land of Gomorrah after its destruction. See also Sodom.

Good Croft, Outseats Db; **Good Field,** Repton Db; **Good Fortune,** Ilsington D; **Good Mickle,** Mansergh We; **Goodness Close,** Darlton Nt; **Goodsale,** Walkern Hrt; **Good Tide Croft,** Hilton Db: complimentary names for fertile fields.

Goodman's Acre, Fulshaw Ch; **Goodman's Close,** Galby Lei; **Good Mans Hey,** Northenden Etchells Ch: if they do not allude to occupiers called Goodman, these names may refer to a piece of waste land enclosed and left to the devil, euphemistically known as Good Man (cf PNCh I, xxi).

Goodins Ox, Great Bowden Lei 1679 (*Goodinges Oxe* 1638, *Goodwyn's Ox* 1655): a name of considerable interest. A document of 1343 refers to a furlong *ubi Godwynesoxe morieabatur* (*sic*), 'where Godwin's ox died'. This is paralleled by two other medieval names; the first is also from Leicestershire: in a terrier of Hoby (1322) one of the furlongs is *Cultura quae vocatur Theretheoxenwereslaine*. The best known example of this type of name is from Northall Bk (13th century) and is quoted by almost every writer on place-names—*Thertheoxlaydede*.

Goose Acre(s), Ashmore Do, Aldsworth Gl, Scraptoft Lei, Slawston Lei 1674, Churchill O, Goring O, Westcot Barton O; **Goose Acre Mead,** Kintbury Brk; **Goose Butts,** Wilsden WRY; **Goose Close,** Crich Db; **Goose Croft,** Hemel Hempstead Hrt, Beechamwell Nf; **Goose Furlong,** Boxford Brk, Iffley O; **Goose Garth,** Beetham We; **Goose Half,** Lambourn Brk; **Gooselands,** Abney Db, Alresford Ha; **Goose Leaze,** Weston Birt Gl; **Goose Marsh,** Fifehead Magdalen Do; **Goose Mead,** Horton Gl; **Goose Meadow,** Cookham Brk; **Goose Mire,** Longsleddale We; **Goose Pingle,** Eyam Db; **Goose Plot,** Speen Brk: 'land on which geese were pastured' [OE *gōs*].

Gooseberry Garden, Bere Alston D, self-explanatory.

Gore Acre, Bullington Ha, see The Goar.

The Gorse, Ashby Folville Lei; **Gorse Break,** Alderwasley Db [OE *bræc*]; **Gorse Close,** Muston Lei, Odstone Lei; **Gorse Low,** Marton Ch (*Le Gorstilowe* 1313) [OE *hlāw*]; **Gorse Meadow,** Halstead Lei; **Nether & Far Gorse,** Dadlington Lei; **Gorses,** Offerton Db; **Gorsey Bank,** Pownall Fee Ch; **Gorsey Close,** Alkmonton Db, Bushby Lei, Evington Lei, Scraptoft Lei, Willoughby Waterless Lei, Piddington O; **Gorsey Field,** North Rode Ch, Abney Db; **Gorsey Knoll,** Alderwasley Db; **Gorsey Slang,** Hampden in Arden Wa; **Gors(t)y Croft,** Eaton Ch; **Gorsty Field,** Barston Wa (*Gorsie Field* 1596); **Gorsty Piece,** Solihull Wa (*Olde Gorsthull* 1347); **Gorsy Holme,** Hope Woodlands Db; **Gorsy Leasow,** Castle Bromwich Wa; **Gosmoor,** Ditcheat So; **Goss Close,** Bleasby Nt; **Goss Covert,** Babworth Nt; **Higher & Lower Gossamore,** East Allington D; **Gossy Close,** Ratcliffe on Soar Nt; **Gossy Leaze,** Iron Acton WRY; **Gosterlow,** Charwelton Nth [OE *hlāw*]; **Gosty Croft,** Woodford Ch; **Gosty Leys,** Bentley Wa: 'land abounding in gorse' [OE *gorst*(*ig*)].

Goshan, Odd Rode Ch, a transferred biblical name alluding to the remoteness of the field.

The Gospel, Cressage Sa; **Gospel Ash Leys,** Kirtlington O; **Gospel Brow,** Chapel en le Frith Db; **Gospel Bush,** Wapley Gl; **Gospel Elem Ground,** Stratford on Avon Wa [OE *elm*]; **Gospel Greave,** Ashford Db, Osmaston Db; **Gospel Hill,** Pucklechurch Gl; **Gospel Oak,** Avington Ha, Selston Nt, Over Whitacre Wa;

Gospel Oak Field, Exhall Wa; *Gospel Place,* Ashover Db 1584; **Gospel Sitch,** Stretton on Fosse Wa; **Gospel Thorn,** Bolsover Db; **Gospels Knap,** Little Compton Wa; **Gosper Bush,** Hawkesbury Gl: 'place where passage from the gospel was read when bounds were beaten'. See also Epistle Field.

Gotham, Osbaston Lei, a derogatory name alluding to the place from which came the proverbially foolish 'wise men' who tried to pen the cuckoo. See Cuckoo Alter.

Grammarian's Field, Brereton cum Smethwick Ch, 'schoolmaster's land', probably endowed for the support of the parish schoolmaster.

Grammers Croft, Highclere Ha; **Grammers Plot,** Hillfield Do; **Grammum's Croft,** Woodford Ch (*Grandmother's Croft* 1766); **Grandmother Meadow,** Bollin Fee Ch; **Grandmother's Meadow,** Burrough on the Hill Lei: 'dower land', ie land assigned to the support of the widow of the late owner.

Granite Piece, Widecombe D, self-explanatory.

Grass Close, Canons Ashby Nth; **Grass Coombe,** Priston So [OE *cūmb*]; **Grass Field,** Arclid Ch; **Grass Flat,** Eaton Ch [ON *flat*]; **Grass Furlong,** Churchill O; **Grass Garth,** Bole Nt, Scallthwaiterigg We, Cridling Stubbs WRY [ON *garðr*]; **Grass Gore,** North Stoke So [OE *gāra*]; **Grass Nether Leaze,** Manston Do; **Grass Pightle,** East Dereham Nf: 'pasture or meadow land' [OE *gærs*].

Gravel Close, Speen Brk; **Gravel Field,** Brightwell Baldwin O; Cottisford O, **Gravel Hill,** Laughton Lei; **Gravel Hole Close,** Bushby Lei, Frisby Lei, Houghton on the Hill Lei, Stoughton Lei; **Gravel Hole Field,** Claughton La, Nateby La; **Gravel Hole Ground,** Hermitage Do; **Gravel Lees,** Stebbing Ess; **Gravel Pightle,** Laleham Mx [ME *pightel*]: **Gravel Pit,** Great Stretton Lei, **Gravel Pit Close,** Botcheston Lei, Wardley R, Preston Montford Sa; **Gravel Pit Field,** Reading Brk, Ware Hrt (*Le Gravel Delf* 15c); **Gravel Pit Furlong,** Newbury Brk; **Gravel Pit Pasture,** Great Dunmow Ess; **Gravel Pit Piece,** Aldborough Nf, Croxton Nf; **Gravel Pit Pightle,** Cantley Nf; **Gravelly Close,** Cookham Brk; **Gravelly Hill,** Rotherfield Greys O; **Gravelly**

Pightle, Burghfield Brk: 'land from which gravel was dug, or with gravel soil' [ME *gravel*].

Great Acre, Stockham Ch [OE *æcer*]; **Great Close,** Buckhorn Weston Do, Coston Lei; **Great Dale,** Haltwhistle Nb; **Great Field,** Haltwhistle Nb; **Great Ground,** Mudford So; **Great Park,** Ashwell R; **Great Piece,** Ashmore Do, Greetham R; **Great Plantation,** Lamberhurst K: self-explanatory names.

Great Jerusalem, Eaton under Heywood Sa; **Great Virginia,** Admonton Mx: transferred names for remote pieces of land.

Greedy Guts, Pyrton O; **Greedy Shoot,** Great Eccleston La: 'land needing much manure'.

Green Acre, Ampney Crucis Gl; **Green Balk,** North Elmsall WRY; **Green Close,** Bucklebury Brk, Kintbury Brk, Alderwasley Db, Holwell Do, Cantley Nf; **Green Croft,** Bollin Fee Ch, St Michaels Hrt; **Green Dell,** Wheathampstead Hrt (*Grenedene* 1305); **Green Field,** Norton Ch, Abbotsham D; **Green Furlong,** Claybrook Lei, Claydon O; **Great Green Gate,** Alexton Lei; **Green Ground,** Idbury O; **Green Hays,** Yockleton Sa; **Green Hedges,** Evington Lei; **Green Heys,** Newton Ch (*Le Grenehey* 1423); **Green Hill,** Hinton Parva Do; **Green Lands,** Chinley Db, Kirby Underdale ERY; **Green Laws,** Houghton le Spring Du [OE *lagu*, 'pool']; **Green Leasow,** Stirchley Sa; **Green Meadow,** Yeardsley Ch, East Anstey D; **Green Mier Pightle,** Cantley Nf; **Green Park,** West Alvington D; **Green Parlour,** Southwick W; **Green Sitch,** Doveridge Db [OE *sīc*]; **Green Sitches,** Hathersage Db; **Green Spots,** Lockington Lei; **Green Whong,** Kneesall Nt [ON *vangr*]: 'notably green piece of land', the colour often indicating marshy ground.

The Grove, Bucklebury Brk, Fifehead Magdalen Do; **Grove Close,** Sall Nf; **Grove Leasow,** Cold Norton St; **Grove Meadow,** Witherley Lei: 'land by a plantation of trees' [OE *grāf*].

The Grub, Watlington O; **Grub Copse,** Chieveley Brk; **Grub Ground,** Bucklebury Brk, Shirburn O; **Grub Hill,** Pyrton O; **Grub Pightle,** Bix O; **Grubbed Close,** Gatherington Ha; **Grubbed Ground,** Kintbury Brk, Shiplake O; **Grubbed Hill,** Harpsden O: 'land from which trees and shrubs have been cleared' [ME *grubbed*].

Guide Post Close, Crich Db; **Guide Post Field,** Eyam Woodlands Db: 'land near a signpost'. See also Fingerpost Close.

Guinea Bean Acre, South Weston O; **Guinea Field,** Allostock Ch; **Guinea Pightle,** Monyash Db: 'land valued at one guinea per annum'. A *guinea bean* was the coin (first issued in 1663) made from Guinea gold; the value was nominally 20 shillings, but from 1717 it was regarded as worth 21 shillings.

Gull Field, Bluntisham Hu; **Gully Mead,** Kintbury Brk; **Gully Meadow,** Enbourne Brk (*The Golly* 1547): 'land by a drainage ditch' [ME *goule*].

Gurr, New Hutton We, 'muddy place' [OE *gor*].

Gutter Acre, Bradley Ha; **Gutter Close,** Ashby Folville Lei; **Gutter Field,** Aldenham Hrt; **Gutter Leasow,** Yockleton Sa: 'land adjoining a drainage channel'.

H

Hackthorne, Sopley Ha, 'thorn-tree', alluding to land by or containing some prominent tree [OE **haca-þorn*].

Had Acre, Cowley O; **The Hades,** Narborough Lei; **Hadland,** Cowley O (*Hevidlond* c 1220): 'the headlands' [OE *hēafod*].

Hagdell, St Michaels Hrt (*Hagdell* t.Eliz 1), St Paul's Walden Hrt; **Agdell,** Harpenden Hrt; **Hag Dell Field,** Hatfield Hrt: 'valley with a sharp bend' [OE *haca*, 'bend'; *dell*]. This topographical feature has been noted frequently in Hertfordshire. In addition to the examples above there are other occurrences of the name in 16–17c documents relating to Berkhamsted and St Peters, and Hagden Lane in Watford looks back to *Hakedellecroft* and *Hagdellefeld* in a deed of 1333. *Haggedelleforlong*, recorded in Hitchin in 1381, survives in Hagdell House and Hagdellshot Cottage.

(The) Hagg, Ashton La, Upper Rawcliffe La, Twycross Lei; **Hagg Meadow,** Kendal We; **Haggs,** Goosnargh La: 'place cleared of trees' [ON *hogg*].

Haggle, Shepperton Mx (*Hoggehell* 1390), 'hog hill' [OE **hogge*, *hyll*].

Hailstones, Repton Db (*Harstones* 1550), '(land near) grey stones'. The sacrosanct immobility of a boundary stone allowed it to become covered with lichen, so that this sort of greyness implies a boundary.

Haisley, Beer D, 'clearing or meadow covered with brushwood' [OE**hǣs, leah*].

Hale Copse, Newton Valance Ha; **Hale Fields,** Thornford Do; **Little & Great Hale,** Aston Rowant O; **The Three Hales,** Upton Lei; **Halladine,** Hope Mansel He [OE *worðign*]; **Big & Little Hallows,** Preston on the Hill Ch: 'land in a secluded nook' [OE *halh*].

(**The**) **Half Acre,** Brinnington Ch, Yeardsley Ch, Belper Db, Alton Pancras Do, Sapperton Gl, Stretton Parva Lei, Ashwell R, Bradford WRY; **Half Acre Peak,** Selborne Ha; **Half Acres,** Newton Ch, Norton Ch, Purston Jaglin WRY: 'land half an acre in area'.

Half Butts Close, Church Broughton Db; **Half Day Math,** Warmingham Ch, Yeardsley Ch; **Half Day Work,** Butley Ch; **Half Demath,** Ashley Ch; **Half Field,** Preston Du, Flaunden Hrt (*Hawfield* 1623) [OE *haga*], Weston Hrt; **Half Ground,** Fifehead Neville Do; **Half Hide,** Great Gaddesden Hrt (*Le Halvehyde* 1325); **Half Piece,** Pitchford Sa; **Half Roods,** Stony Middleton Db; **Half Yard Lands,** Nailstone Lei; **Halfyards,** Breamore Ha: self-explanatory names.

Half Kernal, Pownall Fee Ch; **Half Kernel,** Chorley Ch; (**The**) **Half Moon,** Bowdon Ch, Painswick Gl, Henley O; **Half Moon Plantation,** Worksop Nt: 'semicircular piece of land'.

Halfpence, Ditcheat So; **Halfpence Piece,** Ashmore Do; **Halfpenny Bottom,** South Mimms Mx; **Halfpenny Croft,** Kingsterndale Db; **Halfpenny Field,** Hambledon Sr; **Halfpenny Hale,** Water Orton Wa [OE *halh*]; **Halfpenny Hill,** Barnsley Gl; **Halfpenny Marshes,** Barking Ess (*Halpeny* 1343); **Halfpenny Meadow,** Lower Swell Gl, Kempsey Wo; **Halfpenny Patch,** Newbold Astbury Ch; **Halfpenny Piece,** Ashmore Do: probably derogatory names, suggesting that a low rent was or should be placed upon the land.

Hall Close, Burrough on the Hill Lei, Carlton Curlieu Lei, Shangton Lei, Stoughton Lei, West Langton Lei, Pitchford Sa, Yaxley Sf, Kendal We; **Hall Close Meadow,** Allexton Lei; **Hall Croft,** Andover Ha, Croxton Nf; **Hall Field,** Little Bromby Ess; **Hall Flatt,** Nether Seal Lei; **Hall Furlong,** Stokeham Nt; **Hall Leasow,** Kenley Sa; **Hall Meadow,** Congleton Ch (*Halmede* 1443), North Rode Ch, Belper Db (*Le Hallemedowe* 1415), Newbottle Du, Stony Stretton Sa; **Hall Mire Hill,** Houghton le Spring Du [ON *myrr*]; **Hall Moor,** Norton Ch; **Hall Pasture,** Newbottle Du: 'land attached to the hall, the property of the lord of the manor' [OE (Angl) *hall*].

The Ham(s), Hungerford Brk, West Alvington D, Fifehead Neville Do, Christchurch Ha, Burton Lazars Lei, Churchill O, Mapledurham O; **Ham Close,** Popham Ha; **Ham Field,** Foxton C (*Hamfeld* 14c), Basing Ha; **Ham Meadow,** Passenham Nth (*Le Hamme* 1327), Titchmarsh Nth (*Hamme* 1227), Elstead Sr; **Ham Piece,** Hartlebury Wo; **Great & Little Hams,** Chobham Sr; **Hams Ground,** Holwell Do; **Hams Meadow,** Berrynarbor D: 'enclosure, land beside a river' [OE *hamm*].

Han Acre, Todenham Gl; **Hannaker Field,** Thursley Sr; **Hannicks,** Ash Sr; **Upper Hannicks,** Romsey Ha: 'half acre' [OE (*on*) *healfan æcere*].

The Hand Post, Glen Parva Lei; **Hand Post Field,** Lambourn Brk; **Hand Post Ground,** Bibury Gl; **Hand Post Meadow,** Windsor Brk; **Handing-Post Piece,** Charlbury O: 'land near a signpost'.

Handkerchief, Eaton Ch, Handforth cum Bosden Ch; **Handkerchief Close,** Bishop's Waltham Ha; **Handkerchief Croft,** Bramhall Ch; **Handkerchief Field,** Timperley Ch, Cromford Db, Tottenham Mx; **The Handkerchief Ground,** Bisley Gl, Hailey O; **Handkerchief Mead,** Fair Oak Ha; **Handkerchief Meadow,** Repton Db, Bushby Lei; **Handkerchief Nook,** Dunham Massey Ch; **Handkerchief Piece,** Inkpen Brk, Doveridge Db, Edlaston Db, Matlock Db, Stretton Db, Wemsley & Snitterton Db, Cosham Ha, Romsey Ha, Cadeby Lei, Groby Lei, Shepshed Lei, Feckenham Wo, Hallow Wo: fanciful name for a small piece of land, widely distributed in the Midlands and southern counties.

Handsome, Hannington Ha, a complimentary name for productive and profitable land.

Hang-dog Leys, Wigginton O, a derogatory name for unproductive or otherwise unlucky land.

The Hanger, Beaulieu Ha; **Hanger Hill,** Overton Ha, Ollerton Nt, Skelbrooke WRY; **Hangers Hill,** Cobham Sr; **Middle Hangers,** Beer D: 'tree-covered slope' [OE *hangra*].

Hang Close, Ecchinswell Ha; **The Hanging,** Eckendon O (*Hangingfield* 1606); **Hanging a Long,** Bucklebury Brk; **Hanging Balk,** Hayton Nt; **Hanging Croft,** Aston Db; **Hanging Crows,** Lower Whitley Ch (possibly for *rows*, ie of huts or shelters); **Hanging Field,** Baguley Ch, Ridge Hrt; **Hanging Furlong,** Bathampton So, Fifield O; **Hanging Hills,** Alderwasley Db; **Hanging Lands,** Stoughton Lei, Thorley Wt; **Hanging Lands Field,** Kirtlington O; **Hanging Lands Furlong,** Shipton under Wychwood O; **Hanging Meadow,** Shenley Hrt; **Hangings,** Bray Brk, Hemel Hempstead Hrt, Hassingham Nf, Everdon Nth (*Hangkinde Lond* t.Hy 3), Staverton Nth (*Hangende furlong* t.Ric 2): 'land on a steep slope' [OE *hangende*].

Hangman's Acre, Painswick Gl; **Hangman's Ash,** Alveston Gl, Marshfield Gl; **Hangman's Butts,** Ravenscroft Bridge Ch; **Hangman's Mound,** Fowlmere C; **Hangman's Stone,** Stowell Gl: 'land assigned to the executioner', either for tillage or as a site for executions. The Ravenscroft Bridge land is on record as requiring of its tenant the provision of an executioner for the barony of Kinderton; the mound at Fowlmere is traditionally held to be the site of a gallows on which sheep-stealers were hanged.

Happersnapper, Froxfield Ha (*Hatchersnap* 17c), possibly 'enclosure with a wicket-gate' [OE *hæcc-geat*].

Hard Acre, Bollington Ch; **Hard Acre Close,** Melbourne Db, Lofthouse WRY; **Hard Field,** Butley Ch; **Hard Halves,** Bishopstoke Ha, Stoke Park Ha; **Hard Meadows,** Newnham Nth (*Hardemede* c1275): 'land with hard surface'.

Hard Bargain, Bitterley Sa, a derogatory term for land that has proved too expensive for its owner.

Hard Head Piece, Lydham Sa, a name alluding to a headland, which is likely to become very hard by being used as a field path.

Hard Labour, Coombe Keynes Do; **Hard Work,** Corney Cu: 'land which is difficult to till'.

Hardwick Closes, Normanton le Heath Lei (*Hardwic* 1674); **Upper & Nether Hardwick,** Shangton Lei: 'land (formerly) devoted to livestock' [OE *heord, wīc*].

Hare Butts, Hartington Middle Quarter Db; **Hare Close,** Edlaston Db; **Hare Croft,** Blaston St Michael Lei; **Hare Field,** Chigwell Ess; **Hare Knowle,** Over Alderley Ch; **Hareland Meadow,** Horley Sr; **Haremoor Meadow,** Englefield Brk; **Hare Pingle,** Alderwasley Db; **Hare Shakers,** Longden Sa, Pontesbury Sa; **Hares Toot,** Iron Acton Gl, [OE *tōt*]: 'land on which hares were seen' [OE *hara*]. Hare Shakers may allude to quaking grass (*Briza* spp); an alternative name in Longden, however, is Ash Acres, but it is not possible to establish whether this is an earlier form or merely a rationalisation of the other name.

Harmony Barn, Ashleyhay Db, a complimentary name of uncertain implication. A similar name occurs in a charter of Bengeworth Wo (1003), which mentions a place called *Anmod,* 'harmony, unanimity'.

(The) Harp, Thaxted Ess, Radwinter Ess, Bitton Gl, Hawkesbury Gl, Newent Gl, Westbury on Severn Gl (*La Harpe* 1255), Weston Hrt, Westbury Sa, Corsham W; **Little Harp,** Hanwell Mx; **Near & Far Harp,** Alderbury Sa; **Harp Leasow,** Church Pulverbatch Sa; **Harp Piece,** Bishop's Cleeve Gl, Uckington Gl, Acton Burnell Sa; **Harp Riding,** Clayworth Nt [OE **ryding*]; **Harpscord Field,** Bletchingley Sr; **Harps Croft,** Horley Sr; **Harps Field,** Canewdon Ess; **Harpwell,** Iron Acton Gl; **Harpy Land,** High Ham So: 'triangular piece of land'.

Harrow Barrow, Old Hutton We; **Harrow Down,** Birdbrook Ess (*Harewe* 14c); **Harrow Field,** Hinckley Lei; **Harrow Hill,** Brington Nth: possibly 'land near or containing a pagan sacred grove' [OE *hearg*]. The hill at Brington is thought to have been the hundred meeting place of Nobottle Grove Hundred and was doubtless a religious centre in pre-Christian times.

Hassock Mead, Nursling Ha; **Hassock Meadow,** Osbaston Lei; **Hassock Piece,** Freefolk Ha; **Hassocks,** Braybrooke Nth, Dingley Nth (*Hassokes* 1199); **Hassocky Close,** Burrough on the Hill Lei: 'land characterised by lumps of coarse grass' [OE *hassuc*].

Hatch Close, Sherborne St John Ha, Steventon Ha; **Hatch Croft,** Redbourn Hrt, Great Bookham Sr; **Hatch Field,** Adderley Sa; Artington Sr, Pirbright Sr, Stoke Sr; **Hatch Meadow,** Andover Ha; **Hatchet,** Alwington D; **Little Hatchet Acre,** Ashmore Do; **Hatchet Breck,** Cuckney Nt [OE *bræc*]; **Hatchet Chalk Ground,** Alton Pancras Do; **Hatchet Close,** East Dereham Nf, Sall Nf, Toot Baldwin O; **Hatchet Field,** Berrynarbor D; **Hatchet Flat,** Worksop Nt [ON *flat*]; **Hatchet Furlong,** Kingham O; **Hatchet Marsh,** Hassingham Nf; **Hatchet Piece,** Duffield Db, Ashmore Do, Crowmarsh O; **Hatchett,** Durley Ha; **Hatchett Fields,** Ansterson Ch; **The Hatchett Ground,** Enbourne Brk; **Hatchett Meadow,** Speen Brk, Alton Pancras Do, Sherfield English Ha; **Hatchett Piece,** Somerton So; **Hatchetts,** Feckenham Wo; **Hatch Yatt Piece,** Charlbury O: 'land by a half-gate or wicket gate' [OE *hæcc, hæcc-geat*].

Hatchet Head, Moss WRY, probably alludes to the shape of the field.

Haugh Dale, Haltwhistle Nb, 'land in a nook' [OE *halh*].

Havadrill Bank, Blackden Ch, 'slope on which daffodils grew' [ME *affadille*].

Have a Good Heart, Bishop's Castle Sa, a complimentary name for a fertile field.

Haver Bank, Docker We; **Haver Close Bottom,** Thorpe Thewles Du; **Haver Croft,** Methley WRY; **Haver Flatts,** Cottingham ERY (*Haverflat* 1261); **Haver Lands,** North Elmsall WRY; **Haver Ridding,** Bampton We, Beetham We: 'land on which it was usual to grow oats' [ON *hafri*].

Haver Cakes, Wilsden WRY, 'oat cakes'—possibly a nickname applied to productive land.

Havin Meadow, Boxford Brk (*Halfene Medowe* 1554), 'half meadow'.

Hawkers Head, Minshull Vernon Ch (*Le Haukeserd* 1311); **Hawkesyord,** Wincle Ch; **Hawkshord,** Bradford on Avon W: 'hawk's gap', ie a clearing in woodland where a hawk may be flown [OE *hafoc-scerde*].

Hawkley, Little Downham C (*Haukele* 1309), 'hawk clearing' [OE *hafoc*, *lēah*].

Haycraft, Hook Do; **Hay Groat,** Great Hormead Hrt; **Hay Field,** Lambourn Brk: 'land on which grass was mown for hay' [OE *hēg*].

The Hayes, Passenham Nth (*Le Hammes Hay* 1327); **Hayes Hill,** Ashreigney D; **The Hays,** Belgrave Lei: '(land enclosed by) hedges' [OE *gehæg*].

Hazel Badge, Wildboarclough Ch [OE *bece*, 'valley']; **Hazel Butts,** Bosley Ch, Whinfell We; **Hazel Cross,** Wormingford Ess (*Hasilwodecros* 14c); **Hazel Dell,** Hemel Hempstead Hrt; **Hazeldown Pightle,** Steventon Ha; **Hazel Grove,** Rickmansworth Hrt (*Haselcroft* 1427); **Hazel Holme,** Kentmere We; **Hazel Hough Field,** Hensall WRY [OE *hōh*, 'spur']; **Hazel Mead,** Sherington Bk, Hermitage Do; **Hazel Shaw & Field,** Lamberhurst K [OE *sceaga*, 'wood']; **Hazel Veres,** Long Sutton Ha [OE *fær*, 'path, passage']; **Hazlelonger Mead,** Painswick Gl [OE *hangra*, 'wooded slope']: names referring to the handsome and useful hazel tree (*Corylus avellana*) [OE *hæsel*].

Head Acre, Ashmore Do, Mitcham Sr; **Head Acre Field,** Overton Ha; **Head Field,** Antrobus Ch; **Head Piece,** Ashmore Do: 'land at the top' [OE *hēafod*].

Head Lands, Newbury Brk, 'strips at the edge of a furlong or field'. The headlands were the strips of land on which the plough was turned.

Heald, Alderwasley Db, Eyam Woodlands Db, Underbarrow We; **The Heald** or **Yeld,** Derwent Db: 'slope' [OE *helde*].

The Heart, Wilcot W, alludes to the shape of the field.

Heartache, Swanmore Ha, a derogatory name for land that disappoints.

Hearthstone Field, Curbar Db, alludes to land on which large flat stones could be obtained for use as hearth-stones.

Heater, Dillicar We; **Heater Close,** Sockbridge We; **Heater Croft,** Haddenham C, Marple Ch; **Heater Field,** Barbon We, Beetham We: names alluding to triangular pieces of land, the reference being to the piece of metal formerly used to heat a flat-iron, and of the same shape.

Heath Close, Appleby Lei, Evington Lei, Kirkby Mallory Lei; **Heath End,** Swannington Lei; **Heath Field,** Windsor Brk, Capesthorne Ch, Leese Ch (*Le Hethfeld* 1271), Little Totham Ess (*Hethcrofte* 1502), Froxfield Ha, Flaunden Hrt, Wheathampstead Hrt (*Hathfeld* 1341), Chiddingfold Sr (*Le Hethfelde* 1394), Seale Sr (*Hetherede* 1616); **Heath Fields,** Kings Langley Hrt; **Heath Ground,** Kintbury Brk (*La Bruere* 1250, *Le Heth* 1394); **Heath Piece,** Stony Stretton Sa; **Heath Reeds,** Farnham Sr [OE **rȳd*, **rēod*, 'clearing']; **Heathy Close,** Alkmonton Db; **Heathy Piece,** Monyash Db: 'uncultivated and unproductive land, overgrown with heather and scrub' [OE *hǣð*].

Heathens Close, St Michaels Hrt (*Heath Hearne* 1575, *Hethernes* 1581), 'heath nook' [OE *hyrne*].

Heather Field, Elwick Hall Du, self-explanatory.

Hedge Hog Meadow, Kings Norton Lei, self-explanatory.

Hell Carr, Bamford Db; **Hell Croft,** Bradford WRY; **Hell End,** Stainmore We; **Hell Ford,** Croome D'Abitot Wo; **Hell Ground,** Spelsbury O; **Hell Nook,** Compton Bishop So; **Hell Patch,** Bruern O; **Hell Piece,** Kiddington O: probably 'L-shaped piece of land', though in some dialects *hell* is 'hill'; a derogatory reference is also possible (cf Hell Fire Gate, Hell Hole).

Hell Fire Gate & Lotts, Lower Swell Gl; **Hell Fire Piece,** Bibury Gl; terms of opprobrium for intractable land.

Hell Hole, Newton Ch, Elwick Hall Du, Pauntley Gl, Farnsfield Nt, Elmley Castle Wo; **Hell Hole Spinney,** Odstone Lei; **Hell Hole Wood,** Whitwell We; **Hell Holes,** Wadsworth WRY: 'a dark haunted nook; a den of infamy' [MnE dial. *hell-hole*].

Helm Close, Docker We; **Helm Side,** Lambrigg We: 'land near or containing a shelter' [OE *helm*].

Hemp Croft, Newton Ch, Northenden Ch, Dorchester O; **Hemphay,** Beer D; **Hemphay(e)s,** Bettiscombe Do; Tisbury W;

Hempits, Hinton St Mary Do; **Hempland,** Alkmonton Db, Forncett St Peter Nf, Beetham We, Kirkby Lonsdale We; **North & South Hempland,** North Poorton Do; **Hemplands,** Fairford Gl, Kempsford Gl, Wheatley Nt, Wigginton O; **Hemplands Close,** Lower Heyford O; **Hemp Leasow,** Stirchley Sa; **Hemp Piece,** Ipsden O; **Hemp Pits,** Tabley Superior Ch; **Hemp Yard,** Bamford Db, Stokeham Nt; **Hemp Yards,** Methley WRY; **Hemp Yards Close,** Groby Lei; **Hempen Butts,** Eyam Woodlands Db: 'land on which hemp was grown' [OE *hænep*]. Even when not cultivated on a large scale, hemp was formerly often grown in crofts or home plots to supply the textile needs of the family, but production declined to vanishing point by the mid-nineteenth century.

Hen and Chickens, Doveridge Db, Clifton Hampden O; **Hen and Chickens Plantation,** Shilton O; **Hen and Chicks,** Dorchester O: names which almost certainly refer to some species of wild plant; the expression is used in various parts of the country for a type of double daisy and for London Pride (*Saxifraga spatularis*).

Hen Croft, Sandbach Ch; **Hencroft Butts,** Handborough O; **Henfield,** Mapledurham O (*Hennfield* 1454); **Hen Hill Field,** Abberton Wo; **Hen Holme,** Beetham We; **Hen Mead,** Hendon Mx; **Hen Mires,** Elwick Hall Du; **Hen Pleck,** Smisby Db; **Hen Plot,** Fifield O; **Hen Ridding,** Hutton Roof We; **Hen Wood,** Herriard Ha: names alluding either to domestic fowls or to game birds [OE *henn*].

Hen House Meadow, Tooley Park Lei, 'grassland adjoining or containing poultry houses'.

Hendon, Hempstead Ess (*Hendon* 1271), '(on the) high hill' [OE *hēah*, *dūn*].

Henhogs, Broadwindsor Do, 'land enclosed for cultivation during the fallow course of the remainder of the open field' [ME *inhoke*].

Hermitage, Great Shalford C; **Hermitage Close,** Loughborough Lei; **Hermitage Meadow,** Alton Ha: names alluding to the site of a hermitage.

Herne Field, Castle Bromwich Wa; **The Heron,** Andover Ha; **Herons,** Wharton Ch: '(land in) an angle, a corner' [OE *hyrne*]. See also Hirons Meadow.

Hesland, Desborough Nth (*Heselund* 13c), 'hazel wood' [ON *hesli, lundr*].

Heugh Top, Washington Du, 'summit of spur of land' [OE *hōh*].

The Hide, Chipping Norton O; **Hide Field,** Loughton Ess, Amport Ha: 'hide of land, an area sufficient to support a free family and dependants'. The area is usually estimated at 120 acres, but there was much local variation. See also Hyde.

Hield Field, Pownall Fee Ch, 'land on a slope' [OE *helde*]. See also Heald, The Yeald.

High Close, Knossington Lei, East Dereham Nf (*Le Highe Filde* 1568); **High Crofts,** Askham We; **High Dyke,** Kirkhaugh Nb; **High Field,** Bray Brk, Alkmonton Db, Heworth Du, Layer Breton Ess, Lydney Gl, East Barnet Hrt (*Le Heyefeld* 1346), Kings Langley Hrt, King's Walden Hrt, Hendon Mx, Egham Sr, Withey Sr, Docker We, Levens We; **The High Flatt,** Dufton We; **High Grassing,** Bampton We [OE **gærsing*, 'pasture']; **High Henning,** Bampton We (*Le Heyning* 1323) [ON *hegning*, 'enclosed land']; **Highhill Close,** Feltwell Nf; **High Intack,** Shap We [ON *intak*]; **High Lands,** Bere Alston D; **High Leys,** Blaby Lei; **High Leys Close,** West Langton Lei; **High Meadow,** Great Hucklow Db; **High Pasture,** Crook & Willington Du, Greetham R; **High Reeds,** Frensham Sr [OE **ried*, 'clearing']; **High Thorn,** Coleorton Lei; **High Twelve Acres,** East Anstey D; **High Yard(s),** Hurleston Ch, Crosby Ravensworth We: names applied to land either in a high position relative to the parish as a whole or more elevated than a second field bearing a corresponding name (eg Low Close, Low Leys).

High Field, pre-enclosure great field name in Boynton ERY, Everingham ERY, Rickmansworth Hrt, Braunstone Lei, Stapleford Lei, Radcliffe on Trent Nt, Cold Kirby NRY.

Higher Acre, Bollington Ch; **Higher Close,** Abbotsham D; **Higher Down,** Arlington D, Bampton D, Beaford D; **Higher Field,** Blackawton D; **Higher Forehead,** Beer D; **Higher Meadow,** Berrynarbor D; **Higher Piece,** Fifehead Neville Do; **Higher & Lower Square Close,** East Anstey D: self-explanatory names, particularly common in Devon.

The High Road Field, East Murton Du; **Highway Close,** Burrough on the Hill Lei, Evington Lei, Great Bowden Lei, Twycross Lei, Gunthorpe R; **Highway Piece,** Bampton D: 'land near a main road'.

(**The**) **Hill,** Fifehead Neville Do, Crosby Ravensworth We; **First & Second Hill,** Blackawton D; **Hill Close,** Hook Do, Tring Hrt, Blaston St Giles Lei, Carlton Curlieu Lei, Illston Lei, Knossington Lei, Lubenham Lei, Welham Lei, East Dereham Nf (*Hilwong* 1277), Sall Nf (*Le Hil* 1332, *Hillond* 1343), North & South Wheatley Nt, Southwell Nt (*Hyll Close* 1556), Ashwell R, Croydon Sr (*Hell Close* 1543); **Hill Cop,** Westbury Sa [OE *copp*, 'summit']; **Hill Croft,** Hitchin Hrt (*Hullecroft* 14c), Wheathampstead Hrt (*Hellecroft* 1390); **Hill Field,** Hungerford Brk (*Hullfilde* 1576), Reading Brk, Brindley Ch, Faddiley Ch, Wettenhall Ch, Newbottle Du, Holmer He, Much Cowarne He, North Mimms Hrt, Watford Hrt, Great Ness Sa, Alvechurch Wo; **Hill Flat,** Ossington Nt; **Hill Gaston,** Fifehead Magdalen Do; **Hill Ground,** Enbourne Brk, Kintbury Brk (*La Hull'* c 1220), Newbury Brk, Hermitage Do, Hinton Martell Do, Great Ness Sa, Smethcott Sa; **Hill Leasow,** Smethcott Sa; **Hill Meadow,** Alphington D, Withcote Lei; **Hill Piece,** Great Ness Sa; **Big Hill Piece,** Smethcott Sa: 'land on or near a hill' [OE *hyll*].

Hillock Leas, Minsterley Sa; **Hillocks,** Church Minshull Ch: 'land on or characterised by hillocks' [OE **hylloc*].

Hilly Field, Little Bowden Lei, Farnham Sr (*Hullefeld* 1450), Windlesham Sr (*Hullfeild* 1609); **Hilly Ground,** Enbourne Brk, Newbury Brk, Holwell Do; **Hilly Meadow,** Galby Lei, Illston Lei, Wigston Magna Lei; **Hilly Piece,** Forncett St Peter Nf: self-explanatory names.

The Himpey, Alvechurch Wa; *Himpegarth*, Bolton Cu 1296; *Ympegard*, Forlam Cu 1250: 'sapling enclosure' [OE *impa*, *(ge)hæg*, ON *garðr*].

Hindrance, Alverstoke Ha, a derogatory name for difficult land.

Hinnox, Hawkesbury Gl (*Inhoke* 1450, *Innox* 1639), 'part of an open field enclosed for cultivation during the fallow course'.

Hirons Meadow, Banbury O, 'grassland in, or with, angles or corners' [OE *hyrne*].

Hitch Croft, Elton Ch; **Hitch Field,** Alderwasley Db: 'land enclosed with hurdles' [ME *hiche*].

Hitchen Close, Tring Hrt (*Hitchingeild* t.Jas 1); **Hitching Leys,** Wigginton O; **Hitchins,** Kintbury Brk: 'part of field ploughed and sown while the remainder lies fallow' [OE **heccing*].

Hob Croft, Buglawton Ch, Alston La, Fishwick La; **Hob Field,** Alderwasley Db; **Hob Flat,** Cheswardine Sa; **Hob Iron,** Mere Ch [OE *hyrne*, 'angle, nook']; **Hob Land,** Botley Ha, Bursledon Ha; **Hobs Croft,** Out Rawcliffe La: 'land covered in tussocky grass' [OE **hobbe*].

Hobgoblin, Laughton Lei; **Hobgoblins,** Sutton Bonington Nt: 'land haunted by goblins' [ME *hob*].

The Hoddens, Cawston Nf, possibly 'headlands' [ON *hofuð*].

Hoe Furlong, Smeeton Westerby Lei (*Hofurlong* 1652), 'open-field division on or near a ridge' [OE *hōh*].

Hog Acre, Twyford Ha, Oxford O; **Hog Back,** Stoke Dabernon Sr; **Hog Close,** Cookham Brk; **Hog Common,** Bray Brk; **Hog Gaston,** Romsey Ha; **Hog Hole,** Oddington O; Farnham Sr; **Hog Mead,** Basingstoke Ha; **Hog Meadow,** Taxal Ch; **Hog Moor,** Reading Brk; **Hog Trough,** Cookham Brk, Newbury Brk, Baughurst Ha: names alluding to domestic pigs. Hog Back and Hog Trough may have reference to the surface conformation and the shape of the field respectively [OE **hogg*].

Hogshead Bottom, Cosham Ha; **Hogsheads,** Bollington Ch (*The Hawkes Yord* 1611): 'gaps in woodland where a hawk may be flown' [OE *hafoc*, **scerde*]. See also Hawkers Head.

Holligores Field, Astley Sa; **Hollin Close,** Bilsthorpe Nt; **Hollin Hey,** Dewsbury WRY [OE *(ge)hæg*]; **Hollin Knoll,** Bosley Ch, North Rode Ch; **Hollin Knowl,** Edale Db [OE *cnoll*]; **Hollin Slack,** Kentmere We [ON *slakki*]; **Hollings,** Lambrigg We; **Hollingtree,** Desford Lei; **Holly Acre,** Hinton St Mary Do; **Holly Bush,** Linton C; **Holly Bush Close,** Cookham Brk, Stevenage Hrt, Hugglescote Lei; **Holly Bush Style,** Chieveley Brk; **Holly Close,** Beer D; **Holly Field,** Brackenfield Db, Long Critchell Do; **Holly Hook Field,** Wonersh Sr; **Holly Piece,** Wolstaston Sa; **Holly Tree Close,** Alderwasley Db, Osmaston Db; **Holly**

Wood, Adderley Sa; **Holm Bush,** Hook Do; **Holmbush Piece,** Soberton Ha; **Holney Acre,** Ashmore Do: 'land on which holly grew'. Jeffrey Radley has shown (in *Ag Hist Rev* IX, ii, 89ff) in an interesting article, 'Holly as a winter feed', that holly was an important fodder crop, particularly in the north Midlands [OE *holegn*].

Hollow Ash, East Meon Ha; **Hollow Oak,** Leafield O: 'land marked by a hollow tree of the species named'.

(The) Holme, Baslow Db, Knossington Lei, Bloxham O; **Holme Close,** Alderwasley Db, Medbourne Lei; **Holme Field,** Babworth Nt: 'water-meadow, riverside land, higher dry ground amid marshes' [ON *holmr*].

Holt, Cranage Ch, Little Leigh Ch; **Great & Long Holt,** Great Wymondley Hrt; **Holt Close,** Caddington Hrt, Bilsthorpe Nt, Carlton Nt; **Holt Field,** Sandbach Ch; **Holt Hill,** Billesdon Lei; **Holt Plain,** Clifton Ch (*Le Holt* c 1275): '(land near or containing) a small wood or thicket' [OE *holt*].

Holy Well, Keckwick Ch, Wibtoft Lei, Greasley Nt (*Holwell Croft* c 1500); **Holywell Close,** Wigston Magna Lei; **Holy Well Piece,** Hinckley Lei; **Holywell Syke,** Brandon Du: names possibly referring to springs reputedly with curative powers, but the early form of the Greasley example suggests that it is 'spring in a hollow' [OE *hālig*, 'holy'; *holh, wella*].

Home Ash Park, West Alvington D; **Home Close,** Boxford Brk, Cookham Brk, Enbourne Brk, Englefield Brk, Duffield Db, Fifehead Neville Do, Holwell Do, Froyle Ha, Baggrave Lei, Billesdon Lei, Burrough on the Hill Lei, Carlton Curlieu Lei, Goadby Lei, Halstead Lei, Lubenham Lei, Illston Lei, Knossington Lei, Stretton Parva Lei, Thurnby Lei, Welham Lei, Sall Nf, Bulkington W; **Home Croft,** Alton Ha, Butlington Ha, Longparish Ha, Nether Wallop Ha, Upper Clatford Ha, Kirkby Mallory Lei; **Home Field,** Clewer Brk, Cookham Brk, Windsor Brk, Broxbourne Hrt (*Homfeldgrove* t.Ed 4), East Barnet Hrt (*Le Homfeld* 1267), Hertingfordbury Hrt (*Holmefeld* 1441), Hitchin Hrt (*Homefeld* 1409), Coleorton Lei, Shackerstone Lei, Shepperton Mx, Elstead Sr, Farley Sr (*Homfeld* 1302), Tatsfield Sr (*Homfeld* 1402), Thursley Sr (*Hoomfeld* 1428); **Home Garth,**

Newbottle Du; **Home Ground,** Holwell Do, Claydon O, North Newington O; **Home Hill,** East Anstey D; **Home Mead,** Newbury Brk, Hermitage Do, Hinton St Mary Do, Bisley Sr; **Home Meadow,** Eling Ha, Harbridge Ha; **Home Moor,** Charford Ha; **Home Orchard,** Alton Pancras Do, Wardley R; **Home Park,** Walton Inferior Ch, East Allington D; **Home Pightle,** Tadlow C, Wendy C, Medstead Ha, Sall Nf; **Home Purrock,** Stoke Park Ha: 'land near centre of farm or township' [OE *hām*]. Very common in some counties, apparently non-existent in others, *Home* appears also as a modifier of other names, eg Home Part of Third Close, usually contrasting with Far Part, Higher Part, or Further Part. Occasionally, there is confusion with derivatives of *holmr*, of which *Holmefield*, the early form of Home Field in Hertingfordbury, may be one.

Hone Ground, Hinton Martell Do; **Hone Hill,** Sandhurst Brk (*Le Hone* 1498): 'land from which sharpening stones were obtained' [OE *hān*].

Honey Acre, Coberley Gl; **Honey Bags,** Blaby Lei; **Honey Box,** Boxford Brk; **Honey Butts,** Owthorpe Nt; **Honey Close,** Kintbury Brk, Sandhurst Brk, Church Oakley Ha; **Honey Cut Ditch,** Wolvercote O [OE *cot*]; **Honey Field,** Hurdsfield Ch; **Honey Furlong,** Crowell O; **Honey Gaston,** Marksbury So [OE *gærs-tūn*]; **Honey Grove,** Long Critchell Do; **Honey Ham,** West Littleton Gl, Brize Norton O, Minety W; **Honey Hill,** Oldland Gl, Barrons Park Lei, Desford Lei, Nailstone Lei; **Honey Hole,** Beckingham Nt; **Honeyhole Close,** Laxton Nt; **Honey Hurst,** Leftwich Ch; **Honey Lands,** Hungerford Brk, Broadwas Wo, Owston WRY; **Honey Lease,** Reading Brk; **Honey Leaze,** Burghfield Brk; **Honeyleaze Copse,** Herriard Ha; **Honey Mead,** Hurstbourne Priors Ha, North Stoneham Ha; **Honey Meadow,** Crowley Ch, Minsterley Sa, Wolstaston Sa; **Honey Moons,** Awre Gl; **Honey Piece,** Sudbury Db; **Honey Poak,** Longsleddale We; **Honey Pot,** Catthorpe Lei, Holwell Lei, High Ham So, Beetham We, Holme We; **Honey Pot Field,** Hunton Ha; **Honey Pots,** Andover Ha, Hallaton Lei; **Honey Spot,** Belper Db, Kilburn Db, Goadby Lei; **Honey Spot Meadow,** Hathersage Db; **Honey Spots,** Hope Db: 'honey land' [OE *hunig*]. Three interpretations are commonly suggested for honey names—(1) literal, (2) complimentary and (3) derogatory. Denominatives indicating small pieces of land (eg Butts, Piece, Spot) may refer to the location of beehives; the complimentary interpretation is that some or all of these names refer to good land, with a suggestion that it is flowing with milk and honey; the third possibility is that the name may allude to land with sticky soil.

Hongrill, Bostock Ch, 'land with infertile soil'. See also Hungary [OE *hungor*, *hyll*].

(The) Hook, Northaw Hrt, Burrough on the Hill Lei, Compton Bishop So, Farnham Sr; **Hook Field,** Feering Ess, Hurstbourne Priors Ha, Lamberhurst K, Thames Ditton Sr; **Hook Furlong,** Ipsden O; **Hook Horn,** Hallow Wo; **Hook Meadow,** Kingston Magna Do, Stoke Sr; **Hooked Orchard,** High Ham So; **Hooks,** Tunstall ERY, Great Parndon Ess, Writtle Ess, Gaddesby Lei, Odstone Lei, Frensham Sr (*Hokerede* 1399): 'a spur of land, a spit of land in a river-bend, or a hook-shaped field' [OE *hōc*].

Hop Close, Carlton Curlieu Lei; **Hop Field,** Stebbing Ess (*The Hopgrownde* 1611), Aston Wa; **Hop Furlong,** Alvechurch Wo; **Hop Garden,** Burghfield Brk, Alresford Ha, Alton Ha, Basing Ha, Baughurst Ha, Binstead and Neatham Ha, Eling Ha, Eversley Ha, Fordingbridge Ha, Greatham Ha, Hambledon Ha, Havant Ha, Lockerley Ha, East Meon Ha, Pamber Ha, Yateley Ha, Eye & Dunsden O, Piddington O, Upper Heyford O, Godstone Sr, Ockley Sr, Tisbury W; **Hop Garth,** Haldenby WRY; **Hop Ground,** Hungerford Brk, Inkpen Brk, Sible Hedingham Ess (*Le Hopgrounde* 1596), Burghclere Ha, Shenley Hrt, Spelsbury O, Counthorpe R; **Hophayl,** West Alvington D, [OE *halh*]; **Hop Meadow,** Ellingham Nf; **Hop Pightle,** Bucklebury Brk; **Hop Pound Field,** Lamberhurst K; **Hop Yard,** Aston Grange Ch, Toft Ch, Alkmonton Db, Ashover Db, Fifehead Neville Do, Hook Do, Piddletrenthide Do, Almondsbury Gl, Baggrave Lei, Kings Norton Lei, West Langton Lei, Darlton Nt, Hayton Nt; **Hop Yard Close,** Cadeby Lei, Babworth Nt, Rampton Nt; **Hop Yard Meadow,** Peatling Parva Lei; **Hop Yard Piece,** Islip O; **Hopyard Ridway,** Leigh Wo; **Hopping Close,** Mapledurham O; **Hopping Hill,** Milford Db (*Le Hoppingclif* 1334); **Hopping Piece,** Ashleyhay Db, Bruern O: 'land on which hops were grown' [ME *hoppe*]. This plant (*Humulus lupulus*) was introduced in the sixteenth century 'to the detryment of many Englysshemen', according to a writer of the time, Andrew Boord (quoted by Seebohm in *Evolution of the English Farm*, 220).

Hopeless, Deane Ha; **Hopeless Meadow,** Bootle Cu; derogatory names for unproductive land.

Hoppits, Eastwick Hrt; **Hoppit,** Hunsdon Hrt (*Le Hoppet* 1556): 'small enclosure' [OE * *hoppet*].

Horestone Mear Common, Iffley O, 'common land near boundary marked by a stone'. Literally 'grey stone', the hoarstone was probably so called from an abundance of lichen testifying to its immobility [OE *hār-stān*, *(ge)mære*].

Horne Field, Waltham Holy Cross Ess (*Upperehorncroft* 1408), 'horn-shaped piece of land' [OE *horn*].

Horse Close, Alkmonton Db, Alton Pancras Do, Hook Do, Baggrave Lei, Blaston St Giles Lei, Lubenham Lei, Somerby Lei, Stockerston Lei, Wibtoft Lei, Forncett St Peter Nf, Farnsfield Nt, Kendal We, Skelbrooke WRY; **Horse Close Butts,** Perivale Mx; **Horse Croft,** Hemel Hempstead Hrt, Banstead Sr; **Horse Croft Meadow,** Bakewell Db (Horscroft 1297); **Horse Doles,** Steeple Morden C; **Horse Down,** Long Critchell Do; **Horse Fair Close,** Newbury Brk; **Horse Ground,** Aldborough Nf; **Horse Gussan Close,** Chinnor O (*Horsgarstone* 1220) [OE *gærs-tūn*]; **Horse Hill,** Minchinhampton Gl; **Horse Leys,** Loughton Ess, Alton Ha; **Horse Meadow,** Great Stretton Lei; **Horse Moor,** Lechlade Gl, Croughton Nth (*Horsemor* c 1255), Toot Baldon O; **Horse Park,** Ashreigney D; **Horse Pasture,** Bosley Ch, Lower Withington Ch, Alderwasley Db, Newbottle Du, Lamberhurst K, Bushby Lei, Darrington WRY; **Horse Piece,** Longden Sa; **Horse Plat Furlong,** Hinton Martell Do; **Horse Plot,** Kintbury Brk; **Horsepool Close,** Nether Seal Db; **Horse Roods Close,** Anstey Lei; **Horse Tyning,** Maiden Bradley W [OE *tȳning*]: 'land on which horses were kept or pastured'.

Horse Shoe Field, Forncett St Peter Nf; **Four Horse Shoe Field,** Reading Brk; **Horse Shoe Ground,** Chieveley Brk, Enbourne Brk; **Horse Shoe Piece,** Windsor Brk: names probably alluding to pieces of land shaped like a horse shoe.

The Hospital, Brougham We; **Hospital Close,** Stretton Parva Lei; **Hospital Farm,** East Retford Nt: names alluding to old charitable institutions. The East Retford name refers to Trinity Hospital there, founded in 1665. See also Spital Croft.

Hostage Wood, Blackerwycke Nth. See Aspage.

Hourglass, Ringwood Ha, refers to the shape of the field.

House Close, Alderwasley Db, Alkmonton Db, Belper Db, Barlestone Lei, Billesdon Lei, Bushby Lei, Houghton on the Hill Lei, Illston Lei, Knossington Lei, Osbaston Lei, Scraptoft Lei, Welham Lei, Beal WRY; **House Field,** Aston by Budworth Ch, Cranage Ch, Crowley Ch, Newbottle Du, Washington Du; **House Meadow,** Halstead Lei, Ford Sa, Pontesbury Sa; **House Pasture,** Hylton Du, Illston Lei; **Housen Field,** Blackawton D, West Bergholt Ess: 'land near or containing a house or houses' [OE *hūs*].

Hovel Close, Belper Db, Duffield Db, Barwell Lei, Billesdon Lei, Huncote Lei, Kibworth Lei, Knossington Lei, Lockington Lei, Scraptoft Lei, Wardley R; **Hovel Field,** Peover Superior Ch, Havant Ha; **Hovel Ground,** Chadlington O; **Hovel Lawn,** Hinckley Lei; **Hovel Meadow,** Billesdon Lei: 'land containing a shed for implements or a framework on which a stack is built'.

How Call That Field, Meathop We, refers to land so indifferent as not to be worth naming.

How-so Meadow, Mitcheldean Gl (*Howshold Meadow* 1618), possibly 'land reserved for the domestic needs of the lord of the manor'.

Howler Close, Altofts WRY, 'land adjoining or containing alder trees' [OE *alor*].

Hull Piece, Poulton Gl, 'land containing a shed' [OE *hulu*].

Hundred, Snelston Db; *Hundredfelde*, Macclesfield Ch 1560; **Hundred Hill,** Taverham Nf; **Hundred Path & Ground,** Hawkesbury Gl: possibly 'land on which the people of the hundred assembled' [OE *hundred*].

Hundred Acres, Banstead Sr (*Frithdonus* Sr 1325, *Le ffredowne containing* 100 *acres* 1540), Aldbourne W: 'land of approximately 100 acres in area'. Fields having such a large area are comparatively rare in England, though there are probably some other pieces of land bearing this name which actually have the stated acreage. The ironic application of the name to very small fields is, however, quite common, as the following list indicates; exact areas are given in brackets when known: Bray Brk, Comberton C (1r 36p), Soham C, Steeple Morden C (*Le Hundaker* 13c) (1r 3p), Basing Ha (27p), Binstead & Neatham Ha (3r 7p), Weyhill Ha (2r 23p), Worldham Ha (39p), Aston Hrt, Flamstead Hrt (1r 38p), St Peter's Hrt (3r 3p), Hardhorn with Newton La (2r), Hendon Mx (16p), Carlton in Lindrick Nt, Cowley O, Forest Hill with Shotover O, All Cannings W (2r 1p), Broad Town W (1r 33p), Coulston W (3r), Fittleton W (28p), Heddington W (20p), Hilmarton W (2r 11p), Idmiston W (31p), Boulshot W (3r 38p), Seend W (2r 14p), Sopworth W (1a 2r), Stert & Urchfont W ('very small'), Whiteparish W (3r 9p).

Hundred Year, Brampton Db, fanciful name for a field whose cultivation is likely to occupy an undue length of time.

Hungary, Twyford Ha; **Hungary Field,** Bramshott Ha; **Hungary Hill,** Newbold Astbury Ch, Awre Gl, Berkhamsted Hrt, King's Walden Hrt; **Hunger Bank,** Heage Db; **Hunger Brook Close,** Shirburn O; **Hunger Dale,** Shirley Db; **Hungerdown,** North Weald Basset Ess, Brockenhurst Ha, Sheet Ha; **Hungerdowns,** Great Totham Ess (*Hungerhale* 1287); **Hunger Field,** Solihull Wa; **Hungerford,** Bakewell Db, Bennington Hrt, Marksbury So; *Hungerhil*, Ellington Hu 1322, Flitwick Bd 13c; **Hunger Hill,** Biggleswade Bd, Marston Moretaine Bd, Sherington Bk (*Hungerhul* 1238), Allostock Ch, Bollin Fee Ch, Bollington Ch, Cheadle Ch, Rudheath Lordship Ch, Shipbrook Ch, Somerford Radnor Ch, Tetton Ch, Kirkoswald Cu, Clowne Db, Etwall Db, Eyam Db, Hope Db, Rosliston Db, Beckford Gl, Bulley Gl, Longhope Gl, North Mimms Hrt, Ibstock Lei, Rampton Nt, Walkeringham Nt, Minster Lovell O, Cound Sa, Wolstaston Sa, Drighlington WRY, Wilsen WRY; **Hungerhill Close,** Featherstone WRY (*Hungriha* 1392); **Hunger Hills,** Alderley Gl, North Elmshall WRY (*Hungyrhill* 1392); **Hunger Knowl,** Upton Ch [OE *cnoll*]; **Hunger Land(s),** Oxenhall Gl, Hendon Mx (*Hungerhill* 1574), Old Hutton We; **Hungerley,** Hale Ch (*Hunger Hey* 1637) [OE *(ge)hæg*]; **Hunger Platt,** Dowdeswell Gl; **Hunger Pott,** Middleton We [ME *potte*, 'hole, especially in hillside']; **Hungerstarve Meadow,** Withington Gl; **Hungolds,** Ash Sr (*Hungerhulle*

1385); **Hungrell,** Pontesbury Sa; **Hungrill,** Anderton Ch; **Hungry Acre,** Helsington We; **Hungry Bottom,** Soulby We; **Hungry Close,** Bakewell Db; **Hungry Corner Field,** Chiddingfold Sr; **Hungry Croft,** Lymm Ch; **Hungry Field,** Headley Ha; **Hungry Guts,** Knebworth Hrt; **Hungry Hall,** Hatfield Hrt [OE *halh*]; **Hungry Home Close,** Ashby Folville Lei; **Hungry Hill,** Great Abington C, Sixpenny Handley Do, Siston Gl, Bursley Ha, Mortimer West End Ha, Walkern Hrt, Brigstock Nth (*Hungerhill* 1469), Banstead Sr, Morden Sr, Hartlebury Wo; **Hungry Home Close,** Ashby Folville Lei; **Hungry Lodge,** Up Nately Ha; **Hungry Park,** Withington Gl; **Hungry Well Corner,** Ashwell Hrt: either 'infertile land, requiring much manure' or 'poor land, not likely to provide adequate livelihood for its occupier' [OE *hungor*, *hungrig*].

Hunny Acre, Medbourne Lei 1679 (*Hunniakyr* 1318); **Hunny Hill,** Newport Wt: 'land on which honey was obtained' [OE *hunig*].

Huntitout, Whitchurch Sa, fanciful name for a small, secluded field.

Hurn, Beverley ERY (*The Hyrne* 1677), East Pennard So; **The Hyrne,** Cawston Nf; **Hyrne Close,** Sall Nf: 'nook, corner of land' [OE *hyrne*].

Hurst Furlong, Hallow Wo; **Hurst Leason,** Westbury Sa; **Little Hurst,** Adlington Ch, Barton in the Beans Lei: 'land by a copse' [OE *hyrst*].

Hut Close, Arnesby Lei, Bushby Lei, Foxton Lei, Hallaton Lei, Houghton on the Hill Lei; **Hut Field,** Stretton Ch: 'land containing a hut'.

(The) Hyde, Bucklebury Brk (*Hidehacch* 1348, *Hyde* 1485), Great Henny Ess (*Le Hide* 1600), Hinckley Lei, Shiplake O (*La Hyde* 1275); **Hyde Mead,** Nazeing Ess (*Le Hyde* 1270); **Hyde Meadow,** Boxford Brk, Whitchurch O: 'land approximately 120 acres in extent'; modern fields bearing the name are probably remnants of a piece of land of that area [OE *hīd*].

The Hyrne, Cawston Nf; **Hyrne Close,** Sall Nf: 'nook, corner' [OE *hyrne*].

I

Ice House Plantation, Mere Ch, 'copse near outbuilding used as a cold store'. Before the introduction of chemical refrigeration, food and wine could be chilled and stored in specially designed outhouses into which blocks of ice were brought as required.

The Image, Doddenham Wo; **Image Ground,** Begbrooke O; **Image Mead,** Standon Hrt; **Image Wood,** Sacombe Hrt: 'railed in place'. [ME *inheche*]. Land so named is often near the parish boundary, but the name may also be used of land cultivated when the rest of the field lay fallow.

Imp Yard, Gomersal WRY; **Impudent Garden,** Shalford Ess (*Impyngtongarden* 1491); **Great & Little Impy,** Castle Camps C: 'nursery for saplings' [OE *impa*].

Improved, Whitchurch Sa; **Improved Meadow,** Bostock Ch; **Improved Piece,** Alderwasley Db: names doubtless commemorating eighteenth-century agricultural innovations.

The Inake, Bisley Fl (*Le Inhoke* 1449); **Inhooks,** Hullavington W; **Innex,** Crookham Ha, Colerne W (*Ynhok* 1397), Lacock W (*Le Hinhoc* 13c); **Innicks,** Froxfield Ha, North Wraxall W; **Innicks Close,** Priors Dean Ha; **Innocks,** Buriton Ha, Wrington So; **Innox,** Droxford Ha, Duntisbourne Abbots Gl, Bathampton So, Priston So, Wellow So; **Inox,** Hazelbury Bryan Do: 'land temporarily enclosed for cultivation while the remainder of the great field is fallow' [ME *inhoke*].

Indigo Mead, Noke O, may refer to the colour of the soil, but is unlikely to allude to one of the indigo-bearing plants, since none of these could be grown as a field crop in this country.

Infield, Boughton Nt; **Infield Close,** Rampton Nt, Stokeham Nt; **In Mead,** Driffield Gl: 'land near the homestead or village', such land being enclosed while that beyond would be in open fields [ME *infeld*].

Ing Close, Clayworth Nt, New Hutton We; *Ing Field*, pre-enclosure great field in Skirpenbeck ERY; **Ingmire,** Hurworth Du; **Ings Holm,** Everton Nt; **Ings Meadow,** Adlingfleet WRY: 'pasture land' [ON *eng*].

Inghams Garden, Mickleham Sr; **(The) Inhams,** Holwell Do, Alresford Ha, Bramshott Ha, Werrington Nth (*Le Inham* c 1400), Frensham Sr; **Inhams Field,** Hambledon Ha, Steep Ha, Effingham Sr (*Inhame* 1471); **Inholms Farm,** Dorking Sr; **Inhomes Meadow,** Lubenham Lei: 'land taken in—cultivated land embedded in the waste [OE **innām,* ON *innám*].

Inkerman, Selston Nt, a remoteness name, transferred from the town in the Crimea where the Russians were defeated by the British and French on 5 November 1854.

Inlands, Daventry Nth (*Inlond* 1383), Westbourne Sx (*Inlonde* 1199); **Inn Croft,** Armston Nth (*Incroft* c 1250); **Inn Meadow,** Welford Brk (*Inmede* 1550), Carlton Curlieu Lei; **In Plat,** Abbotsham D; **Inner Close,** Medbourne Lei, Welham Lei: 'land near the homestead' [OE *inland*]. The term *inland* was equivalent to *demesne* in many places.

Innge, Egglescliffe Du; **(The) Inning(s),** King's Walden Hrt (*Innyng* t. Ed 6), North Mimms Hrt (*Innynge* 1429), Hartlebury Wo; **Great Innings,** Harpenden Hrt: 'land taken in and enclosed' [OE **inning*].

Inoculated Meadow, Cound Sa, 'land into which small turves have been set'; this method of conversion to grass began with the ramming in of small pieces of turf during the winter, and was followed by a thin seeding during the spring months following (cf Seebohm, *Evolution of the English Farm*, 296).

Insets Field, Albury Hrt, 'land almost enclosed by a winding parish boundary' [EMnE *inset*].

Intack, Acton Grange Ch, Mere Ch, Wilton Gilbert Du, Egglescliffe Du, New Hutton We; **(The) Intake,** Cheadle Ch, Eaton Ch, Alderwasley Db, Burton Lazars Lei, Bushby Lei, Laxton Nt, Wellow Nt, Worksop Nt, Cold Norton St; **Intake Close,** Church Broughton Db; **Intake Pasture,** Great Heck WRY: 'land taken in and enclosed' [ON *inntak*].

Ireland (Big & Little), Alvechurch Wo; **Irish Bogs,** Isley Walton Lei; **Irish Field,** Marthall cum Warford Ch; **Irish Intake,** Tabley Superior Ch: some or all may allude to settlements of Irish tinkers, though Irish Bogs may be no more than a geographical cliché with reference to particularly boggy land.

Irksum Close, Elkstone Gl, a derogatory name for land that is difficult to work.

Iron Field, Appleton Ch, 'land in a corner' [OE *hyrne*].

Island, Brinnington Ch, High Legh Ch, Crackenthorpe We (*The Yelland* 1510); **Island Close,** Great Stretton Lei; **Island Croft,** Adlington Ch; **Island Field,** West Alvington D; **Island Orchard,** Fifehead Magdalen Do; **Island Platt,** Muston Lei: 'field completely surrounded by water or by other fields' [OE *ēa-land*].

(The) **Isle of Man,** Handforth cum Bosden Ch, Norton Ch, Bletchingdon O, Bradford WRY, Idle WRY; **Isle of Man Dale,** Long Marton We: names alluding either to remoteness or to shape, some of the fields being in the form of a three-pointed star, and so resembling the Manx badge.

Isle of Scilly, Temple Guiting Gl, refers to a remote piece of land.

Isle of Want, Hodnet Sa, a derogatory name for unproductive land.

Isle of Wight, Colesbourne Gl, Arnesby Lei, Ratley Wa; **Isle of Wight Coppice,** Faccombe Ha; **Isle of Wight Meadow,** Speen Brk: names usually referring to land with streams on two or more sides.

Isles, Woodford Ch, 'hillocks' [OE *hygel*].

Itch Hills, Sudbury Db, 'land added to an estate' [OE **ēcels*].

Itchens, East Woodhay Ha; **The Itchings,** Acton Burnell Sa; **New Itchings,** Acton Burnell Sa; 'part of field cultivated while the rest remains fallow' [OE **heccing*].

Ivey Close, Nailstone Lei; **Ivy Bush,** Wareham St Mary Do; **Ivy Close,** Blaston St Michael Lei, Cransley Nth (*Highway Close* 17c), Ashwell R; **Ivy Copse,** Alton Pancras Do; **Ivy Croft,** Lamberhurst K; **Ivy Ground,** Rampisham Do; **Ivy Meadow,** Thornford Do: names alluding to *Hedera helix*. In an area where a Roman settlement has been found, the Thornford name is taken by Barbara Kerr ('Dorset fields and their names', 236) as possibly indicating that there were once ivy-covered ruins in the meadow, and so 'excavation might be profitable' there.

J

Jack Bank, Marple Ch; **Jack Close,** South Croxton Lei; **Jack Croft,** Adlington Ch, Bostock Ch, Woodford Ch; **Jack Field,** Sproston Ch, Twemlow Ch, Warmington Ch; **Jack Flatt,** Coal Aston Db; **Jack Hedges,** Andover Ha; **Jack Hey,** Moore Ch; **Jack Lane Croft,** Little Leigh Ch; **Jack Meadow,** Daresbury Ch; **Jack Ridding,** Pownall Fee Ch; **Jack Riding,** Workshop Nt; **Jacks Croft,** Siddington Ch, Botley Ha: 'vacant, unused land' [MnE dial. *jack*].

Jail Bird, Welford Brk; **Jail Close,** Oddington Gl; **Jail Field,** Bramdean Ha; **Jail Meadow,** Cubley Db: 'land adjoining a prison'. Jail Bird is possibly 'hillside beside a prison' [OE *breord*].

Japan, Fareham Ha, a transferred name for a remote field.

Jay Field, Henbury Ch; **Jay Hay,** North Rode Ch: 'land on which jays were to be found'.

Jericho, Holme St Cuthbert Cu, Bolas Magna Sa; **Jericho Farm,** Cassington O; **Jericho Field,** Clyffe Pypard W: a transferred name for a remote field.

Jerusalem, Coveney C; **Jerusalem Wood,** Chippenham C: transferred name for a remote field.

Jews Bush Furlong, Little Milton O; **Jews Meadow,** Appleton Ch: probably derogatory names for nondescript land.

Jews Trump, Kilburn Db, 'land shaped like a Jew's harp'.

Jig Platt, Adlington Ch (*The Gigge Platt* 1807), 'plot near or containing a gig-mill', referring to a building in which the nap of cloth was raised by means of teasels.

Jillywoods, Rowley ERY (*Suthwode* 1269), 'woods of St Giles', belonging in fact to the Hospital of St Giles in Beverley.

Job's Balk, Tackley O; **Job's Close,** North Aston O; **Job's Piece,** Bosley Ch: derogatory names for intractable land, demanding much patience in its management.

Jointry, Wildboarclough Ch, Edlaston Db: 'land held in jointure', implying a co-tenancy of husband and wife, or entailed property.

Judas, Whitchurch O; **Judas Ground,** Leigh Do; **Judas Slack,** Wyke WRY: probably a derogatory term for land regarded as in some way treacherous, or alluding to the elder, which is occasionally known as the Judas-tree.

Juniper Hill, Abbots Langley Hrt, Crowmarsh O: 'hill on which juniper flourished', alluding to the shrub, which favours chalk and limestone (*Juniperus communis*).

K

Keddle Dock Field, Siddington Ch; **Kedlock Meadow,** Dunham on the Hill Ch; **Kettles Croft,** Brindley Ch: 'land on which charlock was found'. This plant (*Sinapis arvensis*), often abundant on arable land, is known in the Midlands as keddle dock or kedlock.

Keymick Croft, Albrighton Sa, alludes to rest-harrow (*Ononis spinosa*) [OE *cammoc*].

Kid Acre, Plumley Ch (*Kydebuttes* 1345); **Kid Croft,** Cheadle Ch; **Kid Field,** Gawsworth Ch, Presbury Ch; **Kid Mire,** Firbank We; **Kidside,** Preston Richard We: 'land on which sucking calves were kept' [ME *kide*].

Kill Close, Hulland Ward Intakes Db; **Kill Hill,** Old Hutton We; **Kill Pingle,** Bamford Db: 'land by a kiln' [OE *cyln*].

Kill Devils Field, Hatfield Hrt, a derogatory name for land demanding much hard work.

Kiln Close, Bucklebury Brk, Ilsington D, Hursley Ha, Cleveley La, Frolesworth Lei, Kirkby Mallory Lei, Yaxley Sf, Stainforth WRY; **Kiln Croft,** Bollington Ch, Bosley Ch, North Rode Ch, Alderwasley Db, Aston Db, Heptonstall WRY, Sandal Magna WRY; **Kiln Deans,** Ashburton D [OE *denu*]; **Kiln Field,** Chorley Ch, Buckland D, West Buckfastleigh D, Catherington Ha, Ewhurst Ha, Billsborrow La, Bryning La, Out Rawcliffe La, Pilling La; **Kiln Ground,** Sandhurst Brk, Welford Brk; **Kiln Hanger,** Windsor Brk, Gosfield Ess, Steep Ha, Albury Sr [OE *hangra*]; **Kiln Holme,** Firbank We; **Kiln Meadow,** Ashleyhay Db; **Kiln Piddle,** Mortimer Brk; **Kiln Piece,** Edale Db, Selborne Ha; **Kiln Pightle,** Sherborne St John Ha; **Kiln Plot,** Otterbourne Ha: 'land on which a kiln was situated', the purpose being usually brick-making or lime-burning [OE *cyln*].

Kinch Holme, Melbourne Db (*Kingesholm* 1386) [ON *holmr*]; **Kings Close,** Hexton Hrt; **Kings Croft,** Standon Hrt, Leatherhead Sr; **Kings Field,** Hunsdon Hrt (*Kyngesfelde* 13c); **Kings Ground,** Kintbury Brk; **King's Ing,** King's Meaburn We; **Kings Land,** Great & Little Hormead Hrt (*Kingescroft* 13c); **King's Mead,** Alton Ha; **King's Standing,** Ewelme O [ME *standing*, 'hunting stand']: 'land held by (the) King', there being nothing in most forms to indicate whether the holder was the crown or a bearer of the surname King.

Kirk Acre, Bradwell Db; **Kirk Croft,** Warmington Ch, Idridgehay Db; **Kirk Dale,** Glen Parva Lei; **Kirk Field,** Cornsay Du; **Kirk Flatt,** Skelsmergh We [ON *flat*]; **Kirk Ford,** Abney Db, Ashleyhay Db; **Kirkhaugh,** Bollington Ch (*Kirkall* 1611) [OE *halh*]; **Kirk Hey,** Broughton La; **Kirk Hall,** Wildboarclough Ch, Harston Lei; **Kirk Leys,** Langham R; **Kirklands Meadow,** Yeldersley Db; **Kirksteads,** Hayfield Db [OE *stede*, 'site']; **Kirkthwaite,** Millom Cu, Crook We [ON *þveit*]; **Kirk Way Hill,** Walworth Du: 'land by, or belonging to, a church' [ON *kirkja*].

Kirk Field, pre-enclosure great field name in Nunnington NRY, Thirkelby NRY, Kendal We (*Kyrkefeld* 1431), Kirk Deighton WRY, Kirkby Overblow WRY, Ravensfield WRY.

Kiss Arse, Kiss Hill, Rainow Ch (*The Kisse Crofte* 1611); **Kiss Arse Wood,** Wincle Ch: names that may be (in Dodgson's words) 'rude or ironic' (PNCh i, 146), or may allude to particular topographical features, namely a recess and a buttock-shaped hill [ON *kjóss*, OE *ears*].

The Kitchen, Wheatley O; **Kitchen Close,** Bucklebury Brk, Mortimer Brk (*Le Kechyn Croft* 1552), Charford Ha, Rampton Nt, Pishill O, Pyrton O; **Kitchen Croft**(s), Bosley Ch, Butley Ch, Minshull Vernon Ch, Kings Langley Hrt; **Kitchen Field,** Boreham Ess, Colne Engaine Ess, Langenhoe Ess (*Kechenefeld* 1378), Shalford Ess (*Kechenefeld* 1405), Essendon Hrt, Sawbridgeworth Hrt, Harefield Mx, Limpsfield Sr, Merstham Sr, Rowington Wa; **Kitchen Flat,** Derwent Db; **Kitchenhurst,** Hodnet Sa [OE *hyrst*]; **Kitchen Lands,** Dillicar We; **Kitchen Mead,** Holwell Do, Hook Do, Theydon Garnom Ess; **Further & Homeward Kitching,** Ardley O; **Kitching Pasture,** Thorpe Thewles Du: '(land by) a kitchen garden, land on which vegetables were grown for immediate use' [ME *kicchen*].

Kitcumb Wood, Newton Valance Ha (*Ketecumba Helye* 1166) [OE *cumb*, *halh*]; **Kite Corner,** Ashmore Do; **Kite Hill,** Upton Grey Ha; **Kite Meadow,** Winstone Gl; **Kites Hill,** Welford Brk; **Kitlands,** Capel Sr (*Kyttelond* 1487): 'land haunted by kites' [OE *cȳta*].

Klondyke, North Wheatley Nt, Milton Lilborne W; **Klondyke Farm,** Burwell C: transferred name alluding to distant land. Gold was discovered on the Klondike in 1896.

Knap Furlong, Stanton Gl; **(The) Knapp,** Hillfield Do, Stroud Gl, Alton Ha; **Knapp Close,** Tisbury W; **Knapp Hill,** Ampfield Ha, Berkhamsted Hrt; **Knapp Mead,** Christchurch Ha; **Knapps Furlong,** Lechlade Gl: 'land on or containing a hillock' [OE *cnæpp*].

Knave Acre, Catherington Ha; **Knave Holme,** Sedgwick We; **Knaves Acre,** Marton Ch, St Paul's Walden Hrt; **Long Knavery,** Baughurst Ha: 'land assigned to the young men or servants' [OE *cnafa*].

Knave's Conscience, Hurstbourne Tarrant Ha; **Knaw Bone,** Bratton W: derogatory names for difficult or infertile land.

Knees and Elbows, Upper Rawcliffe La, 'land with many angles in the boundary'.

Knole Knap, Long Sutton So; **Knoll Ground,** Littleport C; **The Knoll(s),** Disley-Stanley Ch, Little Addington Nth, Pontesbury Sa; **Knowl Field,** Thelwall Ch; **The Knowle(s),** Ashmore Do, Aldbury Hrt, Habberley Sa; **Knowle End Close,** Markfield Lei: 'land with hillocks' [OE *cnoll*].

The Knooks, North Claine Wo, 'nooks', fancifully spelt.

Knotts, Killington We; **Knotts Hill,** Beetham We (*Le Cnotte* 1332): 'hillocks', usually with the implication of rockiness [ON *knottr*].

Knowsley, Inskip with Sowerby La, name associated with the Earls of Derby, owners of much of the land here.

Konjohns Hole, High Easter Ess (*Conyoneshole* 1401), 'goblin's hollow' [ME *congon*]. See also Congellons, Quindal Hole.

Kuneger, Chinnor O, 'rabbit warren' [ME *coninger*].

L

The L Close, Broughton Astley Lei, 'L-shaped piece of land'.

Labour in Vain, Winterborne Whitechurch Do, Thornbury Gl, Codicote Hrt, Bradmore Nt, Rufford Nt, Bratton W; **Labour in Vain Hill,** Calne W: derogatory names for intractable land.

Labourers Field, Hinton Ampner Ha, Walkern Hrt; **Labouring Poors Allotment,** Milton under Wychwood O; **Labouring Purrock,** Twyford Ha [OE *pearroc*]: 'land allocated to workmen', either in return for the labour, or by way of relief of the poor.

Ladder Close, Privett Ha; **Ladder Stile,** Ashreigney D: 'steep land' [MnE dial. *ladder*].

Ladies Grove, Long Ditton Sr (*Ladycroft* 1498); **Ladies Meadow,** Bushby Lei; **Lady Acre,** Kingham O; **Lady Close,** Hallaton Lei, Hugglescote Lei; **Lady Field,** Crowley Ch, Aston Flamville Lei, Alvechurch Wo; **Lady Furlong,** Wardington O; **Lady Lands,** Layer Bretton Ess (*Ladyland* 1499); **Lady Mead,** Sandhurst Brk, Hillingdon Mx; **Lady Meadow,** Sandbach Ch, Widecombe D, Market Bosworth Lei, Warborough O, North Claine Wo; **Lady Moor,** Thorpe Thewles Du; **Lady Pightle,** Furneux Pelham Hrt; **Lady Wood,** Knossington Lei; **Lady's Corner,** Hinstock Sa: generally, 'land dedicated to the Blessed Virgin' for the maintenance of a chapel or shrine [OE *hlǣfdige*].

Lady Day Close (Great), Owston Lei: 'land whose rent fell due on 25 March'.

Laith Bank, Killington We; **Laith Breck,** Babworth Nt, Warsop Nt, Worksop Nt [OE *bræc*]; **Laith Close,** Brighouse WRY; **Laithe Croft,** Soyland WRY; **Laithe Howe,** Whinfell We [ON *haugr*]: 'land by a barn' [ON *hlaða*].

Lamb Close, Elwick Hall Du; **Lamb Croft,** Kettleshulme Ch, Kings Langley Hrt, Worksop Nt, Hunsworth WRY; **Lambcut(t)s,** Ashby St Ledgers Nth, Blakesley Nth [OE *cot*]; **Lamb Flatt,** Kirkby Lonsdale We; **Lamb Ground,** Toot Baldon O; **Lamb Leys,**

Wickham Bishop Ess (*Lamblese* 1404) [OE *lǣs*]; **Lamb Park,** Ilsington D, Beetham We; **Lamb Piece,** Alderwasley Db; **Lamber Croft,** Warlingham Sr; **Lamber Hey,** Daresbury Ch; **Lamber Leaze,** Ramsden O; **Lamber Leys,** Alkmonton Db; **Lamberstick,** Over Seal Lei [OE *sticce*]; **Lambert,** Brailsford Db (*Lamber Close* 1640); **Lambray,** Walton Superior Ch [OE (*ge*)*hæg*]; **Lammer Piece,** Dummer Ha: 'pastures reserved for lambs'. *Lamber* forms are from *lambra,* the genitive plural of OE *lamb.*

Lamb Pit(s), Northenden Ch, Illston Lei (*Lamputis* 1364); **Lampit Field,** Broxbourne Hrt; **Lampits,** Hoddesdon Hrt; **Lampitt,** Lenchwick Wo; **Lampitts Bottom,** Dorchester O: 'loam diggings' [OE *lām, pytt*].

(**The**) **Lam(m)as,** Windsor Brk, Meesden Hrt, Watton at Stone Hrt; **Great Lammas,** Coston Lei; **Lammas Bridge,** Halton Ch; **Lam(m)as Close,** Stanway Gl, Barton in the Beans Lei, Carlton Curlieu Lei, Catthorpe Lei, Wanlip Lei, Lowdham Nt, Cadlington O, Chinnor O, Ansty Wa; **Lammas Croft,** East & West Tytherley Ha; **Lammas Farm,** Benefield Nth; **Lammas Field,** Longsleddale We; **Lammas Ground,** Ashwell Hrt; **Lammas Lands,** Melksham W; **Lammas Leaze,** Hungerford Brk; **Lam(m)as Mead,** Kemble Gl, Shephall Hrt, Croxton Nf; **Lammas Meadow,** Bromsberrow Gl, Bruntingthorpe Lei, Carlton Curlieu Lei, Newton Unthank Lei; **Lammas Spinney,** Orlingbury Nth; **Lammas Wood,** Aldbury Hrt; **Lammasses,** Shepperton Mx: 'meadow lands used for grazing after 1 August'. The hay harvest occupied the time between 24 June and Lammas, when the fences were removed and the reapers turned their attention to the corn. The cattle were meanwhile allowed to graze on the aftermath. Loaves made from the new wheat were taken to the church at this time for a blessing and a thanksgiving—hence the name *hlāf-mæsse,* 'loaf festival'.

Lamp Acre, Windsor Brk, Churchill O, Hook Norton O; **Lamp Close,** Cheam Sr; **Lampland(s),** Eckington Db, Tiddenham Gl, Broughton Poggs O; **Lamp Meadow,** Ilkeston Db; **Lamp Plot,** Pirbright Sr: 'land whose rent was used to maintain lamps in the parish church'. See also Bell Acre, Dagtail Piece.

Lanches, Tarrant Rawston Do, 'ridges, terraces on a hillside', on the function of which there is much controversy [OE *hlinc*].

(The) Lancott, see Langate.

Land Close, Blaston St Michael Lei, Brooksby Lei, Galby Lei, Knossington Lei, Stockerston Lei, Ashwell R; **Land Croft,** Whatcroft Ch; **Land Field,** Bradwell Ch, Wincham Ch; **Land Meadow,** Burrough on the Hill Lei: 'enclosure consolidating ridges of the open-field strips'. The *land* or ridge was the sub-unit of the strip, which comprised one or more lands, according to the length of the furlong or shot in which the strip was situated [OE *land*].

Land of Promise, Shoreditch Mx, a complimentary name.

Landscore, Alphington D; **Landshare Meadow,** Netherway W: 'allotment or strip intermixed with those of other tenants' [OE *land-scearu*].

Lands End, Lyme Handley Ch, Highworth W: may be a transferred name alluding to distant fields, or merely a reference to the fact that these pieces of land were at the boundary of the ridged arable field.

Lane Close, Welford Brk, Alkmonton Db, Walworth Du, Carlton Lei, Medbourne Lei; **Lane Field,** Halton Ch, Newbottle Du; **Lane Holt,** Kings Norton Lei [OE *holt*]; **Lane Meadow,** Yockleton Sa; **Lane Nep Field,** Benson O; **Lane Piece,** Billesdon Lei, Twycross Lei; **Lane Stead,** Allostock Ch: 'land by a lane' [OE *lane*].

Langate, Chastleton O; **Langett,** Hatherop Gl, Winstone Gl, Oaksey W, Purton W; **The Langhetts,** Hope Mansell He; **Langits,** Rushbury Sa; **Languit,** Feckenham Wo; **Little & Big Lanket,** Waterperry O; **Lankets,** Chieveley Brk; **The Lankett,** Hailey O; **(The) Lancott,** Islip O, Kiddington O, Upper Heyford O: 'long strip of land' [OE **langet*].

Langdale, Goadby Lei; **Lang Delt,** Kentmere We [MnE dial. *dalt*]; **Langdole Field,** Duston Nth (*Le Langdole* 13c) [OE *dǣl, dāl*]; **Langham,** Redbourn Hrt, Hanging Houghton Nth (*Longham* 1465) [OE *hamm*], Ryhill ERY (*Langholme* 1326); **Langholme,** Everton Nt [ON *holmr*]; **Langthornes,** Stratfieldsaye Ha (*Langhorne* 17c) [OE *horn*]: 'long piece of land' [OE *lang*].

Laphole Close, Great Stretton Lei, fanciful name for a secluded piece of land.

Lapwing, Melbourne Db (*Lapwingeflight* 1673); **Lapwing Croft,** Cheadle Ch; **Lapwing Field,** Appleton Ch, Bollin Fee Ch, Lymm Ch, Pott Shrigley Ch, Whettenhall Ch; **Lapwing Hill,** Littleton Ha; **Lapwing Holm,** Sparsholt Ha: 'land on which lapwings were seen'. The reference is to the peewit (*Vanellus vanellus*), which breeds throughout Britain.

Laugherlong (North, South & Homeward), Braybrooke Nth, possibly 'furlong in a woodland clearing' [OE *lēah, furlang*].

Laughing Croft, Gawsworth Ch, Marton Ch; **Laughing Field,** Chapel en le Frith Db; **Laughing Stead,** Stayley Ch: complimentary names for productive land.

Launde Lees, Belton R; **The Launds,** Hylton Du: 'woodland pasture' [OF *launde*].

(The) Lawn(s), Boxford Brk, Hatton Ch, Higher Whitley Ch, Abbotsham D, Abbotsbury Do, Powerstock Do, Offley Hrt, Billesdon Lei, Groby Lei, Medbourne Lei, Ullesthorpe Lei, Monkton Combe So, Wrington So, Broadwas Wo; **Lawn Close,** Everton Nt; **Lawn Croft,** Oxton Nt; **Lawn Field,** Cookham Brk, Alresford Ha, Stockerston Lei; **Lawn Mead,** Bennington Hrt; **Lawn Meadow,** Groby Lei: 'grass ground', though it has been suggested that the name must be interpreted 'arable strips' in some areas (cf. B. Kerr, 'Dorset fields and their names', 251) [OF *launde*, OE *land*].

Lazy Bush, Beaulieu Ha; **Lazy Lands,** Little Somborne Ha; **Lazy Leas,** Wheatley Nt: derogatory names for unproductive land.

Lean Hay, Hook Do, 'arable enclosure' [ME *leyne*].

Leap Hedges, Little Ness Sa, 'land with hedges low enough to be jumped by deer' [OE **hliep*].

Lease Lands, Alderbury Sa; **Leasows,** Millington Ch; **Leasure,** Flagg Db, Earls Barton Nth; **Leasure Close,** Windley Db; **Leisure Copse,** Abinger Sr; **Big & Little Leizure Hill,** Wolstaston Sa; **Lessor Croft,** Peover Superior Ch; **The Lessors,** Hartpury Gl; **Lesure,** Chapel en le Frith Db: 'grasslands', or even (especially in WMidl counties) 'enclosures'. The two-syllabled forms are from *lǣswe*, the dative case of the element [OE *lǣs*].

Leather Close, Heckfield Ha; **Leather Coat,** Tachbrook Wa; **Leather Croft,** Aston Hrt; **Leather Hill,** Holy Cross & St Giles Sa; **Leather Lands,** Merstham Sr; **Leather Meadow,** Bartington Ch; **Leathern Acre,** Merrow Sr: 'land with hard, stubborn soil'.

The Leg, Highcliffe Ha, Knebworth Hrt, Berrow So, Compton Bishop So, Alvediston W; **Leg Ground,** Kington Magna Do; **Legged Field,** Exton Ha: 'land with one or more leg-like projections'.

Leg of Mutton, East Anstey D, West Ashton W, Killington We; **Leg of Mutton Field,** Antrobus Ch; **Leg of Mutton Wood,** Croxton C: fanciful names for triangular pieces of land. Cf Shoulder of Mutton.

Legs, Bosley Ch, Spondon Db, Swannington Lei, Gorwell Paddock So: '(land with) framework of a stack'.

Leipsic, Alston Cu, transferred name (in the 18–19c form) for a remote field. Leipzig was taken by the French in 1806. Cf Corsica, French Flat, Waterloo.

Lemon Doles, Tuxford Nt; **Lemon Field,** Witley Sr; **Lemon Head,** Wadsworth WRY: possibly 'land with artificial watercourses' [ME *leme*].

The Lench, Ellingham Ha; **Lench Field,** Broadwas Wo: same as Linch Field (qv).

Lentil Close, Alderwasley Db, Cossington Lei: 'land on which lentils were grown'. This plant (*Lens esculenta*) seems to have been introduced into England after the Norman Conquest and was at one time much grown in the Midlands and North. It was a part of the diet of the poor in the Middle Ages and was considered in the seventeenth century to be 'excellent sweet fodder' for young cattle (cf Seebohm, *Evolution of the English Farm*, 255).

The Lero, Leicester Lei (*Le Leywro* 1415); **Ley Roe,** Doncaster WRY (*Leywroo* 1562, *Leyrow Field* 1785): 'untilled nook of land' [OE *lǣge*, ON *vrá*].

The Letter L Field, Bramshot Ha, indicates the shape of the field.

Lettuce Field, Crowley Ch, self-explanatory.

Level Close, Atlow Db; **Level Field,** Crowley Ch, Disley-Stanley Ch, Offerton Ch; **Level Leasow,** Minsterley Sa: self-explanatory.

Lewshill, Clipston Nth, 'hill on which pig-sty stood' [OE *hlōse, hyll*].

Ley (Great & Little), Cookham Brk (*La Leyhe* 1371); **Ley Close,** Osbaston Lei, Slawston Lei; **Ley Croft,** Wheathampstead Hrt (*Laypightel* 1390); **Ley Field,** Abbotsham D, Clothall Hrt; **Ley Hill,** Hemel Hempstead Hrt (*Layhill* 1623): 'untilled land' [OE *lǣge*].

The Leys, Little Hadham Hrt, Medbourne Lei; **Leys Close,** Lambley Nt, North Elmsall WRY; **Leys Field,** Nether Wallop Ha: 'meadow lands' [OE *lǣs*].

(The) Lez(z)er, Kiddington O, Alveston Wa, Newbold Pacey Wa: 'meadow lands'. See also Lease Lands [OE *lǣs*].

Lilburne Mead, Halstock Do, an arbitrarily named field, commemorating John Lilburne (?1614–1657), 'the Leveller'. Thomas Hollis, who owned much of the land in Halstock in the late eighteenth century, celebrated several of the men and some of the key ideas of the Puritan Revolution in this way (cf Reasonableness).

Lime Close, Roslinston Db; **Lime Croft,** Bollington Ch; **Lime Field,** Kettleshulme Ch; **Lime Garth,** Old Hutton We; **Lime Grassings,** Strickland Roger We; **Lime Meadow,** Sandhurst Brk; **Lime Piece,** Derwent Db; **Limed Field,** Heptonstall WRY: 'land to which lime has been applied'.

Limekiln Bottom, East Dean Sx; **Limekiln Close,** Alderwasley Db, Eyam Db, Flagg Db, Great Hucklow Db; **Limekiln Field,** Thelwall Ch, Birchanger Ess (*Lymkelne* 1414); **Lime Kiln Furlong,** Lambourn Brk; **Limekiln Ground,** Hillfield Do; **Lime Kiln Meadow,** Evington Lei, Scraptoft Lei; **Lime Kiln Piece,** Harley Sa; **Limekiln Sleight,** Quenington Gl; **Limepit Ing,** Hunsworth WRY: 'land on which lime was dug or burnt'.

Linch Field, Middleton Ess; **Linch Meadow,** Alton Ha, Polebrook Nth (*Le Lynch* 1260); **The Linches,** Thorpe Achurch Nth (*Linches*

1227), Whitchurch O; **Linches Craught,** Alveston Gl [OE *croft*]; **Linchills,** Bozeat Nth; **Lynch,** Mappowder Do, Titherington Gl, Brackley Nth (*La Linche* 1265); **Lynch Land,** Sutton Downes Ch; **Lynchy Field,** Faccombe Ha: 'ridges, terraces on sloping land' [OE *hlinc*].

Lincroft, Aston Db, Kneesall Nt (*Lincroft* 1245), Brackley Nth (*Lyncroft* 1408), Pontesbury Sa; **Line Close,** Gomersal WRY; **Line Garth,** Hof We; **Line Hill,** Acton Burnell Sa, Langley & Ruckley Sa; **Lineleaze,** Horton Gl; **Linnadine,** Hartlebury Wo [OE *worðign*]; **Lin(n)age,** Carlton Lei, Shenton Lei, Long Sutton So; **Linnegar,** Bromfield Sa [OE *æcer*]; **Linton Field,** Lindsell Ess (*Lynton* 1324); **Lions Croft,** St Michaels Hrt (*Linecroft* 1635); **Lymarsh,** Foxearth Ess (*Lynersch* 1374) [OE *ersc*]; **Lym Mead,** Twickenham Mx (*Linmede* t.Hy 6); **Lympsteads,** Thorley Hrt (*Lynstede* 1387) [OE *stede*]; **Lynn Croft,** Sowerby WRY: 'land on which flax was grown' [OE *līn*].

Ling Carr, Goosnargh La; **Lin Close,** Babworth Nt, Dewsbury WRY; **Ling Croft,** Goosnargh La; **Ling Field,** Goosnargh La; **Linghall,** Harlestone Nth (*Linghou* c 1320) [ON *haugr*]; **Ling Heath,** Croxton Nf; **Ling Hill,** Clipstone Nt; **Linghome Hill,** Folkton ERY; **Ling Knobs,** Ruddington Nt; **Ling Leys,** Skelbrooke WRY; **Lingy Field,** Claughton La, Out Rawcliffe La: 'land on which heather grew' [ON *lyng*].

Linhay Field, East Allington D, 'field containing a cattlehouse' [MnE dial. *linhay*].

Lip Gate, Little Barrington Gl (*Lepeȝate* 1327); **Lippiat,** Marshfield Gl; **Lipyeat,** Alveston Gl, East Pennard So, West Pennard So; **Lyppeatt,** Pucklechurch Gl (*Lupihieta* 1189); **Lypyeat,** Wrington So: '(land with) a fence or hedge over which a deer might jump, but which would restrain cattle or sheep' [OE *hlīep-gēat*].

Liquorice Close & Garth, Ferry Fryston WRY: 'land on which liquorice was grown'. The cultivation of liquorice as a field crop seems to have begun in the Middle Ages, and by the early seventeenth century it was well established near Pontefract WRY and Godalming Sr. This herb (*Glycyrrhiza glabra*) requires a dry, loamy soil as free as possible from stones, so that the strong, thick root can develop length as well as thickness.

Little Acres, Orton on the Hill Lei; **Little Bastard,** Breadsall Db; **Little Bit,** Shenton Lei; **Little Bottoms,** East Allington D; **Little Brake,** Blackawton D [OE *bræc*]; **Little Cleeve,** East Pennard So [OE *clif*]; **Little Close,** Arlington D, Alkmonton Db, Billesdon Lei, Holwell Lei, Kibworth Lei, Laughton Lei, Welham Lei; **Little Craught,** Priston So [OE *croft*]; **Little Crofts,** Stoughton Lei; **Little Daywork,** Adlington Ch, Caldbeck Cu; **Little Down,** West Alvington D; **Little Field,** Pownall Fee Ch, Fifehead Magdalen Do, Fifehead Neville Do, Houghton le Spring Du, Hylton Du, Hitchin Hrt (*Lytelfeld* 1409), Kings Langley Hrt, Lamberhurst K, Evington Lei, Glooston Lei, Medbourne Lei, Baschurch Sa, Caterham Sr (*Littelfild* 1500); **Little Furlong,** Fifehead Neville Do, Steep Ha; **Little Gastons,** Priston So [OE *gærs-tūn*]; **Little Ground,** Hillfield Do; *Little Hill*, Kings Norton Lei 1638; **Little Hope,** Poynton Ch [OE *hop*]; **Little Land,** Higher Whitley Ch; **Little Lay,** Fawley Ha; **Little Leasow,** Church Pulverbatch Sa; **Little Meadow,** Abbotsham D, Burton Overy Lei, Kibworth Lei, Owston Lei, Ayston R; **Little Moat,** Evington Lei; **Little Orchard,** West Alvington D; **Little Pasture,** Holt Lei; **Little Worthy,** Weston So [OE *worðign*]: self-explanatory names.

Little Breakfast, Westby with Plumpton La, derogatory name possibly for a large field.

Little Content, Milford Ha, 'disappointingly unproductive field'.

Little Heaven, Henstridge So; **Little Hercules,** Burghfield Brk: presumably complimentary names.

Little Pickle, Southwell Nt (*Picklewonge* 1616); **Little Pightle,** Newbury Brk: 'small piece of land' [ME *pightel*].

Little Profit, Stert & Urchfont W; **Little Worth,** Brimpsfield Gl, Pucklechurch Gl, Ashmansworth Ha, Bletchingdon O, Broad Town W, Brokenborough W, Charlton W, Lydiard Millicent W, Melksham W: derogatory names for unproductive land.

Little 'Un, Hoby Lei (*Litil Eng* 14c), 'small meadow' [ON *eng*].

Loam Close, Wincle Ch; **Loam Holes,** Lamberhurst K; **Loam Pit,** Wandsworth Sr now GL (*Lamputte* 1277): 'land with loamy soil, or from which loam was dug' [OE *lām*].

Lodge Bank, Gawsworth Ch; **Lodge Brow Bottom,** Hurdsfield Ch; **Lodge Close,** Baggrave Lei, Billesdon Lei, Frisby Lei, Illston Lei,

Twycross Lei; **Lodge Field,** Newbury cum Pexall Ch, Bushey Hrt (*Le Logge* 1447), North Mimms Hrt; **Lodge Meadow,** Enbourne Brk: 'land beside a park lodge' [OF *loge*].

London, Heanor Db, Gotham Nt; **Londonderry,** Astley Abbots Sa: transferred names for remote pieces of land.

Long Acre, Bramhall Ch, Sproston Ch, Alphington D, Upham Ha, Berkhamsted Hrt (*Longacre* 1354), Bushey Hrt (*Longeacre* 1473), North Lopham Nf, Castleford WRY; **Long Acres (Lower & Upper),** Snarestone Lei; **Long Balance,** Little Downham Ess [OE *bēan-land*]; **Long Bank,** Crook & Willington Du; **Long Butts,** Tytherington Ch, Over Alderley Db, Redbourn Hrt; **(The) Long Close(s),** Bampton D, Beer D, East Allington D, Alderwasley Db, Bakewell Db, Eyam Woodlands Db, Fifehead Neville Do, Hillfield Do, Hook Do, Hurworth Du, Hitchin Hrt, Coston Lei, Foston Lei, Laughton Lei, Lubenham Lei, Measham Lei, Owston Lei, Scraptoft Lei, Welham Lei, Forncett St Peter Nf, Ashwell R; **Long Crawte,** Selborne Ha [OE *croft*]; **Long Croft,** Bucklebury Brk, Newton Ch, Great Gaddesden Hrt, Hendon Mx (*Longecroft* 1446), Ferry Fryston WRY; **Long Dales,** East Markham Nt, Ferry Fryston WRY; **Long Dole,** South Cerney Gl, Laleham Mx (*Langedole* 1329); **Long Down,** Long Ditton Sr; **Long Field,** West Alvington D, Charlesworth Db, Fifehead Neville Do, Elwick Hall Du, Newbottle Du, Flamstead Hrt, Coulsdon Sr; **Long Fouracres,** Berrynarbor D; **Long Furlong,** Leebotwood Sa, Henstridge So; **Long Ground,** Idbury O; **Long Ground Meadow,** Enbourne Brk; **Long Half,** Selborne Ha; **Long Ham,** Fifehead Neville Do, East Woodhay Ha [OE *hamm*]; **Long Hill Close,** Wardley R; **Long Hold,** Bibury Gl [OE *hold*]; **Long Hyde,** Long Sutton Ha [OE *hīd*]; **Long Ing,** Featherstone WRY [ON *eng*]; **Long Lace,** Mobberley Ch [OE *lǣs*]; **Long Ladders,** St Stephens Hrt; **Long Lands,** Chieveley Brk, Windsor Brk, Abney Db, Hillfield Do, Horton Gl (*Langlond* 1375), Alresford Ha, Basing Ha, Botley Ha, Hemel Hempstead Hrt, Forton La (*Le Langelondes* c 1250), Gaddesby Lei, Hardwick O, Cheam Sr, Alvechurch Wo; **Long Leasow,** Minsterley Sa, Netley Sa, Alvechurch Wo; **Long Leaze,** Hambleton R; **Long Leighs,** Inkpen Brk (*La Lyge* 14c) [OE *lǣge*]; **Long Ley,** East Hatley C; **Long Loons,** Preston on the Hill Ch [OE *land*]; **Long Loont,** Lower Whitley Ch; **Long Mead,** Holwell Do, Tring Hrt,

Ash Sr, Egham Sr; **Long Meadow,** Chieveley Brk, Clewer Brk, Speen Brk, Ilsington D, West Alvington D, Nether Wallop Ha, Stratfieldsaye Ha, Berkhamsted Hrt (*Le Longmed* 1300), Lubenham Lei, Stretton Magna Lei, Sall Nf, Acton Burnell Sa; **Long Park,** East Allington D, West Alvington D; **Long Piddle,** Nuffield O [ME *pightel*]; **Long Piece,** Bampton D; **Long Pightle,** Cantley Nf, Yaxley Sf; **Long Readings,** Hillingdon Mx [OE **ryding*]; **Long Rig(g)s,** Houghton le Spring Du, Walworth Du, Washington Du [ON *hryggr*]; **Long Rood(s),** Eyam Db, Nailstone Lei; **Long Severals,** Cantley Nf; **Long Shot(s),** Stapleford Tawney Ess, Weston Hrt; **Long Slade(s),** Alkmonton Db, Hillfield Do, Eastleach Martin Gl, Wardley R; **Long Slang,** Eaton Ch, Warmingham Ch, Barby Nth; **Long Spinney,** Martinsthorpe R; **Long Storth,** Hayton Nt [OE *steort*]; **Longswath Meadow,** Scaftworth Nt; **Long Thirteen Acre,** Braunston R; **Long Tongue,** Brailsford Db; **Long Vere,** Binstead & Neatham Ha [OE *fær*]; **Long Wong,** Elmton Db, Wellow Nt [ON *vangr*]: 'land of greater length than fields nearby' [OE *lang*].

Long Friday, Kempley Gl, Upper Slaughter Gl; **Long & Short Friday,** Wroxton O: 'unlucky or unproductive land'; Friday connoted both ill fortune and restricted diet. *Long Friday* was Good Friday, but this may not be the sense here [OE *Frīgedæg*].

Long Knavery, Baughurst Ha, a derogatory name for unreliable land.

Long Loved Ground, Shirburn O, a complimentary name.

Longmost Acre, Stockport Ch, 'longest arable strip' [MnE dial. *longmost*, OE *æcer*].

Lonkadine, Waters Upton Sa, 'long enclosure' [OE *worðign*].

Loon Field, Fulshaw Ch; **Loont,** Barnton Ch, Higher Whitley Ch; **Loont Adlands,** Bollington Ch [OE *hēafod-land*]; **Loont Field,** Ollerton Ch: 'enclosures incorporating the ridges of the open field' [OE *land*].

Loose Hay, Tytherington Ch; **Loosehills,** Farnham Sr (*Lowsehill* 1613); **Lordsgrove Field,** Banstead Sr (*Le Losegrovefeld* 1432); **Lousehill Field,** Frensham Sr (*Losehyll* 1570); **Lousey Field,** Corley Wa (*Lucyfeld* 1411); **Lousey Grove,** Standon Hrt (*Loseleye* t.Ed 3); **Lousey Meadow,** Enbourne Brk, Chorley Ch; **Lousey Piece,** Aldsworth Gl; **Lousy Field,** Bostock Ch, Chapel en le Frith Db; **Lousy Ground,** Bournemouth Ha; **Lousy Hill,** Cookham Brk; **Lousy Lands,** Powerstock Do; **Lousy Leys,** Stevenage Hrt (*Luceslond* t.Ric 2); **Lousy Mead,** Ridge Hrt (*Louse Mead* 1623); **Lousy Meads,** Hilton Du; *Lowsie Bush*, Wheatley O 17c; *Lowzie Grove*, Wychwood O 1617 (*Losengrave, Losnegraue* 13c): probably all 'land with a pig-sty', though other senses of *louse* and *lousy* are possible in some examples [OE *hlōse*].

Lords Close, Kendal We (*The Lorde Close* 1568); **Lords Meadow,** Boxford Brk; **Lords Park,** Moulton Ch; **Lords Piece,** Evington Lei: 'land belonging to the lord of the manor, or to a man with the surname Lord' [OE *hlāford*].

Lordship Field, Rudheath Lordship Ch; **Lordship Meadow,** Antrobus Ch: 'land in an extra-parochial demesne' [ME *lordeschip*].

Losing All Field, Colerne W, 'unprofitable land'.

Lost Field, Mobberley Ch, 'secluded piece of land'.

Lot Acre, Cookham Brk; **Lot Mead,** Holwell Do, Bisley Gl, Thames Ditton Sr; **Lot Meadow,** Harpenden O; **Lot Pightle,** Chieveley Brk; **The Lot(t)s,** Chedworth Gl, Painswick Gl, Bix O: 'portions of land allocated by annual ballot' [OE *hlot*].

Lound (Great & Little), Halstead Lei; **Lound Wood,** Rufford Nt (*The Lounds* 1300); **Lount,** Cadeby Lei; **First & Second Lount,** Oadby Lei; **Long Lounts Furlong,** Isley Walton Lei: '(land near or containing) a wood' [ON *lundr*].

Lovelands, Walton on the Hill Sr; **Lovers Field,** Nether Knutsford Ch: 'secluded pieces of land, frequented by lovers'.

Low Field, Hylton Du, Thorpe Thewles Du, Narborough Lei; **Low Hills,** Easington Du: 'land by, or on, a mound' [OE *hlāw*].

Lower Close, Eckington Db, Billesdon Lei, Welham Lei; **Lower Field,** Bollington Ch, Fifehead Magdalen Do; **Lower Ground,** Boxford Brk; **Lower Loons,** Sutton Ch; **Lower Meadow,** Berrynarbor D, Pleasley Db; **Lower Piece,** Fifehead Neville Do: 'land below, or further away from, the village'.

Lucern Field, Windsor Brk, Southminster Ess (*Lucernefeld* 1448); **Lucern Piece,** Croxton Nf; **Lucerne Bit,** Gaddesby Lei; **Lucerne Field,** Marple Ch: 'land on which purple medick was grown'. This leguminous plant (*Medicago sativa*) was introduced into Britain as a fodder crop in the late fourteenth century. The Southminster 15c form is of interest in that it antedates the earliest NED reference by nearly two centuries.

Luceys Field, Great Sampford Ess (*Loshawe* 1300), 'pig-sty enclosure' [OE *hlōse*, *haga*].

Luck Meadow, Chinley Db; **Lucky,** Sherston W: complimentary names.

Luke Stone, Atworth W, '(land beside a) boundary stone at which there was a reading from St Luke's gospel in the Rogationtide ceremonies'. See also Epistle Field.

Lumb, Brampton Db, Brimington Db; **Lumb Close,** Crigglestone WRY; **Lumbley Close,** Calow Db: 'land by a pool' [OE **lumm*].

Lymarsh, see Lincroft.

Lynch, see Linch Field.

M

Machine Close, Cadeby Lei; **Machine Leasow,** Westbury Sa: 'land on which a mechanical implement was used or kept'.

Madcroft, Piddington O, Pyrton O; **Madden,** Hawkesbury Gl (*of Mæddene* 972); **Madgore,** Mappowder Do: 'meadow land' [OE *mǣd*].

Magpie Shaw, Lamberhurst K, 'copse frequented by magpies'.

Maida Hill, Nuneham Courtenay O, transferred name for a remote piece of land, commemorating the British victory over the French at Maida in Calabria, on 4 July 1806.

Maiden Acre, Firbank We; **Maiden Down,** Abbots Anne Ha; **Maidens Balk,** Berkhamsted Hrt (*Mayden Balke* t.Jas 1); **Maids Mead,** Hinton Ampner Ha; **The Maid's Retreat,** Pucklechurch Gl: 'land owned by, or visited by, a maiden or maidens' [OE *mægden*].

Maiden Croft, Wheathampstead Hrt (*Medecroft* 1436), 'small meadow enclosure' [OE *mǣd, croft*].

Main (East & West), East Anstey D; **Main Field,** Dodcott cum Wilkesley Ch, Ollerton Ch, Rostherne Ch; **Main Hey,** High Legh Ch; **Main Meadow,** Pickmere Ch, Pownall Fee Ch; **Main Stones,** Dutton Ch; **Main Wood,** Allostock Ch; **Mains,** Barbon We, Beetham We; **Middle, North & South Manis,** Houghton le Spring Du: 'demesne land, home close' [ME *main*]. See also Means.

Maize Acre, Pownall Fee Ch, 'land on which maize was grown'.

Make Me Rich, Ferry Fryston WRY, a complimentary name for a productive field.

Malaga Slade, Mickleton Gl, a transferred name for a remote field.

Mallow Close, Tur Langton Lei 1638; *Mallow Ford*, Tur Langton Lei 1638; **Mallow Lands,** Austrey Wa: if they do not refer to the very striking plant, the mallow (*Malva sylvestris*), which is large and fine enough to be regarded as a landmark, these names may mean 'land on a gravel ridge' [OE **malu*].

Malm, Compton Ha; **Malm Close,** Bucklebury Brk (*Maum Close* 1791–2), Nursling Ha; **Malm Furlong,** Newbury Brk (*Le Malme* 1439); **Malm Ground,** Bournemouth Ha; **Malm Mead,** Easton Ha; **Malm Meadow Furlong,** Newbury Brk; **Malm Quar Tyning,** Littleton Drew W; **The Malmes,** Redbourn Hrt; **Malms,** Worldham Ha; **Malms Copse,** Binstead & Neatham Ha; **Malmy Field,** Watton at Stone Hrt; **Marm Hill,** Bovingdon Hrt (*Malmehyll* 1603): 'land with light, loamy soil' [ME *malm*].

Malsdon, Westbury on Severn Gl (*Maldon'* 1287), possibly 'speech hill', as it has been suggested that this was the place of assembly for the Westbury Hundred [OE *mæðel, dūn*].

Malthouse Close, Cantley Nf; **Malthouse Croft,** Twycross Lei, Brierley Hill St; **Malthouse Piece,** Forncett St Peter Nf; **Malting Close,** Walkern Hrt; **Malt Kiln Field,** Great & Little Marton La: 'land containing, or adjoining, a house in which malt was prepared or dried'.

Mammocks, Yate Gl, 'untidy heaps' [MnE dial. *mammock*].

Manchips Field, Bishop's Stortford Hrt (*Menshepes* 1396); **Manship,** West Ashton W: 'land held by the community' [OE *gemǣnescip*].

Mancroft, Chieveley Brk, Oveston Gl, Much Hadham Hrt, Bole Nt; **Manland,** Tollard Royal W: 'common land', often used of land on a parish boundary [OE *gemǣne*].

Mangold Field, Newbold Db, 'land on which mangel-wurzels were grown'. This large beet was much favoured by eighteenth-century agrarian improvers.

Manor Close, Stockerston Lei; **Manor House Great Close,** Hallaton Lei: 'land occupied by the lord of the manor, or adjoining the manor house' [ME *maner*].

Manor Pound, Fifehead Magdalen Do, Leafield O, Tetsworth O: 'enclosure for restraint of straying beasts'; the pound or pinfold was in the charge of a manorial officer, the pinder, who personally received and kept the fines due on impounded animals.

Mans Leg, Kendal We, alludes to the shape of the field.

Many Butts, Carrington Ch; **Many Leys,** Huncote Lei: 'enclosure consolidating numerous pieces of land from the arable or grassland of the unenclosed fields'.

Mapit Field, Ruislip Mx (*Marlputfeld* 1436), 'marlpit field'. See Marl Churl.

Maple Close, Herriard Ha; **Maple Croft,** Stebbing Ess (*Mapulcroft* 1577); **Maple Field,** Leese Ch, Hambledon Ha, Great Gaddesden Hrt; **Maple Ing,** Morley WRY; **Maple Stubbs Field,** Croydon Sr: 'land with maple tree(s)'. The field maple (*Acer campestre*) is a native English tree and is widely distributed, though it is most common in SE counties [OE **mapul*].

Mardale, Braunston Nth; **Mar Furlong,** Ashmansworth Ha; **Margate,** Kilsby Nth; **Mar Hill,** Burrough on the Hill Lei; **Marlands,** Albury Sr (*Merelande* 1362), Monks Kirby Wa; **Mare Crates,** Hinton Ampner Ha [OE *croft*]; **Mare Field,** Winchen Ch (*Le Meyrfeld* 1490); **Mare Furlong,** Piddington O; **Mare Ing,** Everton Nt [ON *eng*]; **Mareland,** Chiddingfold Sr (*Merelond* 1548); **Mareland Copse,** Godalming Sr; **Mare Meads,**

Leatherhead Sr: it is hard to separate, without early forms for each, names meaning 'land on a boundary' [OE (*ge*)*mǣre*] from those which are 'land on which mares grazed' [OE *mere*]; it is likely that the former are in the majority.

Mare's Nest, Marple Ch, 'disappointing land'.

Mark Field, Sandbach Ch, Bishop's Sutton Ha, Berkhamsted Hrt, Leatherhead Sr; **Mark Furlong,** Stanwell Mx; **Mark Hays,** Minsterley Sa [OE (*ge*)*hæg*]; **Mark Oak Close,** Northington Ha; **Mark Piece,** Highclere Ha: 'land on a boundary '[OE *mearc*].

Marl Churl(s), Carrington Ch, Yeardsley Ch; **Marl Churr,** Marple Ch; **Marl(ed) Julls,** Clifton Ch [EMnE *ear*, 'ploughing']; **Marl Close,** Kington Magna Do; **Marl Croft,** Baschurch Sa; **Marl Earth,** Chapel en le Frith Db; **Marl Field,** Minshull Vernon Ch, Rudheath Lordship Ch, Cerne Abbas Do, Little Bookham Sr; **Marl Hay,** Barrow Ch, Cubley Db; **The Marl Lands,** Norwood Green WRY; **Marl Marsh,** Cantley Nf; **Marl Piece,** Stoughton Lei; **Marld Field,** Bollington Ch, Bosley Ch, Dunham Massey Ch; **Marl'd Lont,** Hale Ch; **Marle,** Beechenwell Nf (*Marledewong* 1218); **Marled Hays,** Elton Ch; **Marles,** Beer D; **Marlpit,** Lambley Nt; **Marlpit Close,** Barwell Lei, Upton Lei, Dersingham Nf, Sutton Bonington Nt; **Marlpit Field,** Bilsborrow La, Elston La, Goosnargh La, Hothersall La, Inskip La, Adderley Sa, Newdigate Sr; **Marlpit Leasow,** Church Pulverbatch Sa; **Marlpit Meadow,** Burton We: 'land on which marl was spread, or from which it was dug'. Marl consists of clay mixed with calcium carbonate; it was spread on sandy soils by the Celtic inhabitants of Britain before the Roman occupation, and its value was realised—and its use revived—by the 'improvers' of the seventeenth and eighteenth centuries [OF *marle*].

(The) Marsh, Boxford Brk, Arclid Ch, Belstone D, Manston Do, Oundle Nth (*Le Mersh* 1287); **Marsh Croft,** Mobberley Ch; **Marsh Field,** Over Knutsford Ch, Timperley Ch, Bakewell Db (*Le Mersch* 1290), Artington Sr, Mitcham Sr, Hook WRY; **Marsh Furlong,** Speen Brk, Broxbourne Hrt, North Newington O; **Marsh Holmes,** Saundby Nt [ON *holmr*]; **Marsh Hook,** Ashby Folville Lei; **Marsh Mead,** Holwell Do; **Marsh Meadow,** Ollerton Ch; Marsh Pightle, Enbourne Brk: 'boggy land' [OE *mersc*].

Mawkin, Macclesfield Forest Ch, Preesall with Hackinsall La; **Mawkin Hey,** Bilsborrow La; **Mawkin Holes,** Macclesfield Forest Ch; **Mawkinshire Lane,** Cotgrave Nt (*Malkynshire* 1546): 'land on which hares were seen' [MnE dial. *malkin*].

May Acre, Carrington Ch; **May Croft,** Redbourn Hrt (*Mayefeld* 1543), Standon Hrt (*Maicrofte* 1556); **May Field,** Cound Sa; **Maylands Wood,** Hemel Hempstead Hrt (*Mayefeld* 1543); **May Plash,** Hitchin Hrt: ambiguous names, possibly referring either to May festivities, or to the hawthorn or may tree.

May Day Field, Preston La; **May Day Meer,** Over Haddon Db; **Maypole Bank,** Kenley Sa; **Maypole Close,** Sevenhampton Gl; **Maypole Ground,** Whitchurch O; **Maypole Hill,** Bilsborrow La; **Maypole Meadow,** Newnham Gl; **Great & Little May Pool,** Odd Rode Ch (*Maypole Bank* 1680): 'land on which May festivities took place'.

Mead Field, Haslemere Sr (*Meddemefeld* 1280, *Medefeld* 1388), 'middle field' [OE *medume*].

Mead Field, Anstey and Barkway Hrt (*Litilmadfeld* 1362), Furneux Pelham Hrt (*Litilmedfeld* 1479), Harpenden Hrt (*Madfeld* 1393), Hemel Hempstead Hrt, Ridge Hrt, St Peters Hrt (*Madcroft* 1438); **Mead Furlong,** Bedfont Mx; **Mead Lands Close,** Spelsbury O; **Mead Platt,** Rickmansworth Hrt; **Mead Plot,** Burghfield Brk; **Mead Shott,** Redbourn Hrt [OE *scēat*]: 'grassland mown for hay' [OE *mǣd*].

The Meadow, Berrynarbor D, Ashby Folville Lei, Burton Overy Lei, Foxton Lei, Illston Lei, Medbourne Lei; **Meadow Close,** Holt Lei, Ayston R; **Meadow Eyes,** Wincham Ch [OE *ēg*]; **Meadow Field,** Elwick Hall Du, Hylton Du, Haltwhistle Nb; **Meadow Flatt,** Kelsall Ch; **Meadow Garth,** Heworth Du [ON *garðr*]; **Meadow Gate Field,** Sutton Bonington Nt (*Le Medueweigates* 1247); **Meadow Head,** Underbarrow We; **Meadow Orchard,** Alphington D; **Meadow Parlour,** Barwell Lei; **Meadow Pleck,** Solihull Wa; **Meadow Spot,** Hayfield Db: 'grassland mown for hay'; *mead* is from *mǣd*, nominative case of the OE word, and *meadow* from the dative case, *mǣdwe*.

Mean Close, Maplebeck Nt; **Mean Croft,** Hambledon Ha, Holme We; **Mean Field,** Rostherne Ch, Edale Db, Coulsdon Sr, Thornton WRY (*Le Menefeld* 1421); **Mean Hey,** Hatton Ch [OE (*ge*)*hæg*]; **Mean Holme,** Cleveley La, Lytham La; **Mean Piece,** Oxton Nt; *Meane Meadowe,* Marston on Dove Db 1617; **Minlands,** Bletchingley Sr (*Le Meanelande* 1567): 'land held in common' [OE *gemǣne*].

Means, Wybunbury Ch; **Means Close,** Eynsham O; **Means Meadow,** Cold Norton St: 'demesne land; home close' [ME *main*]. See also Main.

Mear Oak Field, Smisby Db; **Meer Close,** Snarestone Lei; **Meeres,** Tabley Superior Ch; **Mereach,** Staverton Nt [OE *hæcc*, 'wicket-gate']; **Mere Ash,** Bratton W; **Mere Close,** Willoughby Waterless Lei; **Mere Stone Close,** Ticknall Db; **Merfield,** Winsley W (*Merefelde* 1341); **Merry Croft,** Hendon Mx; **Merry Field,** Durley Ha, Froxley Ha; **Merry Lands,** Whitchurch Wa; **Merry Oak,** Feckenham Wo; **Merry Orchard,** Winchfield Ha: 'land by a boundary' [OE (*ge*)*mære*].

Melon Ground, Crowmarsh O, possibly 'land by a mill' [OE *myl*(*e*)*n*].

Merciful, Soberton Ha, arbitrary and enigmatic name, possibly complimentary.

Mesne Close, Abney Db, Mansfield Nt; **Mesne Field,** Curbar Db; **Mesne Intake,** Brinnington Db; **Mesne Piece,** Oxton Nt: 'demesne land, home close'. See also Main (East & West) [AF *mesne*].

Methodist Nook, Out Rawcliffe La, 'land near a Methodist chapel'.

Mexico, Dufton We, a transferred name for a remote piece of land.

Mexo Close, Gawsworth Ch; **Mexon Field,** Dunham Massey Ch: 'land by or with a dung-heap' [OE *mixen*].

Miccle Holme, Staythorpe Nt (*Le Michilholm* 1300) [ON *holmr*]; **Michael Heath,** St Michaels Hrt; **Michael Meadow,** Lowdham Nt; **Michelholme,** Moreton Pinkney Nth (*Muchelholme* c 1200); **Mickla Bridge,** Woolaston Gl (*Mickley Meadow* 1620); **Mickle Dale,** Bilsthorpe Nt, Rufford Nt; **Mickle Field,** Brereton cum

Smethwick Ch; **Mickleland Field,** Thorganby ERY (*Micheland* 13c); **Micklemead,** Siston Gl; **Mickle Meadow,** Elwick Hall Du, Stanley Pontlarge Gl (*Muchlemede* 12c), Hill Croome Wo; **Micley,** Hulse Heath Ch, Feckenham Wo [OE *lēah*]; **Mickling,** Belton Lei [ON *eng*]; **Mickling Swathes,** Girton Nt: 'large piece of land' [OE *micel*, ON *mikill*].

The Middle Acres, Pickworth R; **Middle Close,** West Anstey D, Alderwasley Db, Baggrave Lei, Billesdon Lei, Gaddesby Lei, Illston Lei, Knossington Lei, Medbourne Lei, Stretton Parva Lei, Welham Lei, Ayston R, Martinsthorpe R; **Middle Field,** Kinderton Ch, Great Hucklow Db, Hinton St Mary Do, Hylton Du, Newbottle Du, Chilbolton Ha, Hemel Hempstead Hrt (*Middlefeild* 1200), North Witham L, Brooksby Lei, Stoughton Lei, Thurnby Lei, Ashwell R, Adderley Sa, Leatherhead Sr, Wilton W, Ansley Wa, Castle Bromwich Wa (*Le Middelfeld* 13c), Norton WRY; **Middle Field Close,** Burghwallis WRY; **Middle Furlong,** Boxford Brk, Stanwell Mx, Long Ditton Sr; **Middle Ground,** Gunthorpe R, Kenley Sa; **Middle Hill,** Great Longstone Db; **Middle Hook,** Henstridge So; **Middle Mead,** Burghfield Brk (*Middelmade* 1380); **Middle Meadow,** Alkmonton Db; **Middle Park,** West Alvington D; **Middle Rows,** Kirkhaugh Nb: 'land between, or in the midst of, other pieces of land' [OE *middel*].

Middle Field, pre-enclosure great field name in Salford Bd, Bierton Bk, Swaffham Prior C, Shotton Du, West Wick Du, Etton ERY, Harpham ERY, Faccombe Ha, Folksworth Hu, Scotter L, Kirkby Bellars Lei, Walton & Kimcote Lei, Cold Kirby NRY, Eskrick NRY, Nunnington NRY, Kirton Nt, Hardingstone Nth, South Stoke O, Tinwell Ru, Angmering Sx, Dinton W, Quidhampton W, Wylye W, Darfield WRY, West Tanfield WRY.

Midge Hole, Whitwell We; **Midge Holme,** Killington We; **Midge Mire,** Over Staveley We: either 'land infested by midges or gnats' [OE *mycg*] or 'land into which seepage from a manure heap drained' [OE *micge*].

Midsummer Leys, Willersey Gl, possibly 'grassland where mid-summer games took place'; the hay harvest commenced on St John's day (24 June) and when it had been completed the summer festivities were held. Alternatively, the name might imply that service on these leys had to be performed on Midsummer Day itself.

Milestone, Kibworth Lei, Swannington Lei; **Milestone Field,** Hinton Martell Do; **Milestone Ground,** South Stoke So; **Milestone Leasow,** Leebotwood Sa; **Milestone Piece,** Hinton Martell Do: 'land near a milestone', the named closes being adjacent to roads.

Milham, Churchill O (*Milnehamme* 1298, *Mulleham* 1299); **Millhams,** East Meon Ha: 'enclosure containing a mill' [OE *myln, hamm*].

Milkhill, Hursley Ha, Ashtead Sr, Ewhurst Sr (*Milkhilles* 1435), Woldingham Sr; **Milk Hills,** Thursley Sr; **Milk House Mead,** Chinnor O; **Milk House Plot,** Ellingham Ha; **Milking Bank Field,** Adderley Sa; **Milking Close,** Abney Db; **Milking Croft,** Alderwasley Db; **Milking Field,** Northenden Ch; **Milking Hill Moss,** Old Hutton We; **Milking Hillock,** Castleton Db, Green Fairfield Db; **Milking Holm,** Lambrigg We; **Milking Place,** Hathersage Db; **Milking Plot,** Fifehead Neville Do; **Milking Stead Bank,** Whinfell We; **Milking Yard,** Yaxley Sf; **Milkings Close,** Houghton on the Hill Lei: 'land by building where cows were milked'.

Milkwell, Fifehead Magdalen Do; **Milk Well Field,** Great & Little Wymondley Hrt; **Milk Well Ground,** Newton Purcell O (*Milkwell Furlong* 1601): complimentary names for grassland producing good milk.

Mill Acre, Kemble Gl, Empshott Ha; **Mill Brow,** Docker We; **Mill Close,** Bray Brk, Welford Brk, Melbourn C (*Le Mellefeld* 1385), Newbottle Du, Bushey Hrt, Alexton Lei, Barwell Lei, Billesdon Lei, Foxton Lei, Goadby Lei, Laughton Lei, Medbourne Lei, Cotgrave Nt, Mansfield Nt, Worksop Nt; **Mill Croft,** Milford Ha, Great & Little Munden Hrt; **Mill Field,** Newbottle Du, Easington ERY, East Mersea Ess (*Mellefelde* 1421), Hatfield Broad Oak Ess, Shalford Ess, Stanford le Hope Ess (*Mellefeld* 1414), Wickford Ess (*Melnfeld* 1299), Hayling Ha, Liss Ha, Steep Ha, Anstey & Barkway Hrt, Hexton Hrt, Ickleford Hrt (*Mulnelond* t.Ed 3), Lea La (*Mulnefeld* 1265), Carlton Curlieu Lei, Coleorton Lei, Medbourne Lei, Dersingham Nf, Laxton Nt, Esher Sr, Great Bookham Sr, Woldingham Sr (*Mullfeld* 1386),

Barston Wa (*Milfeld* 1490), Hampton in Arden Wa (*Milfeld* 1490), Great Heck WRY, Hensall WRY, Whitley WRY; **Mill Fields & Meadow,** Cobham Sr; **Mill Five Acres,** Alton Pancras Do; **Mill Furlong,** Treswell Nt; **Mill Ground,** Wolstaston Sa; **Mill Ham,** Longstock Ha, South Stoke So; **Mill Hanger,** Froyle Ha [OE *hangra*]; **Mill Hill,** Houghton le Spring Du, Norton ERY (*Milneholm* 1252), Billesdon Lei; **Mill Holme,** Medbourne Lei, Warmington Nth, Holme We; **Mill Howe,** Crook We [ON *haugr*]; **Mill Intack,** Heworth Du; **Mill Mead,** Hungerford Brk, Beer D, Alton Pancras Do, Codicote Hrt, Stanton Prior So, Artington Sr, Farnham Sr; **Mill Meadow,** Boxford Brk, Sandhurst Brk, Longparish Ha, Watford Hrt, Castle Bromwich Wa; **Millmoot,** East Brent So [ME *mote*]; **Mill Orchard,** Alphington D; **Mill Plain,** Christchurch Ha; **Mill Spot,** Knossington Lei; **Mill Tongue,** East Allington D; **Millway Tyning,** Littleton Drew W: 'land on or near which a mill was built' [OE *myln*].

Mill Field, a pre-enclosure great field name in Everingham ERY, Wilberfoss ERY, Weston Hrt, Keyston Hu, Aylstone Lei, Blaby Lei, Catthorpe Lei, Countesthorpe Lei, Foxton Lei, Glenfield Lei, Medbourne Lei, Nether Broughton Lei, Oadby Lei, Saxelby Lei, Sharnford Lei, Stonton Wyville Lei, Twyford Lei, Terrington NRY, Finmere O, Handborough O, Tutbury St, Aberford WRY, Bolton Percy WRY, Garforth WRY, West Tanfield WRY.

Mill Stone Meadow, Marthall cum Warford Ch; **Mill Stone Piece,** Kintbury Brk; Hinton Martell Do: 'land from which mill stones could be obtained'.

Millers Butts, Newbottle Du; **Millers Close,** Newbottle Du, Hatherop Gl; **Millers Ing,** Out Rawcliffe La: 'land allocated to the miller'.

Millin Dene, Michelmersh Ha [OE *denu*, 'valley']; **Milnflatt,** Kendal We; **Miln Holme,** Farndon Nt; **Miln Parrock,** Beetham We: 'land on which the mill was situated' [OE *myln*].

Million Roods, Temple Normanton Db; **Millions Meadow,** Rushbury Sa: ironic names for small fields.

Mince Croft, North Weald Basset Ess (*Mynchynhopes* 1480) [OE *hop*]; **Minchen Croft,** Long Sutton Ha; **Minchins Seven Acres,**

Itchen Abbas Ha; **Minchinton Orchard,** Mudford So: 'land owned by nuns' [OE *myncen*].

Minster Field, Godalming Sr (*Oldmynstrefeld* 1441), 'land near a monastery or church' [OE *mynster*]; it is not far from an old chapel at Tuesley.

Mire Squadge Close, Smisby Db; **Mirey Hill,** Goadby Lei; **Mirey Spinney,** Bushby Lei; **Miry Meadow,** Billesdon Lei; **Miry Moor,** Somerhal Herbert Db: 'boggy land'. *Squadge* seems to be a dialect form of *squash* (ie 'squashy') and reinforces the sense of the specifier [ON *mýrr*].

Mirk Slack, Whinfell We, 'dark or muddy hollow' [ON *myrkr, slakki*].

Misfortune Field, Hesket Cu, a derogatory name for poor land.

Missey Croft, Mobberley Ch; **Mizey Meadow,** High Legh Ch; **Mizzey,** Rostherne Ch: 'muddy land' [MnE dial. *misy*, *mizzy*].

Mixil, Harbury Wa; **Mixnams,** Chertsey Sr (*Mixtenhammes* 675): 'land with dung-hills' [OE *mix(en), hyll, hamm*].

Mizmaze, Long Sutton So; **Mizmaze Hill,** Salisbury W; **Mizmaze Wood,** West Ashton W: 'labyrinth, land with perplexing obstructions' [MnE dial. *mizmaze*].

Moat Bank, Alkmonton Db; **Moat Close,** Evington Lei, Scraptoft Lei, Alvechurch Wo; **Moat Field,** Hunsdon Hrt (*Mote Hoppetts* 1675); **Moat Furlong,** Claybrook Lei; **Moat Intack,** Broughton La; **Moat Meadow,** Appleton Ch, Little Leigh Ch, Scraptoft Lei; **Moat Piece,** Plumley Ch; **Moat Yard,** Shackerstone Lei: 'land by a moat'; this term seems not to have been limited to the water surrounding a castle, but to have been applied also to mill pools.

Mockbeggar, Ibsley Ha; **Mockbeggar Hall,** Werneth Ch: derogatory names for land on which a beggar might find neither shelter nor sustenance.

Monday Croft, Sheldon Wa; **Mondayshill,** Siston Gl, Wick & Abson Gl; **Munday Corn,** Pownall Fee Ch; **Mundays Row,** Catherington Ha: 'land on which service due was performed on Mondays' [OE *monandæg*].

Money Ash, Hale Ch; **Money Lows,** Ashford Db (*Monyloes* 1617): 'many ash trees' and 'many mounds' respectively [OE *manig*, *æsc*, *hlaw*].

Money Bank, Atcham Sa; **Money Breck,** Wellow Nt [OE *bræc*, 'scrub']; **Money Croft,** Therfield Hrt; **Money Field,** Takeley Ess (*Monyfeld* 1348), Buckland Hrt (*Monefeld* 13c), Great Munden Hrt (*Monewode* 1354); **Money Furlong,** Churchill O; **Money Meadow,** Aldershot Ha; **Money Pot Hill,** Roydon Ess (*Moneye* 1277): 'land subject to a special money payment'. The rent from the Therfield land provided a fund for a bread charity. The Roydon name may allude to a buried hoard.

Monk Croft, Barton Stacey Ha; **Monk Holes,** Winchcombe Gl; **Monka Meadow,** Batsford Gl (*Monke Meadow*, 1630); **Monken Mead,** Binstead & Neatham Ha; **Monks Acre,** Bowden Ch; **Monks Close,** Lubenham Lei 1670, Ashwell R; **Monks Croft,** Stalmine La (*Le Monekedike* c 1250); **Monks Hayes,** Stoneleigh Wa [OE *(ge)hæg*]; **Monks Mead,** Therfield Hrt; **Monks Orchard,** Sawston C; **Monks Wood,** Tuxford Nt: 'land held by a community of monks' [OE *munuc*]. The Batsford land was held by Tewkesbury Abbey, that at Bowden by Birkenhead Priory, and that at Therfield by the monks of Royston; Monk Holes at Winchcombe marks the site of the quarry used by the local monastic community in building their church.

Monkey Corner, Shiplake O; **Monkeys Horn,** Beaulieu Ha: possibly 'land on which young hares were seen' [MnE dial. *monkey*, 'young hare'].

Montserrat, Muston Lei, a transferred name for a remote piece of land, probably commemorating the restoration of the island of Montserrat to British rule in 1783.

Moon Field, Great & Little Munden Hrt (*Monefildole* 1416, *Monefeld* 1463), a name not yet satisfactorily explained. It may allude to a location favoured for moonlight activities, such as poaching.

Moonlight, Great Barrington Gl, Bullington Ha: an enigmatic name. In the eighteenth century the term was used of illicit or smuggled spirit (cf MnE *moonshine*), and this may be the sense here. Cf Rummer's Hill and Smuggler's Hole, both in Cawston Nf.

(The) **Moor,** Exton Ha, Wherwell Ha, Adderley Sa, Egham Sr (*Le Morforlong* 1333); **Big & Little Moor,** North Rode Ch; **Moor Acre,** Newton Ch; **Moor Close,** Boxford Brk, Wimpole C (*Mordole* 1231), Hinton St Mary Do, Lubenham Lei 1670, Stretton Parva Lei, Forncett St Peter Nf, Farnfield Nt, Fledborough Nt, Flintham Nt, Kelham Nt, Forest Hill with Shotover O; **Moor Croft,** Greatham Ha, Odiham Ha; **Moor Field,** Wildboarclough Ch, East Anstey D, Sheet Ha, Bruntingthorpe Lei, Hillingdon Mx; **Moor Furlong,** North Stoneham Ha; **Moor Hatch,** Woking Sr; **Moor Hill,** Sparsholt Ha; **Moor Ings,** Clayworth Nt; **Moor Lands,** Fair Oak Ha; **Great Moorlands Copse,** Otterbourne Ha; **Moor Head,** Hinton St Mary Do, Twickenham Mx; **Moor Meadow,** Milford Ha; **The Moors,** East Anstey D, Tring Hrt: 'barren waste land' [OE *mōr*].

Morning Dell, Basing Ha, 'valley particularly favoured in the morning', possibly because of an eastern aspect [OE *dell*].

The Morrey, Kilmerton Ha; **Morrif,** Foleshill Wa (*Le Moreyf, Le Moreyife* 1411), 'piece of land given by a man to his bride on the morning after their marriage' [OE *morgen-gifu*].

Morris, Beetham We (*Morrass Ford* 1763), 'boggy land' MnE *morass*].

Morris Ground, Clifford Chambers Gl, either 'boggy land' or 'land on which morris dancers performed'.

Morter Pit Furlong, Hensington O (*Morter Pyttes* 1606), 'land from which limestone was dug for making mortar' [ME *morter*].

Moscow, Alston Cu; **Moscow Hall,** Bramhall Ch: a transferred name for a remote piece of land, no doubt celebrating Napoleon's retreat in 1812. See also Leipsic.

Moss, Adderley Sa; **Far & Near Moss,** Kendal We; **Upper & Lower Moss,** Preston Montford Sa; **Moss Bottom,** Somerford Booths Ch; **Moss Close,** Gawsworth Ch, Old Hutton We; **Moss Field,** Birtles Ch, Henbury Ch, Twemlow Ch; **Moss Hill,** Nether Staveley We, Whitwell We; **Moss Piece,** Eaton Ch; **Mossthwaite,** Lambrigg We [ON *þveit*, 'clearing']; **Mossy Close,** Hugglescote

Lei: 'land covered with moss' or 'swampy land' [OE *mos*, ON *mosi*].

Mot Close, Thurlaston Lei; **Mot Meadow,** Thurlaston Lei; **Mott Lands,** Kingsley Ha: possibly 'land on which assemblies took place' [OE *mōt*].

Mothers Croft, Butley Ch, 'land assigned to the widow'.

Moths Croft, Longparish Ha, 'land on which many moths were seen'.

Mount Copse, Ropley Ha: **Mount Meadow,** Beaulieu Ha; **Mount Piece,** Hinckley Lei: 'land on a slope' [ME *mont*, *munt*].

Mount Folly, Boarhunt Ha, Southwick Ha; **Mount Misery,** Porchester Ha; **Mount Poverty,** Ashton on Mersey Ch; **Mountain of Poverty,** Nether Alderley Ch, Forton La: derogatory names for unproductive hilly land.

Mount Pleasant, Baguley Ch, Hockenhill Ch, Middlewich Ch, Nether Alderley Ch, Offerton Ch, Tarvin Ch, Werneth Ch, Wildboarclough Ch, Ashleyhay Db, Great Hucklow Db, Hermitage Do, Bramshott Ha, Goosnargh La, Arnesby Lei, Blidworth Nt, Edwinstowe Nt, Greasley Nt, Styrrup Nt, West Stockwith Nt, Hinstock Sa, Rowton Sa, Berkswell Wa; **Mount Pleasant Farm,** Marthall cum Warford Ch; **Top, Bottom & Second Mount Pleasant Close,** Peatling Magna Lei: a complimentary name that may at times, however, be bestowed ironically. See also Pleasant Piece.

Mount Sinai, Great Hicklow Db, transferred name for remote land.

Mountain, Snelson Ch; **Mountain Piece,** Alderbury Sa: 'hilly land'.

Mouse Bank, Norland WRY; **Mouse Field,** Leebotwood Sa; **Mouse Furlong,** Newbury Brk (*Musfurlong* 1247–8); **Mouse Hill,** Caterham Sr; **Mouse Hill Spring,** Lilley Hrt; **Mouse Hills, Spring,** Lilley Hrt; **Mouse Hills,** South Weston O; **Mouse Park,** Newbold Db; **Mouse Riding,** Over Alderley Ch; **Mouse Tippett,** Inkpen Brk; **Mouses Nest,** Ringwood Ha: 'land infested by mice', though the last two names are almost certainly derogatory labels for small fields.

Mow Flatt, Leftwich Ch; **Mow Plot,** West Alvington D; **Mowstaddle Field,** Beaford D; **Muffolands,** Shipbrook Ch; **Mugborrow,** Aldbury Hrt (*Mogborowe* 1548): 'land on which a stack stands' [OE *muga*].

The Mowed Wong, Scalford Lei; **Mowing Slang,** Twycross Lei: 'small strip mown for hay' [ON *vangr*; MnE *slang*].

The Mowwell, Illston Lei, 'land producing good hay'.

Much Close, Sutton on the Hill Db; **Much Field,** Mere Ch: 'big piece of land' [OE *micel*, ME *much*].

Muchado, North Poorton Do, derogatory name for land requiring a disproportionate amount of labour.

Much Lay On, Sheldon Wa, 'land requiring a great deal of manure'.

Muck Close, Desford Lei, Shepshed Lei, Milburn We; **Muck Earth,** Bosley Ch; **Muckfield,** Lach Dennis Ch, Stanthorne Ch, Longden Sa; **Muck Hill Gate,** Gaddesby Lei; **Muck Hill Ground,** Kibworth Lei; **Muck Leasow,** Leebotwood Sa: 'land on which manure was heaped or spread'.

Mud Land, South Stoneham Ha; **Mud Lands,** Farlington Ha; **Mud Parrick,** Bratton W [OE *pearroc*]: self-explanatory.

Mug Down, West Pennard So, 'land by or with a heap of earth' [OE *muga*].

Mushroom Close, Bradley Db; **Mushroom Field,** Chinley Db: 'land on which mushrooms abounded'.

Mustard Close, Tideswell Db, 'land on which mustard was grown'.

Mythe Close, Witherley Lei; **Mythe Lands,** Sheepy Magna Lei; **Mythe Meadow,** Witherley Lei: 'land by a river confluence' [OE *mȳðe*].

N

Nab Field, Carleton La; **Nab Nook,** Larbreck La; **Nabbings Close,** Kneesall Nt [ON *eng*]; **Nabby End,** Hylton Du: 'land on or by a hillock' [ON *nabbi*].

Le Naccok, Walton on Thames Sr 1342; **Naddocks,** Greatworth Nth (*Nattokes* 1271); **Nadhooks,** Hullavington W (*Le Nattok* 1445); **Nattock,** Kemble Gl; *Nattok*, Malmesbury W c 1400; *atte Nattoke* Tolworth Sr 1350; **Nattox Mead,** Nazeing Ess; **Nothooks,** Thornbury Gl: 'isolated patch of cultivable ground in a swampy area'. This interpretation is based on evidence from Northamptonshire and Essex; this somewhat intractable form may have arisen from a phrase such as ME *atten *eit-hoke*, 'at the island corner', postulating a compound of OE *ēgeð* and *hōc* and later coming to have the special meaning proposed above.

Nackerty, Bovingdon Hrt (*Nookity* 1623), 'land with many nooks or corners' [ME *nokede*, 'cornered'].

Nadder Hey, Ashley Ha, 'land infested with vipers' [OE *nædre*].

Nameless Field, Lymm Ch, 'indifferent piece of land'.

The Nap, Windsor Brk (*La Knaipe* 1335); **Long Nap,** West Anstey D; **Nap Ground,** Holwell Do; **Nap Mead,** Hook Do; **North & South Napps,** Berrynarbor D: '(land on) a steep hillside' [OE *cnæpp*].

Napple Piece, Hope Mansel He, 'land near an apple-tree', from misdivision of ME *atten appel*(*tre*) [OE *æppel*].

Narrow Close, Barlestone Lei, Billesdon Lei; **Narrow Field,** Carrington Ch, Bere Alston D; **Narrow Scribe,** Newbottle Du; **Narrow Shred,** Burrough on the Hill Lei; **Narrow Slip,** Bollin Fee Ch: names alluding to abnormally narrow land. It should be noted that *scribe*, *shred* and *slip* generally bear this sense.

Nash Field, Little Hadham Hrt; **Nash Hill,** Redbourn Hrt: 'land near the ash tree', from the common misdivision of ME *atten asche* [OE *æsc*].

National Patent, Wharton Ch, doubtless alludes to the introduction of machinery into agriculture. 'Numerous patents were taken out between 1788 and 1816 for drills, reaping, mowing, haymaking, and winnowing machines, as well as for horse-rakes, scarifiers, chaff-cutters, turnip-slicers, and other mechanical aids to agriculture' (Ernle, *English Farming Past and Present*, 208).

Navigation, Barrow Ch; **Navigation Close,** Findern Db, Lubenham Lei: 'land adjoining a canal'.

Navigation Pingle, Smisby Db, cannot refer to a canal, since it is on high ground; it may allude to some other artificial water-course.

Neap Hill, Garsdon W; **The Neaperies,** Pontesbury Sa; **Further Neaplands,** Henley O: 'land on which turnips were grown' [OE *nēp*].

Near Breach, Twycross Lei; **Near Calf Close,** Ratby Lei; **Near Garden Close,** Witherley Lei; **Near Holt,** Kings Norton Lei; **Near Ploughed Close,** Bushby Lei; **Near Rook Close,** Ashwell R; **Near Stobbs,** Upton Lei: 'part of a divided piece of land nearest the village; piece of land adjacent to a named feature'. *Near* and *Far* as correlative specifiers occur commonly in some counties (eg Leicestershire), but hardly ever in others. It is worth noting that *Far* occurs rather more frequently than *Near;* a single close established at the enclosure of a parish might be subsequently divided into two, one part retaining the original name, the other becoming the Far part; division into three parts might result in the addition of Near, Middle and Far. Thus, an original close called Ten Acres might be divided into three small pieces called Near Ten Acres, Middle Ten Acres, and Far Ten Acres.

Neat Marsh, Preston ERY (*Notmersk* 1344), 'cattle marsh'. The early form represents ON *naut* with the Scandinavianised form of OE *mersc* added. These forms were in due course replaced by the normal English words.

The Neck, Freefolk Ha, 'narrow strip of land'.

Neckcloth, Feckenham Wo, 'triangular piece of land, shaped like a neckerchief'.

Neednotts, Awre Gl, a complimentary name for productive land.

The Nell, Takeley Ess (*La Knel* 1208), 'mound' [OE **cnell*].

Nelson, Elwick Hall Du, one of a group of commemorative names alluding to the Napoleonic wars. See Duke.

Neltro, Bisley Sr (*Le Eltrowe* 1345, *Nelltrow* 1605), '(at the) elder tree', with initial *N* from ME *atten*, 'at the'. Cf Le Naccok, Napple Piece, Ninlands.

Nest Field, Windsor Brk, 'land on which birds' nests were to be found'.

Nether Close, Halstead Lei, Huncote Lei, Gunthorpe R; **Nether Field,** Alderwasley Db, St Paul's Walden Hrt (*Neitherfeild* t.Hy 8); **Nether Furlong,** Goadby Lei; **Nether Ground,** Knossington Lei, Shangton Lei, West Langton Lei; **Nether Knoll,** Alkmonton Db; **Nether Lands,** Fareham Ha; **Nether Meadow,** Little Hucklow Db, Goadby Lei, Lubenham Lei, West Langton Lei; **Nether Park,** East Allington D: 'land further from the village, or lower in elevation'; *Nether* and *Higher* or *Upper* are frequently used as correlatives.

Nettlebed, Dersingham Nf 1545; **Nettlebeds,** Tetbury Gl; **Nettledale,** Hitchin Hrt, Farnsfield Nt; **Nettle Field,** Hemel Hempstead Hrt; **Nettle Hole Field,** Houghton le Spring Du; **Nettleholmes,** Hatfield WRY [ON *holmr*]; **Nettle Piece,** Broadwell O; **Nettle Slack,** Kendal We [ON *slakki*]: 'place where nettles grew'. These names refer to the stinging nettle (*Urtica dioica*) which, though a very freely growing wild plant, was not necessarily regarded as a weed since it provided a dyestuff and had pharmaceutical uses [OE *netel*].

Never Gains, West Littleton Gl; **Never Worse,** Meathop We: derogatory names for infertile land.

New Berry Field, Berrynarbor D; **New Break,** Alderwasley Db; **New Broken Grounds,** North Newington O; **Newbrook or Newbroke Land,** Lower Heyford O; **New Close,** Carnanton Co, West Anstey D, Hillfield Do, Elwick Hall Du, Hylton Du, Billesdon Lei, Gaddesby Lei, Nailstone Lei, West Langton Lei; **New Croft,** Croydon Sr; **New Earth,** Kendal We; **New Field,** Crowley Ch, North Rode Ch, Alderwasley Db (*Newefeld* 1415), Bradley Db, Galby Lei, Holwell Lei; **New Ground,** West Alvington D, Churchill O; **New Ing(s),** Hayton Nt, Misson Nt; **New Laid Down Close,**West Langton Lei; **New Laid Field,** Belmont Du, Spennymoor Du 1717; **New Land Furlong,** Shipton under Wychwood O; **Newlands,** Castle Hedingham Ess (*Newelond* 1331), Millbrook Ha, Owlesbury Ha, East Barnet Hrt (*Le Newland* 1296), St Stephens Hrt (*Newelond* 1291), Shepperton Mx (*Newelond* 1329), Croydon Sr, Beetham We; **Newlands Field,** Newton Valance Ha; **New Leasow,** Baschurch Sa, Leebotwood Sa; **New Leaze,** Fareham Ha; **New Leys,** Alton Ha [OE *lǣs*]; **New Meadow,** Bennington Hrt, Bushby Lei, Galby Lei, Knossington Lei, Shawell Lei,

Cold Norton St, Alvechurch Wo; **New Orchard,** Fifehead Neville Do, Kings Norton Lei; **New Park,** Berrynarbor D, West Alvington D; **New Pasture Lands,** Adderbury O; **New Piece,** Hope Woodlands Db, Dadlington Lei, Hether O; **(The) Newtake-in,** Ampney Crucis Gl, Castle Eaton W; **New Tinding,** Leebotwood Sa; **New Tining(s),** Cound Sa, Priston So; **New Tyning,** North Wroxall W [OE *tyning*]; **New Wong,** Stretton R [ON *vangr*]: 'land newly taken into cultivation, or newly enclosed' [OE *nīwe*].

New England, Balsham C, Swaffham Bulbeck C, Tadlow C, Basford Ch, Halstock Do, Aston Hrt, Wyddial Hrt, Hammersmith Mx, Mansfield Nt, Ollerton Nt, Aston Botterell Sa, Potterne W: transferred name for land in a remote part of the parish. The name was originally bestowed, by Captain John Smith, on the six north-eastern colonies of the American seaboard. There is a slight possibility that some of these names may be variants of ME *inland*.

Newfoundland, Wensley & Snitterton Db, Chilbolton Ha, Fordingbridge Ha, Clothall Hrt, Swepstone Lei, Crowmarsh O, Baschurch Sa, Ellesmere Sa, Hughley Sa, Prees Sa, Ryton Sa, Stokesay Sa, Wem Sa; **Newfoundland England,** Lyme Handley Ch [ME *inland*]; **Newfoundland Field,** Marden He; **Newfoundland Furlong,** Chedlington O: probably a transferred name for a remote field, though in some instances the expression *newfound* (current from the fifteenth century) may be intended as a literal attribution, without reference to the island of Newfoundland itself.

New Line England, Rainow Ch, 'land which has received a dressing of lime', possibly representing *new liming land*.

New South Wales Field, East Barnet Hrt, a transferred name for a remote piece of land, which is in fact on the parish boundary.

New World Farm, Ely C, fanciful name for a remote field.

New York, Ilmington Wa; **New Zealand,** Bourn C, Croxton C, Theydon Ess, Harpenden Hrt, Waterperry O, Hilmarton W, Lydiard Tregoze W, Harbury Wa; **New Zealand Farm,** Little Cheverell W, Napton on the Hill Wa: transferred names for remote pieces of land.

Nigher Field, Cressage Sa, 'nearer piece of land'.

Nightless, Stamford Rivers Ess (*Night Leaze* 1631); **Nightless Field,** Capel Sr; **Nightleys,** Cheshunt Hrt (*Night Lease* 1650), Rampton Nt: 'pastures used at night' [OE *lǣs*].

Nine Acre Wood, Essendon Hrt (*Nynacres* 1360); **Nine Acres,** Chorley Ch, Abbotsham D, Arlington D, Berrynarbor D, Bradley Db, Duffield Db, Alton Pancras Do, Fifehead Neville Do, Hillfield Do, Holwell Do, Thorpe Thewles Du, Walworth Du, Bibury Gl, Arnesby Lei, Knossington Lei, Welham Lei, Stretton R, Bagington Wa, Alvechurch Wo; **Butty Nineacres,** Clifton Ch; **Lower & Upper Nine Acres,** Cold Norton St; **Nine Acres Close,** Lubenham Lei: 'land nine acres in area, or adjoining such a piece of land' [OE *nigon æcer*].

Nine Ashes, Wirksworth Db, Hunsdon Hrt; **Nine Elms,** Lydiard Millicent W: self-explanatory.

Nine Butts, Cranage Ch; **Nine Corners,** Havant Ha; **Nine Day(s) Math,** Adlington Ch, Tetton Ch, Dowdeswell Gl, Pontesbury Sa, Solihull Wa; **Nine Day Work,** Hulme Walfield Ch; **Nine Guards,** Hale Ch [ON *garðr*]; **Nine Hills,** Hatfield Hrt; **Nine Lands,** Alderwasley Db, Rosliston Db, Frolesworth Lei, Bentley Wa; **Nine Leys,** Overseal Lei; **The Nine Ridges,** Elvaston Db; **Nine Standards,** Wharton We [EMnE *stander*, 'pillar', ie a boundary mark]; **Nine Stiles,** Enbourne Brk; **Nine Well Close,** St Paul's Walden Hrt (*Nynewells* t.Hy 8); **Nine Wells,** Great Shelford C: 'land containing the nine named features' [OE *nigon*].

Ninepenny Cut, Feckenham Wo, probably an allusion to the rent of the land.

The Nineteen Acre, Harston Lei; **Nineteen Acres,** Weston Underwood Db: 'piece of land nineteen acres in area'.

Nineteen Lands, Repton Db; **Nineteen Lands Piece,** Drayton O: 'consolidation of nineteen ridges of an arable open field'.

Nineveh, Hampton Lucy Wa, Crook We; **Nineveh Close,** Holbeck WRY; **Nineveh Farm,** Nuneham Courtenay O, Idlicote Wa; **Nineveh Meadow,** Lamberhurst K: a name suggesting remoteness. The later capital of the Assyrian empire was being excavated in the early nineteenth century; this topicality possibly led to the use of the name from that time.

Ninham, Brading Wt; **Ninhams,** Pattiswick Ess (*Inname* 1289); **Ninnings,** Flamstead Hrt (*Le Innyng* 1509): 'land taken in or enclosed' [OE **innam, *inning*].

Ninlands, East Clandon Sr (*Le Inlond* 1350), 'land near a residence'. This name, like Ninham, Ninhams and Ninnings, owes its initial letter to a wrong division of a phrase including *atten* ('at the'), ME *atten inlond* becoming *atte-ninlond* etc [ME *inland*].

No Gains, Soberton Ha, a derogatory name for unprofitable land.

No Man's Ball, Ludgershall W; **No Man's Bush,** Tur Langton Lei; **No Man's Common,** Reading Brk (*No Mans Land* t.Ed 6); **No Man's Down,** Monxton Ha; *No Mans Furlong*, Barkestone Lei 1579; *No Man's Gapp*, Elsfield O 1629; **No Man's Gore,** Alton Pancras Do, Drayton St Leonard O; **No Mans Heath,** Heather Lei; **Nomans Hill,** Ladbroke Wa; **No Man's Land,** Thorney C (*Nomanneslond* 1191), Aldworth Gl, Barnsley Gl, Little Barrington Gl, Stanton Gl, Chilcomb Ha, Nether Wallop Ha, Yateley Ha, Caldecote Hrt, Great Munden Hrt, Hitchin Hrt, Offley Hrt, Wheathampstead Hrt (*Bruera de Nomanlond* 1428), Kingsbury Mx, Edwinstowe Nt, Wellow So, Bratton W, Kimpsey Wo; **No Man's Nook,** Ansty Wa, Walsgrave on Sowe Wa; **No Man's Patch,** Northmoor O; **Nomans Wood,** Bengeo Hrt, Sutton in Ashfield Nt 1609 (*Nomannes Wode* t.Ed 3): 'boundary land, land claimed by more than one parish or private owner'.

No Man's Friend, Aldbury Hrt, St Stephens Hrt, Watton at Stone Hrt, Wigginton Hrt: a derogatory name for poor land, for which no one has a good word to say.

Noah, Crofton Ha; **Noah Field,** Cosham Ha; **Noah's Ark,** Over Alderley Ch; **Noah's Ark Close,** Bradbourne Db; **Noah's Flood,** Soberton Ha; **Noar Hill,** Newton Valance Ha: possibly 'land on the bank of a river', the initial letter resulting from the misdivision of *atten oran* (cf Ninnings, Ninlands); the Cheshire and Derbyshire names may have a merely fanciful origin [OE *ora*].

Noble Hey, Peover Superior Ch, 'land rented at one noble per annum'. The noble was a gold coin, current in England until the seventeenth century and worth 6s 8d.

The Nook(s), Timperley Ch, Clifton & Compton Db, Heanor Db, Hognaston Db, Morley Db, Peckleton Lei; **Nook Close,** Quarndon Db, Bushby Lei, Odstone Lei, Car Colston Nt, Girton Nt; **Nook Croft,** Alvanley Ch; **Nook Field,** Toft Ch, Sale Ch; **Nook Heath,** Elton Ch; **Nook Meadow,** Barrons Park Lei; **Nook Shotten Field,** Stoneleigh Wa; **(The) Nooking(s),** Thorpe Thewles Du, Much Hadham Hrt, Cuckney Nt, Misson Nt, Oxton Nt, Wellow Nt; **Nooking Close,** Bleasby Nt, Fiskerton Nt; **Nooking Piece,** Mansfield Nt; **Nooking Whong,** Kneesall Nt [ON *vangr*]: 'land in a secluded corner, or land with many corners' [ME *noke*, EMnE *nooking*].

Nooked Close, Kingsterndale Db; **Nooked Field,** Norley Ch; **Nookerty,** Kings Langley Hrt: 'land with many corners' [ME *nokede*].

Nor Croft, Eakring Nt (*Northcroft* c 1200); **Norden Meadow,** West Alvington D; Nordens Sparsholt Ha [OE *denu*]; **The Nore,** Almondsbury Gl; **Normead,** Bitton Gl (*North Meade* 1575), Coulston & Edington W, Lacock W (*Normede* 1536); **Normeadow,** Beckford Gl; **Norwood,** Winsley W: 'land on the north side of the township' [OE *norð*].

Norman Field, Fritwell O; **Norman's Field,** Elberton Gl, Bengeo Hrt, Letchworth Hrt, Widford Hrt; **Normans Land,** Aston by Budworth Ch: possibly variants of *No Man's* names, but see Great Normans, Banstead Sr.

North America, Helsington We, a transferred name for a remote field.

North Close, Fifehead Neville Do, Newbottle Du; **North Close for the Use of the Poor,** Fifehead Neville Do; **North Crates,** Priors Dean Ha; **North Croft,** Bray Brk, Bentworth Ha, Chippenham W; **North Down,** Ashmore Do; **North Drove,** Hermitage Do; **North Field(s),** Reading Brk (*Northfeld* 1273), Welford Brk, Timperley Ch, Kirk Ireton Db, Hinton Martell Do, Holwell Do, Mappowder Do, Houghton le Spring Du, Newbottle Du, Cowley Gl, Holybourne Ha, Essendon Hrt, Great Gaddesden Hrt, Ware Hrt, Burton Overy Lei, Banstead Sr, Mere & Zeals W, Seagry W, Allesley Wa (*Le Northfelde* 1311), Harbury Wa, Hemsall WRY; **North Flat,** Little Marton La; **North Furlong,**

Totley Db, Wolstaston Sa; **North Gore,** Alton Pancras Do; **North Ground,** Abbotsham D; **North Hill,** Kingston Magna Do; **North Leasow,** Whichford Wa; **North Leaze,** Broad Town W; **North Mead,** Burghfield Brk (*Northemed* 13c); **North Moor,** Kington Magna Do; Elstead Sr; **North Naps,** Berrynarbor D [OE *cnappa*]; **Great & Little Northwards,** Takeley Ess (*Nortwud* c 1225): 'land to the north of the parish' [OE *norð*].

North Field, pre-enclosure great field name in Houghton Regis Bd, Souldrop Bd, Southill Bd, Toddington Bd, Claydon St Botolph Bk, Hulcot Bk, Wingrave Bk, Great Coxwell Brk, Stanford in the Vale Brk, Stoke Brk, Boxworth C, Chippenham C, Foxton C, Harlton C, Wilburton C, Glapwell Db, Shirebrook Db, Eastington Do, Nyland Do, Bolam Du, Langton Du, Summerhouse Du, Wolviston Du, Bewick ERY, Ganton in the Wolds ERY, Hessle ERY, Holme on Spalding ERY, Huggate ERY, Kirby Gridelythe ERY, Kirby Underdale ERY, Rowley ERY, Cherrington Gl, Sherborne Gl, Tresham Gl, Yanworth Gl, Enham Ha, Faccombe Ha, Claxby L, Halburgh L, Scotter L, Stainton L, Stubton L, Upton L, Aylestone Lei, Billesdon Lei, Carlton Lei, Cossington Lei, Easton Lei, Edmondthorpe Lei, Goadby Lei, Harston Lei, Peatling Parva Lei, Saltby Lei, Sapcote Lei, Skeffington Lei, Sproxton Lei, Stockerston Lei, Forncett St Peter Nf, Elvington NRY, Kirton Nt, Knighton Nt, Walkeringham Nt, Brackley Nth, Culworth Nth, Drayton Nth, Fawsley Nth, Harleston Nth, Preston Nth, Radstone Nth, Southorp Nth, Weedon Nth, Enstone O, Hensington O, Milcombe O, Rollright O, South Stoke O, Oakham R, Brompton So, Charlton Musgrove So, Eartham Sx, Aldbourne W, Chilhampton W, Dichampton W, South Newton W, Stanton W, North Ugford W, Binley Wa, Compton Wa, Harbury Wa, Hinsworth WRY, Leathley WRY, Sherburn WRY, Wroxall Wt.

North East Close, Cossington Lei; **North East Field,** Long Critchell Do; **Northern Close,** Foston Lei; **Northward Close,** Shangton Lei; **Northward Field,** Shangton Lei; **North West Close,** Cossington Lei; **North West Field,** Newbottle Du: self-explanatory names.

Nothing, Mobberley Ch; **Nothing Field,** Priors Dean Ha; **Nothing Hill,** Ecchinswell Ha; **Nothings Nook,** Lockington Lei: enigmatic but probably derogatory names.

Nova Scotia, Ealing Mx, Dillicar We: a transferred name for a remote field.

Nun Ings, York; **Nun Wood,** Ashdon Ess; **Nunnery Farm,** Cheshunt Hrt; **Nuns Path,** Warminster W; **Nuns Piece,** Sherfield English Ha; 'land owned or used by a religious community of women' [OE *nunne*].

Nursery, Ripley Db, Hillfield Do, Kings Norton Lei; **Nursery Field,** Matlock Bath Db; **Nursery Ground,** Adderbury O; **Nursery Orchard,** Alton Pancras Do; **Long Nursery,** Market Bosworth Lei: 'land on which young trees were planted'.

Nut Binns, St Paul's Walden Hrt; **Nut Croft,** Everton Ha, Long Sutton Ha; **Nuthangers,** Hurstbourne Priors Ha [OE *hangra*]; **Nut Ing,** Outseats Db [ON *eng*]; **Nutshell Field,** Coston Lei; **Nut Tree Plat,** Inkpen Brk; **Nut Wood,** Beechamwell Nf; **Nuttinger Hill,** Holt Wo [OE *hangra*]; **Nutts Field,** Bosley Ch: 'land with nut trees' [OE *hnutu*].

O

Oak and Elm Piece, Waterperry O; **Oak Close,** Duffield Db (*Le Okefeld* 1415), Barwell Lei, Ambrosden O; **Oak Field,** Bollington Ch, Hylton Du, Stebbing Ess (*Okefeld* 1422); **Oak Flatts,** North Elmsall WRY; **Oaklands,** Berrynarbor D; **Oak Leasow,** Minsterley Sa; **Oak Leaze,** Almondsbury Gl; **Oakley,** Bisley Gl; **Oak Piece,** Woodthorpe Db; **Oakshott Coppice,** Wonersh Sr [OE *scēat*]; **Oak Slade,** Mortimer Brk; **Oak Tree Close,** Alderwasley Db, Barwell Lei; **Far & Near Oak Tree Close,** Desford Lei; **Oak Tree Ground,** Ardley O, Spelsbury O; **Oak Tree Meadow,** Windsor Brk; **Oaken Copse,** Northmore O; **Oakenshaw Field,** Butley Ch; **Oaks Meadow,** Wolstaston Sa; **Oaky Leasow,** Feckenham Wo; **Oaky Means,** Cold Norton St [ME *main*]: 'land near, or containing, oak trees, [OE *āc*].

Oat Arrish, Ilsington D [OE *ersc*]; **Oatash Field,** Martyr Worthy Ha [OE *ersc*]; **Oat Close,** Alderwasley Db, Alkmonton Db, Ford Du, Stanwell Mx (*Otecroft* 1450); **Oat Croft(s),** Laleham Mx (*Otlond* 1329), Wheatley O; **Oat Edditch,** Monks Coppenhall Ch; **Oat Etch,** Walton on the Hill Sr [OE *edisc*]; **Oat Field,** Helion Bumpstead Ess, East Tisted Ha, Baggrave Lei; **Oat**

Furlong, Sherston W; **Oat Ground,** Cotesbach Lei; **Oat Hill(s),** Appleby Lei, Eydon Nth (*Otehul* c 1200), Preston Capes Nth, Lewknor O, Spelsbury O; **Oathill Field,** Hungerford Brk; **Oat Hill Furlong,** Aldsworth G; **Oatlands,** Tetton Ch, Standlake O, Hankerton W (*Otegarstone* c 1300); **Oatlands Furlong,** Poulton Gl; **Oat Leaze,** Box W; **Oatley,** Butley Ch; **Oatnell,** Longdon Wo [OE *hyll* or *halh*]; **Oat Pightle,** Colne Engaine Ess (*Oteland* 1225); **Oat Plat,** Thame O (*Hotlande* 1250); **Oatenhams,** Iron Acton Gl: 'land on which oats were grown' [OE *āte*].

Ochre Ground, Forest Hill with Shotover O; **Ocre Kiln & House,** Horspath O: 'land from which yellow-brown earth was dug, or on which it was processed, for use as a pigment'.

Old Bake, Durnford W (see The Bake); **Old Barn Close,** Barwell Lei; **Old Breach Close,** Belton R; **Old Bury,** Kimpron Hrt; **Old Bury Meadow,** Headley Sr (*La Eldeburi* 1313) [OE *eald, burh*]; **Old Close,** Frisby Lei, Goadby Lei, Slawston Lei, Stockerston Lei, Ashwell R; **Old Coalpit Field,** Stapleton Sa; **Old Croft,** Whitwell Db; **Old Earth,** Dillicar We; **Old Enclosure,** Long Critchell Do; **Old England,** Welham Lei [ME *inland*]; **Old Field,** Fooloe Db, Houghton le Spring Du, Bedfont Mx (*Elderfelde* 1438), Beal WRY; **Old Garston,** Sparsholt Ha [OE *gærs-tūn*]; **Old Gore,** Daventry Nth (*Oldegore* 1314), Towcester Nth (*Elde-gore* 1419) [OE *gāra*]; **Old Ground,** Burghfield Brk; **Old Ground Pasture,** Sall Nf (*Oldeyherd* 1340 [OE *geard*]); **Old Heath,** Stretton R; **Old Hill Sleight,** Corston So [OE *slæget*]; **Old House Close,** Frolesworth Lei; **Old House Croft,** Dunham Massey Ch; **Old House Piece,** Wolstaston Sa; **Old Lands,** Stapleford Abbots Ess (*Eldelond* t.Hy 6), Long Ditton Sr; **Old Lands Ground,** Inkpen Brk; **Old Meadow,** Tytherington Ch, Normanton Db (*Oldmedo* 1450), Houghton on the Hill Lei, Stockerston Lei, Minsterley Sa, Cuddington Sr (*Oldemede* 1408); **Old Moor,** Stretton R; **Old Orchard,** Bray Brk, Kintbury Brk, Alderwasley Db, West Langton Lei; **Old Park,** Hook Do; **Old Pasture,** Burrough on the Hill Lei; **Old Ploughed Field,** Arnesby Lei; **Old Redens,** Farnham Sr [OE **ryden*]; **Old Rough Close,** Ashby Folville Lei; **Old Rush Hay,** Preston on the Hill Ch; **Old Ryegrass,** Little Ness Sa; **Old Sainfoin Ground,** Ardley O, Idbury O; **Old Sainfoin Piece,** Welford Brk; **Old Sedge Fen,** Feltwell Nf; **Old Seed,** Fifield O; **Old Severals,** Overton Ha [ME *several*]; **Old**

Turf Piece: 'land formerly used for the stated purpose, or containing the buildings'.

The Old Gentleman, Nursling Ha; **Old Jane Pingle,** Bakewell Db; **Old Man's Croft,** Twemlow Ch; **Old Man's Field,** Baschurch Sa; **Old Wife Ing,** Liversedge WRY; **Old Womans Close,** Isley Walton Lei; **Old Womans Croft & Meadow,** Marple Ch; **Old Womans Dowry,** Chapel en le Frith Db; **Old Woman's Field,** Butley Marple Ch; **Old Woman's Meadow,** Marple Ch, Pott Shringley Ch, Rostherne Ch: names which sometimes commemorate occupation by an elderly person, but sometimes refer to an insignificant piece of land.

Old Man's Hat, Hursley Ha, probably alludes to the shape of the field.

Old Mary's Field, Plumley Ch, possibly alludes to the celebrated seventeenth-century lady of the manor, Dame Mary Cholmondley, James I's 'bold lady of Cheshire' (cf PNCh ii, 94).

Old Wife's Smock, Moss WRY, is probably not of the same type as Smock Close etc (see Smoak Acre), but refers to the shape of the field.

Oldery Field, Newbold Astbury Ch; **Oller Field,** Nether Wyresdale La; **Ollar Hey,** Preston La; **Ollars,** Cleveley La; **Oller Carr,** Dutton Ch; **Oller Field,** Marton Ch, Brockholes La; **Oller Hey,** Little Marton La; **Ollery Croft,** Betchton Ch: 'land on which alder trees grew' [OE *alor*, *-ig*]. See also Oular Croft.

(The) One Acre, Higher Whitley Ch, Marston Montgomery Db, Kings Norton Lei, Shawell Lei: 'land of approximately one acre in area' [OE *æcer*].

One Bush Ground, Kiddington O; **One Crop Field,** Chesterton O; **One Stone Close,** Great Hucklow Db: curious but self-explanatory names.

One Hole, Sherington Bk, 'lonely pit'; this land was formerly called *Pokeput*, 'goblin pit', alluding to the stonepit there [OE *ān*, *pūca*, *pytt*].

One Thousand Acres, Horley Sr, ironic name for a piece of land 1 rood 4 perches in area. See also Thousand Acres.

Onion Close, Great Hucklow Db, self-explanatory.

Onyx Close, Wool Do, 'land enclosed for cultivation during the fallow course of an open field' [ME *inhoke*].

Open Pasture, Coston Lei; **Open Piece,** Wirksworth Db: 'land left open after a general enclosure of the parish'.

Orange Hill, Hendon Mx, possibly commemorative of William III.

(The) Orchard, Chapel en le Frith Db, Darley Db, Wotton Bassett W; **Orchard Close,** Houghton le Spring Du, Damerham W, Sturt & Urchfont W; **Orchard Field,** Charlesworth Db, Elwick Hall Du; **Orchard Meadow,** Pownall Fee Ch, Stanthorne Ch; **Orchard Park,** Berrynarbor D; **Orchard Pingle,** Worksop Nt: 'land containing, or adjoining, a plantation of fruit trees' [OE *orceard*].

The Orles, Kempley Gl; **Upper & Lower Orles,** St John in Bedwardine Wo; **Orley,** Bransford Wo: 'land on or near which alder trees grew' [OE *alor*].

Osier Beds, Boughton Nth (*Osierwelle* 1397); **Osier Close,** Shearsby Lei; **Osier Ground,** Pownall Fee Ch; **Ozier Bed,** Dadlington Lei; **Ozier Car(r),** Dersingham Nf, East Dereham Nf; **Ozier Ground,** Fifehead Magdalen Do; **Ozier Holt,** Croxton Nf: 'land on which osier willows were grown'. The osier willow (*Salix viminalis*) is usually grown as a coppice crop (ie the trunks are cut down to ground level to encourage sucker growth) beside streams and in marshy districts. The thin stems are used for basket-making [OF *osier*].

Other Bit, Lymm Ch, a derogatory name for an inconsiderable piece of land.

Otter Close, Tansley Db; **Otterdale Pasture,** Orton We; **Otter Down Meadow,** Hatherton Ch; **Otter Holes,** Barlborough Db: probably 'land on which otters had been seen', but the surname Otter cannot be disregarded as a possible source of at least one of these names.

Oular Croft, Lostock Gralam Ch; **Ouler Field,** Crowley Ch; **Oulery Croft,** Anderton Ch; **Oulery Field,** Allostock Ch: 'land on which alders grew' [OE *alor*, *-ig*]. See also Oldery Field, The Orles, and The Owler.

Out Broom, Betchton Ch; **Out Close,** North Poorton Do; **Out Field Common,** Debden Ess (*Le Outfeld* 1353); **Out Furlong,** Swerford O; **Outland(s),** Edale Db, Ampney Crucis Gl (*Le Outlonge* 1275); **Out Lees,** Bradbourne Db [OE *lǣs*]; **Outrage Close,** Egham Sr (*Owtreddes* 1548), [OE **rȳd*, 'clearing']; **Outshot,** Aston Grange Ch, High Legh Ch [OE *scēat*]; **Outskirts,** Edale Db; **Outer Half,** Sarisbury Ha; **Outer Showl Broad,** Wrington So [ME *shovel-brade*]: 'land further out' [OE *ūt*, *ūterra*].

Outgang, Cuckney Nt, Manham Nt, Tuxford Nt, Asby We, Bampton We, Brough Sowerby We, Crosby Ravensworth We, Kaber We, Newbiggin We, Orton We; **Outgang Close,** Blyth Nt, Kneesall Nt, Rampton Nt: 'exit, path taken by cattle from enclosed land to common' [OE *ūtgang*].

(The) Outlet(t), Audlem Ch and many other places in Ch; **Outlet Field,** Woodcott Ch: 'pasture adjoining winter cattle-sheds'.

Outrake, Wolstaston Sa, Warcop We: 'exit path' [OE *ūt*, *hraca*]. It is the custom in some places to enclose temporary pens on this path, so that sheep returning from upland pastures can be sorted and claimed by their owners.

Ouzel, Hope Mansel He, possibly refers to the blackbird [OE *ōsle*].

Oven Field, Butley Ch; **Oven Pits,** Oddington Gl: 'land on which a furnace was sited' [OE *ofen*].

Over Close, Alkmonton Db, Duffield Db, Fifehead Neville Do; **Over Croft,** Great Hucklow Db; **Over Croft & Field,** Bosley Ch; **Over Field,** Wharton Ch (*Overeforlong* c 1230), Bamford Db, Rockhampton Gl; **Over Ground,** Shawell Lei; **Over Meadow,** Holwell Lei: 'land beyond or across other land' [OE *ofer*].

Overthwart, Alderwasley Db, Castleton Db, Sowerby WRY; **Overthwart Bank,** King's Meaburn We; **Overthwart Close,** Little Longstone Db; **Overthwart Field,** Ballingdon Ess;

Overwart, Wimbish Ess (*Ouerwhartlonde* 1566); **Overwart Field,** Liston Ess: 'field lying at right angles to another, and crossing its boundaries at each side' [OE *ofer,* ON *bverr*].

(The) Owler(s), Hathersage Db, Newbold & Duston Db, Wingerworth Db, Norland WRY; **Owler Car(r),** Hope Db, Outseats Db, Westby with Plumpton La; **Owler Field,** Butley Ch, Over Alderley Ch; **Owler Hag,** Derwent Db [ON *hogg*, 'part of wood marked off for felling']: 'land on which alder trees grew'. See also Oldery Field, The Orles.

Oxall, Eastleach Martin Gl [OE *halh*]; **Oxbourn,** Wawne ERY (*Oxenburne* 12c) [OE *burna,* 'stream']; **Ox Briggs,** Weeton with Preece La; **Ox Butts,** Great Singleton La [ME *butte*]; **Ox Carr,** Hardhorn with Newton La [ON *kjarr*]; **Ox Close,** Alderwasley Db, Blackwell Db, Callow Db, Tansley Db, Egglescliffe Du, Out Rawcliffe La, Pilling La, Stalmine with Staynall La, Snarestone Lei, Skelbrooke WRY, Stainforth WRY; **Ox Croft,** Wheathampstead Hrt (*Oxencroft* 1343), Goosnargh La; **Oxen Croft,** Broughton La, Whittingham La; **Oxen Holme,** Little Marton La; **Oxen Park,** Berrynarbor D; **Oxey,** Braunston Nth (*Oxehay* 1255) [OE *(ge)hæg*]; **Oxeys Meadow,** Fawley Ha; **Oxhall,** Arnesby Lei [OE *halh*]; **Oxhay Meadow,** Cadlington O; **Ox Hey,** Nether Alderley Ch, Alston La, Barnace La, Claughton La, Elston La, Haighton La, Hardhorn with Newton La; **Ox Hey Meadow,** Bosley Ch; **Ox Hill,** Clifton with Salwick La; **Oxlands Bank,** Skeffling ERY (*Oxland* 1339); **Ox Lease Meadow,** Burghfield Brk; **Ox Leasow,** Frodesley Sa, Pontesbury Sa, Yockleton Sa, Broadwas Wo; **Ox Leasows,** Dumbleton Gl; **Ox Leaze,** Reading Brk, Welford Brk, Acton Turville Gl, Mangotsfield Gl, Sapperton Gl, Basing Ha, Itchen Abbas Ha, Crowmarsh O (*Oxeleaze* 1605); **Oxleaze Farm,** Romsey Ha; **Oxleys,** North Mimms Hrt (*Oxlees* 1370), Rickmansworth Hrt, Edmonton Mx; **Ox Mead,** Britford W (*Exemede* 1383); **Ox Meadow,** Heather Lei; **Ox Pasture,** Great Budworth Ch, Alkmonton Db, Great Hucklow Db, Great Longstone Db, Elwick Hall Du, Polesworth Wa, South Elmsall WRY; **Lower & Upper Oxpens,** Pyrton O; **Ox Piece,** Alderbury Sa; **Oxyard,** Ashby Folville Lei: 'land on which an ox was kept, or where oxen were pastured' [OE *oxa*].

Oxhead Close, Muston Lei, may be an instance of the type of name recalling the impalement of an animal's head in heathen sacrificial ceremonies; it is more likely, however, that the *-head* represents *headland*, an area occasionally used for pasturing animals [OE *oxa, hēafod*].

Oyster End, Little Hadham Hrt (*Oystreherne* 1382); **Oyster Well,** Bagendon Gl: 'land on which a sheepfold was sited' [OE *eowestre*].

P

Packhorse Close, Ashleyhay Db; **Packhorse Ground,** South Stoke So; **The Packway Pightle,** Yaxley Sf: 'land on which packhorses were kept, or adjoining roads used by packhorses'.

Packsaddle, Swannington Lei; **Packsaddle Bank,** Weston Ch: probably allude to the shape and conformation of the field.

(The) Paddock, Enbourne Brk (*Le Parocke* 1547), Reading Brk (*Le Padoke* 1551), Wharton Ch, Brassington Db, Marston O, Hambleton R; **Lower, Middle & Road Paddock,** Lutterworth Lei: 'grass enclosure' [OE *pearroc*].

Pail Piece, Drayton Sa; **Pails Close,** Ripley Db; **Big & Little Pale,** Church Minshull Ch; **Pale Field,** Stapeley Ch; **Pale Piece,** Hartlebury Wo; **Big & Little Palin,** Wardle Ch; **Palings Field,** Wettenhall Ch: 'land enclosed by a paled fence'.

Pan (Large & Little), Idbury O; **Pan Croft,** Therfield Hrt: possibly 'depression in the surface of an otherwise flat area'.

Pancake, Out Rawcliffe La, 'round, flat field'.

Paradice, Hughill We; **Paradice Marsh,** Barking Ess; **Paradise,** Abington Piggotts C, Chesterton C, Antrobus Ch, Brereton cum Smethwick Ch, Clifton & Compton Db (*Parodys* 1557), Doveridge Db, Green Fairfield Db, Holmesfield Db, Holwell Do, Motcombe Do, Minsterworth Gl, Breamore Ha, Hursley Ha, Cheshunt Hrt, Shepshed Lei, Greenford Mx, Gotham Nt, Hailey O, Swinbrook O, Chelmarsh Sa, Cheswardine Sa, High Ham So, North Wootton So, Pitminster So, Somerton So, Tisbury W, Chilvers Coton Wa, Coventry Wa, Tachbrook Wa, Bampton We, Crackenthorpe We, Tebay We, Brighouse WRY, Challe Wt; **Paradise Croft,** Soberton Ha; **Paradise Farm,** Easington Du; **Paradise Field,** Docott cum Wilkesley Ch, Rownhams Ha; **Paradise Meadow,** Appleton Ch, Edale Db,

Goosnargh La; **Paradise Ten Acres,** Burnham So: a name generally indicating approval, but sometimes, like Mount Pleasant, it may be bestowed ironically—eg at Motcombe Do, where it designates a steep, bracken-covered hill (cf B. Kerr, 'Dorset fields and their names', 248).

Parcel Meadow, Barleston Lei, 'grassland divided into allotments'.

Paring Field, Little Strickland We, 'land on which paring and burning was practised'. See also Burn Bake, Denshers Meadow, and Push Ploughed Field.

Parish Leasow, Leebotwood Sa; **Parish Pound,** Mappowder Do: 'common or official land owned by the parish'. See also Manor Pound.

(**The**) **Park,** Buglawton Ch, Kermincham Ch, Therfield Hrt, Carlton Curlieu Lei, Foxton Lei, Stoughton Lei, Kirkby in Ashfield Nt, Thurgarton Nt, Hambleton R, Alvechurch Wo; **Park Croat & Field,** Ardeley Hrt (*Parkefeild* 1559) [OE *croft*]; **Park Field,** White Notley Ess (*Perkfeld* 1385), Bushey Hrt (*Le Oldpark* 1447), Shenley Hrt; **Park Ground,** Burghfield Brk; **Park Leasow,** Leebotwood Sa; **Park Mead,** Bray Brk, Hook Do; **Park Meadow,** Boxford Brk, Clifton Ch, Marton Ch, Donington Lei, Nuneham Courtenay O (*Parcum de Nywenham* 1396); **Park Plantation,** Croxton Nf: 'land enclosed for hunting or as a pleasure ground' [ME *park*].

Parliament, Leese Ch; **Parliament Close,** Ayston R: possibly 'land enclosed by act of parliament'.

(**The**) **Parlour,** Burghfield Brk, Willoughby Waterless Lei, Solihull Wa; **Parlour Croft,** Dutton Ch; **Parlour Field,** Agden Ch, Newbold Astbury Ch, Little Bedwyn W; **Parlour Furlong,** Stony Stretton Sa; **Parlour Ground,** Shipton under Wychwood O; **Parlour Meadow,** Enderby Lei: 'small piece of ground' [ME *parlur*].

Parsley Close, Ticknall Db, 'land on which parsley was grown', alluding to the herb *Petroselinum crispum,* which has been more widely cultivated than this single example of the name would suggest.

Parsonage Close, Ambrosden O; **Parsonage Cowleaze,** Mappowder Do; **Parsonage Field,** Alton Pancras Do; **Parsonage Hill,** Inkpen Brk; **Parsonage Mead,** Kintbury Brk; **Parsonage Wood,** Berrynarbor D; 'land adjacent to the parsonage, or for the use of the parson'.

Parsons Acre, Cowley O; **Parsons Breach,** South Leigh O; **Parsons Breeches,** Burton We [OE *brǣc*]; **Parsons Bush,** Banstead Sr; **Parsons Close,** Berrynarbor D, Long Critchell Do, Nailstone Lei, Ambrosden O; **Parsons Croft,** Newbold Astbury Ch; **Parsons Ease,** Eaton Ch; **Parsons Eyes,** Leftwich Ch [OE *ēg*, 'waterside land']; **Parsons Field,** Buglawton Ch, Pottisford O; **Parsons Ground,** Shawell Lei; **Parsons Grounds & Tithe Piece,** Normanton le Heath Lei; **Parson's Ings,** Beckingham Nt [ON *eng*]; **Parson's Marsh,** Fontmell Magna Do, Manston Do; **Parson's Mead,** Yetminster Do, Beddington Sr (*Personesdene* 1375); **Parsons Meadow,** Duffield Db, Sandford St Martin O; **Parsons Moor,** Rampisham Do; **Parsons Piece,** Welford Brk, Glen Parva Lei, Minster Lovell O, North Leigh O; **Parsons Pightle,** Eckendon O; **Parson's Pingle,** Stoneleigh Wa, Westleigh Wa: 'land for the use, or the benefit, of the parson'.

Partables, Headon Nt, 'land privately owned'.

Partridge Close, Beechamswell Nf; **Partridge Flatt,** Babworth Nt: names possibly alluding to the game bird, though they may embody the surname Partridge.

(The) Pasture, Over Haddon Db, Harston Lei; **Pasture Close,** East Allington D, Heworth Du, Lockington Lei; **Pasture Field,** Mellor Db, Newbottle Du; **Pasture Pingle,** Little Longstone Db: 'grazing land' [ME *pasture*].

Pasty Crust, Caynham Sa, a fanciful name alluding to brittle soil.

(The) Patch, Baguley Ch, Kermincham Ch, Minshull Vernon Ch, Moston Ch, Rope Ch, Sandbach Ch, Darley Db, Foolow Db; **Patch Field,** Hemel Hempstead Hrt; **Patch Meadow,** Alsager Hrt; **The Patchet,** Marston O (*Le Patchet* 1488): 'small piece of ground'.

Paternoster, Sherston W; **Paternoster Croft,** Chapel Ess; **Paternoster Field,** Great Bookham Sr: either 'land on boundary near a place where the Lord's prayer was said during the Rogationtide ceremonies' or 'land held by service of saying one paternoster daily for the soul of the donor'.

Pavement Field, Alpraham Ch, Church Minshull Ch, Faddiley Ch, Rudheath Lordship Ch; **Pavement Hey,** Foulk Stapleford Ch; 'land near or beside a paved road'.

Peahill, Brigham ERY (*Pighill* 1565), 'small field' [ME *pightel*].

Peak Field, North Mimms Hrt (*Pekefeld* 1467); **Peaked Acre,** Bover W; **Peaked Close,** Boxford Brk, Bucklebury Brk, Hinton Parva Do, Sheldon Ha; **Peaked Field,** Alresford Ha, Farnham Sr (*Pykemede* 1447); **Peaked Ground,** Cirencester Gl; **Peek Field,** Castleton Db: 'land which comes to a point' [OE *pīc*, **pīced*].

Pear Close, Nettlebed O; **Pear Garth,** Cliburn We; **Pear Tree Close,** Ash Db, Market Bosworth Lei, Muston Lei, Narborough Lei, Greetham R, Darrington WRY; **Pear Tree Croft,** Hemel Hempstead Hrt; **Pear Tree Field,** Rudheath Lordship Ch, Walworth Du, Layer Breton Ess (*Periton* 1499), North Mimms Hrt (*Peryfeld* 1553), Ridge Hrt, Long Ditton Sr (*Pyrihagh* 1235); **Pear Tree Ground,** Burghfield Brk; **Pear Tree Hill,** Lenchwick Wo; **Pear Tree Leasow,** Harley Sa, Kenley Sa; **Pear Tree Marsh,** Barking Ess; **Pear Tree Meadow,** Yeldersley Db; **Pear Tree Means,** Cold Norton St [ME *main*]; **Pear Tree Piece**, Chadlington: 'land planted with pear trees' [OE *pyrige*].

Peas Bonges, Hope Db [ME *banke*]; **Peas Croats,** Watton at Stone Hrt [OE *croft*]; **Peascroft,** North Rode Ch, Alkmonton Db, Hemel Hempstead Hrt, Sydenham O; **Peasdales,** Casterton We; **Peas Field,** Bovingdon Hrt (*Peascroft* 1623); **Peas Furlong,** Chadlington O; **Peasland(s),** Hunsterson Ch, Ugley Ess (*Peselondfeld* 1344); **Peas Leaze,** Minchinhampton Gl, Tortworth Gl; **Pease Ash,** Breamore Ha [OE *ersc*]; **Pease Bank,** Beetham We; **Peaseberry Hill,** Ottringham ERY (*Peseberch* 13c) [OE *beorg*]; **Pease Close,** Burghfield Brk, Belstone D, Alderwasley Db, Castleton Db, Hook Do; **Pease Field,** Birtley Ch, Marston Ch; **Pease Furlong,** Eyam Db; **Pease How,** Strickland Roger We [ON *haugr*]; **Pease Leys,** Rockingham Nth (*Peseleie* 1203); **Peasewell,** Stratfieldsaye Ha; **Peasy Close,** Bushby Lei; **Peasy Flat,** Repton Db (*Pissyflat* 14c); **Peazens,** Beer D [OE *hamm*]: 'land on which peas were grown' [OE *pise*].

Peat Close, Bradley Db; **Peat Delf,** Elstesd Sr [OE *(ge)delf*]; **Peat Hill,** Hugill We; **Peat Ing Intack,** Kentmere We; **Peat Moor & Mead,** Kintbury Brk; **Peat Moss Fcild,** Dufton We; **Peat Pots,** Stainmere We [ME *potte,* 'pit']; **Peethill Plantation,** Bakewell Db: 'land from which peat was obtained' [ME *pete*].

Pebble Close (Great & Little), Arncott O; **Pebley Croft,** Bucklebury Brk; **Pebley Furlong,** Chadlington O: 'land with stony soil' [ME *peble*].

Pecket, Inskip La; **Pecket Leasow,** Alvechurch Wo: 'land coming to a point' [OE **piced*].

Pellet Royd Wood, Huddersfield WRY (*Pilaterode* c 1210), 'clearing in which pill-oats are grown' [OE **pil-āte, rod*]. Pill-oats, otherwise known as pilled oats or pilcorn, are a species of oat (*Avena nuda*) in which the husks or glumes do not adhere to the grain. Cf Ekwall, *Studies on English Place-Names,* 105.

The Pen, Melksham W; **Pen Close,** Billesdon Lei, Bushby Lei, Halstead Lei, Holwell Lei, Hugglescote Lei, Scraptoft Lei; **Pen Corner,** Donington Lei; **Pen Ham Dale,** Kensworth Hrt [OE *hamm*]: 'land containing an enclosure for animals' [OE *penn*].

Pennsylvania, Little Eaton Db, Church Stretton Sa, Prees Sa, Market Lavington W, Marston W, Monkton Farleigh W; **Pennsylvania Meadow,** Burford Sa: a transferred name applied to remote pieces of land.

Penny Cake, Oxenhope WRY, a fanciful name alluding to the smallness (and probably also the round shape) of the field.

Penny Bank, Chapel en le Frith Db; **Penny Close,** Kirk Langley Db, Ringwood Ha, Adderbury O, Kendal We, Liversedge WRY; **The Penny Close,** South Elmsall WRY; **Penny Croft,** High Legh Ch, Sandbach Ch, Takeley Ess, Tortworth Gl, Winterbourne Gl, Staines Mx (*Pennecroft* 1275); **Penny Field,** Tolleshunt Major Ess, Fairford Gl, Eye & Dunsden O (*Pendenemed* 1271), Marley Wo; **Penny Furlong,** Wroxton O; **Penny Hill,** Hathersage Db, Elvetham Ha; **Penny Lands,** Barnsley Gl, Charlbury O; **Penny Mead,** Cromhall Gl; **Penny Meads,** Charfield Gl; **Penny Meadow,** Oundle Nth (*Penymedouwe* 1300); **Penny Moor,** Longden Sa; **Penny Pasture Common,** Eakring Nt; **Penny Patch,** Wrenbury cum Frith Ch; **Penny Piece,** Cosham Ha; **Penny Pingle,** Witcham

C; **Penny Pleck,** Church Broughton Db; **Penny Prick,** Eyam Db [ON *brekka,* 'slope']; **Penny Wood,** Alton Pancras Do: 'land on which a penny rent was payable' [OE *pening*].

Penny Pot Garth, Preston Du; **Penny Pot Hall,** Cheshunt Hrt (*Penyngs Pytte* 1353): probably 'land on which a hoard of coins was found' [OE *pening,* ME *potte*].

Pennyless Pinch, Brimpsfield Gl; **Pennyworth,** Fifehead Magdalen Do; **Pennyworth of Cheese,** Duntisbourne Rouse Gl: derogatory names for small pieces of land.

Pepper Bottom, Great Wymondley Hrt (*Pepper Acre Bushe* t.Hy 8); **Pepper Combe Down,** Alwington D; **Pepper Corn,** Brough & Shatton Db, Casterton We; **Peppercorn Hey,** Tintwistle Ch; **Western & Eastern Pepperern Wells,** West Alvington D; **Pepper Hill,** Arnfield Ch; **Lower Pepper Land,** Priors Dean Ha; **Pepper Leys,** Tur Langton Lei; **Pepper Mill Hill,** Bulmer Ess: names of varied origin and significance. Besides Peppercorn Hey, others possibly allude to a nominal rental. Pepperern Wells contained or adjoined a building [OE *ærn*] connected with the preparation of pepper. Yet another origin may be in plant names such as peppermint (*Mentha piperita*) or field pepperwort (*Lepidium campestre*).

Peril Field, Feckenham Wo; **The Perils,** Horspath O (*Pyrihale* 1308) [OE *halh*]; **Perry Acre,** North Stoke So; **Perry Croft,** Cheshunt Hrt, Great Munden Hrt; **Perry Field,** Bocking Ess, Feering Ess (*Pyrifelde* 1289), Fordham Ess (*Piryzefelde* 1391), Great Horsley Ess (*Pyrifelde* 1391), Magdalen Laver Ess, Shalford Ess, Newent Gl, Much Cowarne He, Hendon Mx; **Perry Garden,** Fareham Ha; **Perry Ground,** Little Ness Sa; **Perryhill,** Cranfield Bd (*Piriecroft* 13c); **Perry How,** Malden Sr [OE *hōh*]; **Perry Lane & Moor,** Aston Wa; **Perry Mead,** Puttenham Sr; **Perry Moor,** Hartlebury Wo: 'land on which pears were grown' [OE *pirige*].

Perlieu, Hope Mansel He; **Perlieu Plantation,** Hankerton W: 'land on the edge of a forest' [ME *purley*]. See also Purleigh.

Pescot Field, Greenford Mx (*Peasecroft* 1625); **Pessill,** Husbands Bosworth Lei; **Pessle Syke,** Laughton Lei [OE *sīc*]: 'land on which peas were grown' [OE *pise, croft, hyll*].

The Pest-house, Chipping Norton O; **Pest House Close,** Highworth W; **Pest-house Field,** Steeple Aston O: 'site of a hospital for plague or fever victims'.

Pet Field, White Notley Ess (*Ye Petfeild* 1627), 'land containing a quarry' [OE *pytt*].

Pheasant Pingle, Alderwasley Db; **Pheasants Meadow,** Burnaston Db: 'land on which pheasants were preserved'.

Philadelphia, Hasland Db, a transferred name for a distant field.

Philbarn Hill, Bix O, a complimentary name (with whimsical spelling) for productive land.

Pica Hill, Hillbeck We; **Picardy Lawn,** Alvechurch Wo; **Piccadilly,** Grafton W, Hullavington W, Lacock W; **Pickaxe,** South Warnborough Ha (*Pickhatch* 19c); **Picked Acre,** Ashmore Do; **Picked Ball Croft,** Sparsholt Ha [OE **ball*, 'mound of earth marking boundary']; **Picked Close,** Bucklebury Brk, Burghfield Brk, Hinton Martell Do, Sherborne St John Ha, Crowmarsh O; **Picked Common,** Weston So; **Picked Field,** Banstead Sr; **Picked Ground,** Highclere Ha, Whitchurch O, Hennington W, Stretton on Fosse Wa; **Picked Heath,** Eye & Dunsden O; **Picked Hill,** Steventon Ha; **Picked Hokum,** Sparsholt Ha [OE *āc hamm*, 'oak enclosure']; **Picked Lands,** Ampney Crucis Gl; **Picked Mead,** Newbury Brk, Faccombe Ha, Stanton Fitzwarren W; **Picked Meadow,** Inkpen Brk (*Pykedhalue* 14c) [OE *healf*], Little Gaddesden Hrt, Sandford St Martin O; **Picked Piece,** Ashmore Do, Cliddesden Ha, Cadlington O; **Picked Pightle,** Bucklebury Brk; **Picked Riddance,** Silchester Ha [OE **ryden*]; **Picket Close,** Steventon Ha, Tring Hrt, Eye & Dunsden O; **Picket Piece,** Wychwood O; **Picquet Close,** Hayton Nt: 'land which comes to a point' [OE **pīced*].

Pickhill Bank, Snaith WRY; **Pickle,** Old Hutton We; **Pickle Close,** Birstall WRY; **Pickle Pasture,** Orwell C; **Pickle Worthy,** Wapley Gl [OE *worðign*]; **The Pickles,** Shardlow Db; **Pickoe,** Thelwall Ch; **Pickow,** Higher Whitley Ch: 'small piece of land' [ME *pichel*].

Pickpocket, Pucklechurch Gl, Siston Gl, Winterslow W; **Pick Pockets,** Walkern Hrt; **Pickpockets Mead,** Essendon Hrt: derogatory names for unprofitable land.

Piddle Meadow, Inkpen Brk; **Pie Dell,** Stevenage Hrt (*Pyedell-acre* 1409); **(The) Pightle,** Chieveley Brk (*The Piddle* 1550), Enbourne Brk (*Le Piddill, Le Pudle* 1547): 'waterlogged land' [OE *pidele].

Pie Priests Mead, Otterbourne Ha, 'land owned by monks or friars wearing a parti-coloured habit', eg the Dominicans or Carmelites.

Piece, Newton Ch, self-explanatory.

Pied Leys Piece, Edale Db, 'land with parti-coloured surface' [ME *pied*].

Pig Garth, Hamphall Stubbs WRY; **Pigs Croft,** Ridgewell Ess (*Pygges Croftys* 1483); **Pigs Field,** East Allington D; **Pigs Louse,** Buckland Newton Do [OE *hlōse*, 'pig-sty']; **Pigs Park,** Billesdon Lei: 'land on which pigs were kept' [OE *pigga].

Pig Hill, Crigglestone WRY; **Pighill Close,** Crofton WRY; **Pig Hill Head,** Hunsworth WRY; **(The) Pightle,** Kelvedon Ess (*Le Pitle* 1560), Adderbury O, Chinnor O, Pishill O, Coulsdon Sr: 'small piece of land' [ME *pichel, pightel*].

Pigeon Coat Croft, Great Eccleston La; **Pigeon Cote Field,** Little Singleton La; **Pigeon House Close,** Burghfield Brk, Windsor Brk; **Pigeon House Ground,** Kintbury Brk, Harpsden O; **Pigeon House Land,** Handborough O; **Pigeon House Meadow,** Newton Ch; **Pigeon Park,** West Alvington D: 'site of a pigeon house'. See also Dove Coat [OE *cot*].

Piggledy Peers Croft, Coventry Wa (*Pykedeperefeld* 1306, *Picardy Pere* 1538), 'pointed pear orchard' [OE *pīced]. See Pica Hill.

Pike Field, Norton Ch; **Piked Ground,** Beoley Wo; **Pikes Meadow,** Windlesham Sr (*Longpik* 1609); **Pikey Piece,** Leebotwood Sa: 'pointed piece of land' [OE *pīc*].

Pildash (Far, Middle), Nailstone Lei, Odstone Lei: 'barked ash tree'. A form of sugar may be extracted by cutting into the bark of an ash tree [ME *piled*, OE *æsc*].

Pile Mead, Fifehead Neville Do; **Pill Croft,** Great Waltham Ess (*Pylcroft* 1400): 'land by a pool' [OE *pyll*].

Pilhough, Stanton Db (*Pilethhalch* c 1290) [OE *halh*]; **Pillet Shaw,** Lamberhurst K; *Pillitland*, Bruntingthorpe Lei 1606; **Pillow Croft,** Carrington Ch, Ault Hucknall Db, Willington Db, Pudsey WRY (*Pilotrecroft* 13c, *Pilatecroft* 1638); **Pilly Tough,** Holmesfield Db (*Pelethhalgh* 1498) [OE *halh*]; **Pilot Field,** Falfield Gl (*Pilatefeilds* 1638); **Pilot Hill,** Faccombe Ha: 'land on which pill-oats were grown' [OE **pil-āte*]. See Pellet Royd Wood.

Pin Croft, Kintbury Brk; **Pin Meadow,** Waterperry O; **Pin Plot,** Hermitage Do: 'land with an animal enclosure' [OE *penn*].

Pinchgut, Blunsden W, Lacock W; **Pinchgut Hall,** Holwell Hrt; **Pinch Park,** Haltwhistle Nb; **Pinchpoor,** Siston Gl, Nettleton W; **Pinching House,** Elland WRY: derogatory names, ambiguously referring to parsimony and torture.

Pincushen Hill, Ambleside We; **Pincushion,** Ashmore Do: 'convex piece of land'.

Pinder Close, Moss WRY; **Pinder Flatt,** Eggborough WRY; **Pinders,** Ropley Ha; **Pinder's Field,** Rampton Nt: 'land allocated to the keeper of the parish pound' [OE **pundere*].

Pine Acres, Beer D, 'land near or containing pine trees'.

Pine Belly, North Elmsall WRY; **Pine Belly Hill,** Gildersome WRY, Pudsey WRY: derogatory names, referring to the pains of starvation. By way of contrast, there is a Full Belly Dale in Gildersome.

(The) **Pinfold,** Dunham Massey Ch, Hale Ch, Lymm Ch, Mobberley Ch, Great Singleton La, Hambleton La, Lytham La, Pilling La, Ribby La, Illston Lei, Muston Lei, Stokeham Nt, Burton We, Kentmere We; **Pinfold Bottom,** Boxford Brk; **Pinfold Close,** Hinckley Lei; **Pinfold Croft,** Preston on the Hill Ch, Broughton La; **Pinfold Field,** Appleton Ch, Aston by Budworth Ch, Newton Ch, Plumley Ch, Sandbach Ch, Toft Ch, Alston La, Barnacre La, Broughton La, Nether Wyresdale La; **Pinfold Hill,** Crossthwaite We; **Pinfold Meadow,** Alston La, Claughton La, Burrough on the Hill Lei: 'land by a pound for stray animals' [OE **pynd-fald*].

(The) **Pingle,** Hatherton Ch, Hunsterson Ch, Wybunbury Ch, Bradwell Db, Castleton Db, Chapel en le Frith Db, Goosnargh

La, Inskip La, Woodplumpton La, Barwell Lei, Bushby Lei, Evington Lei, Upton Lei, Babworth Nt, Darlton Nt, Hodsock Nt, Kneesall Nt, Laxton Nt, Kingsbury Wa; **Pingle Meadow,** Billesdon Lei; **Pingo,** Chorlton Ch; **Pingot(t),** Antrobus Ch, Church Coppenhall Ch, Hurdsfield Ch, Lymm Ch, Millington Ch, Rostherne Ch, Timperley Ch: 'small piece of land' [ME *pingel*].

Pink Croft, Kintbury Brk; **Pink Field,** Lamberhurst K; **Pink Knowle,** Elwick Hall Du; **Pink Meadow,** Feckenham Wo: of uncertain origin and meaning; if the allusion is not to the colour of the soil, the name may represent 'land on which finches were seen' [OE **pinca*].

Pippen Field, Eyam Db, possibly 'land on which apples were grown' [ME *pippin*].

Pippins Park, Rufford Nt, see Pittance Park.

Piss Furlong, Warborough O (*Pusefurlong* 1321), 'land on which peas were grown' [OE *pise*].

Pith Hill, Hunsworth WRY, Wooldale WRY; **Pithill Close,** Skipwith ERY (*Pichel* 12c): 'small piece of land' [ME *pightel*, *picel*].

Pit Close, Kintbury Brk, Welford Brk (*La Pette* 1180, *La Putte* 1392), Alderwasley Db, Alkmonton Db, Fifehead Magdalen Do, East Dereham Nf, Willoughby Waterless Lei; **Pit Croft,** Hemel Hempstead Hrt; **Pit Field,** Windsor Brk, Abbotsham D, Houghton le Spring Du, Newbottle Du, Compton Sr (*Putlonde* 1320), Merstham Sr (*Pytfelde* 1500); **Pit Furlong,** Daventry Nth (*Putfurlong* c 1300); **Pit Lands,** Coulsdon Sr; **Pit Leasow,** Leebotwood Sa; **Pit Meadow,** Boxford Brk, Hatfield Hrt (*Putlegh* 1277), Dadlington Lei; **Pitt Meads,** Berrynarbor D: 'land containing or adjoining a pit or quarry' [OE *pytt*].

Pittance Park, Rufford Nt (*Pittanes Closes* 1609, *Pippins Park* 1826), was probably land endowed for the benefit of Rufford Abbey; a pittance was a pious bequest for the provision of special food etc on particular occasions.

Pityful Meadow, Bakewell Db, a derogatory name for poor land.

The Pix, Adderbury O, 'land with a point' [OE **piced*].

Pixy, Ringwood Ha, possibly alludes to haunting by a fairy.

Plain Close, East Anstey D; **Great & Little Plain Down,** West Alvington D: 'flat meadowland' [ME *plain*].

Plaistow, Deerhurst Gl; **Plaster Croft,** Burland Ch; **The Plasters,** Bromfield Sa; **Plastow Green, Great Plaster Pightle,** Kingsclere Ha; **Plastows,** Cookham Brk (*Plaisters* 1609); **Plastows Mead,** Essendon Hrt (*Pleystowe* 1461): 'sport place' [OE *pleg-stōw*]. The assembly was sometimes more serious; the Deerhurst land was the site of the manor and hundred court meetings.

Plane (East, Middle), Hugglescote Lei; **Plane Tree Field,** Houghton le Spring Du; **Plane Tree Hill Homestead,** Elwick Hall Du: 'land on which plane trees grew' [OE *plāna*]. The western or London plane is cultivated widely (*Platanus acerifolia*), but usually for ornamental purposes.

Plantation Close, Buckminster Lei, Illston Lei; **Plantation Field,** Abbotsham D, Houghton le Spring Du: 'land with a clump of young trees'.

Plash Field, St Michaels Hrt (*Plashfeld* t.Hy 6), Mytholmroyd WRY; **Plash Wood Field,** Newton Valance Ha, Southwick Ha (*Plashett* 16c); **Plashets,** Sheering Ess: 'marshy place' [OE **plæsc*, ME *plashet*].

The Plat, Chinnor O; **The Platt,** Pishill O; **Inner Platt,** Chertsey Sr; **Platt Meadow,** Great Stretton Lei: 'small piece of ground' [ME *plat*].

Plato, Halstock Do, commemorative name celebrating the author of *The Republic*. See also Aristogyton, Lilburne Mead.

Play Cross, Hazelbury Bryan Do; **Play Ground,** Pownall Fee Ch: 'land for recreation' [OE *plega*]. This possibly has the same implication as Plaistow (qv).

Playing Close, Charlbury O; **Playsteds Ground,** Westbury on Severn Gl; **Pleasure Ground,** Adderbury O, Great Haseley O, Harpsden O; **Pleasure Grounds,** Henley O: 'land for recreation'.

Pleasant Piece, Astley Abbots Sa, self-explanatory.

The Pleck, Doddenham Wo; **Pleck Green,** Holwell Do; **Plick,** Hook Do: 'small plot of ground' [ME *plek*].

The Plot, Halstock Do, Medbourne Lei, Welham Lei: 'small piece of ground' [OE *plot*].

Plough Close, Knossington Lei; **Plough Grounds,** Beer Hackett Do; **Plough Sitch,** Whittington Db; **Ploughed Bitten,** Stretton on Fosse Wa [OE *bytme*]; **Ploughed Close,** Bushby Lei, Foxton Lei, Galby Lei, Holwell Lei, Illston Lei; **Ploughed Field,** Hillfield Do, Blackfordby Lei; **Ploughed Noah's** or **Nores,** Bennington Hrt [OE *ōra*, 'bank']; **Ploughed Piece,** Witherley Lei; **Ploughing Field,** Walworth Du; **Ploughland,** Welwick ERY (*Plughelande* 1540); *Ploulondes* Dersingham Nf 1300: 'land under arable cultivation'. It is likely that the Welwick name, Ploughland, represents one of the *ij plogeland on þorp* mentioned in Cnut's grant of Patrington (1033), in which case it is the measure of land, regarded as the amount of ground a team of oxen could plough in a year [OE *plōg*, *plōh*, *plōg(a)-land*].

Plowsters, Culmington Sa, possibly 'ground for recreation' [OE *pleg-stōw*]. See also Plaistow.

Pluff Hill, Rencomb Gl, 'arable hilly land' [OE *plōh*].

Plum Close, Kintbury Brk; **Plum Field,** Shalford Ess (*Plomfelde* 1501); **Plum Furlong,** Bushwood Wa; **Plum Greaves,** Haldenby WRY; **Plum Mead,** Dagenham Ess; **Plum Tree Hill,** Windsor Brk; **Plumb Bush Furlong,** Icomb Gl; **Plumb Tree Wong,** Clowne Db; **Plumbs Pightle,** Burghfield Brk: 'land on which plum trees were grown' [OE *plūme*, *plūm-trēow*].

Plum Cake, Parwich Db; **Plum Cake Corner,** Elvetham Ha; **Plum Pudding Meadow,** Ockbrook Db, Stoke Dabernon Sr: names alluding either to the coloration or the consistency of the soil.

Plutarch, Halstock Do, arbitrary name. See Aristogyton.

Pocket Patch, Walton Inferior Ch; **Pockett Field,** Thelwall Ch: 'nook of land'.

Poets Close, Manston Do, an unexplained name.

Poison Piddle, Mortimer Brk; **Poison Piece,** Alderwasley Db: 'land with sterile soil'.

Policy Field, Panfield Ess (*Pollardeshey* 1252); **Pollard Furlong,** Shipton under Wychwood O (*Pollard Hill Coppice* 1608): 'land containing or adjacent to pollarded trees'. *Pollarding* was (and is) the removal of all tree branches above about six feet from the ground, causing the growth of numerous slender poles, of great use in hurdle-making, basketry and other crafts.

Pomfret Mead, Hempstead Ess (*Pountfrett* 1484), 'land by broken bridge' [OF *pont freit*].

Pond Close, Newbury Brk, Hinton Martell Do, Greetham R; **Pond Field,** East Allington D, Houghton le Spring Du, Bushey Hrt (*Pondacre* 1425), East Barnet Hrt, Elstead Sr; **Pond Mead,** Ashreigney D, East Anstey D; **Pond Meadow,** West Alvington D, Hook Do, Tring Hrt; **Pond Plot,** Welford Brk: 'land containing a natural or artificial pool' [ME *ponde*].

Pondicherry, North Wingfield Db, a transferred name for remote land.

Pool Close, Beer D, Ashby Folville Lei, Scraptoft Lei; **Pool Field,** Capesthorne Ch, Drayton in Hales Sa, Hinstock Sa, **Pool Piece,** Cressage Sa, Alvechurch Wo; **Pool Pleck,** Hartlebury Wo: 'land containing or adjoining a pool' [OE *pōl*].

Poopal Meadow, Clungunford Sa; *Popleyclose*, Shaw Brk 1547; *Popple Mede,* Blewbury Brk 1548; *Poppley Yate*, Winterbourne Brk 1550: possibly 'pebbly land' [OE *popel*].

Poor Allotment, Windsor Brk; **Poor Allotments,** Enbourne Brk; **Poor Folks Pasture Gate,** Bedley & Stowood O; **Poor House Field,** Newhall Ch; **Poor Land,** Rampton Nt; **Poor Leys,** Alvechurch Wo; **Poor Man a Peny,** Cookham Brk; **Poor Mans Friend,** Edwinstowe Nt; **Poor Mans Piece,** Everton Nt, Mansfield Nt; **Poors Close,** Billesdon Lei, Nailstone Lei, Shipton under Wychwood O; **Poors Ground,** Northmoor O; **Poors Knapp,** Evenlode Gl; **Poor Land,** Barley Hrt; **Poors Piece,** Swarkestone Db, East Norton Lei; **Poors Plot,** Wolvercote O: most of these names probably refer to charitable endowments for the benefit of the poor, though one or two may allude to land of bad quality; Poor Mans Friend may be a more general complimentary name.

Poor Close, Hulland Ward Intakes Db, Illston Lei, Stretton Magna Lei; **Poor Ground,** Buckhorn Weston Do; **Poor Field,** Antrobus Ch; **Poor Tining,** Chippenham W: ambiguously named pieces of land; in the absence of evidence that they refer to charitable endowments, these names may be taken to relate to the quality of the soil.

Poor Peter, Grimsargh La; **Poor Rachael,** Shepperton Mx; **Poor Robin,** Chaldon Sr: probably derogatory names.

Pope Furlong, Bloxham O; **Popes Hole,** Odiham Ha: probably alluding to the common red poppy, *Papaver rhoeas* [MnE dial. *pope*].

Popple Field, Curdridge Ha, possibly 'pebbly land' [OE *popel*].

Poppy Field, West Anstey D; **Poppy Home,** Hugglescote Lei [ON *holmr*]; **Poppy Lot Drove,** Feltwell Nf (*Popilholt* 14c): 'land on which poppies grew'.

Port Mahon Garden, Oxford, a transferred name for a remote piece of land. Port Mahon is the capital of Minorca, which changed hands fairly frequently during the eighteenth century and so must have often been mentioned in the news.

Potash Four Acres, Havant Ha, alludes to a field on which potash was regularly used.

Pothook Mount, Dawley Magna Sa, 'sloping field shaped like a pothook'.

Pot Kiln Brake, Croxton Nf; **Pot Kiln Meadow,** Inkpen Brk: 'land on which a pottery kiln was sited'.

Potlids, Witham Ess, probably 'land characterised by shallow mounds resembling saucepan-lids'.

Potato Piece, Alderwasley Db, Wykin Lei; **Potatoe Bed,** Pott Shrigley Ch; **Potatoe Brow,** Kingsley Ch; **Potatoe Croft,** Cold Norton St; **Potatoe Fiel(d),** Charlesworth Db, Newbottle Du; **Potatoe Pleck,** Warmingham Ch; **Potatoe Plot,** Billesdon Lei: 'land on which potatoes were grown'.

Potters Croat, Brent Pelham Hrt [OE *croft*]; **Potters Field,** Otterbourne Ha, Headley Sr (*Potterscroft* 1218); **Potters Mead,**

Whitchurch Mx: 'land used or occupied by a potter', the use being normally the provision of clay for pottery.

Potters Piece, Alderwasley Db, probably land occupied by the family of Thomas Potter, recorded locally in 1637.

Pound Acre, Holme We; **Pound Close,** Mortimer Brk, Welford Brk, Hinton Martell Do, Holwell Do, Laleham Mx, Iffley O, Kendal We; **Pound Field,** Feering Ess, Hadlow K, Headington O, Wolvercote O, Hambledon Sr; **Pound Field Piece,** Stebbing Ess (*Pundfalde* 1441); **Pound Piece,** Hungerford Brk, Sapperton Gl; **Pound Pightle,** Aldborough Nf; **Pound Pleck,** Alvechurch Wo; **Pound Wood,** Banstead Sr: 'land by an enclosure for stray animals' [OE **pund, pundfald*].

Prae Wood, St Michaels Hrt (*Le Preye* 1342); **Pray Field,** Thorpe Sr; **Prey Acre,** Elmeley Castle Wo; **Preylands,** Artington Sr; **Prey Meadow,** Cheriton Ha, Wonersh Sr: '(land adjoining) a meadow' [ME *pre*].

The Prebend, Avon Dassett Wa; **Prebend Down,** Itchen Abbas Ha: 'endowed land providing the stipend of a canon'.

Presmore Common Meer, Cowley O; **Press Field,** St Michaels Hrt, Hillingdon Mx, Solihull Wa (*Prestfild* t.Ed 6); **Pressgate Close,** Burton Overy Lei; **Press Mead Furlong,** Cookham Brk; **Prest Stile,** Priston So: 'land assigned to the priest' [OE *preost*].

Pretty Close, Alderwasley Db; **Pretty Field,** Lower Whitley Ch: either derived from the surname Pretty or complimentary names.

Priest Acre, Great Hucklow Db; **Priest Croft,** Saffron Walden Ess; **Priestdown,** Compton Abdale Gl; **Priest Earth,** Heptonstall WRY; **Priest Field,** Minshull Vernon Ch, Sutton Downes Ch, Felsted Ess, Newent Gl, Kilmeston Ha, Rickmansworth Hrt (*Prestfeilds* 1594), Chertsey Sr (*Prestelese* t.Hy 3); **Priest Hill,** Kempsey Wo; **Priest Holme,** Skelsmergh We; **Priest Ings,** Walkeringham Nt; **Priest Intack,** Kentmere We; **Priestlands,** Earls Colne Ess (*Prestyslondlane* 1390), Itchen Abbas Ha, Bloxham O; **Priestley Field,** Wilnecote Wa (*Le Preestmedew* 1436); **Priestly Field,** Felsted Ess (*Presteshai* 1200) [OE *(ge)hæg*]; **Priest Mead,** Fifehead Neville Do; **Priest Meadows,** Gateshead Du; **Priest Top,** Hook Norton O (*Prestefeld* 1153); **Priestwells,**

Greetham R; **Priests Acre,** Bisley Gl; **Priests Land,** Kelvedon Ess (*Prestesland* 1318); **Priest's Meadow,** Twyford Ha: 'land owned by a priest' [OE *prēost*].

Primrose, Foolow Db; **Primrose Field,** Goosnargh La; **Primrose Field Whath,** Dukinfield Ch [ON *vað*, 'ford']; **Primrose Greaves,** Weeton with Preece La [OE *grǣfe*, 'thicket']; **Primrose Hill,** Cuddington Ch, Arnesby Lei; **Primrose Meadow,** Haighton La; **The Primrose Pasture,** West Hartlepool Du; **Primrose Shaw,** Crowmarsh O [OE *sceaga*, 'copse']: 'land on which primroses grew'. The primrose (*Primula vulgaris*) is common in woods and other shady places [ME *primerole*].

Pringle, Claughton La, Inskip La, Preston La, Dawley Magna Sa, Wroxall Wa (*The Pingle* 1713); **Great & Little Pringle,** Altofts WRY: 'small piece of land' [ME *pingel*].

Prior Close, Whitwell Db; **Prior Field,** Breedon on the Hill Lei; **Prior Leys,** Hollington Db; **Prior Piece,** Elmton Db; **Priors Close,** Barton C; **Priors Field,** Newton Ch (*Pryors Feild* 1423); *Priors Karre*, Dersingham Nf 16c [ON *kjarr*]; **Priors Lees,** Stanstead Abbots Ess (*Pryers Leaze* 1556); **Pryors,** Rickling Ess (*Prioureshach* 1361) [OE *hæcc*]: 'land held by a prior'. The Whitwell name refers to the prior of Worksop, the Hollington one to Tutbury priory; Prior Piece in Elmton was the property of the prior of Thurgarton, Priors Close in Barton that of the prior of Merton, and Priors Field in Newton that of Norton Priory. The Dersingham land was held by the prior of Bynham. Waltham Abbey held land in Stanstead Abbots, and the prior of Berden in Rickling.

Prison Bar Field, Brereton cum Smethwick Ch, 'land used for the children's game of prisoner's base'.

Procession Mere, Dersingham Nf 1560, 'boundary path used in the ceremony of beating the bounds'. See also Amen Corner.

Profitable Field, Lingfield Sr, self-explanatory.

Prospect (Near, Middle, Far), Coleorton Lei, 'land commanding a fine view'.

Providence, Eaton under Heywood Sa; **Providence Farm,** Blidworth Nt: complimentary names for profitable land.

Proxies, Bosden Ch, alluding to land whose rent was used to commute an incumbent's obligation to procure or provide lodging for the bishop.

The Psalms, Bromfield Sa, 'land on which the psalms were recited during the bound-beating ceremony'. See also Amen Corner.

Puck Acre, Daglingworth Gl; **Puck Close,** Feckenham Wo; **Puck Field,** Ewhurst Sr; **Puck Hay,** Crudwell W [OE *(ge)hæg*]; **Puck Lands,** Witley Sr; **Puck Mead,** Croydon Sr; **Puck Moor,** Dymock Gl; **Puckpit Meadow,** Aston Somerville Gl; **Puckpits,** Filton Gl, Ditcheat So; **Puckwell Farm,** Niton Wt; **Pucks Croft,** Rusper Sx; **Pux Pit,** Bleadon So: 'land haunted by a goblin' [OE *pūca*].

Puddenham, Willersey Gl (*Poddenhomme* 709, *Pudnam Field* 1637), 'Puda's enclosure' [OE *hamm*].

Pudding Acre, Cookham Brk, Little Bedwyn W; **Pudding Bag,** Harston Lei; **Pudding Bag Close,** Cromford Db; **Pudding Bush,** Ackworth WRY; **Pudding Bush Close,** Adderbury O; **Pudding Close,** Burghfield Brk, Lydiard Millicent W, Lea Marston Wa; **Pudding Croft,** Charlwood Sr, Hatfield WRY; **Pudding Field,** Hope Woodlands Db, Upton Grey Ha, Mitcham Sr; **Pudding Hill,** Bibury Gl, Alvechurch Wo; **Puddinghole,** Betchworth Sr; **Pudding Holme,** Sutton C (*Puddynholm* 1438) [ON *holmr*]; **Pudding Mead,** Shurdington Gl, Wellow So, Brokenborough W; **Pudding Meadow,** Hadlow K; **Pudding Patch,** Matlock Bath Db, **Pudding Pie Field,** Wheston Db; **Pudding Poke,** Scarcliffe Db, Laxton Nt (*Puding Roodes* 1625), Barbon We, North Elmsall WRY; **Pudding Poke Close,** Darrington WRY; **Pudding Poke Wood,** Eakring Nt: a fanciful name for soft, sticky land.

Pulse Hill, Rosliston Db, 'land on which peas and beans were grown' [ME *pouls*].

Purchase Croft, Little Horkesley Ess (*New Purchas* 1584), 'land obtained by purchase'.

Purgatory, Appleton Ch, Breamore Ha, Alston La, Carleton La, Poulton La, Steeple Barton O, Wentnor Sa, Minety W, Alvechurch Wo: 'land requiring painful and tedious labour'.

Purleigh (Upper & Lower), Charlton W; **Purley,** Takeley Ess, Siddington Gl, Marston Meysey W; **Purley Grove,** Awre Gl;

(The) **Purlieu,** Bagendon Gl, Lydney Gl, Soberton Ha, Sopley Ha, Litchborough Nth, Cricklade W, Minety W; **Purlieu Mead,** Awre Gl; **Purlieu Piece,** Eling Ha; **Purlieu Waste,** Wychwood O: 'land on the edge of a forest' [ME *purley*].

Purrance, Leafield O (*Purveaunce* 1300, *Perryans, Purrans* 1551), 'land whose rent was used to offset demands for provisions by the royal household' [ME *purveance*].

Push Ploughed Field, Agden Ch, Appleton Ch, Keckwick Ch, Woodford Ch; **Push'd Ploughed Meadow,** Barnton Ch: 'land from which the turf was pared and burnt'. See also Paring Field.

Pye Close, Hambledon Ha; **Pyegrave,** Butley Ch [OE *grǣfe*]; **Pye Greave,** Lambrigg We; **Pye Mead,** Priston So: 'land on which magpies abounded' [ME *pīe*].

Pylons, Lytchett Minster Do, Whitchurch Canonicorum Do: 'land on which structures for supporting electric power cables were sited'.

Pyrcroft, Chertsey Sr (*Piricroft* t. Hy 3), Weybridge Sr: 'land on which pear trees were grown' [OE *pyrige, croft*].

Q

Quab Close, Hulland Ward Intakes Db; **Quab Meadow,** Hinstock Sa, Preston Montford Sa; **Quabbs,** Dymock Gl; **Quag Field,** Chessington Sr; **Quag Meadow,** Walton Inferior Ch; **Quaggy Leasow,** Stapleton Sa; **Quobbs,** Wolstaston Sa: 'boggy land' [OE *cwabba*, EMnE *quag*].

Quake Field, Darlton Nt, 'land with unsteady surface'.

Quaker Close, Killamarsh Db; **Quaker Field,** Lymm Ch; **Quakers Close,** Melbourne Db, Somerby Lei; **Quakers Field,** Pyrton O; **Quakers Land,** Henley O; **Quakers Piece,** Watlington O: names of several possible origins and meanings. The Melbourne land was owned by the Society of Friends, and some of the other fields named here may have the same history; another possible meaning is 'land on which quaking grass grew', usually implying the common quaking-grass or totter grass (*Briza media*), which grows widely throughout Britain. A less likely possibility is that the name may refer to land with a quaking surface.

Quar Bush, Camerton So; **Quar(r) Close,** Holwell Do, Kingston Magna Do, West Pennard So; **Quar Furlong,** Stanton Prior So; **Quarhill Field,** Churchill O; **Quar(r) Ground,** Sevenhampton Gl (*Quarre Feld* 1532), Stanton Fitzwarren W; **Quarr Leaze,** Garsdon W; **Quarr Tyning,** Bratton W; **Quarry Close,** Arlington D, Ashreigney D, Hermitage Do, Billesdon Lei; **Quarry Field,** Abbotsham D, East Anstey D, Ilsington D, Thorpe Bulmer Du; **Quarry Furlong,** Spelsbury O; **Quarry Hole,** Ferry Fryston WRY; **Quarry Holes,** Ashwell Hrt (*Quarrepette* 1444); **Quarry Meadow,** Forton La; **Quarry Moor,** Billesdon Lei; **Quarry Park,** West Alvington D; **Quarry Pit,** Goosnargh La; **Quarry Shaw,** Lamberhurst K: 'land containing or adjoining a quarry' [ME *quarrere*].

Quarrelsome, Clifton & Compton Db, a derogatory name for difficult land.

The Queach, Rickmansworth Hrt; **Queach Grove,** Great Oakley Ess; **Queats,** Ewhurst Sr; **(The) Queeches,** Eastwick Hrt (*Le Queche* 1349), Watford Hrt (*Le Queche* t.Ed 3): 'a thicket' [ME *queche*].

Queen Anne's Bounty, Hailey O; **Queen Annes Bounty Field,** Willaston Ch: 'land whose rent was applied to the fund for the support of poor clergy, called Queen Anne's Bounty'.

Queen Croft, Standon Hrt (*Eldequencroft* 1342); **Queens Close,** East Dereham Nf; **Queens Croft,** High Easter Ess (*Eldequenecroft* 1342); **Queens Pightle,** East Dereham Nf: the East Dereham names may be associated with a queen, but the Standon example is 'old woman's croft' and the High Easter name 'old women's croft' [OE *ēald*, *cwēne*, *croft*].

Querne Acre, Colerne W (*Querneacres* 1363); **Questers (Great),** Little Sampford Ess; **Questers (Little),** Great Sampford Ess (*Quernstede* 13c); **Quorn Field,** Pattiswick Ess: 'land from which were obtained stones suitable for handmills' [OE *cweorn*].

Quick Bean, East Anstey D, '(land containing) juniper' [OE *cwic-bēam*].

Quick Close, Wroxton O; **Quick Hills,** Marton Ch; **Quicksets,** Kingsterndale Db, Pleasley Db: 'land by a hawthorn tree, or with a hawthorn hedge'. The hawthorn hedge is called *quick* or *live*, by contrast with hurdle or wattle fencing, sometimes referred to as *dead hedges;* but the plant has been called 'live' or 'lively' since Anglo-Saxon times, doubtless on account of its readiness to root [OE *cwic*].

The Quire, Broadwell O, 'land endowed for the upkeep of the quire of the parish church'. See also Lamplands.

Quisters Hey, Dutton Ch, 'bleaching ground' [EMnE *quister*, 'bleacher'].

The Quor, Elmley Castle Wo, 'quarry' [ME *quarrere*].

R

Rabbit Bank, Wincle Ch; **Rabbit Borough,** Solihull Wa; **Rabbit Close,** Alderwasley Db, Desford Lei; **Rabbit Croft,** Mytholmroyd WRY; **Rabbit Hill,** Elwick Hall Du; **Rabbit Holes,** Elmton Db; **Rabbit Holes Meadow,** Burton Overy Lei; **Rabbit Warren,** Northenden Ch, Holt Lei; **Rabbits Hill,** Eweleme O: 'land on which rabbits were found'. Much rarer than names of the Conery, Coneygree type (qqv), names compounded with Rabbit are likely to be of recent origin, since *cony* was the usual term for the animal until the late Middle Ages, *rabbit* being originally applied only to the young [ME *rabet*].

Rack Close, Sandhurst Brk, Bagendon Gl, Box W, Horningsham W; **Rack Field,** Nether Wyresdale La; **Rack Ground,** Priston So; **Rackhay,** Fifehead Magdalen Do; **Rack Hill,** Fairford Gl, Painswick Gl, Rodborough Gl, Stroud Gl, Woodchester Gl; **Racknap,** Windrush Gl; **Rack Piece,** Crawley O; **Racks,** Easton Grey W: probably 'land containing frames used in finishing cloth'. See also Tenter Close.

Radish Closes, Litton Db (*Ruhedisse* 1254), 'rough enclosures' [OE *ruh*, *edisc*].

Radmoor Close, Welton Nth (*Rodemor* 1365), 'marshland on which reeds abounded' [OE *hrēod*, *mōr*].

Rag (Long), Beer D; **Rag Mead,** Buckhorn Weston Do; **Raggmires,** Egglescliffe Du: 'land on which rough stone was found' [ME *ragge*].

Rail Close, Little Eaton Db, Barton in the Beans Lei, Yaxley Sf, Featherstone WRY; **Rail Field,** Ash Sr; **Rail Leasow,** Wolstaston Sa; **The Rails,** Isley Walton Lei: 'land enclosed with a rail fence'.

Railway Close, Abbotsham D, Swannington Lei; **Railway Field,** Newbottle Du; **Railway Piece,** Bollin Fee Ch, Crich Db, Ullesthorpe Lei: self-explanatory.

Rain Close, Moss WRY, Owston WRY; **Rain Meadow,** Longden Sa; **Raine,** Dufton We: 'land on a boundary' [ON *reinn*].

(The) **Rainbow,** Burghfield Brk, Sandhurst Brk, Eversley Ha, Stapleton Sa, Longbridge Deverill W; **Rainbow Acre,** Charlbury O; **Rainbow Close,** Allesley Wa; **Rainbow Field,** Wellow So, Charlwood Sr; **Rainbow Hill,** Hankerton W; **Rainbow Piece,** Longdon Wo: 'land ploughed concentrically with a curved boundary'.

Rake Field, Newbottle Du; **Rake Head,** Goosnargh La, **Rake Heads,** Abney Db; **Rake Hill,** Alton Pancras Do; **Rake Meadow,** Ribby with Wrea La; **Rakestitch,** Morton Corbet Sa [OE *stycce*]: 'land near or containing a narrow hill-path' [OE *hraca*].

Ram(s) Close, Elmesthorpe Lei, Holt Lei, Swalcliffe O, Gunthorpe R; **Ram Field,** Baggrave Lei; **Ram Mead & Close,** Chalgrave O (*Rameker* 1278) [OE *æcer*]; **Ram Meadow,** Bittesby Lei, Illston Lei, Kings Norton Lei; **Ram Paddock,** Rotherby Lei: 'enclosure for ram(s)' [OE *ramm*].

Rampant Down, West Horsley Sr; **Ramper Down,** Elstead Sr; **Romping Downs,** Ash Sr, Shalford Sr: 'terraced land' [MnE dial. *ramp*, 'to make a series of inclined drops'].

Rampart Close, Scarcliffe Db; **Rampart Field,** Inskip La, Upper Rawcliffe La; **Ramparts,** Great Horkesley Ess; **Ramper,** Thornton La, Wesham La; **Ramper Meadow,** Upper Rawcliffe La: 'land beside a causeway or part of a Roman road' [MnE dial. *rampart*]. Cf Wainwright, *FN Amounderness*, 202.

(The) **Rand,** Ellingham Nf, Darrington WRY; **Rands,** Finningley Nt: '(land on) border' [OE *rand*].

Ranget, Goosnargh La, Great Eccleston La, Out Rawcliffe La, Roseacre La, Woodplumpton La; **Ranglet,** Broughton La:

'irregularly shaped land' [MnE dial. *ranget*, 'small field of irregular shape', from ON *vrangr*, 'crooked'].

Ranglands, Cossington Lei, 'crooked arable strips' [ON *vrangr*].

Rape, Holwell Do; **Rape Breck,** Babworth Nt; **Rape Close,** Ashover Db, Kirk Langley Db: 'land on which rape was grown'. The plant alluded to may be either *Brassica napus*, a fodder crop, or *Brassica campestris oleifera*, the seeds of which are crushed for oil.

Raspberry Brake, Wigginton O, 'scrubland on which wild raspberries grew' [OE *bræc*].

Rats Castle, Lechlade Gl, 'land containing or adjoining a derelict building'.

Raven Field, Audlem Ch, Blakenhall Ch, Overton Ha; *Raven Flatt*, Belmont Du 1650; **Ravensbank,** Windermere We; **Ravenscout,** Beetham We [ON *skúti*, 'rock']: 'land on which ravens were seen' [OE *hræfn*].

Raw Bones, Tandridge Sr (*Rawbones* 1670), a derogatory name suggestive of pain and emaciation resulting from working such unproductive land.

Ray Cragg, Underbarrow We; **Ray Croft,** Grimsargh La; **Ray Field,** Bispham with Norbreck La; **Ray Hey,** Great Singleton La, Upper Rawcliffe with Tarnacre La: 'land in a nook or corner' [ON *vrá*].

Ray Field, Hatfield Broad Oak Ess; **Ray Mead,** Fetcham Sr; **Ray Meadow,** Shiplake O: 'land beside a river', the initial letter originating from the misdivision of a phrase [ME *atter*, OE *ēa*].

Raydon Hill, Wroxton O (*Ruedenehull* 1242–3, *Reydown Hill* 1768), 'hill beside the rye valley' [OE *ryge*, *denu*, *hyll*].

Reading, Bushwood & Layworth Wa (*Ruddyng* 1552); **Readings,** Shudy Camps C (*Le Redinge* 1313), Layer Marney Ess (*Le Redene* 1331), Little Clacton Ess, Sible Hedingham Ess (*Readinge* 1534), Harpenden Hrt (*Reddyng* 1379), King's Walden Hrt, Watford Hrt; **Readings Field,** West Wickham C (*Redings* 1650); **(The) Reddings,** Abbots Langley Hrt (*Reddinges* 14c), Longsleddale We, Alvechurch Wo: 'cleared land' [OE **ryding*].

Ready Furlong, Breaston Db, 'reed-infested land' [OE *hrēodig*].

Reasonableness, Halstock Do; **Republic,** Halstock Do; **Revolution,** Halstock Do: arbitrary names applied by Thomas Hollis, to celebrate moral and political ideas associated with the Commonwealth. See Appendix 3.

Rector's Close, Buckminster Lei; **Rector's Field,** Leftwich Ch; **Rector's Wood,** East Allington D: 'land belonging to a rector'.

Red Acre, Selborne Ha; **Red Bank,** Gawsworth Ch; *Redbanks*, Kings Norton Lei 1638; **Red Barn Field,** Houghton le Spring Du; **Red Brink Close,** Dersingham Nf; **Red Croft,** Alvechurch Wo; **Red Earth,** Charlesworth Db, Ludworth Db, Buckminster Lei, Wymondham Lei; **Red Earth Hern,** Freethorpe Nf [OE *hyrne*, 'corner']; **Red Flatt,** Hope Db; **Redgap Riggs,** Elwick Hall Du; **Red Hill,** Clayworth Nt, Towcester Nth, Forest Hill with Shotover O, Tadmarton O, Bentley Wa; **Red Hill Field,** Abinger Sr; **Red Hill Mead,** Crowhurst Sr (*Redheld'* 1418) [OE *hielde*, 'slope']; **Redlands,** Welford Brk, Caldwell Db, Holwell Do, Feering Ess, Barnsley Gl, Stow on the Wold Gl, Newton Burgoland Lei; **Red Mead,** Mortimer Brk (*Redemede* 1224–5): 'land with red soil' [OE *rēad*].

Redlands, Idmiston W (*Rudlonde* 1518), 'strips on which reeds grew' [OE *hrēod, land*].

Redricks, Writtle Ess (*Retherwyke* c 1300), 'ox farm' [OE *hrȳther, wīc*].

Reed Fen, Little Thetford C; **Red Ground,** Cantley Nf; **Reed Meadows,** Bruen Stapleford Ch (*Le Reddemede* 1510); **Reed Moss,** Skelsmergh We (*Reddmosse* 1241): 'land on which reeds grew' [OE *hrēod*].

Reeve Shot, Steeple Morden C (*Le Reueaker* 13c); **Reeves Croft,** Thorley Hrt; **Reeves Field,** Great Sampford Ess; **Reeves Green,** Ware Hrt; **Reeves Ground,** Bagot Wa (*Revelond* 1545); **Reves Hay,** Crudwell W [OE *(ge)hæg*]: 'land assigned to the reeve of the manor' [OE *(ge)refa*]. The reeve or bailiff was the villein appointed (or often elected) to have general charge of the manorial husbandry. For a full account of the duties and privileges of the reeve see G. C. Homans, *English Villagers of the Thirteenth Century*, 296–307.

Reform, Ormside We, an isolated arbitrary name of the type applied to fields in Halstock Do (cf Reasonableness).

(The) Reins, Cornsay Du, Brough We, Newbiggin We, Stainmore We, Alvechurch Wo; **Long Rein,** Haslington Ch: '(land on) boundary' [ON *reinn*].

Remedy Close, Hillfield Do, a complimentary name for productive land.

Reservoir Close, Alderwasley Db; **Reservoir Meadow,** Shackerstone Lei: self-explanatory.

Revel Mead, Hampton Gay O, Horspath O: 'pleasure ground'.

Rhyme Acre, Northmoor O, possibly 'boundary strip' [OE *rima*, 'edge'].

Rich Dale, Boyleston Db; **Rich Field,** Great Waltham Ess; **Rich Flatt,** Bradford WRY; **Richland,** Standlake O; **Rich Leasow,** Smethcott Sa; **Rich Nook,** Edale Db: 'productive land'.

Rick Close, Ashreigney D, Flagg Db, Peckleton Lei; **Rick Field,** Brierley Hill St; **The Rickstead Close,** East Norton Lei; **Rick Yard,** Hartington Middle Quarter Db, Broughton Astley Lei; **Rick Yard Close,** Crich Db; **Rick Yard Mead,** Enbourne Brk: 'land containing a stack of corn or hay' [OE *hrycce*].

Riddance Meadow, Silchester Ha; **Riddens,** Witley Sr; **The Ridding,** Polesworth Wa (*Rudyng Stile Hull* 1387); **Ridding Meadow,** Sheldon Wa (*Olderiddinge* t.Hy 7); **(The) Riddings,** Haslington Ch, Whitegate Ch, Ashford Db, Chapel en le Frith Db (*Rydynges* 1330), Winster Db, Brockholes La, Cabus La, Cleveley La, Aston Wa (*The Ruddyng* 1461), Balsall Wa (*Ruddyng* 1540), Bentley Wa, Bransford Wo; **Riding,** Coventry Wa; **Riding Fields,** Beverley ERY; **Ridings,** Cookham Brk (*La Rydynges* 1389), Foleshill Wa: 'cleared land' [OE **ryding*].

Ridge Close, Artington Sr; **Ridge Field,** Hitchin Hrt (*Le Redge* 1460); **Rigg Meadow,** Woodplumpton La; **Riggs,** Thorngumbald ERY (*Le Rigge* 1339): 'ridged land', ie land formerly in strip cultivation, the well-defined ridged 'lands' being still observable often after centuries of being laid down to grass [OE *hrycg*, ON *hryggr*].

Ring, Out Rawcliffe La; **Ring Field,** Audlem Ch, Carleton La; **Ring Meadow,** Elkstone Gl: 'circular enclosures' or, possibly, 'land containing ancient stone circles' [OE *hring*, ON *hringr*]. (Cf Wainwright, *FN Amounderness*, 194).

Ringlands, Warter ERY (*Wrangland* 12c), 'twisted arable strips' [ON *vrangr*].

Rioth, Little Longstone Db (*Rie Earth* 1611), 'land on which rye was grown' [OE *rȳge*, *erð*].

River Acre, Kintbury Brk; **River Field,** Goldington Bd; **River Pasture,** Welford Brk; **River Slipe,** Whaddon C [ME *slipe*, 'strip']: 'land beside a river'.

Rix Acre, Foolow Db, 'land overgrown with rushes' [OE *risc*].

Road Close, Sherington Bk, Crich Db, Burrough on the Hill Lei, Bushby Lei, Laughton Lei, Nailstone Lei, Wardley R; **Road Field,** Matlock Bath Db, Kenley Sa; **Road Meadow,** Appleby Lei; **Road Piece,** Offcote & Underwood Db; **Road Slang,** Buerton Ch; **Roads,** Hognaston Db; **Roads Close,** Ashreigney D: 'land adjoining a road or roads' [OE *rād*].

Roast, Baguley Ch (*Rhuehurst* c 1300), 'rough hillock' [OE *rūh*, *hyrst*].

Robin, Blackawton D; **Robin Croft,** Derwent Db; **Robin Intake,** Charlesworth Db; **Robins Croft,** Gawsworth Ch; **Robins Mead,** Alton Pancras Do: names possibly alluding to the redbreast, though some may embody the personal name Robin or the surname Robins.

Robin Hood Bank, Edwinstowe Nt; *Robin Hood Buttes*, Farlam Cu 1598; **Robin Hood Close,** Newstead Nt; **Robin Hood Field,** Helsby Ch; **Robin Hoods Butts,** Cuddington Ch; **Robin Hoods Meadow,** Perlethorpe Nt: arbitrary names celebrating some association with Robin Hood; in view of this, the Butts are probably fields where archery was practised.

Rock Close, Great Hucklow Db; **Rocky Field,** Widecombe D: self-explanatory.

Rock Pit Field, Wincham Ch, Winnington Ch, Witton cum Twambrook Ch: 'field near or containing a salt mine', distinguished from a brine pit, from which the salt was extracted in solution.

Rockwells, North Mimms Hrt (*Rokedell* 1380), 'little valley haunted by rooks' [OE *hrōc, dell*].

Roddle, West Haddon Nth (*Redewellhull* 1260), 'hill above Redewell, ie the reedy spring' [OE *hrēod, wella, hyll*].

Rodmore, Lechlade Gl, 'marshland on which reeds grew' [OE *hrēod, mor*].

The Roe, Eckington Db (*The Wroe* 1609); **Roe Close,** Rampton Nt; **Roe Meadow,** Norton juxta Twycross Lei; **Rose Mead,** Netteswell Ess (*Wroesmad* 1408); **The Rows,** Higham Ferrers Nth (*Le Wro* 1313): 'nook of land' [ON *vrá*].

Rokefield, Dorking Sr, 'land on which rooks abounded'.

Roley Poley Bank, Didbrook Gl, a name light-heartedly descriptive of the gradient of the land.

Roman Field, Fyfield Ha, 'land containing Roman remains'. It is the site of a villa.

The Roman T, Wrockwardine Sa, alludes to the shape of the field—that of a capital T.

Rood Field, Audlem Ch; **Roodlings,** Dunchurch Wa (*Rodeland* c 1150); **Rood Piece,** East Dereham Nf: 'land having an area of a quarter of an acre' [OE *rōd*].

Rook Cliff, Barford Wa (*Rueclive* 14c), 'rough bank' [OE *rūh, clif*].

Rook Hill, Baunton Gl; **Great & Little Rooker,** White Colne Ess (*Le Rokho* 1390) [OE *hōh*, 'ridge']; **Rookery Meadows,** Ford Sa; **Rookery Wood,** Capesthorne Ch; **Rookley Field,** Tanworth Wa (*Rokeley* 1464): 'land on which rooks nested or fed'.

Rope Close, Wirksworth Db; **Rope Walk,** Bollington Ch, Bakewell Db, Castleton Db, Derby Db; **Rope Yard,** Bonsall Db: 'long, narrow pieces of land used as rope-walks', ie where rope was twisted.

Rose Close, Unstone Db; **Rose Hey,** Thwelwall Ch; **Rose Orchard** Hoff We; **Rose Pasture,** Alkmonton Db; **Rose Pightle,** Shiplake

O; **Rosey Bottom,** Windsor Brk; **Rosy Park,** Berrynarbor D: 'land on which wild roses grew'.

Rose Mead, Nettlewell Ess (*Wroesmad* 1408), 'grassland in a nook' [ON *vrá*].

Rotherfield Park, East Tisted Ha; **Rotherwick Mead,** Egham Sr (*Rutherwyk* 1336); **Rutherhook,** Cottesbrooke Nth: names alluding to cattle [OE *hrȳðer*].

Rotten Ing, Rishworth WRY; **Rotten Marsh,** Cantley Nf; **Rotten Meadow,** Spurstow Ch, Frolesworth Lei; **Rotton Hill,** Church Lawford Wa; **Rotton Lays,** Crowmarsh O; **Rotton Moor,** Curbridge O: derogatory names usually applied to soft, boggy land.

Rough, Bunbury Ch; **Rough Bottom,** Thorpe Thewles Du; **Rough Close,** North Wingfield Db, Whitwell Db, Barwell Lei, Lowesby Lei; **Rough Dene,** Houghton le Spring Du; **Rough Dumble,** Walton Db; **Rough Ground,** Enbourne Brk, Alton Pancras Do; **Rough Hams,** Ringwood Ha; **Rough Lands,** Shalbourne W; **Rough Leasow,** Minsterley Sa; **Rough Leigh,** Crook & Willington Du; **Rough Mead,** Cookham Brk; **Rough Meadow,** North Mimms Hrt (*Rowmedfeld* t.Ed 1), Newton Purcell O, Nuneaton Wa, Tanworth Wa; *Rough Nook*, Hylton Du 1750; **Rough Pasture,** Windsor Brk, Callow Db; **Rough Piddle,** Mortimer Brk; **Rough Piece,** Woodthorpe Db, Burton Lazars Lei, Walsgrave on Sowe Wa; **Ruff Hill,** Rencomb Gl: self-explanatory [OE *rūh*].

Round Acre, Ashleyhay Db; **Round Close,** Welford Brk, Barton C, Ilsington D, Callow Db, Therfield Hrt, Great Stretton Lei; **Round Coppice,** Alton Pancras Do; **Round Croft,** Finchingfield Ess, Stapleford Hrt (*Roundfelde* 1413); **Round Field,** Kintbury Brk, Sandbach Ch, Kings Langley Hrt, Sheepy Magna Lei, Adderley Sa, Berkwell Wa (*Roundruding* 1316); **Round Ham,** Bagendon Gl [OE *hamm*]; **Round Hey,** Thelwall Ch [OE (*ge*)*hæg*]; **Round Ing,** Sandal Magna WRY [ON *eng*]; **Round Mead,** Mortimer Brk, St Michaels Hrt (*Roundemede* t.Hy 6) Shenley Hrt; **Round Meadow,** East Allington D, Sandon Hrt, Catthorpe Lei; **Round Oak Piece,** Windsor Brk; **Round Piece,** Langley & Ruckley Sa; **Round Shaw,** Lamberhurst K [OE *sceaga*, 'copse']: 'land approximately circular in shape'.

(**The**) **Roundabout,** Chippenham C, Bradwall Ch, Buerton Ch, Buglawton Ch, Cheadle Ch, Church Lawton Ch, Lymm Ch, Moston Ch, Sandbach Ch, Smallwood Ch, Tabley Superior Ch, Wybunbury Ch, Charlesworth Db, Church Broughton Db, Harthill Db, Markheaton Db, Elvetham Ha, Romsey Ha, Bovingdon Hrt, Stanstead St Margarets Hrt, Ashby Folville Lei, Greenford Mx, Staines Mx, Mapledurham O, Newton Purcell O, Acton Burnell Sa, Cound Sa, Shepton Mallet So, Lacock W, Lee Marston Wa, Solihull Wa, Water Orton Wa, Hallow Wo; **Roundabout Copse,** Ewhurst Ha; **Roundabout Croft,** Elton Ch; **Roundabout Field,** Windsor Brk, Kinderton cum Hulme Ch, Mobberley Ch, Lamberhurst K; **Roundabout Search,** Hurstbourne Tarrant Ha [ME *assart*, 'clearing']; **Roundabout Warths,** Bredbury Ch [OE *waroð*, 'streamside meadow']; **Roundabouts,** Mortimer Brk, Chilworth Ha, St Stephens Hrt, Upton Lei, Aston Rowant O, Banbury O, Kiddington O, Oxford O, Burstow Sr, Little Bookham Sr, Bentley Wa: 'piece of land surrounded by streams, trees, or roads', or, occasionally, 'piece of land with an isolated clump of trees within its boundaries'.

Roundey, Albury Hrt; **Roundy,** Belstone D; **Roundy Field,** Berrynarbor D: 'round enclosure' [ME *rond*, OE *(ge)hæg*].

Rowborough, Abthorpe Nth (*Rouburgh* 1367) [OE *beorg*]; **Rowler,** Weedon Lois Nth (*Rowlow* 1593) [OE *hlāw*]: 'rough hill' [OE *rūh*].

Row Fields (Little & Great), Bampton O (*Rugheueld* 1239); **Rowham,** Braybrooke Nth (*Ruholm* c 1250) [ON *holmr*]; **Row Lees,** Horndon-on-the-Hill Ess (*Rowlese* 1555) [OE *lǣs*]; **Rowley,** Grimley Wo; **Row Mead,** Cobham Sr: 'rough arable or grassland' [OE *rūh*].

Row Nooking, Everton Nt (*Wroe* 1716); (**The**) **Rows,** Higham Ferrers Nth (*Le Nether Wro*, *Le Midel Wro*, *Over Wro* 15c): 'nook(s) of land' [ON *vrá*].

Royal Meadow, Brinnington Ch; **Roylance,** Toft Ch [OE *land*]; **Royle(s),** Acton Ch, Over Alderley Ch [OE *hyll*]: 'land on which rye was grown' [OE *rӯge*].

Rubbish Meadow, Acton Burnell Sa; **Rubbishing Shutt,** Bakewell Db: 'land on which refuse was tipped'.

Rubborough Meadow, Farnborough Wa (*Rouburgh* 1246), 'rough hill' [OE *rūh, beorg*].

Rudd Mead, Nursling Ha (*Hriod Eg* 10–11c); **Rudmead,** Burbage W (*Rodmed* 1264); **Rutland,** Martin W (*Rudlonde* 1518), possibly 'land on which reeds grew' [OE *hrēod*].

Rudding Field, Eakring Nt (*Riddyngstygh* 1355); **Ruddings,** Stillingfleet ERY (*Waltef Riding* 1219), Milburn We, Strickland Roger We: 'clearing(s)' [OE **ryding*]; the medieval form of the Stillingfleet name alludes to a man called Waltheof.

Rue Close, Aldbury Hrt (*Rewe Close* 1593), Market Bosworth Lei; **Rue Lane,** Edleston Ch (*Roo Lane* 1690): 'land on which rue grew'. Rue (*Ruta graveolens*) was cultivated for its (real or imagined) value as a disinfectant, being strewn liberally in courts of law to protect the judges and counsel from the germs carried by prisoners from unhealthy prisons. Its present pharmaceutical use, through its derivative rutin, is in the treatment of high blood pressure.

Rug Field, Moston Ch; **Rug Hay,** Broadwas Wo; **Rug Moors,** Longden Sa; **Rug Piece,** Chastleton O, Enstone O; **Rug Spinney,** Shipton under Wychwood O: 'land covered in large stones' [MnE dial. *rug*].

Ruins, Netherbury Do, refers to land with a particularly uneven surface, not unlike ruined buildings in appearance (cf B. Kerr, 'Dorset fields and their names', 233).

Rumbland, Chesterton C (*Rumelonde* 1228); **Rumstead,** Meesden Hrt (*Rumstedefeld* 1347), 'empty, unoccupied land' [OE *rūm*].

Rumps and Buttocks, Walworth Du, a fanciful name alluding to convex configurations.

Run Mead, Toller Pocorum Do, interpreted by B. Kerr ('Dorset fields and their names', 239) as 'meadow where assembly was held' [OE *rūn*, 'council'].

Runaway Field, Church Oakley Ha, probably alludes to steeply sloping land.

Rundown Field, Higher Whitley Ch, a derogatory name for worn-out land.

Running Furrow, Muston Lei, possibly 'arable land the soil of which lacks cohesion'.

Rush Close, Barlestone Lei, Bushby Lei, Forncett St Peter Nf, Eggborough WRY; **Rush Croft,** Wimbish Ess (*Rosshe Croft* t.Hy 8), Haldenby WRY; **Rush Greaves,** Melbourne Db (*Le Russhegreues* 1367) [OE *grǣfe*, 'thicket']; **Rush Mead,** Kintbury Brk, Mortimer Brk; **Rush Meadow,** Weston Hrt, Wheathampstead Hrt (*Russhemede* 1521); **Rush Nook,** Odstone Lei; **Rush Plat,** Malmesbury W; **Rush Plecks,** Bentley Wa [ME *plek*, 'small plot of ground']; **Rushey Close,** Piddington O; **Rushey Leaze,** Hungerford Brk [OE *lǣs*]; **Rushey Piddle,** Mortimer Brk; **Rushy Bottom,** Worksop Nt; **Rushy Close,** Kniveton Db, Donington Lei, Bleasby Nt, Bedworth Wa; **Rushy Field,** Poynton Ch, West Anstey D, Edale Db; **Rushy Leasow,** Dawley Magna Sa [OE *lǣs*]; **Rushy Mead,** Holwell Do; **Rushy Meadow,** Minsterley Sa, Britford W (*La Ruysche* 1323), Arrow Wa, Rowington Wa; **Rushy Orchard,** Beaford D; **Rushy Pasture,** Houghton le Spring Du; **Rushy Piece,** Sible Hedingham Ess (*Rusheia* 14c): 'land abounding in rushes' [OE *risc*]. A plentiful growth of rushes (*Juncus* spp) is evidence of badly drained land. Of little agricultural value, these plants were nevertheless put to various domestic uses as floor-coverings and as illuminants. They were plaited for use as chair seats and were occasionally used for thatching.

Russets, Chingford Ess (*Risset* 1222); **Rusletts,** Manningford Bruce W; **Russlett,** North Newnton W (*Riscslæd* 892): 'rushy land'; the Chingford name has the suffix *-ett*, signifying 'characterised by . . .'; the Wiltshire examples probably both contain the element *slæd*, '(damp) valley'.

Ruworth (Upper & Lower), Woodeaton O (*Ruyworþe* 1264), 'rye enclosure' [OE *rȳge, worð*].

Rye Acre, North Poorton Do, Stebbing Ess; **Rye Bank,** Norbury Ch; **Rye Close,** Alderwasley Db, Highcliffe Ha, Catthorpe Lei, Farnham Sr, Minety W, Studley Wa; **Rye Croat,** Great Hormead Hrt [OE *croft*]; **Rye Croft,** Butley Ch, Great Warford Ch, Rainow Ch, Abney Db, Alderwasley Db, Great Hucklow Db, Halstead Rural Ess, Highcliffe Ha, Sparsholt Ha, Appleby Lei (*Ryecroft* 15c), Farnham Sr, Limpsfield Sr (*Reyecroft* 1312),

Skelsmergh We, Eggborough WRY; **Rye Eddish,** Cholmondeston Ch; **Rye Eddish Field,** Sheldon Wa [OE *edisc*, 'enclosure']; **Rye Field,** Hylton Du, Kelvedon Ess (*Reyfeld* 1318), Hitchin Hrt (*Reyfurlong* 1381), Finchley Mx; **Rye Flatt,** Yeardsley cum Whaley Ch; **Rye Furlong,** Kintbury Brk, Mickleton Gl, Kirtlington O, Pyrton O (*Ruyfurlong* c 1280), Swerford O; **Ryfurlong,** Bourton O; **Rye Garth,** Over Staveley We; **Rye Ground,** Mortimer Brk; **Rye Hill,** Gawsworth Ch, Glen Parva Lei, West Haddon Nth (*Ryehul* 1200), Church Lawford Wa, Alvechurch Wo; **Rye Hill Mead,** Washington Du; **Rye Hulse,** Burland Ch [OE *hyll*]; **Ryeland,** Bourton O, Hinton St Mary Do, Sandford St Martin O; **Ryelands,** North Poorton Do, Hook Norton O; **Rye Leasow,** Church Pulverbatch Sa; **Rye Mead,** Grafton & Radcot O; **Rye Piece,** Boxford Brk; **Rye Plat,** Elvetham Ha [ME *plat*, 'small piece of ground']; **Rye Riddings,** North Elmsall WRY [OE **ryding*]; **Rye Roods,** Shackerstone Lei: 'land on which rye was grown' [OE *rȳge*].

Ryegrass, Rayne Ess; **Rye Grass Bit,** Alderwasley Db; **Rye Grass Close,** Alkmonton Db, Glenfield Lei; **Rye Grass Field,** Bunbury Ch, Peover Superior Ch, Hylton Du, Smethcott Sa; **Rye Grass Leasow,** Acton Burnell Sa: 'land on which common ryegrass grew'. This species (*Lolium perenne*) is a valuable pasture grass, and one of the first to be deliberately cultivated on sown meadows.

Rye Loaf, Blackwell Db, probably so called from its shape.

S

Saffran Bank, Sowerby WRY; **Saffron Beck,** Walkeringham Nt; **Saffron Butts,** Condover Sa; **Saffron Close,** Sall Nf, Denton O, Ewelme O; **Saffron Field,** Thaxted Ess; **Saffron Garden,** Horndon on the Hill Ess, Maiden Bradley W; **Saffron Garth,** Rawcliffe WRY; **Saffron Ground,** High Easter Ess (*Safforne Grounde* 1572), Little Hadham Hrt (*Le Saffron Garden* 1589); *Safrongardyn*, Widdington Ess 1467: 'land on which saffron was cultivated [ME *safron*]. The saffron crocus (*Crocus sativus*) is the species referred to, the culinary herb being prepared from the dried stigmas of this plant, which is not to be confused with the poisonous meadow saffron (*Colchicum autumnale*). The saffron crocus was introduced into England about the year 1340.

Sage Piece & Acre, Ewelme O, 'land on which sage was grown' [ME *sauge*]. Sage (*Salvia officinalis*) was brought to Britain by the Romans; it is still much used as a culinary herb.

Sainfoin Close, Aldbury Hrt, Darrington WRY, Skelbrooke WRY; **Sainfoin Hill,** Croxton Nf, Kirtlington O; **Sainfoin Piece,** Kintbury Brk; **Saintfoil Ground,** Enstone O; **Saintfoin Close,** Ault Hucknall Db, Cromford Db, Muston Lei; **Saintfoin Field,** Essendon Hrt; **Saintfoin Ground,** Newton Purcell O; **Old Saint Foin Ground,** Broadwell O; **Saint Foyne Field,** Hendon Mx; **Sanfoin Field,** Albury Hrt (*Cinquefoil Field* c 1840); **Sangfoil Field,** St Marthe's Sr: probably all allude to sainfoin, the leguminous plant, *Onobrychis viciifolia,* though the confusion with cinquefoil (*Potentilla* spp) may be significant. The value of this deep-rooting legume on thin soils in limestone areas was early realised by agricultural improvers (cf M. A. Havinden 'Agricultural progress in open-field Oxfordshire', AHR IX, ii, 73–83) [F *sainfoin*, 'healthy hay'].

St Catherine's Field, Little Wilbraham C, alludes to land formerly belonging to St Catharine's College, Cambridge.

St Giles Croft, Beverley ERY, *alias* **Gillycroft** (*Croftum Sancti Egidii* 1407, *Seint Gilicroft* 1413), alludes to land which formerly belonged to the Hospital of St Giles in Beverley.

St James Close, Dadlington Lei 1674, refers to glebe land pertaining to the church of St James.

St John & Half a St John, Stanton St John O (*Syngett* 1522); **St John Ground,** Burford O; **St John Leys,** Broadwell O; **St John's Bank,** Marbury cum Quoisley Ch; **St John's Close,** Enderby Lei; **St Johns Field,** Walkern Hrt (*Sanget*, *Sangetfeld* 1381); **St John's Ley,** Ashley C: of various origins, some of these names being allusions to the dedication of the local church, others to ownership by the Hospitallers of St John, but at least two seem to relate to the midsummer bonfires on St John's day (24 June), as the alternative early names *Synget*, *Sanget* ('burnt') confirm.

St Marys Croft, Earls Colne Ess; **St Mary's Hill,** Eckington Db: names referring to churches dedicated to the Blessed Virgin.

Sale, Hungerford Brk; **Old Sale,** Beaumont Chase R; **Upper Sale,** Market Bosworth Lei; **Sale Car Close,** Stanton Db [ON *kjarr*]; **Sale Field,** High Easter Ess (*Salfeld* 1280); *Sale Furlong*, Stathern Lei 16c; **Sale Meadow,** Alvechurch Wo; **Sales Hill,** Wheathampstead Hrt (*Salyswyk* 16c): a name discussed in PNNth 157, under Britain Sale, where the interpretation 'division of a wood, of which the underwood is cut down and sold' is rejected, and some doubt cast on a derivation from OE *salh*, 'willow'. The latter seems possible, however, in the Stanton name, in view of the association with Car, 'wet ground', a term which is specified by tree-names, eg Alder Car. *Sale* is obviously a name which must await explanation in the light of examples yet to be collected.

Salgasson, Godalming Sr (*Chalnegarston* 14c, *Charlgarston* t.Eliz 1), 'calf paddock' [OE *cealf*, *gærs-tūn*].

Sallad Royd, Horbury WRY, 'willow clearing' [OE **saliht* 'abounding in willows'; *rod*].

Sallow Bed, Burrough on the Hill Lei; **Sallow Close,** Aldbury Hrt, Flamstead Hrt, Buckminster Lei, Freethorpe Nf; **Sallow Hill,** Tadlow C; **Sallow Holt**, [illegible]erwasley Db; **Sallow Nooking,** Oxton Nt; **Sallow Pit Close,** Sall Nf; **Sallow Sale,** Beaumont Chase R; **Sallowtree Close,** Mansfield Nt; **Sallows,** Kentmere We; **Sally Beds,** Toddington Gl: 'land containing willow trees' [OE (Angl) *salh*]. The wood from these trees was (and still is) put to various craft uses.

Sallow Hill, Ely C (*Seuelowes* 1251), 'seven mounds' [OE *seofon*, *hlāw*].

Salt Acre, Bowdon Ch; **Salt Coat,** Larbreck La, Out Rawcliffe La; **Salthouses Field,** Bispham with Norbreck La; **Salt Mead,** Hook Do; **Salt Meadow,** Acton Grange Ch, Norton Ch; **Salt Pits Meadow,** West Langton Lei; **Salt Rand,** Freethorpe Nf; **Salt Rushes,** Northern Etchells Ch; **Salter Ridings,** Cheadle Ch; **Saltersford,** Middlewich Ch: names alluding to land from which salt was extracted or which was connected in some other way with this industry.

Saltpie, Sutton Downes Ch; **Saltpie Close,** Calverley WRY: 'land containing a lean-to shed' [MnE dial. *saltpie*].

Sandacre Meadow, Billesdon Lei; **Sand Beck,** Bisthorpe Nt [ON *bekkr*]; **Sand Bed(s),** Alderwasley Db, Tebay We, Altofts WRY; **Sand Close,** Baggrave Lei, Rawcliffe WRY; **Sand Crofts,** Great Maplestead Ess; **Sand Field,** Burland Ch, Elsfield O; **Sand Furlong,** Headington O; **Sand Holes,** Hallaton Lei; **Sand Lands,** Over Ch, Newton Solney Db, Milburn We; **Sandmoor,** Hinton St Mary Do; **Sand Park,** Ashreigney D, Belstone D; **Sand Piece Shot,** Carshalton Sr (*Sande* 1229); **Sand Pightle,** Goring O; **Sand Sho(a)rd,** Bratton W, Upton Scudamore W [OE *sceard*, 'gash']; **The Sands,** Enbourne Brk, Little Ness Sa; **Sands Furlong,** Aynho Nth; **Sandy Acres,** Boreham Ess (*Sandæcere* 1062); **Sandy Brae,** Elsdon Nb [ME *brae*, ON *brá*]; **Sandy Breck,** Dersingham Nf [OE *bræc*, 'thicket']; **Sandy Butts,** Bollington Ch (*Soundibootes* 1611); **Sandy Carrs,** Easington Du; **Sandy Close,** Greetham R, Chilmark W; **Sandy Earths,** Hayfield Db; **Sandy Flat,** Melbourne Db; **Sandy Furlong,** Ipsden O; **Sandy Hearns,** Harefield Mx [OE *hyrne*, 'corner']; **Sandy Hill,** Preston Bagot Wa; **Sandy Lane Pightle,** East Dereham Nf; **Sandy Lease,** Bray Brk [OE *lǣs*]; **Sandy Leys,** Knossington Lei; **Sandy Piece,** Boxford Brk, Alderwasley Db, Leafield O: 'land with sandy soil' [OE *sand*, *sandig*].

Sand Field, pre-enclosure name of one of the great fields in Welton ERY and Wadsworth WRY.

Sandal Common, Henham Ess (*Le Sandhelle* 13c); **Sandell's Copse,** Symondton Ha; **Sandle Inclosure,** Nether Alderley Ch; **Sandle Piece,** Maugersbury Gl: 'sand hill' [OE *sand*, *hyll*].

Sandhill Close, Coventry Wa; **Sandhill Common,** Holwell Do; **Sandhills,** Earls Colne Ess; **Sandhole,** Hurleston Ch, Barnacre La, Goosnargh La, Barwell Lei; **Sandhole Field,** Henbury Ch, Houghton le Spring Du; **Sandhole Meadow,** Alston La; **Sandhole Piece,** Out Rawcliffe La; **Sandpit Close,** Mickleover Db, Cossington Lei, Sall Nf (*Le Sondpit* 1332); **Sandpit Field,** Broughton La, Cold Norton St; **Sandpit Furlong,** Ashmore Do, Horspath O, Iffley O; **Sandpit Leasow,** Alvechurch Wo; **(The) Sandpits,** Shackerstone Lei, Grittleton W, Bushwood & Lapworth Wa: self-explanatory.

Sangfoil Field, St Martha's Sr, see Sainfoin Close.

Sart Field, Islip O, 'woodland cleared for cultivation' [OF *assart*].

Sattercross, Strickland Roger We; **Saturay,** Natland We: names alluding to shielings, or summer pastures, at (or with) a cross and a mound respectively [ON *sǽtr*, OI *cros*, ON *haugr*].

Saturday Piece, Monyash Db; **Saturdays,** Poole Ch: 'land for which service was rendered on Saturdays' [OE *Sæterndæg*].

Saunt (Little), Ullesthorpe Lei, probably 'sand' [OE *sand*].

Sawforth, Rastrick WRY, 'willow ford' [OE *salh, ford*].

Saw Pit Bank, Whettenhall Ch; **Saw Pit Close,** Hungerford Brk, Shirley Db, Wessington Db, Broughton Astley Lei, Tooley Park Lei, Bruern O; **Saw Pit Close & Field,** Windsor Brk; **Saw Pit Field,** Prestbury Ch, Green Fairfield Db, Lamberhurst K, Grimsargh La, Out Rawcliffe La, Alvechurch Wo; **Saw Pit Ground,** Mortimer Brk; **Saw Pit Hills,** Ellingham Nf; **Saw Pit Leasow,** Kenley Sa; **Saw Pit Mead,** Holwell Do: 'land near, or containing, a sawpit'. The longitudinal cutting of large pieces of timber was possible in the days before power-saws only by placing one of the wielders of the two-handed saw below ground level in the pit designed for the purpose.

Scale Close, Kirkby Lonsdale We; **Scale Meadow,** Newton La; **Scales,** Whittingham La, Crosby Ravensworth We, Kentmere We; **Scaley Hill,** Greyrigg We: 'land on which there was a hut' [ON *skali*].

School Broad, Bonsall Db, 'shovel's breadth—narrow piece of land' [ME *shovel-brade*].

School Croft, Witton cum Twambrook Ch; **School Field,** Norbury Ch, West Anstey D, Chinley Db, Dronfield Woodhouse Db; **Schoolham Close,** Cotgrave Nt (*Scholewong* 1585); **School House Field,** Bere Alston D; **School Leasow,** Baschurch Sa; **School Loont,** Weaverham cum Milton Ch [OE *land*]: 'land belonging to, or adjoining, a school' [OE *scōl*].

Scissors, North Stoneham Ha, alludes to the bifurcated shape of the field.

Scorch in 'Ell Hills, Norton Hrt (*Scotchin Hills* 1657), a derogatory name in its modern form, but apparently a development of an earlier name of uncertain meaning.

Scotch Banck, Great Longstone Db; **Scotch Danes,** Clothall Hrt (*Scotesdenfurlong* 1638); **Scotch Field,** Cranage Ch, Edmonton Mx (*Scottesgraf* 13c); **Scotch Groats,** Eastwick Hrt (*Scotch Croft* c 1840) [OE *croft*]; **Scotch Pightle,** South Mimms Mx: possibly all derived from the name of former owners, though the allusion may be to some tax payable on the land [ME *scot*].

Scotack Close, Killamarsh Db [OE *æcer*]; **Scot Field,** Eckington Db; **Scot Ground,** Naunton Gl; **Scotland,** Papworth St Agnes C, Darley Db, Kemble Gl, Burton Overy Lei, Hallaton Lei, Osbaston Lei, Evenley Nth (*Scotte Furlong* 1210), Tong WRY; **Scotland Close,** Hugglescote Lei; **Scotland Common,** Sandhurst Brk; **Scotland Farm,** Bourn C, Dry Drayton C, Odiham Ha; **Scotland Field,** Addington Sr; **Scotland Flatt,** Carsington Db; **Scotland Meadow,** Inkberrow Wo; **Scotland Nook,** Kirkby Lonsdale We; **Scotland Wood,** Maidwell Nth; **Scotlands,** Bishop's Waltham Ha, Malmesbury W, Skelsmergh We; **Scot Laughton,** Eckington Db [OE *lēactūn*, 'kitchen garden']; *Scotwra*, Levens We 1200 [ON *vrá*]: 'land subject to tax'; many of these are in fact boundary fields, which possibly accounts for the payment [ME *scot*].

The Scraggs, Taddington Db, 'rough ground' [MnE dial. *scrag*].

Scrape Bone, Malmesbury W, derogatory name for infertile land.

Scratch Croft, Therfield Hrt (*Scotteslane* 13c, *Scottescroft* 1455, *Scotch Croft* 1636): the early forms indicate that this is of the same type of name as Scotch Danes (qv); perhaps coincidentally a derogatory name seemed in order, whence the alteration to *Scratch*, a local name for the Devil.

Scratter, Little Longstone Db (*Scrattehard* 1570); **Scratters,** Hayton ERY (*Scrathou* 13c): 'devil-haunted mound' [ON *skratti*, *haugr*].

Scroggs, Norton Db, Barbon We, Crosby Ravensworth We, Tebay We: '(land covered with) brushwood' [ME *scrogge*].

Scutchen, Mobberley Ch, '(land infested with) couch grass'; *scutch* is one of the quite large number of different terms for *Agropyron repens*, this abundance of synonyms being doubtless a measure of the weed's unpopularity and evidence of its ubiquity.

Sea Field, Great Clacton Ess (*Seeland* 1459); **Sea Flatts,** Frodsham Lordship Ch (*Le See Flat* 1441): 'arable land near the sea' [OE *sǣ*].

Seaches, West Felton Sa, 'meadow-land beside a stream' [OE *sīc*].

Seal Tree Parrock, Docker We; **Seall Stubbs,** Lupton We; **Sill Carr,** Beetham We [ON *kjarr*]: 'land with or near willow trees' [ON *selja*].

Seavy Carr, Eastington ERY (*Seyve Closes* 1590); **Seavy Side,** Shap Rural We: 'land on which sedge grew' [ON *sef*].

Seckup, Warmingham Ch, 'flat-topped hill' [OE **set-copp*].

Second Close, Billesdon Lei, Houghton on the Hill Lei; **Second Croft,** Horsley Woodhouse Db, Shirland & Higham Db; **Second Field,** Castleton Db, Kirkby Mallory Lei: an unimaginative name of no significance except to indicate that the field lay between the first and the third of the series.

Secrets, Sandridge Hrt (*Sea Croft* 1689), ie Seed Croft, 'an area of sown grass' [OE *sǣd*].

Sedcups, Hornchurch Ess; **East & West Sedcups,** Cheshunt Hrt: see Seed Cobs.

Sedge Holme, East Drayton Nt; **Sedge Meadow,** Frodsham Lordship Ch; **Sedgy Spring,** Bakewell Db: 'land on which sedge grew' [OE *secg*]. The sedges, which are perennial grass-like herbs of the *Cyperaceae* family, generally grow in wet and swampy places.

The Seech, Middle Aston O, 'piece of meadow along a stream' [OE *sīc*].

Seed Acre, Crook We; **Seed Close,** Gaddesby Lei, Knossington Lei; **Great Seed Field,** Thorpe Thewles Du; **Seed Hill,** Nailstone Lei, Hillbeck We; **The Seeds,** Hallaton Lei, Slawston Lei; **Seeds Close,** Walton Lei: 'area of sown grass' [OE *sǣd*].

Seed Cobs, Little Canfield Ess; **Seedcotts,** King's Walden Hrt, Wheathampstead Hrt (*Settecoppe* 1305); **Seed Croft,** St Paul's Walden Hrt (*Sedcop Close*, t.Chas 1); **Seedcups,** Nazeing Ess (*Sedycomp* 1475); **Seed Gaps,** Matching Ess (*Setecuppe* 1288); **Seedskips,** High Easter (*Setecoppe* 1409); **Seeds Cup Plantation,**

Gilston Hrt: 'flat-topped hill'; this recurring name, with numerous variants in both early and modern forms, was first studied in detail by Reaney (PN Ess 589), who observes that the fields are all on high ground, 'generally on isolated rounded hills and the same is true of Sidcup K' [OE **set-copp*].

Segg Furlong, Flintham Nt (*Segfurlong* 13c); **Segholme,** Lockington Lei: 'water-meadow on which sedge grows' [ON *holmr*, OE *secg*].

Sein Acre, Minshull Vernon Ch; **Sein Buttes,** Eaton Ch; 'seven acres', 'seven butts'. *Seven* undergoes erosion in much the same way as *croft*, by loss of the middle consonant [OE *seofon*].

Seldom Seen, Patney W, indicates a remote piece of land.

Semilong, Kingsthorpe Nth (*Southmyllewong* 15c), 'enclosure by the south mill' [OE *suð*, *myln*, ON *vangr*].

Senacre, North Lopham Nf; **Senaker,** Norbury Db; **Senecas,** Horsley Woodhouse Db; **Senex Meadow,** Allostock Ch; **Senichar,** Marton Ch: 'seven acres' [OE *seofon*, *æcer*]. See also Sein Acre.

Senna Field, Froxfield Ha; **Senna Meadow,** Longford Db; **Senna Park,** Weston Underwood Db: if this name relates to a plant, it is not one of the genus *Cassia*, species of which provide pharmaceutical senna, since this is a tropical genus. It is doubtful whether shrubby bladder-senna occurs frequently or abundantly enough to be the source, either; this plant (*Colutea arborescens*) was once valued for the purgative property of its leaves.

Sentry Field, Widecombe D: almost certainly 'sanctuary field'; the land adjoins the churchyard.

Sepulchre, Newby We, possibly alluding to the discovery of human remains on the land.

Sermon Acre, Goring O, 'land (on the boundary) where the sermon was preached', alluding to the ceremonies of beating the bounds.

Setcopfelde, Misterton Nt t.Hy 6; **Setcup,** Sutton cum Duckmanton Db; **Settcock Hill,** Hayton Nt; *Settcoppe,* Wheathampstead Hrt 1222–46; **Settcutts,** Great Wymondley Hrt: 'flat-topped hill' [OE **set-copp*].

The Setts, Whittlesey Rural C, Coates Gl: 'parcels of meadow land'.

Seven Acre Meadow, Bradbourne Db, Stoughton Lei; **Seven Acre Piece,** Coleorton Lei; **(The) Seven Acres,** Macclesfield Forest Ch, Pott Shrigley Ch, Abbotsham D, Berrynarbor D, Blackawton D, East Anstey D, Bradley Db, Crich Db, Pentrich Db, Alton Pancras Do, Hillfield Do, Holwell Do, Newbottle Du, Barwell Lei, Desford Lei, Evington Lei, Hallaton Lei, Illston Lei, Knossington Lei, Norton Lei, Scraptoft Lei, Welham Lei, Spelsbury O, Bushwood Wa (*Sevenacres* 1421); **Seven Acres Furlong,** Sibford Ferris O: 'piece of land having an area of seven acres' or 'meadow, etc, adjoining such a piece of land' [OE *seofon, æcer*].

Seven Butts Furlong, Isley Walton Lei; **Seven Lands,** Temple Normanton Db, Buckminster Lei; **Seven Lands Close,** Elvaston Db; **Seven Leys,** Hoby Lei, Wykin Lei, Exhall Wa; **Seven Ridges,** Gilmorton Lei; **Seven Rood Field,** Castleton Db; **Seven Roods,** Repton Db: names transferred from open-field cultivation, utilising the units appropriate to the earlier arrangement.

Seven Day(s) Math, Rudheath Lordship Ch, Tetton Ch, Alkmonton Db; **Seven Day Work,** Marton Ch, Pott Shrigley Ch: see Eight Day Math.

Seven Greaves, Lockington Lei; **Seven Wells,** Naunton Gl: 'land containing seven copses/seven springs' [OE *seofon, grǣfe, wella*].

Seven Halves, Wilcot W, probably 'seven half-acre strips'.

Seven Measures Sowing, Barrow Ch, Mouldsworth Ch: names alluding to the area of the field by reference to the quantity of seed required.

Seven Men's Mowth, Turkden Gl; **Seven Mowers,** Adderbury O: 'meadow providing work for seven men'.

Seven Rakes, Matlock Bath Db: '(land containing) seven paths' [ME *rake*].

Seven Shilling Worth, Allostock Ch; **Seven Shillings,** Weston Ch: names referring to the rent paid for the land.

Seventeen Acre(s), Alton Pancras Do, Mappowder Do, Stoughton Lei; **Seventeen Acre Close,** Holyoak Lei; **Seventeen Acre Lings,** Walworth Du [ME *ling*, 'heather']: names alluding to the area of the named fields, or of land immediately adjacent.

Several, Chinnor O, Shalbourne W; **(The) Severals,** Fowlmere C, Saffron Walden Ess, Bibury Gl, Henbury Gl, Brent Pelham Hrt, Croxton Nf, East Dereham Nf, Hatfield WRY; **Big Severals,** Latton W; **Upper & Lower Severals,** Lilley Hrt: 'plot of privately owned land, especially enclosed pasture'. This is another term surviving from common-field agriculture [ME *several*].

Severn Barrass, Cressage Sa; **Severn Close,** Codnor & Loscoe Db; **Severn Leasow,** Cressage Sa; **Severn Meadow,** Cressage Sa: the Cressage names allude to the river Severn, *barrass* being a defensive river-bank; the Derbyshire example, however, probably embodies the surname Severn.

Sewage Field, Alphington D, self-explanatory.

Shady Close, Crich Db; **Shady Meadow,** Hinckley Lei: self-explanatory.

Shake Croft, Antrobus Ch; **Shaking Flat,** Longford Db: names probably alluding to unstable marshy ground.

Shamble Butts Furlong, Markeaton Db; **Shambles,** Wharton Ch; **Shambles Close,** Wigginton O; **Shan Field,** Standon Hrt (*Shamelfeld* 1342): 'land containing a stall for displaying goods, especially meat, for sale'. The sense 'shelf of land' is by no means impossible and may accord with the topography of some of the examples [OE *sceamol*].

Shameful, Bennington Hrt, a derogatory name for infertile land.

Sharbra, Preston Capes Nth (*Shardeborow* 1433), 'cloven hill' [OE *sceard*, 'cleft', *beorg*].

Sharp Croft, Stony Middleton Db; **Sharpland,** Hellidon Nth (*Scharplond* 1402), 'steep land' [OE *scearp*, *land*].

Sharrag Hill, Castle Ashby Nth; **Shear Hogs Close,** Illston Lei: the allusion is to *shearhogs*, ie lambs after their first shearing.

Shaw, Chapel en le Frith Db, Offerton Db, Whitwell We; **Shaw Close,** Wirksworth Db; **Shaw Croft,** Selston Nt; **Shaw Dale &**

Wood, Longsleddale We (*Le Schagh* 1332); **Shaw Field,** Poole Ch; **Shawfield Close,** Weston Underwood Db; **Shaw Hay,** Charlesworth Db [OE *haga*]; **Shaw Meadow,** Washington Du; **Shaw Pightle,** Burghfield Brk; **Shaw Shott,** Woodford Ch; **Shaws Wood,** Ripley Db: 'land near, or containing, a copse' [OE *sceaga*].

The Shawl, Ashford Bowdler Sa; **Shawl Mead,** East Pennard So; **Shawls,** Baltonsborough So: 'a narrow piece of land', a 'shovel' [OE *scofl*].

Shear and Go, Evershot Do, is said by B. Kerr ('Dorset fields and their names', 254) to be the 'watchword' of itinerant sheep shearers, who 'worked from dawn to dusk and insisted on dancing half the night'. This may indeed be so, but it is possible that the name may have been altered from Shearing Gore [OE *gāra*] under the influence of such a watchword. *Gore* is found elsewhere reduced to *Go* (cf Woman's Go, Compton Abdale Gl). But cf Clip and Go, Broad Town W (PNW 495).

Sheb Big Meadow, Abbotsham D, 'land on which sheep were kept' [OE *scēap*].

Shed Meadow, Brailsford Db, 'land containing a small building'.

Sheep Brecks, Hodsock Nt [OE *bræc*, 'scrub']; **Sheep Close,** Alderwasley Db, Neville Holt Lei; **Sheep Close Meadow,** Nailstone Lei; **Sheep Down,** Marlborough W (*Shepedoune* 1570); **Sheep Down Furlong,** Boxford Brk; **Sheep Field,** Ashreigney D, Hope Woodlands Db, Kendal We; **Sheep Haugh,** Leatherhead Sr (*Schephale* 1331) [OE *halh*, 'nook']; **Sheep Hill,** Buckland Gl; **Sheepland,** Great Henny Ess (*Sheppelond* t.Ed 3); **Sheeplands,** Limpsfield Sr (*Schepeland* 1312); **Sheep Lane,** Stanton St John O [ME *leyne*, 'tract of arable land']; **Sheep Lea,** Great Hucklow Db; **Sheep Lease,** Hinton St Mary Do; **Sheep Leaze,** Thornbury Gl, Highcliffe Ha; **Sheep Leys,** Aldbury Hrt, Babworth Nt [OE *lǣs*]; **Sheep Shaw,** Blakenhall Ch [OE *sceaga*]; **Sheep Sleight,** Broad Town W; **Sheepslight,** North Poorton Do [OE **slæget*, 'sheep pasture']; **Sheep Stile Field,** Lamberhurst K; **Sheep Thorn Thicket,** Carlton Curlieu Lei: 'land on which sheep were kept' [OE *scēap*].

Sheepcot(e) Field, Mortimer Brk, Crowton Ch, Dodcott cum Wilkesley Ch, Takeley Ess (*Shipcottfeild* 1491), St Peters Hrt (*Shipcotcroft* 1485), Goring O (*Shepecott Furlong* t.Hy 8); **Sheepcote Leasow,** Wattlesborough Sa; **Sheepcote Pightle,** Saffron Walden Ess; **Sheep Cubs,** Whittington Gl [MnE dial. *cub*, 'shed']; **Sheep Pen Close,** Barlestone Lei; **Sheep Pen Meadow,** Bentley Wa: 'shelters/small enclosures for sheep' [OE *cot*, *penn*].

Sheephouse Close, North Newnton W (*Shippingclose* 1570), 'land adjoining, or containing, a cowshed' [OE *scypen*].

Sheep Walk, Bridgemere Ch, Wirswall Ch; **Sheep Walk Field,** Effingham Sr: 'unfenced sheep pasture'.

Sheep Wash, Heage Db; **Sheepwash Meadow,** Elvetham Ha: 'land adjoining place where sheep were dipped' [OE *scēap-wæsce*].

Sheer Ash, Minster Lovell O; **Sheer Croft,** Limpley Stoke W: 'land on county or hundred, etc, boundary', such a boundary often being marked by a prominent tree [OE *scīr* or *scearu*].

Shelboard, Osmaston Db; **Shell Broad,** Chapel en le Frith Db (*Shoe Broad* 1633): 'narrow strip of land' [ME *shovel-brade*].

Shelf, Mudford So, Banstead Sr (*Le Shulf* 1369); **Shelf Ridge,** Wrington So; **The Shelves,** Southam Wa (*Sulf* 1206): 'ledge' [OE *scelf*].

Shepherdcroft, Willoughby on the Wolds Nt; **Shepherds Bush,** Dorking Sr; **Shepherds Close,** Cookham Brk, Godington O; **Shepherds Croft,** Normanton Db (*Schepeherdcroft* 1450); **Shepherds Meadow,** Windsor Brk, Abbotsham D: 'land occupied by a shepherd'. Land might be assigned to a shepherd in payment for his services; Shepherds Bush, however, was probably a place of shelter in the course of the shepherd's pastoral duties [OE *scēap-hirde*].

Shew Bread, Bramhall Ch, Wentnor Sa; **Shewbut,** Chinley Db: 'narrow strip of land' [ME *shovel-brade*].

Shifting Meadow, Little Longstone Db, 'land with unstable surface'.

Ship Close, South Leigh O (*Sheepehouse Close* 1619); **Ship Croat,** Thorley Hrt [OE *croft*]; **Ship Field,** Frodsham Ch (*Le Schepisfeld* 1321, *Le Schipfeld* 1349); **Shipley Flat,** Linby Nt (*Shepeleyfeld* 1540); **Ship Mead,** Long Sutton So; **Ship Walk,** Wimpole C: 'land on which sheep were kept' [OE *scēap*].

Shipcoat Yeat, Kendal We; **Upper & Lower Ship Coops;** Ewhurst Ha: names alluding to sheep houses [OE *scēap*, *cot*, *gēat*].

Shippen Field, Goosnargh La; **Shippen Hey,** Wesby with Plumpton La; **Shippen Park,** Billesdon Lei; **Shippon Croft,** Marton Ch; **Shippon Field,** Allostock Ch (*Sheponfeld* 1465), Hartford Ch; Great Marton La; **Shippon (Shippum) Meadow,** Lower Whitley Ch: 'land containing, or adjoining, a cowshed' [OE *scypen*].

Shire Field, Checkley cum Wrinehill Ch, Harpenden Hrt (*Schyrlonde* 1305); **Shire Mier,** Melbourne Db (*Schireland* 1482) [OE (*ge*)*mære*]; **Shireoaks Wood,** Kirkham ERY; **Shireowlers,** Derwent Db [OE *alor*]: 'land on county boundary' [OE *scīr*].

Shittleheugh, Elsdon Nb [OE *hōh*]; **Shuttle Close,** Long Sutton So: 'unstable land' [OE **scytel*].

Shivery Sham, Marston O, 'land with unsteady surface'.

Shoe Broad, Sale Ch, Ashford Db, Buxton Db, Green Fairfield Db (*Should Broad* 1682): 'narrow piece of land' [ME *shovelbrade*].

Shoot, Mellor Db, 'division of a common field' [OE *scēat*].

Shop Close, Lambrigg We; **Shop Field,** West Lulworth Do, Hylton Du, Mytholmroyd WRY; **Shop Leasow,** Church Pulverbatch Sa, Stony Stretton Sa; **Shop Leaze,** Rangeworthy Gl: 'land containing a shed' [OE *sceoppa*].

Short Acre, Eyam Db; **Short Acres,** Little Hucklow Db; **Short Brodds,** Great Longstone Db [OE *brǣdu*]; **Short Butt,** Monyash Db; **Short Close,** Hinton St Mary Do, Forncett St Peter Nf; **Short Croft,** Hatfield Broad Oak Ess (*Shortcroft* 1438); **Short Earths,** Dewsbury WRY; **Short Flatt,** Foolow Db; *Short Furlong*, Dersingham Nf 16c; **Short Lands,** Cerne Abbas Do, Holwell Do, Pattiswick Ess, Ash Sr (*Shortland* 1385), Skelsmergh We; **Short Pightle,** Yaxley Sf; **Short Shoot,** Great Eccleston

La; **Short Wong,** Rampton Nt [ON *vangr*]; **Shortworthy,** East Pennard So: self-explanatory [OE *sceort*].

Short Cake Field, Thorpe Bulmer Du, an allusion either to the shape or to the consistency of the soil of the field.

Shortfridayes, Glooston Lei 17c; **Short Saturday,** Newent Gl: names probably alluding to the days of the week when service was rendered.

Shot Ends, Eastoft WRY, 'irregular pieces of land at the edge of a furlong' [OE *scēat, ende*].

Shotland Field, Duffield Db (*Shortlandefelde* 1415), 'arable field with short strips' [OE *sceort, land, feld*].

Shouldbreads, Kings Norton Lei 1638; **Shoulder Broad,** Bamford Db: 'narrow piece of land' [ME *shovel-brade*].

Shoulder of Mutton, Sherington Bk, Windsor Brk, Alsager Ch, Edleston Ch, Henhull Ch, Mobberley Ch, Moston Ch, Offerton Ch, Plumley Ch, Ridley Ch, Sandbach Ch, Eyam Db, Whittington Db, Houghton le Spring Du, Hylton Du, Newbottle Du, Thorpe Bulmer Du, Alveston Gl, Barnsley Gl, South Cerney Gl, North Mimms Hrt, Bilsborrow La, Billesdon Lei, Illston Lei, Knossington Lei, Nailstone Lei, Shepshed Lei, Swannington Lei, Withcote Lei, Ealing Mx, Friern Barnet Mx, Hendon Mx, Ickenham Mx, Carlton Nt, Bix O, Cuddesdon O, Henley O, Wheatley O, Brierley Hill St, Hilperton W, Orcheston St Mary W, Aston Wa, Helsington We, Alvechurch Wo, Darrington WRY, Tong WRY; **Shoulder of Mutton Close,** Melbourne Db, Cadeby Lei, Coleorton Lei, Hugglescote Lei, Scraptoft Lei; **Shoulder of Mutton Field,** Nantwich Ch; **Shoulder of Mutton Grove,** Woodchester Gl; **Shoulder of Mutton Piece,** Cookham Brk, Blaby Lei; **Shoulder Mutton Field,** Lymm Ch, Thorpe Thewles Du; **Shoulder Mutton Ground,** Tetsworth O: 'land shaped like a shoulder of mutton'. See also Leg of Mutton.

The Shoule Land, Horspath O; **The Shoules,** Hook Norton O; **Shouls,** Wroxton O; **(The) Shovel,** Widecombe D, Wykin Lei; **Shovel Acre,** Uckington Gl (*Souelakere* 1248); **Shuflands Field,** Hursley Ha: 'land shaped like a shovel' [OE *scofl*].

Shovel Broad Furlong, Southwell Nt (*Shovelbordes* 17c); **Shovel Broads,** Treswell Nt, Gomersal WRY: 'narrow piece of land, the breadth of a shovel' [ME *shovel brade*]. See also School Broad, Shelboard, Shew Bread, Shoe Broad, Sill Bread.

Showell, Staverton Nth (*Le Schouele* 1320), 'shovel', alluding either to shape or to narrowness [OE *scofl*].

Shrog (Little), Altofts WRY; **Shrog(g)s,** Hope Db, Carleton La, Hollet & Forton La, Medlar La, Nateby La: 'brushwood' [ME *shrogge*].

Shurrocks, Buckland Hrt, '(land reserved for) shearhogs'. See Sharrag Hill.

Shut Flatt, Drayton in Hales Sa; **Shut Furlong Meadow,** Stirchley Sa; **Great Shutes,** Broughton La; **Shutt Close,** Owston WRY; **Shutt Croft,** Castle Bromwich Wa (*Shutecroft* 1371), **Shutts,** Derwent Db: names alluding to the shot or block of strips or selions constituting the main division of the great field under the open-field system of agriculture [OE *scēat*].

Siberia Nursery, Darley Db, alluding to the remoteness of the land (in this instance, on the eastern edge of the parish).

Sich Orchard, Leigh Wo; **Siche Close,** Chelmorton Db: 'meadow land beside a stream'. See also Seaches, The Seech, Sick, The Sitch, Sixch, Sutch (Little), Syke Close [OE *sīc*].

Sick, Flintham Nt, Hucknall under Huthwaite Nt; **Sick Close,** Southwell Nt, Warsop Nt; **Sick Hollow,** Hockerton Nt: see Sich Orchard.

Side of the Hill, Goadby Lei, Norton Juxta Twycross Lei: self-explanatory.

(The) Side Land(s), Naunton Gl, Charlbury O, Kiddington O, North Wootton So, Wellow So; **Great & Little Sideland,** Milton under Wychwood O; **Side Land Ground,** Newbury Brk, Bremhall W; **Sidelay Furlong,** Wolford Wa (*Sydlyngges* 1347); **Sidelings,** Beer D; **The Sidelong,** Hope Mansel He; **Sidelong Meadow,** Feckenham Wo: 'land alongside (another piece of land or a stream)' [OE **sīdling*].

Sign Board Piece, Inkpen Brk; **Sign Post Close,** Welham Lei; **Sign Post Field,** Peover Superior Ch: 'land near a sign post'. Cf Finger Post Close.

Signal Hill, Babraham C, self-explanatory.

Sike Close, Holme Pierrepont Nt: see Sich Orchard.

Sike Field, pre-enclosure great field name in Harby Lei and Foston NRY.

Silage Pit Field, East Allington D, 'land on which green fodder is specially stored for winter forage'. In the silo, or silage pit, young grass and other green crops are compressed and sprayed with a sugar solution. The process has been widely used only since the end of the nineteenth century.

Silence, Great Gaddesden Hrt, probably identical with *Selewyns-lond,* recorded in 1432 and embodying the name of a medieval holder of the land.

Silk Mill Meadow, Hesland Db, 'land adjoining a silk factory'.

Sill Bread, Beetham Wc, probably 'narrow piece of land' [ME *shovel-brade*].

Silver Close, Kintbury Brk; **Silver Croft,** Barbon We; **Silver Field,** Mooresbarrow Ch, Derwent Db, Sowerby WRY; **Silver Hill,** Walworth Du; **Silver Streak,** Eyam Db: names of uncertain reference a[illegible] meaning. Some may allude to wild plants. Others may refe[illegible] the finding of silver coins; it is known that this happene[illegible] on the land in Sowerby.

Silver Tree Wong, Bilsthorpe Nt, probably alludes to a birch tree in a prominent position.

Sim Butts, Elton Ch, 'seven detached ends of land' [ME *butte*].

Sin Acre, Mobberley Ch, Marden He: 'seven acres of land'.

(The) Sitch, Clifton & Compton Db, Hathersage Db, Great Longstone Db, Broughton Astley Lei; **Sitch Close,** Barrow on Trent Db, Broughton Astley Lei; **Sitch Field,** Hough Ch, Yeard-sley Ch, Drayton in Hales Sa; **Sitch Meadow,** Idridgehay Db; **Six,** Pinxton Db: see Sich Orchard.

Six Acre Close, Elwick Hall Du; **Six Acre Crate,** Andover Ha [OE *croft*]; **Six Acre Mead,** Hermitage Do; **Six Acre Meadow,** Great Stretton Lei; **Six Acre Piece,** Offcote & Underwood Db; **Six Acre Reeding,** Long Sutton Ha [OE **ryding*]; **Six Acres,** Pott Shrigley Ch, Abbotsham D, East Anstey D, Alkmonton Db, Bradley Db, Alton Pancras Do, Fifehead Neville Do, Hermitage Do, Hillfield Do, Holwell Do, Appleby Lei, Billesdon Lei, Hinckley Lei, Illston Lei, Laughton Lei, Willoughby Waterless Lei, Alderbury Sa, Westbury Sa, Corley Wa (*Sexacres* 1411): 'piece of land having an area of six acres, or adjoining such a piece of land' [OE *sex*, *æcer*].

Six Butts, Walgherton Ch, see Seven Butts.

Six Day(s) Math, Barrow Ch, Edleston Ch, Minshull Vernon Ch, Habberley Sa, Langley & Ruckley Sa; **Six Day(s) Work,** Mooresbarrow Ch, Siddington Ch, Alderwasley Db, Hope Db, Shirley Db, Solihull Wa: see Day Math, Day Work.

Six Lands, Brough Db, Castleton Db, Osmaston Db; **Six Leys,** Slawston Lei; **Six Lunds,** Greenhalgh La [OE *land*]; **Six Pightles,** Checkendon O: 'enclosed land consolidating six smaller units'.

Six Measures Sowing, Helsby Lei, alluding to the extent of the land by reference to the amount of seed required.

Six Men's Mead, Spelsbury O, 'grassland requiring six men to mow it'.

Sixch, Scarcliffe Db, see Sich Orchard [OE *sīc*].

Le Sixpeniwurthe of Land, Lach Dennis Ch 1548; **Sixpenny Close,** Tiddington with Albury O; **Sixpenny Ham,** Shifford O; **Sixpenny Mead,** Spelsbury O: 'land valued at sixpence'. If this is the purchase price, the name is likely to be derogatory, but it might be the annual rent.

(The) Sixteen Acres, Beer D, Hook Do, Burton Lazars Lei, Eastwell Lei, Houghton on the Hill Lei, Laughton Lei, North Witham L: see Six Acres.

Sixteen Day Math, Clotton Hoofield Ch; **Sixteen Days Work,** Solihull Wa: see Seven Day Math.

Sixteen Pound Meadow, Clifton & Compton Db, alludes to value or rent.

Sixty-foot Field, Steeple Aston O: 'land measuring sixty feet across'.

Skarewits, Alfold Sr, associated in some way with Thomas Skyrewyt, named in a document of 1332.

Skinny Flint, Bootle Cu, a derogatory name for ungenerous land.

Skirt, Bradley Db, '(land on) a boundary'.

Le Skouilbrad, Lowther We 1317, see Shovel Broad Furlong [ME *shovel-brade*].

Slack Bank Plantation, Coleorton Lei: 'copse beside heap of small coal' [ME *slak*].

Slack Close Head, Hope Woodlands Db; **Slack Field,** Crowley Ch, Hope Db, Goosnargh La; **Slack Ing,** Casterton We; **Slack Meadow,** Aston La, Broughton La, Woodplumpton La; **Slack Moor,** Westby La: 'land in a valley' [ON *slakki*].

Slad Piece, Hope Mansel He, Inkberrow Wo; **(The) Slade,** Hatherton Ch, Abney Db, Winstone Gl, Great Bowden Lei, Snarestone Lei, Sutton Bonington Nt, Ditcheat So; **Slade Acre,** Batcombe So; **Slade Bottom,** Darmerham W (*Sladisheued* c 945, *La Slade* 1518); **Slade Close,** Tysoe Wa (*Le Slade* 13c) Ashwell R; **The Slade Field,** South Weston O; **Slade Furlong,** Stoke Lyne O; **Slade Hill,** Belstone D; **Slade Meadow,** Stretton Parva Lei, Wykin Lei; **Slade Piece,** Leebotwood Sa; **Slady Meadow,** Carlton Curlieu Lei: 'land in a (marshy) valley' [OE *slæd*].

(The) Slang, Shavington cum Gresty Ch, Walgherton Ch, Brough & Shatton Db, Castleton Db, Codnor & Loscoe Db, Great Stretton Lei, Upton Lei, Bentley Wa, Polesworth Wa; **Top & Bottom Slang,** Dadlington Lei; **Slang Meadow,** Buglawton Ch, Leebotwood Sa: 'small, narrow (sinuous) strip of ground' [ME *slang*].

Slate Hill, Groby Lei; **Slate Lands,** Bamford Db; **Slate Meadow,** Alderwasley Db; **Slate Nick,** Belper Db; **Slate Pit Field,** Chinley Db; **Slate Pit Furlong,** Swerford O; **Slate Quar,** Aldsworth Gl: 'land from which slate or similar stone was quarried'.

Slaughter, Oxenhope WRY; **Slaughter House Field,** Little Warley Ess (*Slougwatere* 1485, *Slowatre* 1488); **Slaughter Moor,** Buerton Ch: 'land on or near which a sloe tree grew' [OE *slāh, trēow*]. It is worth remarking the extreme length which popular etymology has taken the Little Warley name.

The Slay, Tidcombe W; **Slay Down,** Enford W (*La Slee* 1212); **Slay Furlong,** Pyrton O; **Slay Shaw,** Swyncombe O; **The Sleagh,** Freefolk Ha; **Upper, Middle & Lower Sleigh,** Cuddesdon O: 'a slope; a lane cut through whin or broom cover to admit a vehicle to receive the cuttings' [OE **slēa*].

Sleates, Selston Nt; **Sleights,** South Cave ERY: 'smooth, level fields' [ON *sléttа*].

Sleepy Field, Cuddington Sr, a derogatory name for a field which is a long time coming into activity.

The Sleight, Coates Gl, Horton Gl; **Sleights,** Buckhorn Weston Do, Wellow So: 'sheep pasture' [OE **slæget*].

The Slenge or **Slinge,** Headington O; **(The) Sling,** Southwick W, Kingsbury Wa (*Slynge* 1545), Packwood Wa, Solihull Wa; **Sling Meadow,** Oxford O, Leigh Wo: 'small, narrow strip of land' [ME *sling*].

Slight Marsh, Ryhill ERY (*Sleight Marsh* 1583), 'boggy land in level terrain' [ON *slétta*].

Slip, Newbury Brk; **(The) Slipe,** Aldenham Hrt, Chinnor O; **Slipes,** Steeple Morden C: 'small strip of land' [ME *slīpe*].

Slither, Steep Ha, 'slippery place'. The land is, in fact, on a very steep slope.

Slobeards, Stoneleigh Wa, 'plantations of sloe trees' [OE *slāh, bedd*].

Sloe Croft, Henley O; **Sloe Land Field,** North Elmsall WRY; **Sloethorn Field,** Hunsworth WRY; **Slow Field,** Toppesfield Ess; **Slow Hill,** Great Gaddesden Hrt: 'land near, or containing, sloe trees'. The sloe or blackthorn (*Prunus spinosa*) is useful as a hedging shrub, by reason of its forbidding spines [OE *slāh*].

Slough, Winkfield W (*Le Sloo* 1432); **Slough Close,** Breaston Db; **Slough Corner,** North Wootton So; **Slough Field,** Hatfield Broad

Oak Ess (*Sloefeld* 1420), Standon Hrt (*Slofeld* 1342); **Slough Meadow,** Thundridge Hrt (*Slou* 1294): 'mire' [OE *slōh*].

Slovens Acre, Minchinhampton Gl; **Slovens Hill,** Quenington Gl: probably a derogatory name.

Small Beer Field, Lambourn Brk [OE *bere*]; **Small Close,** Enderby Lei; **Small Combe,** Batcombe So; **Small Ground,** Boxford Brk; **Small Leys,** Stokeham Nt; **Small Meade,** Cookham Brk (*Smalmed* 1471); **Small Park,** Billesdon Lei; **Small Piece,** Frisby Lei; **Small Stitch,** Ilsington D [OE *sticce*, 'strip of land']: self-explanatory.

Small Gains, Kintbury Brk, Lambourn Brk, Steeple Morden C, Albury Hrt, Little Hadham Hrt, Shephall Hrt, Watton at Stone Hrt, Berwick St John W, Corsham W, Donhead St Mary W, Inglesham W, Marlborough W, Mildenhall W, Pewsham W, Whiteparish W, Gatcombe Wt; **Small Gains Furlong,** Chadlington O; **Small Games,** Much Hadham Hrt (*Small Gains Pasture* 1742): ruefully derogatory name for unproductive land. Cf Small Profit.

Small Glass Furlong, Desborough Nth (*Smalgras* c 1320), 'land on which thin grass grew' [OE *smæl, gærs*].

Small Hopes, Furneux Pelham Hrt, possibly 'small enclosed valley(s)', though the derogatory implication of the present form may be more than coincidental [OE *smæl, hop*].

Small Profit, Beer D, see Small Gains. Cf Little Profit.

Small Thorn, Cotton Ch; **Small Thorns,** Aston juxta Mondrum Ch (*Le Smalethornfeld* 14c), Cholmondeston Ch, Bourton on the Hill Gl; **Small Wergs,** Churchill O: 'land on which slender trees grew'. *Wergs* is a local term for willows.

Smear Hill, Farmington Gl (*Smyrehill* 1621); **Smear Lands,** North Elmsall WRY; **Smear Pots,** Itchen Abbas Ha: 'fat land' implying either richness of soil, or that the grass produced good butter; a further possibility, connected in a vague way with the other interpretations, is that it alludes to land so productive that the farmer can expect to live on butter [OE *smeoru*].

Smeeth, Newton C (*Le Smeth, Le Smith* 1395); **Smeeth Field,** Beechamwell Nf (*Smethefeld* 1218); **Smeeth Hay,** Dawley Sa

[OE *(ge)hæg*]; **Smeeth Plantation,** Beechamwell Nf; **Smith Mead,** Standlake O; **Smith Meadow,** Welton Nth (*Smethemede* 1409): 'smooth land' [OE *smēðe*].

Smithy Close, Cossington Lei; **Smithy Field,** Chinley Db; **Smithy Mead,** Walkern Hrt: 'land containing, or adjoining, a forge' [OE *smiððe*].

Smoak Acre, Ringwood Ha; **Smoak Lands,** Martyr Worthy Ha; **Smoake Acres,** Banbury O; *Smocaker*, Hilmarton W c 1220; **Smock Acre,** Clifton Gl, Charlbury O (*Smokacre* 1272), Crowmarsh O, Codford W (*Smoake Acre* 1632), Upton Scudamore W; **Smock Close,** Pentrich Db, Blaston St Michael Lei, Frolesworth Lei, Welham Lei; **Smock Furlong,** Chippenham W, Highworth W; **Smock Hedges,** Hallaton Lei; **Smock Hill,** Pyrton O; **Smock Land,** Limpley Stoke W; **Smock Meadow,** Aston Flamville Lei; *La Smokacre*, Broad Chalke W 1276; **Smoke Acre,** Daglingworth Gl, South Cerney Gl, Oxford O, Bradford on Avon W, Great Bedwyn W; **Smoke Furlong,** Broadwell Gl; **Smoke Ground,** Langley Burrell W; **Smoke Hams,** Exton Ha, Henstridge So [OE *hamm*]; **Smoke Letches,** Washington Du [ME *leche*, 'boggy stream']: 'land on which the rendering of tithewood was replaced by the payment of money'.

Smoothing Iron Field, Timperley Ch, alludes to the triangular shape and flatness of the land.

Smyrrell Meadow, Lechlade Gl (*Smerehilham* 1448), 'grass enclosure on Butter Hill' [OE *smeoru*, *hyll*, *hamm*].

Snagholes, Chipstead Sr, 'snake hollows' [OE *snaca*, *hol*].

Snagtails, Great Burstead Ess (*Snaketeilleslond* 1229), 'snake tails', possibly alluding to the shape of the field [OE *snaca*, *tægl*].

Snailcroft, Great Maplestead Ess (*Snelmedwe* 1489); **Snail Hays,** Lower Whitley Ch; **Snail House Meadow,** Cold Norton St; **Snailscroft,** Wardington O; **Snailsome,** Hursley Ha [OE *hamm*]: 'land on which snails abounded' [OE *snægl*].

Snake Field, Childs Ercall Sa; **Snake Land Furlong,** Hinton Martell Do; **Snakes Croft,** Chelsham Sr; **Snakes Field,** Felsted Ess (*Snakepot* 1367); **Snakes Horn,** Seale Sr; **Snakes Meadow,** Cantley Nf; **Snakes Pightle,** Rotherfield Greys O; **Snakes Tail,**

Henbury Gl: names alluding to snakes in various ways [OE *snaca*] Most probably indicate the presence of serpents, but Snakes Tail refers to a field of sinuous shape. Snakes Croft may be an altered form of *Snapes Croft* in a document of 1568, but other forms are lacking to confirm this identification.

Snap Dragon Spring, Bloxham O, refers to the yellow toadflax, *Linaria vulgaris.*

Snape, Church Hulme Ch; **Snape Close,** Southwell Nt; **Snape Field,** Poulton La, Bilsthorpe Nt; **Snape Meadow,** Odd Rode Ch; **Snapes,** Toller Porcorum Do, Ellerton ERY (*Northsnapp* 1252); **Snapes End,** Hassingham Nf: 'marshy land' [OE **snæp*].

Sneddle Carr, Little Marton La [ON *kjarr*]; **Sniddle Field,** Lytham La: 'land covered in coarse grass or rushes' [MnE dial. *sneddle*].

Snipe Close (Great & Little), Newton Burgoland Lei, alluding to the presence of the common snipe (*Capella gallinago*), a bird of the marshes and damp meadows.

Snout Close, Ely C; **Snout Fen,** Willingham C: 'projecting piece of land', this term usually being applied to dry land on the edge of fens [ME *snōte*].

Snow Ball Hill, Bix O; **Snow Down,** Priors Dean Ha; **Snow Hill,** Fifield O; **Snowtons,** Ballingdon Ess (*Snoudune* 13c): 'hills often covered with snow (in winter)' [OE *snāw*].

Sodom, Holwell Do, Holbeck WRY; **Sodom Field,** Brampton Db: emphatically derogatory name for unproductive land (see Genesis 19).

Sogs, Whitchurch Canonicorum Do; **Soggy Ground,** Bettiscombe Do: 'water-logged land'.

Soldiers Close, Hermitage Do, probably a place of enlistment.

Soon Field, Higher Whitley Ch; **Soond Field,** Plumley Ch; **Soond Hill Field,** Marton Ch; **Soonds,** High Legh Ch: 'sandy field', showing the local phonetic change which similarly gives 'loon' or 'loond' for *land* [OE *sand*].

Sops, Gillingham Do, 'boggy land'.

Sorrel Croft, Bradwell Ch; **Sorrel Dale, (Upper, Middle, Nether),** Coston Lei; **Sorrel Field,** Farnborough Ha; **Sorrel Ground,** Highcliffe Ha: 'land infested with sorrel'. Common sorrel (*Rumex acetosa*) is an abundant weed in most parts of Britain [ME *sorele*].

Sorrow Close, Whitwell Db, derogatory name for a disappointing field.

Sough Close, Blackwell Db; **Sough Garden,** Cossington Lei; **Sough Piece,** Brailsford Db: 'swampy land' [ME *sogh*].

Sought, Churcham Gl, probably alludes to a secluded field.

Sound Heath, Millington Ch, 'sandy waste land'; see also Soon Field [OE *sand, hǣð*].

Sour Acre, Broughton La; **Sour Acres,** Spelsbury O; **Sour Butts,** Ashover Db, Skelsmergh We; **Sour Close,** Barrow on Trent Db, Weston Hrt (*Sower Land* 1597), Old Hutton We; **Sour Croft,** Claughton La; **Sour Dale,** Pownall Fee Ch; **Sourdown,** Overton Ha [OE *dūn*]; **Sour Ends,** Westby La; **Sour Field,** Higher Whitley Ch, Minshull Vernon Ch, Nether Peover Ch, Stublach Ch, Lilley Hrt, Claughton La, Inskip La; **Sour Ing,** Featherstone WRY, Harshead WRY, Wyke WRY [ON *eng*]; **Sour Lands,** Great Hucklow Db; **Sour Leasow,** Stirchley Sa; **Sourley Row,** Nutley Ha; **Sourmead,** Weston Birt Gl, Pyrton O; **Sour Meadow,** Anderton Ch, Marton Ch, Duffield Db, Barnacre La, Whittingham La; **Sour Moor,** Withington Gl; **Sour Mounts,** Pyrton O; **Sour Patch,** Rockhampton Gl; **Sour Ranglet,** Broughton La [OE *wrang*, ON *vrangr*, 'crooked']: 'land with coarse, worked-out, or acid soil' [OE *sūr*].

Sour Ale & Sweet Ale, Cuxham with Easington O, possibly with reference to differing qualities of barley produced in adjacent pieces of land.

Southall, Stirchley Sa [OE *halh*, 'nook']; **South Close,** Boxford Brk, Abbotsham D, Newbottle Du, Norton juxta Twycross Lei; **South Croft,** Welford Brk, Egham Sr (*Southecroft* 1333); **South East Close,** Cossington Lei; **South End Close,** Litlington C; **South Field,** Butley Ch, Holwell Do, Newbottle Du, Washington Du, Preston ERY, Bovingdon Hrt, Broxbourne Hrt, Wigginton Hrt, Burton Overy Lei, Haltwhistle Nb, Laxton Nt, Walkeringham

Nt (*Le South Felde* c 1300), Chaldon Sr (*Le Sudfeld* 1350), Tandridge Sr, Adlingfleet WRY; **South Field Meadow,** Yaxley Sf; **South Furlong,** Holwell Do, Dersingham Nf 1560; **South Hay,** Fifehead Magdalen Do; **South Ings,** Everingham ERY (*Southenge* 1338) [ON *eng*]; **South Intack,** Heworth Du; **Southland,** Tandridge Sr (*Sowthelondes* 1523); **South Lands,** Leigh Sr (*Southlonde* 1516); **South Mead,** Farnham Sr (*Suthmed* t.Hy 7); **South Moor,** Whitley WRY; **Southover,** Baltonsborough So; **South Park,** Abbotsham D [ME *park*]; **South Side,** Berrynarbor D, **Great South West Field,** Long Critchell Do: 'land on the south (or SE or SW) of the parish or of another piece of land' [OE *sūð*].

South America, Helsington We, **South Carolina,** Cromford Db: transferred names for remote pieces of land.

South Field, pre-enclosure great field name in: Houghton Regis Bd, Southill Bd, Stoke Bk, Bockhampton Brk, Coleshill Brk, Boxworth C, Chippenham C, Wilburton C, Glapwell Db, Nyland Do, Langton Du, Long Newton Du, Summerhouse Du, Wolviston Du, Cherrington Gl, East Leach Gl, Tresham Gl, Yanworth Gl, Andover Ha, Butlington Ha, Enham Ha, Overton Hu, Claxby L, Haburgh L, Stainton L, Stubton L, Great Bowden Lei, Freeby Lei, Melton Mowbray Lei, Walton & Kimcote Lei, Kirton Nt, Brackley Nth, Culworth Nth, Drayton Nth, Fawsley Nth, Radstone Nth, Bensington O, Bicester O, Milcombe O, Tackley O, Oakham R, Aldbourne W, Ebbesborne Wake W, Hilperton W, Stanton Fitzwarren W, Compton Wa, Wroxall Wt.

South Sea, Lydiard Tregoze W, a fanciful name for a remote field. There may also be a suggestion that the land is a doubtful investment, possibly alluding to the 'South Sea Bubble', an unprecedented bout of speculation centred on the South Sea Company in 1720.

Sow Briggs, Shackerstone Lei; **Sowbrook,** Daventry Nth (*Suthbroc* 1255); **Sow Close,** Forest Hill with Shotover O; **Sow Croft,** Abbots Langley Hrt (*Sowe Croft* 1551); **Sowditch Thicket,** Harleston Nth (*Suȝdic* c 1312); **Sow Field,** Widdington Ess (*Le Southfeild* 1529), Meesden Hrt (*Le Suthfeld* 1347); **Sow Leasow,** Kenley Sa; **Sow Moor,** Pytchley Nth (*Suthemor* 1461): names of various origins and meanings. As there is uncertainity with some, particularly of course with those lacking in early forms, all examples of *Sow* names have been given together. Many are 'land in the south' [OE *sūð*] (eg Sowbrook, Sow Field and Sow Moor cited here); at least one example is 'boggy land'—Sowditch Thicket, the fourteenth-century form of which, *Suȝdic*, indicates a derivation from ME *sogh*. Lastly, some of these names almost certainly embody *sow*, 'female pig', but early forms to confirm this are lacking.

Sowdils, Offley Hrt (*Southull* 1326), 'south hill(s)' [OE *suð, hyll*].

Sowrelands, Kingsthorpe Nth (*Sourland* t.Ric 2), 'arable strips with coarse, worked-out or acid soil' [OE *sūr*].

Spa Close, Thorpe Arnold Lei; **Spa Field,** Derby Db, Broughton La; **Spa Meadow,** Broughton La; **Spaw Well,** Broughton La: 'land containing, or adjoining, a medicinal spring'. Strictly, this is a transferred name, since the English common noun *spa* is derived from the Belgian place-name Spa.

Spade Furlong, Warborough O, may allude to the shape of the land or to its being cultivated by means of the spade rather than the plough.

The Spang, Donington Lei, 'long, narrow strip of land' [OE *spang*, 'fastening of a belt'].

Spanish Hays (Big & Little), Cressage Sa; **Spanish Liquorice,** Bere Regis Do; **Spanish Piece,** Clowne Db: the Dorset name alludes to experimentation with unusual crops in the middle of the eighteenth century and onward through the Napoleonic period; the other names are possibly similar.

Spark Field, Bledington Gl, 'land covered with shrubs or brushwood' [OE **spearca*].

Sparrow Bill Piece, Kintbury Brk; **Sparrow Bills,** Ecchinswell Ha: possibly 'a sharp projection on a boundary', taking Cockbill, Southam Wa, as an analogous form [OE *spearwa, bill*].

Sparrow Castle, Teversal Nt; **Sparrow Castle Field,** Cridling Stubbs WRY; **Sparrow Flatt,** Church Broughton Db: possibly all derogatory names, though Sparrow Flatt may be simply 'land on which sparrows abounded', referring almost certainly to the house sparrow (*Passer domesticus*). *Sparrow Castle* is a term usually applied to a tumbledown building.

Spectacles, Henley O, alluding to the shape of the field.

Spicecake Close, Walton Db, a complimentary name for productive land.

Spinney Close, Barwell Lei, Bushby Lei, Desford Lei, Galby Lei, Houghton on the Hill Lei, Kibworth Beauchamp Lei, Shangton Lei, Stretton Magna Lei; **Spinney Field,** Stoughton Lei; **Spinney Hill,** Evington Lei, Scraptoft Lei; **Spinney Holme,** Tur Langton Lei: 'land containing, or adjoining, a copse' [ME *spinney*].

Spioncop, Wheatley O, transferred name commemorating the battle during the Boer War at Spion Kop, a hill in Natal, in January 1900.

Spital Croft, Cheshunt Hrt; **Spital Meend,** Tiddenham Gl [OW *minid*]; *Spitelenge*, Papcastle Cu 1281 [ON *eng*]; **Spittal Field,** Mottram St Andrew Ch, Hitchin Hrt; **Spittal Meadow,** Holton O; **Spittle Acre,** Liversedge WRY; **Spittle Croats,** Ardeley Hrt [OE *croft*]; **Spittle Crofts,** Melbourne Db; **Spittle Fields,** Nafferton ERY; **Spittle Flat,** Brough & Shatton Db; **Spittle Garth,** Kilham ERY (*Spyttilegarth* 1546); **Spittle Green,** Garsington O: 'land owned by a hospital, or on which a hospital was built' [ME *spitel*]. Medieval hospitals, charitable institutions caring for the poor and aged as well as (or rather than) the sick, depended for their support on gifts and endowments.

Spite Field, Disley Stanley Ch; **Spiteful Yards,** Ipsden O: derogatory names for intractable land.

Splash Furlong, Abberton Wo; **Splash Meadow,** Painswick Gl: 'land near a shallow ford' [MnE dial. *splash*].

Splashetts, Almondsbury Gl (*Plaishetts* 1756), 'marshy pools' [OF *plaschiet*].

Splats, Yate Gl; **Splatts,** St Mary Bourne Ha; **Near, Far, Home & Hillocky Splatts,** Chastleton O (*The Splatts* 1596): 'patches of land' [ME *splot*].

Spleck Coppice, Thursley Sr; **Little Spleck,** Abinger Sr: 'small piece of ground'. This seems to be a local variant of *pleck* [ME *plek*].

Split (Home & Further), Birdbrook Ess (*Spretefeld* 1294–1300), 'land from which poles were obtained' [OE *sprēot*].

Spoil Bank, Baddington Ch, Swannington Lei, Selston Nt, Kellington WRY: 'land adjacent to, or containing, a heap of excavated soil'.

Spondhurst, Stapleton Sa; **Spoondale,** Kensworth Hrt (*Spondell* 1561); **Spoonley Copse,** Crawley O (*Sponden* 1300); **Spoonley Field,** Drayton in Hales Sa; **The Spoons,** Walton Lei: 'land from which timber was obtained for roof shingles' [OE *spōn*].

Spong Field, Hassingham Nf; **Long Spong,** Bradden Nth: 'long, narrow strip of land'. See also The Spang [OE *spang*].

Sport Field, Rostherne Ch, 'land for recreation' [ME *disport*].

Spreading Tree Close, Barwell Lei, self-explanatory.

Spring Close, Cookham Brk, Snibstone Lei; **Spring Field,** Basford Ch, Birtles Ch, Haslington Ch, Abbotsham D, Bere Alston D, East Allington D, Belmont Du, Abbots Langley Hrt, Watford Hrt, Ewelme O, Rollright O; **Spring Flat,** Worksop Nt; **Spring Hill,** Market Bosworth Lei; **Spring Land,** Hunsworth WRY; **Spring Leasow,** Stirchley Sa; **Great Spring Leasow,** Harley Sa; **Spring Plantation,** Alderwasley Db; **Springsfield,** Forncett St Peter Nf: probably 'land adjoining, or containing, a wood', though some of the names may mean 'land adjoining, or containing, a well or the source of a stream'; the common idea is of bursting forth or jutting out, and it is not certain which of the two meanings is the older [OE *spring*].

Spruce Field, Idbury O, alludes to the spruce fir (*Picea abies*), an important component of many modern forests in Britain. It was originally imported from northern Europe in the seventeenth century; the English name is an altered form of *Pruce*, 'Prussia'.

The Spung, Heyford Nth, 'long, narrow strip of land'. See also The Spang and Spong Field [OE *spang*].

Square Close, Ashreigney D, Belstone D, Alderwasley Db, Belper Db, Great Hucklow Db, Fifehead Magdalen Do, Long Critchell Do, Narborough Lei, Owston Lei, Thurnby Lei, Witherley Lei; **Square Cover,** Gopsall Hall Lei; **Square Croft,** Siddington Ch; **Square Field,** Ridley Ch, East Allington D, Abney Db,

Hinton Parva Do, Thorpe Thewles Du, Arnesby Lei, Haltwhistle Nb; **Square Fouracres,** Berrynarbor D; **The Square Ground,** Hermitage Do; **Square Heath,** West Alvington D; **Square Hide,** Churchill O [OE *hīd*]; **Square Leasow,** Langley & Ruckley Sa, Minsterley Sa; **Square Meadow,** Somerford Booths Ch, Welham Lei; **Square Piece,** Walton upon Trent Db, Hinckley Lei; **Square Pike,** Narborough Lei [OE *pīc*, 'point']; **Square Shaw,** Lamberhurst K: self-explanatory.

Squirrel Field (Lower, Further & Upper), Yaxley Sf; **Squirrels Close,** Thriplow C: names probably embodying the surname Squirrel. A John Squirel is referred to in a 1320 Thriplow document.

Squitch, Badby Nth; **Squitch Field,** Syresham Nth, Minster Lovell O; **Switchley Gutter,** Bugbrooke Nth: 'land infested with couch grass'. Couch (*Agropyron repens*) rejoices in numerous local names, including Quick, Creeping Wheat, Twitch, Quickens, and Scutch; although it is a troublesome weed on arable land, it is by no means unwelcome as grazing for cattle, the shoots from the underground stems being particularly nutritious.

Stable Close, Upton Lei; **Stable Field,** Presbury Ch, Chinley Db; **Stable Mead,** Enbourne Brk; **Stable Meadow,** Somerford Booths Ch: 'land adjoining, or containing, a stable' [ME *stable*].

Stack Butts, Over Ch; **Stack Close,** Egglescliffe Du; **Stack Garth,** Hambleton La, Little Eccleston La, Out Rawcliffe La, Asby We, Warcop We, Beal WRY; **Stackyard,** Woodford Ch, Heanor Db, Offcote & Underwood Db; **Stackyard Close,** Codnor & Loscoe Db, Crich Db, Peatling Magna Lei, Peckleton Lei, Stretton R; **Stackyard Field,** Worleston Ch, Barrow on Soar Lei, North Witham L: 'land containing a stack of corn or hay' [ON *stakkr*].

Stackley Field, Glen Magna Lei 17c, 'great field at Stackley, ie clearing where stakes were cut', a pre-enclosure great field name.

Stadfield, Ashby St Ledgers Nth; **Stadfold,** Melbourne Db (*Le Stotfolde* 1522); **The Stadfolds,** Upton Lei: 'horse enclosure' [OE *stōd-fald*].

Stagdell, Brington Nth (*Stakedale* 1297), 'valley marked by a stake' [OE *staca, dæl*].

Staggering Close, Sherington Bk (*Scregethornhul* c 1300, *Scragen Hill* 1580), 'land containing stumps of thorn trees [ME *scrag*, 'stump'].

Staggering Field, Garsington O, possibly 'land with uneven surface'.

Stagwell, Northwood Wt, 'spring used by stags' [OE *stagga*, *wella*].

Stair Field, Wincle Ch, 'steep land' [OE *stǣger*].

Stakenses Field, Sawston C, named from the *stakings* or staked-out allotments belonging to various individuals and to the town itself.

Stall Close, Hillfield Do, 'land containing a cattle shed' [OE *stall*].

Stanchill, Eydon Nth (*Stainihthulles* 13c), 'rocky hill' [OE *stāniht*].

Standall Pitts, Fritwell O; **Standells,** Spratton Nth; **Standhill,** Great Longstone Db, Boxwell Gl, Hitchin Hrt (*Stondelfeld* 1556); **Standles,** Gretton Nth; **Upper & Lower Standles,** Alnc Wa: 'stone quarry/quarries' [OE *stān-(ge)delf*]. See also The Stannel.

Stank End Garth, Barton We; **Stank Leasow,** Church Pulverbatch Sa, Condover Sa, Kenley Sa; **Stanks Meadow,** Rowington Wa; **Stankwell Field,** Newbottle Du: 'land containing a pond' [ME *stank*].

The Stannel, Kingsbury Wa; **The Stannels,** Bretby Db (*Stainhulfeld* 1353); **Stannill Close,** Rampton Nt: 'stone hill(s)' [OE *stān*, ON *steinn*, OE *hyll*].

Stanthill Furlong, Lower Heyford O (*Standhill* 1685); **Stanthills,** Weedon Lois Nth: 'stony hill(s)' [OE *stāniht*, *hyll*].

Star Brow, Orton We; **Star Close,** Burghfield Brk; **Star Croft,** Sutton Downes Ch; **The Star Field,** Elvetham Ha; **Star Mead,** Mere & Zeals W: some of the northern examples are probably 'land on which sedge grew' [ON *storr*], but those in southern counties possibly allude to the shape of the field.

Star Chamber, Woodplumpton La, Heptonstall WRY: a derogatory name, suggesting that work on the field resembles an encounter with the tribunal suppressed in 1640.

Starch, Litchborough Nth; **Starch Hill,** Dallington Nth: 'tail ends of land'; Starch is an altered form of Starts [OE *steort*].

Starks Nest, Edmonton Mx (*Storkesnest* 13c), 'land on which storks nested'.

Starling Close, Hitchin Hrt; *Starlingescroft*, Dersingham Nf c1300; **Sterling,** Therfield Hrt (*Starlingesden* 1294): 'land haunted by starlings'; the bird referred to is *Sturnus vulgaris*, known in North America as the European starling [OE *stærlinc*].

Start Holes, Ridge Hrt (*Stertefeld* 1332); **Start Meadow,** Somersal Herbert Db; **Starthe,** Brooksby Lei: see Starch.

Starvation Hill, Great Hormead Hrt; **Starve Acre,** Broadwindsor Do, Hook Do, Winchcombe Gl, East Tinsted Ha, Froxfield Ha, Hawley Ha, Selborne Ha, Tichborne Ha, St Stephens Hrt, Ealing Mx; **Starve All,** Didmarton Gl, Horton Gl, Pucklechurch Gl, Redbourn Hrt, Holton O, Baltonsborough So, Weston So, Biddestone W, Blunsden W, Colerne W, Leigh Delamere W, Malmesbury W; **Starveall Barn,** Fairford Gl, Highworth W; **Starveall Corner,** Ockley Sr; **Starveall Field,** Hurstbourne Tarrant Ha; **Starveall Meadow,** Shawell Lei; **Starvealls,** Highcliffe Ha; **Starve Croft,** St Stephens Hrt; **Starvecrow,** Westbury on Severn Gl; **Starvecrow Field,** Great Hormead Hrt; **Starved Croft,** Bremhill W; **Starved Lot,** Pilling La; **Starve Goose Close,** Bourn C, Girton C; **Starvehall,** Church Lawford Wa; **Starve Land,** Buckhorn Weston Do; **Starvelarks Field,** Little Berkhamsted Hrt; **Starvington Downs Furlong,** Milton under Wychwood O: derogatory names for unproductive land.

Steart, High Ham So; **Stearts,** North Wootton So; **Little Stearts,** Corston So: see Starch.

Steep (First & Second), East Anstey D; **Steep Break,** Beaford D; **Steep Copy,** Calverley WRY; **Steep Meadows,** Alwington D: self-explanatory.

Steeping (Over & Nether), Wardley R; **Steepings,** Peterborough Nth (*Ballestibbunges* 1198), 'clearing' [OE **stybbing*].

Steeple Pightle, Ellingham Nf, possibly an endowment for the cost of maintenance of the church steeple.

Steer Croft, Monyash Db; **Steer Park,** Abbotsham D: 'land on which young bullocks were kept' [OE *stēor*].

Steins, Merrow Sr, 'stony place' [OE **stǣne*].

Stell Field, Walworth Du, possibly 'land adjoining a place for catching fish' [OE *stell*]. There is in fact a stream running through this field.

Stembre, Cotterstock Nth (*Stemborough* 1815), 'rock hill' [ON *steinn*, ON/OE *berg*].

Stepping-Stone Ing, Norton WRY, self-explanatory [ON *eng*, 'meadow'].

Steppings, Cottingham Nth (*Le Newestybbing* c 1400), 'clearing' [OE **stybbing*].

Stert Meadow, Aston Rowant O; **Stert Piddle,** Eye & Dunsden O [ME *pightel*]; **Sterts,** Manston Do; **The Stirts,** London Wo; **Sturt Six Acres,** Newdigate Sr; **Sturts,** Mappowder Do; **Great Sturts,** Manston Do, Mappowder Do: see Starch [OE *steort*].

The Stew, Hulme Walfield Ch; **Stew Meadow,** Smisby Db; **Stew Potts,** Lamberhurst K [ME *potte*, 'hole, water-hole']: 'land containing a pond or tank for keeping fish until needed for the table' [ME *stewe*].

Stile Meadow, Enbourne Brk, 'grassland adjoining a stile' [OE *stigel*].

Still Stays, Malmesbury W, complimentary name for a reliable field.

Stink to Tetbury, Didmarton Gl, indicates that the smell was very powerful since Tetbury is about five miles away.

Stinyard, Melbourne Db (*Steanard* 1620), Repton Db (*Steanerde* 1593): probably 'stone enclosure' [ON *steinn*, OE *geard*].

Stock Field, Great Clacton Ess (*Stokkefelde* 1438); **Stock Piece,** Tanworth Wa; **Stockey Loons,** Carrington Ch [OE *land*]; **Stocks Close,** Barton C (*Stocfurlang* 1203); **Stocks Field,** St Peters Hrt (*Stockfeld* t.Jas 1): 'land with tree-stumps left standing on it' [OE *stocc*].

(The) Stocking, Shudy Camps C (*Stokinge* 13c), Hartwell Nth (*Stockyng* 14c), Ardley O, Elmley Castle Wo; **Stocking Balk,** Headon Nt; **Stocking Close,** Hempstead Ess (*Stockings* t.Eliz 1), Knowle Wa (*Stocking* 1490); **Stocking Croft,** Guilden Morden C; **Stocking Ground,** Oddington O (*Stockinge* 1231); **Little & Big Stocking,** Sherington Bk, Hinckley Lei; **Lower & Upper Stockings,** Pyrton O, Longden Sa: 'land cleared of tree-stumps' [OE **stoccing*].

Stocking Foot, Grimsargh La, Ingol & Cottam La, Roseacre La: fanciful name for an L-shaped field.

Stomacher Patch, Milton under Wychwood O; **Stomacher Piece,** Sheepy Magna Lei: 'land of irregular shape' [MnE dial. *stomacher*].

Stone Acre, Beer D, Otterbourne Ha; **Stone Acre Meadow,** Handborough O (*Stone Acres* 1606); **Stonebed,** Haltwhistle Nb; **Stonebow Fouracres,** Lympsham So; **Stone Bridge Road,** Croxton Nf; **Stone Close,** Snibstone Lei; **Stone Croft,** Wakes Colne Ess (*Le Stonecroft* t.Eliz 1), Thursley Sr (*Stonycroft* t.Hy 6); **Stone Dale,** Kirby Underdale ERY (*Stayndale* 1250) [ON *deill*]; **Stone Delf Field,** Lymm Ch [OE (*ge*)*delf*]; **Stone Delph,** Green Fairfield Db; **Stonego Close,** Great Hucklow Db [OE *gāra*]; **Stone Hayes,** Itchen Stoke Ha [OE (*ge*)*hæg*]; **Stonehell Copse,** St Mary Bourne Ha [OE *hyll*]; **Stone Hill,** Poulton Gl; **Stonehill Field,** Mortlake Sr now GL, Windlesham Sr; **Stonelands,** Crosby Ravensworth We; **Stone Marsh,** Cantley Nf; **Stone Park,** Abbotsham D, Ashreigney D, Beaford D; **Stone Piece,** Little Longstone Db; **Stone Pit Close,** Cold Overton Lei, Eastwell Lei, Holwell Lei, Snarestone Lei, Stretton R; **Stonepit Hill,** Kirby Grindalythe ERY (*Staynepitflat* 13c); **Stone Quarry Ground,** Kiddington O; **Stoney Acre,** Higher Whitley Ch; **Stoney Close,** Yaxley Sf; **Stoney Field,** Hitchin Hrt, St Peters Hrt (*Stonyfeld* 1455), Farnham Sr; **Stoney Riggs,** Haltwhistle Nb [ON *hryggr*]; **Stony Butts,** Askham We; **Stony Close,** Burghfield Brk, Tring Hrt, Bix O; **Stony Croft,** Bovingdon Hrt, St Michaels Hrt, Watford Hrt (*Stancroft* 1436); **Stony Delph,** Coventry Wa [OE (*ge*)*delf*]; **Stony Field,** Belmont Du, Thorpe Thewles Du, South Weston O, Pirbright Sr; **Stony Flats,** Houghton le Spring Du; **Stony Flatt,** Ferry Fryston WRY; **Stony Furlong,** Tichborne Ha; **Stony Hills,**

Campsall WRY; **Stony Lands,** Mappowder Do, Harlington Mx; **Stony Lane & Furlong,** Pyrton O; **Stony Leasow,** Stapleton Sa; **Stony Leys,** Cookham Brk [OE *lǣs*]; **Stony Meadow,** Send Sr; **Stony Nap,** Upper Slaughter Gl; **Stony Tang,** Alderwasley Db [OE *tang*, 'spit of land']; **Stony Wong,** Askham Nt [ON *vangr*]: 'land with stony soil, or from which stone was excavated, or adjoining stone buildings' [OE *stān*, ON *steinn*].

Storth, Hutton Roof We; **Storth Field,** Offerton Db, Hayton Nt: 'land adjoining, or containing, a young wood' [ON *storð*].

Stotfold (Low & Middle), Elwick Hall Du (*Stotfold* c 1200): 'horse enclosure' [OE *stōd-fald*].

Straight Fold, Muston Lei; **Straight Piece,** Claughton La; **The Strait,** Cornsay Du; **Strait Meadow,** Alston La: 'land adjoining a (Roman) road' [OE *strǣt*].

The Strap, Ditcheat So, Gorewell Paddock So; **Strapp,** Ashreigney D: 'long narrow piece of land' [OE *strop*].

Straw Hall, Laxton Nt, a derogatory name for land that produced straw rather than ear in the corn [OE *strēaw*, *halh*].

Strawberry Bank, Wessington Db, Liversedge WRY; **Strawberry Close,** Belstone D; **Strawberry Dale,** Barbon We; **Strawberry Field,** Bere Alston D; **Strawberry Grove Coppice,** Artington Sr; **Strawberry Hanger,** Steep Ha [OE *hangra*]; **Strawberry Hill,** Adderley Sa; **Strawberry Lee,** Great Longstone Db [OE *lēah*]; **Strawberry Lines** or **Linces,** Benson O [OE *hlinc*]: 'land on which strawberries were grown'.

Strawberry Hill Shot, Twickenham Mx, as preceding. This name is of some interest because of its association with Horace Walpole. When Walpole bought 'Chopped Straw Hall' in 1748 he noticed this field-name mentioned in the deeds of the property and renamed the house *Strawberry Hill.*

Street Acre, Yenworth Gl; **Street Field,** Great Marton La, Preesall with Hackinsall La; **Street Furlong,** Mortlake Sr (*Stratfurlong* 15c): 'land by a Roman road' [OE *strǣt*].

Street Field, Cranleigh Sr (*Le Sterte* 1419); **Streets Meadow,** East Clandon Sr (*Le Sturtes* 1350); **Long Straight,** Ham Sr (*Long*

Stert 1650); **The Streights,** Cornbury Park O: 'elongated projection, or tail, of land' [OE *steort*].

Stripe, Elwick Hall Du; **Stripe Field,** Walworth Du; **Stripes,** Holmesfield Db, Shap Rural We: 'narrow piece of land' [OE **strīp*].

Stroud, Compton Bishop So; **Strouds,** Nutfield Sr; **Strouds Field,** Enfield Mx (*Le Strode* t.Ed 3); **Strouds Wood,** Kings Somborne Ha: 'marshy land overgrown with brushwood' [OE *strōd*].

Stroudhams, Byfleet Sr (*Stroutham* 1548); **Strut Field,** Idbury O; **Strutt Mead,** Dunkerton So: 'land in dispute' [OE **strūt*].

Stub Furlong, Chieveley Brk; **Stubb Cutts,** Harpenden Hrt (*Stub Croft* c 1840) [OE *croft*]; **Stubbing Land,** Forncett St Peter Nf; **Stubbs,** Pownall Fee Ch; **Upper Stubbs,** Kintbury Brk: 'land covered with tree stumps' [OE *stubb*, **stubbing*].

Stubble Close, Pittington Du, Ashby Folville Lei, Aston Flamville Lei; **Stubble Hill,** Shenton Lei; **Stubble Meadow,** Burghfield Brk: names alluding to land upon which the stubble was allowed to remain for an abnormally long time.

Sturt Six Acres, Newdigate Sr; **Sturts,** Chieveley Brk, Farnham Sr; **Sturts Field,** Shalford Sr; **Sturts Meadow,** Brughfield Brk: 'tails of land' [OE *steort*].

Stutch Close, Greatworth Nth; **Big & Little Stytch,** Drayton in Hales Sa: 'small plot of land' [OE *stycce*].

Sub-chanters Dole, North Wootton So, 'endowment of a succentor'; this land was owned by Glastonbury Abbey.

Subpoena, Pilling La, probably a derogatory term.

Sucklesome, Catton Db, complimentary name for land producing good milk.

Sugar Acres, Kingham O; **Sugar Close,** Nuffield O; **Sugar Hills,** Calverley WRY; **Sugar Tump,** Newham Gl: complimentary names for sweet land.

Sugar Loaf, Turnditch Db, 'hillock resembling a sugar loaf'.

Summer Croft, Alton Pancras Do; **Summer Dell,** Harpenden Hrt; **Summer Eating Ground,** Fifield O; **Summerer,** Great

Singleton La [ON *erg*]; **Summerer Meadow,** Weeton La; **Summer Hays,** Swinbrook O, Wychwood O; **Summer Land,** Lechlade Gl; **Summer Lands,** Finchley Mx; **Summer Leaze,** Cookham Brk, Holwell Do, Doddington Gl, Southrop Gl; **Summer Leazows,** Rollright O; **Summerleys,** Chinnor O, Ewelme O; **Summerlys Meadow,** St Mary Bourne Ha: 'land used in summer'.

Summer Work Field, Bollin Fee Ch, Handforth Ch: 'land left fallow during the summer'.

Sun Acres, Northenden Ch; **Sun Field,** Marton Ch, Waltham Holy Cross Ess (*Sonefeld* 1408); **Sun Flat,** Bramhall Ch; **Sunhills,** Woking Sr; **Sun Ing,** Churwell WRY [ON *eng*]; **Sun Meadow,** Hungerford Brk; **Sun Paddock,** Cookham Brk; **Sun Shoot,** Little Leigh Ch [OE **sciete*]; **Sun Side,** Hope Woodlands Db; **Sunny Bank,** Wolstaston Sa; **Sunny Brow,** Rainow Ch; **Sunny Meadow,** Whitchurch Wa; **Sunny Shoot,** Twycross Lei: 'land facing the sun'.

Sunday Close, Milton under Wychwood O; **Sunday Field,** Mobberley Ch, High Easter Ess (*Sundayeshawe* c 1400); **Sunday Flatt,** Yeardsley cum Whaley Ch: probably all embodying the surname Sunday. The explanation of the Mobberley name, 'said to be so named as the best field in Mobberley, Sunday being the best day of the week' (cf PNCh, ii, 71) would be more convincing if it could be confirmed by a wide range of other examples. An allusion to feudal service (cf Monday Croft) is not likely, either, since the day of rest is inappropriate for such obligations.

Sunderhill, Nettleton W; **Sunderlands,** Babraham C (*Surderland* [*sic*] 1141–7), Foston Lei, Lupton We: 'private or detached land' [OE *sundorland*].

Swallow Dell, Hemel Hempstead Hrt; **Swallow Nest,** Cheadle Ch, Heckmondwike WRY; **Swallows Acre,** Hatton Ch: 'land frequented by swallows' [OE *swalwe*].

Swallow Hole Close, Greetham R, Stretton R; **Swallows,** Walkern Hrt: 'land by or containing swallow holes' [OE **swalg*], ie depressions in a river bed, into which much of the water flows in dry weather, to pursue its course below ground.

Swallow Tail, Cound Sa, Little Strickland We, Morland We: alludes to land so shaped.

Swamp, Bibury Gl; **Swamp Close,** Eyam Db; **Swamp Mill,** Liversedge WRY: 'boggy land' [MnE *swamp*].

Swan Carr Pond, Thorpe Thewles Du; **Swan Field,** Elvetham Ha, Rickmansworth Hrt (*Swonneslond* t.Ric 2); **Swan Flatt,** Stokeham Nt; **Swans Nest,** Fifehead Magdalen Do; **Swans Nest Pasture,** High Easter Ess (*Swannesnest* 1449): 'land on or near which swans were to be found' [OE *swan*].

Swanback Field, Adderley Sa; **Swan(s) Neck,** Mobberley Ch, Rudheath Lordship Ch, Latton W: names alluding to the shape or contours of the land.

Sweedentree Plain, Shorthampton O; **Sweetentree Close,** Spondon Db; **Sweetentree Piece,** Fawler O: 'land on which sweet apples were grown' [ME *sweting*, 'sweet apple'].

Sweet Bit(t), Somersal Herbert Db, Elswick La; **Sweet Close,** Bradley Db, Chirbury Sa; **Sweet Field,** Little Leigh Ch, Mere Ch, Snelson Ch, Upton Ch, Durley Ha; **Sweet Green,** Ash Db; **Sweet Hill,** Dersingham Nf; **Sweet Hills,** Hope Woodlands Db; **Sweet Leys,** Melbourne Db; **Sweet Nap,** Batcombe So; **Sweet Piece,** Brough & Shatton Db, Chastleton O; **Sweet Pot,** Claydon O: 'land whose soil was well constituted and fertile' [OE *swēte*].

The Sweeting, Treswell Nt; **Sweetings,** Rampton Nt: if not an allusion to sweet apples (see Sweedentree Plain), 'pleasant grassland' [OE *swēte*, ON *eng*].

Sweet Tooth, Greenhalgh La, Medlar La: complimentary name for productive land.

Swine Carr, Clayworth Nt; **Swinedale,** Bakewell Db; **Swine Hollins,** Scaftworth Nt [OE *holegn*, 'holly']; **Swine Park,** Ilsington D, Liversedge WRY; **Swine Parrock,** Firbank We; **Swingfield,** Banstead Sr (*Swynefeld* 1363): 'land on which pigs were kept' [OE *swīn*].

Swinehead, Froxfield Ha; **Swineshead,** North Mimms Hrt (*Swyneshevedlond* 1311); **Swinsead Homestead,** Cookham Brk (*Swineshead* 1470): an allusion to the custom of erecting the head of a sacrificed animal on a pole to mark the site of pagan ceremonies is possible, but that *head* means simply 'headland' seems even more likely.

Swineherd Hill, Hook WRY; **Swineherd's Close,** Hurstbourne Tarrant Ha: 'land assigned to the pig-keeper'.

Swinnow Close, Wheatley Nt; **Swinnow Wood,** Harworth Nt (*Boscum de Swnehaga* c 1175): 'wood into which pigs were turned for feeding' [OE *swīn*, *haga*].

Swire Close, Cleckheaton WRY, 'neck of land' [OE *swēora*].

Sycamore Close, Alderwasley Db, Chelmorton Db; **Sycamore Field,** Lambourn Brk: 'land on which, or near which, sycamore trees grew'. The sycamore (*Acer pseudo-platanus*) was introduced into Britain in the early sixteenth century.

Sych, Wincle Ch; **Syke,** Carleton La, Goosnargh La, Greenhalgh La, Preston La, Warton La; **Syke Close,** Kneesall Nt; **Syke Foot,** Barton We: 'meadow land beside a stream' [OE *sīc*, ON *sík*].

Syxteneakres, Catton Db 1328, 'furlong or consolidated holding comprising sixteen strips of arable land', an interesting early example of what was later to be a very common type of field-name.

T

T Acres, Elwick Hall Du, see Tea Close.

Tadborough Close, Norton juxta Twycross Lei, 'land on hill infested with toads' [OE *tāde*, *beorg*].

Taffy Meadow Road, Breadsall Db, probably alludes to the stickiness of the soil.

Tainter Field, Bocking Ess (*Le Teynter Leyes* 1559); **Tainters,** Cound Sa; **Teinter Close,** Wootton Wawen Wa: 'land on which cloth-finishing was carried out' [ME *teyntour*, 'frame on which cloth was stretched'].

Tallow Meadow, Longford Db, 'land likely to produce fat cattle'. *Tallow* is obtained from the hard fat of ruminant animals and is, or has been, used in the manufacture of candles and soap.

Tanhouse Field, Somerford Booths Ch, Bispham La, Layton La, Pilling La; **Tanners Plank,** Ardley O [ME *planke*, 'narrow field']; **Tannes,** Wickwar Gl (*Tannhouse Lease* 1661); **Tan Pit(t) Field,** Broughton La, Hothersall La, Woodplumpton La; **Tan Pit Ing,**

Gomersal WRY; **Tan Yard,** Davenham Ch, Great Eccleston La; **Tanyard Field,** Alphington D: 'land used in the manufacture of leather'. See also Barker Ing and Barkhouse Close.

Tansey Close, Islip O; **Tansy Field,** Chapel en le Frith Db: names referring to the common wild flower (*Chrysanthemum vulgare*).

Tanter Field, Catterall La, see Tainter Field.

Tare Close, Duffield Db; **Tare Croft,** Thaxted Ess, Limpsfield Sr (*Tarefeld* 1445): 'land on which vetches were grown'. The vetch (*Vicia sativa*) is a common fodder plant.

Tarn Acre, Pilling La; **Tarn Field,** Nateby La, Wilsden WRY; **Tarn Lands,** Casterton We: 'land near, or containing, a pond' [ON *tjorn*].

Tea Close, Blaston St Giles Lei; **Tea Tining,** Priston So; **T Acres,** Elwick Hall Du; **Tee,** Hope Db; **The Tee Bank,** Martley Wo; **Tee Field,** Mobberley Ch; **Tee Ground,** Hailey O; **Tee Piece,** Alderwasley Db: 'T-shaped piece of land'.

Teakettle Handlepiece, Belper Db, fanciful name for a curving field.

Teg Down Plantation, Godsfield Ha; **Teggs Field,** Little Bookham Sr: 'land on which young sheep were pastured' [OE **tagga*].

Temple Carr, Kellington WRY; **Temple Close,** Gaddesby Lei; **Temple Field,** Dowdeswell Gl (*Old Temple* 1577); **Upper & Lower Temple,** Addington Sr: 'land formerly owned by the Knights Templars'. The range and extent of the land owned by this military religious order (suppressed in 1312) may be observed by the occurrence of *Temple* in both major place-names and field names [ME *temple*].

Ten Acre Close, Flagg Db; **Ten Acre Marsh,** Beaford D; **Ten Acre Mead,** Hermitage Do; **Ten Acre Meadow,** Foxton Lei; **Ten Acre Piece,** Coleorton Lei, Hinstock Sa; **Ten Acre Side,** Hope Db; **Ten Acres,** Bray Brk (*Tyneacre* 1388), Clewer Brk, Norton Ch, Mappowder Do, North Poorton Do, Bibury Gl, Long Sutton Ha, Peatling Magna Lei, Upton Lei, Stretton R, Yaxley Sf, Southam Wa (*Tienacres* 1302): 'land with an area of ten acres, or adjoining such a piece of land'.

Ten Days Math, Twemlow Ch, Coberley Gl, Minsterley Sa; **Ten Day(s) Work,** Bosley Ch, Buglawton Ch, Crosby on Eden Cu: see Five Day Math.

Ten Farundels, Clanfield O (cf *Tria Fordella* c 1240, *þrefertlendels* 15c): 'ten quarters'. The early forms mean 'three quarters', and the modern name may result from a mistaken alteration or may indicate an actual change in the field's size [OE *fēorða-dǣl*, 'fourth share'].

Ten Feet Ground, Feltwell Nf 1642; **Ten Foot Meadow,** Frolesworth Lei; **The Ten Lands,** Carlton Lei; **Ten Leys,** Wardington O; **Ten Measures Sowing,** Helsby Ch; **Ten Swathes,** Castleton Db: names variously alluding to the size of the fields.

Ten Groats Field, Hursley Ha; **Ten Pound Field,** Oulton Lowe Ch, Rudheath Lordship Ch; **Ten Pound Piece,** Foston Lei: alluding to the actual or merited rent of the piece of land. The last British groat was issued in 1662, but a silver fourpenny piece current in the early nineteenth century was colloquially referred to by this term.

Tenantry Down, Compton Chamberlayne W, Edington W, Figheldean W, Langford W, Sherrington W, Winterbourne Stoke W; **Tenantry Field,** Fovant W; **Tenants Car Plantation,** Callow Db; **Tenants Down,** Long Critchell Do; **Tenants Hill,** Alton Pancras Do: 'pasture land occupied by tenants and not forming part of the lord's demesne'.

Tenter Bank, Brockholes La, Haltwhistle Nb, Norland WRY; **Tenter Close,** Melbourne Db, Cadeby Lei, Haltwhistle Nb, Old Hutton We; **Tenter Croft,** Millington Ch, Nether Alderley Ch, Woodford Ch, Duffield Db, Barnacre La, Broughton La, Goosnargh La, Hartshead WRY, Sandal Magna WRY; **Tenter Field,** Chapel en le Frith Db, Earls Colne Ess (*Teyntor Croft* 1390), Great Coggeshall Ess (*Teynterplot* 1535), Bilsthorpe Nt, Barbon We; **Tenter Green,** Middleton We; **Tenter Ing,** Rishworth WRY [ON *eng*]; **Tenter Hey,** Aston La; **Tenter Loon,** Newbold Astbury Ch [OE *land*]; **Tenters,** Killington We; **Tenters Field,** Keswick Cu, Rampton Nt; **Tentholme,** Everton Nt (*Tyntholme* t.Hy 8) [ON *holmr*]; **Tentry Croft,** Barthomley Ch, Nether Peover Ch; **Tentry Field,** Marton Ch: 'land containing cloth-stretching frames' [ME *teyntour*].

Terrible, Dunham Massey Ch, a derogatory name. Cf Dreadful.

Tessil Croft, Walthamstow Ess now GL, 'land on which teasels were grown'. The fuller's teasel (*Dipsacus fullonum*) grows wild in Britain and has been cultivated in the past; the hooked seed-heads were used for combing wool and for raising the nap on cloth [OE *tǣsl*].

Tewitt Close, Tuxford Nt; **Tewitt Hill,** Hartshorne Db: 'land frequented by lapwings'. This bird (*Vanellus vanellus*) is also known as the green plover or peewit.

Thackholm(e), Laxton Nt, Atherstone Wa; **Thackmire,** Beetham We (*Thakmyre* 1524) [ON *mýrr*]; **Thackracks,** Cossington Lei [OE *racu*, 'hollow, bed of stream']; **Thackrigg,** Keswick Cu [ON *hryggr*]: 'land from which thatch-reeds were obtained' [ON *þak*].

Thames Furlong, Lechlade Gl, South Cerney Gl; **Thames Shot(t),** Staines Mx, Wandsworth Sr now GL (*Temeshote* 1413): 'land adjoining the river Thames'.

Thanky Furlong, Mylton under Wychwood O, complimentary name for productive land.

Thatch Croft, Newton Ch; **Thatch Field,** St Michaels Hrt; **Thatch Ground,** Ardley O: 'land from which thatch-reeds were obtained' [OE *þæc*].

Thick Thornes, Holwell Do, Staines Mx (*Thikthorne* 1446), self-explanatory, and in contrast to Small Thorns.

Thieves Acre, East Dereham Nf; **Thieves Close,** Brooksby Lei; **Thieves Clough,** Minshull Vernon Ch [OE **clōh*]; **Thieves Dale,** Reedness WRY [OE *dæl*]; **Thieves Den,** Harthill Db; **Thieves Meadow,** Brooksby Lei: derogatory names for unproductive or otherwise unattractive land.

Thimble Hall, Warsop Nt; **Thimble Hole,** Hope Woodlands Db: 'small piece of land', perhaps a small hollow so shaped [OE *þymel, hol, halh*].

Thin Porridge, Oxenhope WRY, a derogatory name indicating either soil that might be so described or, rather more probably, land that produces only sufficient oats to make very watery porridge.

Thirteen Acre Debdale, Evington Lei (see Debdale); **Thirteen Acre Piece,** Hinstock Sa; **Thirteen Acres,** Alton Pancras Do, Hillfield Do, Stretton R: 'land of, or adjoining, the stated area'.

Thirteen Doles, Staveley Db, 'consolidated piece containing thirteen shares'.

Thirtfield, Ashreigney D; **Thirtlands,** Amport Ha: 'strips lying at right angles to others' [ME *þwert*].

Thirty Acre Farm, Swine ERY (*Thirty Acres* 1541); **Thirty Acres,** Mappowder Do, East Norton Lei, Stockerston Lei, Stoughton Lei, Stretton R: 'land thirty acres in area'.

Thirty-four Acres, Foxton Lei, self-explanatory.

Thistlands Mead, South Stoke So; **Thistle Close,** Walworth Du, Sheepy Magna Lei, Crigglestone WRY; **Thistle Downs,** Willingale Doe Ess (*Thisteldownes Lande* t.Hy 8); **Thistle Field,** Ipsden O; **Thistle Goit,** Askern WRY [OE **gota*, 'stream']; **Thistle Hill,** Inkpen Brk, Shirburn O; **Thistles Clough,** Nether Alderley Ch [OE *clōh*]; **Thistl(e)y Close,** Bucklebury Brk, Melbourne Db, Washington Du, Popham Ha, Illston Lei, Nailstone Lei; **Thistl(e)y Field,** Barrow Ch (*Thyslifeld* 1296), Edleston Ch, Hylton Du, Gestingthorpe Ess (*Thistleffeilde* 1592), Goldhanger Ess (*Thistle Croft* 1418), St Michaels Hrt, Helsington We; **Thistley Hay,** Frodsham Ch; **Thistley Hill,** Longhope Gl; **Thistley Pingle,** Duffield Db: 'land on which thistles abounded' [OE *þistel*].

Thistle Dyke, Yelvertoft Nth (*Thurkeles Dik* 1318), '(land at) Thurketill's dyke' [OE *dīc*].

Thong, Long Sutton So; **Thongs,** Great Saling Ess (*Le Thwonge* 1398), Somerton So: 'narrow strip of land' [OE *þwang*].

Thorn Close, Fifehead Magdalen Do, Aston Flamville Lei; **Thorn Croft,** Bovingdon Hrt; **Thornhanger,** Boxford Brk [OE *hangra*]; **Thornhill,** Welton Nth (*Thirnehil* 1303); **Thornlands,** Nazeing Ess; **Thorney Close,** Blaston St Michael Lei; **Thorny Field,** Broughton Astley Lei; **Thorny Leys,** Houghton on the Hill Lei: 'land containing, or hedged by, hawthorn bushes [OE *þorn*]. The hawthorn (*Cratægus oxycantha*) is the characteristic shrub of English hedges, ensuring that they are both self-renewing and stock-proof, but it readily invades neglected pastures.

Thorn Tree Balk, Rampton Nt; **Thorntree Close,** Alderwasley Db, Snarestone Lei; **Thorntree Field,** Houghton le Spring Du: 'land containing, or adjoining, thorn trees'. Unclipped, the hawthorn will grow to a height of about twenty feet; its characteristic outline and indestructibility caused it to be named as a land-mark in boundary charters of the Anglo-Saxon period.

Thor's Copse, Ashburton D, alludes to a traditional or fancied association of isolated woods with heathen holy places.

Thousand Acres, Whitchurch Canonicorum Do, Ringwood Ha, Rickmansworth Hrt: ironic name for very small fields. In Whitchurch the name is applied to four fields, each of less than one acre; the Ringwood land is described as 'very small', and the Rickmansworth field scarcely exceeds an acre. See also One Thousand Acres.

Threaphurst, Marple Ch [OE *hyrst*]; **Threap Lands,** Newby We; **Threap Lee(s),** Barton We, Morland We [OE *lēah*]; **Threapleton,** Wyke WRY (*Threapelondes* 1602); **Threap Wood,** Buerton Ch: 'land in dispute' [OE *þrēap*].

Three Ackers, Lupton We; *Threeacre*, Lower Rissington Gl c 1180; **Three Acre Close,** Belper Db; **Three Acres,** Norton Ch, Lower Whitley Ch, Bradley Db, Shirley Db, Alton Pancras Do, Holwell Do, Hook Do, Mappowder Do, Barnsley Gl, Stoughton Lei: 'land of the stated area'.

Three Angles, Aston by Budworth Ch, 'triangular field'.

Three Ashes, Silchester Ha, 'land marked by three ash trees'.

Three Butts, Dunham on the Hill Ch, Newbold Astbury Ch, Hope Db: 'enclosed land consisting of three butt-ends of the open strips'.

Three Cocked Hat, Irthington Cu, fanciful name for a triangular field.

Three Corner Bit, Prestbury Ch; **Three Corner Close,** Holwell Do, Bruntingthorpe Lei, Braybrooke Nth, Gunthorpe R; **Three Corner Field,** Arnesby Lei; **Three Corner Moor,** Hinton Mary Do; **Three Corner Piece,** Ilsington D; **Three Corner Pightle,** Bucklebury Brk; **Three Corner Platt,** Peckleton Lei; **Three Cornered Church Field,** Odstone Lei; **Three Cornered Close,** Ashleyhay Db,

Dadlington Lei, Evington Lei, Groby Lei, Holwell Lei, Lubenham Lei, Market Bosworth Lei, South Croxton Lei, Stoughton Lei, Adderbury O; **Three Cornered Croft,** Bollin Fee Ch, Pownall Fee Ch, **Three Cornered Debdale,** Shawell Lei (see Debdale); **Three Cornered Field,** Aston Db, Bakewell Db, Chinley Db, Writtle Ess (*Thriehornedecroft* 14c); **Three Cornered Haw,** Enderby Lei [OE *haga*]; **Three Cornered Meadow,** Butley Ch, Great Stretton Lei; **Three Cornered Patch,** Thornbury Gl (*Thracornardscroft* 1497); **Three Cornered Piece,** Windsor Brk, Chorley Ch, Bradley Db, Great Stretton Lei, Hallaton Lei, Stoughton Lei, Norton juxta Twycross Lei, Pontesbury Sa; **Three Cornered Pightle,** Burghfield Brk; **Three Cornered Pildash,** Odstone Lei (see Pildash); **Three Cornered Plot,** Hillfield Do; **Three Cornered Spinney,** Mollington O; **Three Corners,** Abbotsham D, Belstone D, Bere Alston D, East Allington D, East Anstey D, Ilsington D: 'triangular piece of land'.

Three Crawts, Hadlow K (*Three Crofts* 1610); **Three Croats,** Watton at Stone Hrt: 'enclosure consolidating three small pieces of land' [OE *croft*].

Three Day Math, Hurlestone Ch, Minshull Vernon Ch, Rudheath Lordship Ch, Tetton Ch; **Three Day(s) Work,** Bosley Ch, Newbold Astbury Ch, Hope Db, Norton Db 1704, Outseats Db, Corley Wa, Bradford WRY: see Day Math.

Three Devils, Westbury on Severn Gl, a derogatory name for intractable land.

Three Farndels, Twyning Gl [OE *feorða-dǣl*]; **Three Fields,** Claydon O; **Three Hales,** Upton Lei [OE *halh*]; **(The) Three Halves,** Enbourne Brk, Ashmore Do, Long Sutton Ha, Sherfield English Ha, Savernake W; **Three Halves Ground,** Ecchinswell Ha; **Three Lands,** Outseats Db, Eastleach Martin Gl; **Three Lands Close,** Chinnor O; **Three Lays,** Hilton Db, Twycross Lei; **The Three Leasows,** Little Ness Sa; **(The) Three Quarters,** Chorley Ch, Norton Ch, Warburton Ch; **Three Roods,** Belper Db, Curbar Db, Fooloe Db, Hope Db, Kingsterndale Db, Dadlington Lei, Scaftworth Nt; **Three Swathes,** Great Marton La: 'enclosure comprising the three named units of land'.

Three Nook, North Bierley WRY; **Three Nook Close,** Belper Db; **Three Nook Field,** Lyme Handley Ch; **Three Nooked Bank,** Old

Hutton We; **Three Nooked Field,** Edleston Ch, Abney Db, Hope Db, Egglescliffe Du 1742, Kendal We; **Three Nooked Piece,** Eaton Ch, Ashleyhay Db; **Three Nooked Pingot,** Lyme Handley Ch [ME *pingel*]; **Three Nooks,** Kingsley Ch, Bakewell Db, Kingsterndale Db, Alston La, Ashton La, Bispham La, Bryning La, Grimsargh La, Lea La, Evington Lei: 'triangular piece of land'.

Threepenny Close, Ilsington D; **Threepenny Copse,** Wychwood O: possibly derogatory names alluding to the actual or estimated rent of the land.

Three Pound Meadow, Hyde Ch, name alluding to the price of the land.

Three Shires, Marshfield Gl, 'land at the meeting place of three counties'. This land is at the junction of Gloucestershire, Wiltshire and Somerset [OE *scīr*].

Three Square, Barton in the Beans Lei; **Three Square Close,** Osbaston Lei: 'triangular field'.

Three Trees Closes, Mollington O; **Three Trees Leasow,** Kenley Sa: self-explanatory.

The Thrif, Shutlanger Nth; **Thrift Close,** Harringworth Nth; **Thrift Mead,** Barking Ess; **Thrift Meadow(s),** Burghfield Brk (*Frithmore* 1231), Perivale Mx; **Thrift Wood,** Thaxted Ess (*Eldfrith* 1348), Ayot St Peter Hrt: 'woodland' [OE (*ge*)*fyhrð*].

Thriving Land, Finchley Mx, complimentary name for productive land.

Thoroughts, Aston Subedge Gl; **Through Shoots,** Kemble Gl; **Through Shoots Close,** Buxton Db; **Throughter Piece,** Didbrook Gl; **Throughters,** Elmley Castle Wo; **Throughters Furlong,** Stanway Gl: 'land whose boundaries project across neighbouring fields' [OE *þurh, scēte*].

Throstle Nest, Bradford WRY; **Thrush Close,** Whitwood WRY: 'land on which thrushes nested' [OE *þrostle, þrysce*].

Thunder Field, Eaton under Heywood Sa; **Thunderhedge Flat,** Breedon on the Hill Lei 1730; **Thunder Piece,** Hallow Wo; **Thunderwell,** Islip O; **Thunderwell Slip,** Islip O: 'land associated in some way with thunder'; the connexion may be with actual thunderstorms or with topographical features causing a roar of wind or water. Absence of early forms precludes confident derivation from the name of the god Thunor.

Thurn Close, South Croxton Lei, 'nook'. The name is probably a development of *Th' Hurn* [OE *hyrne*].

Thurspit, Heyford Nth; **Thrush Pits,** Measham Lei; **Thruss Pits,** Eakring Nt (*Thrussepittes* 1520): 'demon-haunted holes' [OE *þyrs*].

Thwaite, Dufton We, 'clearing' [ON *þveit*].

Tile Barn Field, Lambourne Brk; **Tile Barrow Field,** Edmonton Mx (*Tichelberch* 1252) [OE *beorg*]; **Tilebeds,** Farnham Sr; **Tilefield,** Send Sr; **Tile Garth,** Newbottle Du; **Tile Kiln Field,** Broxbourne Hrt (*Tygilhous* 1391); **Tile Kiln Wood,** Welbeck Nt (*Tylekylncroft* t.Ed 3); **Tile Shade Field,** Newbottle Du [OE *sceadu*, 'shelter']; **Tillery Field,** Wisbech St Peter C (*Le Tyllerie* 1351); **Tilmore Farm,** Petersfield Ha (cf *Tigel Leah* 10c): names alluding either to the manufacture of tiles or to buildings roofed or hung with them [OE *tigel*].

Tillage Close, Belgrave Lei; **The Tillage Holme,** Aislaby Du: 'land enclosed for arable use'.

Tiltland (Great), Copford Ess (*Tedelond* 1438, *Tendelond* 1441), 'enclosed land' [OE *tȳned*].

Timber Mead, Enfield Mx (*Tymberfeld* 1464), 'land containing, or adjoining, a wood from which timber was obtained' [OE *timber*].

Time of Day, Nether Alderley Ch, fanciful name for a very small field—of a size comparable to a greeting rather than a dialogue.

Timothy Flat, Longford Db, 'land on which cat's-tail grass grew'. Timothy grass, or meadow cat's tail (*Phleum pratense*) is grown throughout the British Isles and was introduced into the United States by Timothy Hanson—hence the name. See also Catstail.

Tin Mead, Hatfield Broad Oak Ess (*Tendemed* 1322); **Tin Park,** East Allington D: 'enclosed land' [OE *tȳned*].

The Tindings, North Claine Wo; **Big & Little Tining,** Minsterley Sa; **The Tinings,** Grimley Wo: 'enclosure' [OE *tȳning*].

Tinker Flatt (Great & Little), Norton Juxta Twycross Lei; **Tinker Furlong,** Benson O; **Tinker's Close,** Coleorton Lei; **Tinker's Croft,** Middlewich Ch; **Tinkers Field,** Newhall Ch; **Tinker's Pool Patch,** Yockleton Sa; **Tinkler Croft,** Milburn We: 'land on or near which itinerant tinkers camped'.

Tint Field, Oxted Sr (*Teyntfeild* 1475); **Tinter Croft,** Stebbing Ess (*Teyntourcrofte* 1422): 'land on which cloth-finishing frames were set out' [ME *teyntour*].

Tippenny Meadow, Bloxham O, derogatory name, suggesting that the land was worth only twopence.

Tipperary, Brougham We, transferred name for remote land.

Tit Field, Leese Ch; **Titfurlongs,** North Poorton Do; **Titty Mouse Green,** Brereton cum Smethwick Ch: 'land on which titmice abounded'. A number of species of birds of the *Paridae* family are very common throughout Britain, including the great tit (*Parus major*), the blue tit (*Parus caeruleus*), and the coal tit (*Parus ater britannicus*).

Tithe Barn, Greenhalgh La; **Tithe Barn Close,** Repton Db; **Tithe Barn Croft,** Carrington Ch, Elston La, Hardhall La, Preesall La; **Tithe Barn Field,** Great Eccleston La, Thornton La; **Tithe Barn Meadow,** Ashton La; *Tithe Barne Yarde*, Dersingham Nf 1560; **Tithebarns,** Send Sr; **Tythe Barn Close,** Spondon Db, Burton We: 'land containing, or adjoining, the building in which the tithes of corn were stored'.

Tithe Copse, Hatfield Broad Oak Ess; **Tithe Croft,** Duffield Db; **First, Middle & Top Tithe Field,** Arnesby Lei; **Tithe Garth,** Crosby Ravensworth We; **Tithe Lands,** Beaford D, Bibury Gl; **Tithe(s) Meadow,** Mouldsworth Ch, Aston Db, Barwell Lei: 'land reserved for the payment of tithe' [OE *tēoðung*].

Tithing Man's Acre, Painswick Gl; **Tithing Man's Ground,** Islip O; **Tithing Man's Hill,** West Anstey D; **Tithing Man's Tilt,** Burghclere Ha [OE *tȳned*]; **Tithing Man's Yard,** Bucklebury Brk 1604, Buckhorn Weston Do; **Tythesman's Plot,** Shipton under Wychwood O: 'land assigned to parish constable or to the collector of tithes'. The ambiguity arises from the term *tithing* being used of a small administrative district as well as in the sense of an ecclesiastical tax.

Toad Carr Meadow, Adlington Ch (*Todelache* 1280) [ON *kjarr*, OE *læcc*, 'bog']; **Toad Hole,** Gawsworth Ch, Wincle Ch, Babworth Nt, Drighlington WRY, Whitwood WRY: 'land on which toads were found' [OE **tāde*].

Toad Pipe Meadow, Carleton La, Roseacre La; **Toad Pipe Parrock,** Pilling La: 'land on which horsetail grew'. Field horsetail (*Equisetum arvense*), a curious deep-rooted but flowerless plant which grows in damp meadows, is known in the north of England as toadpipe.

Toft Dale, Coston Lei; **Toft Flats,** Scrayingham ERY; **East & West Toft Rigs,** Cassop Du; **Tofts,** Carnaby ERY (*Le Toftes* 1306): 'site of a building' or 'hillock in flat country' [ON *topt*].

Toll Bar Field, Cranage Ch; **Tollgate Close,** Billesdon Lei, Norton juxta Twycross Lei; **Tollgate Meadow,** Clifton & Compton Db, Foston Lei: 'land adjoining a place for the payment of road-tolls' [OE *toln*].

Tom o' th' Hall Piece, Edale Db, a name embodying an early form of surname; similar field names are **John a Meadow Close,** Repton Db, and (perhaps) **Little Jack in the Wood,** Laindon Ess.

Tom Pasture, Sutton Downes Ch; **Tom Yard Meadow,** Mathall cum Warford Ch: 'common pasture', shared among all the dwellers in the village [OE *tūn*].

(The) Tongue, Elton Ch, Over Alderley Ch, East Allington D, West Alvington D, Brigstock Nth (*Tonge* 1307), Whinfell We, Norland WRY, Soyland WRY; **Tongue Croft,** Worksop Nt; **Tongue Field,** Ilsington D; **Tongue Piece,** Ashreigney D: 'projecting piece of land' [OE *tang*, *tong*].

Toot (Broad), Rangeworthy Gl; **Toot Field,** West Bradley So; **Toot Hill,** Horsley Gl, Calverton Nt, Cotheridge Wo; **Toothill Butts Furlong,** Headington O; **Toot Hill Close,** Groby Lei; **Toot Hill Round,** Beechamwell Nf; **Toota,** Corney Cu [ON *haugr*]; **Nearmost, Middle & Furthest Tootal,** Nether Wyresdale La [OE *hyll*]; **Tooth Hill,** Bowdon Ch; **Tootle,** Paulerspury Nth; **Tuttle,**

Claughton La, Woodford Halse Nth: 'land on a look-out hill' [OE **tōt*]. See also Total Hill.

Top Cliff, Bonsall Db (*Topcliff* 1415); **Top Close,** Odd Rode Ch, Matlock Bath Db, Billesdon Lei, Kibworth Lei, Scraptoft Lei, Stretton Parva Lei, Thurnby Lei; **Top Croft,** Offerton Ch, Shackerstone Lei; **Top Field,** Sherington Bk, Alphington D, Berrynarbor D, Blackawton D, East Anstey D, Clifton & Compton Db; **Top Forty Acres,** Stockerston Lei; **Top Hill,** East Anstey D; **Top Leys,** Normanton le Heath Lei; **(The) Top Meadow,** Dukinfield Ch, Kirk Hallam Db, Mellor Db, Offcote Db, Wensley Db, Billesdon Lei, Evington Lei, Goadby Lei, Lubenham Lei, Stoughton Lei; **Top of All,** Hope Woodlands Db, Todmorden WRY; **Top of the Hill,** Goadby Lei, Norton juxta Twycross Lei; **Top o' th' Hill,** Lyme Handley Ch; **Top o' th' Wood,** Marple Ch, Romiley Ch; **Top Orchard,** Peckleton Lei; **Top Piece,** Bampton D; **Top Slang,** Sheepy Magna Lei; **Top Twenty,** Shawell Lei (ie twenty acres): 'land at the summit of a hill, or far from the village'.

Total Height, Out Rawcliffe La, an ironic name for land in a depression (cf Wainwright, *FN Amounderness*, 194).

Total Hill, Beal WRY, 'look-out hill' [OE *tōt, hyll*]. See also Toot.

Town Close, Aldbury Hrt, Burton Overy Lei, Croxton Nf, Hayton Nt; **Town Croft,** Bollington Ch, Eaton Ch, Totley Db, Stretton Parva Lei; **Town Field,** Bradwell Ch, Sandbach Ch, Eckington Db, Holmesfield Db, Whittington Db, Shangton Lei, Shuckburgh Wa (*Tunfurlong* c 1200); **Town Furlong,** Newbold Pace Wa; **Town Haggs,** Stretton Parva Lei; **Town Leaze,** Ashley Gl; **Town Meadow,** Longford Db, Huncote Lei, Hoveringham Nt, Selston Nt, Brighwell Baldwin O, Frodesley Sa, Longden Sa; **Town Moor,** Aston Wa; **Town Park,** Billesdon Lei; **Town Piece,** Bonsall Db, Enstone O (*Tunfurlong* 1280); **Town Rigg,** Crackenthorpe We; **Towns Close,** Ashreigney D; **Towns Meadow,** Misson Nt: 'land near the village, or shared by all its inhabitants' [OE *tūn*].

Town End, Heath Db, Milburn We; **Townend Butts,** Barlborough Db; **Town End Close,** Cookham Brk, Carburton Nt, Chilwell Nt, Kneesall Nt, Laxton Nt, Crofton WRY; **Towns End,** North

Cerney Gl, Evington Lei, Galby Lei, Stoughton Lei, West Langton Lei, Chinnor O, Condover Sa, Kenley Sa; **Townsend Close,** Buckhorn Weston Do, Hallaton Lei, Knossington Lei, Norton juxta Twycross Lei, Snarestone Lei, Welham Lei, Beechamwell Nf; **Townsend Flat,** Markeaton Db; **Town's End Piece,** Ashwell Hrt, Kiddington O: 'land at the end of the village'.

Town Field, pre-enclosure great field name in Shirebrook Db, Rillington ERY, Bolton Percy WRY, Keighley WRY, Goldsbrough WRY.

(The) Township, Baggrave Lei, Bittesby Lei, Elmesthorpe Lei: 'the site of a village' [OE *tūnscipe*].

Trafalgar Farm, Temple Guiting Gl, transferred name commemorating the naval battle in 1805.

Traitors Meadow, Speen Brk, a derogatory name for unreliable land.

Tram, Barbon We, Beetham We, Firbank We, Kendal We, Mansergh We, Middleton We, Scalthwaiterigg We; **Tram Roods,** Crich Db; **Trams Close,** Skelsmergh We: 'long, narrow, tapering field' [MnE dial. *tram*].

Treacle Nook, Spondon Db, fanciful name alluding to sticky soil.

Tree Close, Callow Db, Market Bosworth Lei; **The Tree Ground,** Chieveley Brk; **Tree Piece,** Brierley Hill St: self-explanatory.

Trefoil, Pownall Fee Ch, Shirland & Higham Db; **Trefoil Close,** Hinckley Lei: 'land on which clover grew'. Various clovers (*Trifolium* spp) have been grown as fodder crops since the seventeenth century.

Triangle, Aston by Budworth Ch, Macclesfield Forest Ch, Northenden Ch, Bradwell Db, Darley Db, Alton Pancras Do, Galby Lei; **Triangle Bit,** Broughton Astley Lei; **Triangle Close,** Ashleyhay Db; **Triangle Croft,** North Rode Ch; **Triangle Field,** Newbottle Du, Bradford WRY; **Triangle Piece,** Eyam Woodlands Db, Wykin Lei, Croxton Nf; **Triangular Croft,** Eyam Woodlands Db; **Triangular Field,** Norton Db, Pittington Du; **Triangular Piece,** Windsor Brk, Horton cum Studley O: 'three-cornered piece of land'.

Trinity Dole, Macclesfield Ch (*Le Trinite Acre* 1414); **Trinity Farm,** Retford Nt: respectively 'endowment of the chantry of the Holy Trinity' and 'land owned by Trinity College, Cambridge'.

Troublesome, Oldland Gl, derogatory name for poor land.

Trough, West Hallam Db; **Trough Acre,** Wirksworth Db; **Trough Close,** Codnor & Loscoe Db, Ripley Db, Sutton cum Duckmanton Db, Tapton Db; **Trough Field,** Bollin Fee Ch, East Allington D, Holmesfield Db; **Trough Stones,** Eaton & Alsop Db: 'a valley' [OE *trōg*].

Trouzers Field, Gatcombe Wt, fanciful name alluding to the shape of the field.

True Field, Feltwell Nf (*Trehowefeld* t.Ed 1), 'land on Trehowe, ie tree-clad hill' [ON *tré, haugr*].

Tucking Mill, Beaford D, Rushall W: 'land containing or adjoining a cloth-finishing factory'.

Tundish, Saintbury Gl, 'funnel-shaped piece of land'; a tun-dish is a shallow vessel with a tube in the bottom, for attaching to the bunghole of a cask.

Tunnel Close, Swannington Lei; **Tunnel Field,** Preston on the Hill Ch: 'land adjacent to a canal or railway tunnel'.

Tup Close, Welby Lei; **Tup Croft,** Marple Ch, Stretton Db; **Tup Hill,** Clayworth Nt (*Tupcroft* 1548): 'land on which rams were kept' [ME *tup*, 'breeding ram'].

Tupping Dale, Everton Nt, 'land on which rams and ewes were turned out together'.

Turbary Croft, Warmingham Ch; **Turfberry,** Cliburn We: 'land where turf or peat can be got' [ME *turbarye*].

Turf Banks, Gawsworth Ch (*Turberhurste* 1561); **Turf Close,** Tur Langton Lei; **Turf Common,** Hook Do; **Turf Cot Field,** Crowley Ch [OE *cot*]; **Turf Dole(s),** Sutton C, Cantley Nf; **Turf Fen,** Ely C, East Dereham Nf; **Turf Moor,** Matlock Bath Db; **Turf Pits,** Hattesley Ch, Walton Inferior Ch: 'land containing or adjoining peat beds' [OE *turf*].

The Turn, Norton Db; **Turn Croft,** Eaton Ch, Millington Ch, Unstone Db; **Turn Meadow,** Bradwell Db; **Turn Wood,** Firbank We: 'circular piece of land' [OE **trun*].

Turnabout, Pilsley Db; **Turnabout Ley,** Pontesbury Sa; **Turning But Flat,** Frodsham Ch; **Turning Holme,** Snelstone Db; **Turning Leasow,** Church Pulverbatch Sa: 'land on which a plough may be turned'.

Turn Penny Field, Buglawton Ch, complimentary name for land from which a quick profit may be gained.

Turnep Croft, Disley-Stanley Ch; **Turnip Close,** Widecombe D, Tibshelf Db, Blaston St Giles Lei, Broughton Astley Lei, Huncote Lei, Walton Lei; **Turnip Hill,** Hylton Du; **Turnip Hill,** Hylton Du; **Turnip Piece,** Offcote Sa, Yockleton Sa; **Turnip Pingle,** Middleton by Wirkworth Db; **Turnip Plot,** North Poorton Do; **Turnips Close,** Duffield Db; **Turnup Hold,** Cassop Du [ME *hold*, 'store']: 'land on which turnips were grown' [OE *næp*]. Though the name of Charles, second viscount Townshend (1674–1738), is indelibly associated with this crop, he did not in fact introduce it into England, for it had been grown as a garden crop in Tudor times and was used occasionally for fodder in the seventeenth century. But Townshend's great innovation was the use of roots as the fourth course in crop rotation, thus avoiding the wasteful fallow year (see Lord Ernle, *English Farming Past and Present*, 172 ff).

Turnpike Close, Alderwasley Db, Walton Db, Barwell Lei, Twycross Lei; **Turnpike Field,** Cheadle Ch, Dalbury Lees Db, Elwick Hall Du; **The Turnpike Ground,** Drayton O; **Turnpike Meadow,** Arnesby Lei, Billesdon Lei; **Turnpike Piece,** Cardiston Sa; **Turnpike Road Field,** Stockport Etchells Ch: 'land adjacent to a main road'. The turnpike was, of course, the barrier or toll bar across the road, which prevented passage until the toll had been paid.

Tuttle, see Toot Field.

Tweenabrooks, Ilsington D; **Tween Dikes,** Carlton Curlieu Lei; **Tween Eyes,** South Cerney Gl [OE *ēa*, 'stream']; **Tweengates,** Greetham R [ON *gata*]; **Tween Towns,** Steeple Morden C; **Tween**

the Ways, Repton Db; **Tween Yeats,** Meathop We [OE *gēat*]: 'land between the stated features' [OE *betwēonan*].

Twelmin, Morland We (*Twelveman Rigg* 1704), 'land requiring the service of twelve men'.

(The) Twelve Acre(s), Brailsford Db, Eckington Db, Holwell Do, Mappowder Do, Castle Bytham L, Arnesby Lei, Thurlaston Lei, Stretton R; **Twelve Acre Close,** Elwick Hall Du, Hylton Du; **Twelve Acre Meadow,** Peatling Magna Lei; **Twelve Acre Riddance,** Silchester Ha; **Twelve Acre Ridge,** Bradley Db; **Twelves,** Rockhampton Gl: 'land having an area of twelve statute acres, or adjoining a piece of land of that area'.

Twelve Butts, Rudheath Lordship Ch; **Twelve Days Work(s),** Buglawton Ch, Ilkeston Db, Walworth Du; **Twelve Demath,** Ridley Ch; **Twelve Lands,** Buxton Db, Caldwell Db, Matlock Bath Db; **Twelve Leys,** Norton juxta Twycross Lei; **Twelve Roods,** Ilkeston Db: 'land having an area of twelve units as named'.

Twelve Pence, Moston Ch; **Twelve Penny Piece,** Lower Withington Ch; **Twelve Pound Close,** Walworth Du, Sysonby Lei: names alluding to the value of the land.

Twentiaker, Asby We 1239; *Twentiakre,* Oxford O c 1220; **Twenty Acres,** Pott Shrigley Ch, Beer D, Swarkestone Db, Gaddesby Lei; **Twentys,** Rockhampton Gl (*Twentyacres* 1400): 'land having an area of twenty acres'.

Twenty Bushel Piece, Charlbury O; **Twenty Butts,** Morton Db; **Twenty Dork,** Birker Cu (see Day Work); **Twenty Lands,** Alkmonton Db, Barton Blount Db, Boyleston Db, Eakring Nt, Fringford O, Idbury O; **Twenty Lands Plantation,** Thrumpton Nt (*Twenty Lands* 15c): 'land with area calculated in twenty units of various kinds'.

Twenty Pits, Shackerstone Lei, self-explanatory.

Twenty-four Acres, Foxton Lei, 'land having an area of twenty-four acres'.

Twenty Shilling Field, Agden Ch; **Twenty Shillings Pasture,** Washington Du: names alluding to the value of the land.

Twisted Ash Piece, St Mary Bourne Ha; **Twisten Allers,** Hillfield Do [OE *alor*]: 'land marked by a deformed tree or trees'.

Twistgut, Boxwell Gl, derogatory name for intractable land.

Twistle Close, Lyneham W; **Twizzle Acre,** Batcombe So; **Twizzle Close,** Tur Langton Lei: 'land in a fork, between two roads or streams' [OE *twisla*].

Twitch Common, Hollowell Nth; **Twitch Dole,** Unstone Db; **Twitchfield,** Yardley Hastings Nth; **Twitch Piece,** Duffield Db: 'land infested with couch grass'. *Twitch* is one of the more common synonyms of couch-grass, (*Agropyron repens*), which is also known as *quick*, *scutch* and *stroil*.

Twitchel, Kirk Langley Db; **Twitchell,** Berkswell Wa (*Twichefeld* 1452); **Twitchells,** Claverley Sa; **Twichen,** Berrynarbor D; **Twitchen Plantation,** East Anstey D; **Twitcher Meadow,** Hyde Ch: 'land in a fork between two roads or streams' [OE *twicen*].

Twixt Hedges, Kings Norton Lei, self-explanatory.

Twizzle Ash, Grittleton W, 'land marked by a forked ash tree' [OE *twisla, æsc*].

Two Acre, Crowley Ch (*The Two Acres* 1651); **Two Acre Pightle,** Enbourne Brk; **(The) Two Acres,** Norton Ch, Alderwasley Db, Pentrich Db, Hermitage Do, Barwell Lei, Billesdon Lei, Dadlington Lei, Illston Lei, Knossington Lei, Stretton Parva Lei; **Two Acres and a Half Close,** Matlock Bath Db; **Two and Half Acre Meadow,** Glen Parva Lei; **Two and a Half Acres,** Abbotsham D: 'land having the stated area, or adjoining such a piece of land'.

Two Dark, Bewcastle Cu; **Two Day Math,** Marton Ch, Tetton Ch; **Two Day(s) Work,** Bosley Ch, Buglawton Ch, Eaton Ch, Kilburn Db, Brough We; **Two Lands,** North Wingfield Db, Tansley Db, Selston Nt; **Two Loonts,** Comberbach Ch [OE *land*]; **Two Shoots,** Bradley Db; **The Two Swaths,** Hallow Wo: 'land with an area measured in the stated conventional units'.

Two Dell Field, St Peters Hrt (*Twodelfeld* t.Ed 4); **Two Ditches,** Eastleach Martin Gl; **Two Hedges,** Shawell Lei; **Two Hill Closes,** Evington Lei; **Two Knows,** Ashton on Mersey Ch [OE *cnoll*]; **Two Moors,** Adderley Sa; **Two Paddocks,** Hermitage Do; **Two**

Pit Close, Hungry Bentley Db; **Two Pool,** Scraptoft Lei; **Twopool Ground,** Fifield O; **Two Road Close,** Scraptoft Lei: 'land having or adjoining the stated features'.

Twopenneworth, Stublach Ch; **Twopenny Close,** Hartshorne Db; **Twopenny Pasture,** Warmingham Ch; **Twopenny Patch,** Bollington Ch: possibly derogatory names alluding to the value of the land.

Two Withens, Hulse Heath Ch, 'land containing or adjoining two willow trees (or willow copses)' [OE **wiðign*].

Tye Croft, Fingringhoe Ess (*Tyecroft* 1502); **Tye Field,** West Mersea Ess: 'small enclosure' [OE *tēag*].

Tynin, Bulkington & Keevil W; **(The) Tyning,** Bratton W, Coulston & Edington W, Hullavington W, Luckington W, Monkton Farleigh W, Sherston W; **(The) Tynings,** Heytesbury W, Melksham W: 'an enclosure' [OE *tȳning*].

Tyrant, Betchton Ch, Brereton cum Smethwick Ch: 'nook of land'. It is suggested that the name is a development of *t' iron*, ie 'the iron' [OE *hyrne*].

U

Under Acre, Forncett St Peter Nf; **Underbank,** Marton Ch; **Underflatt,** Murston We [ON *flat*]; **(The) Underhill,** Shackerstone Lei, Hartley We; **Under Hill Field,** Great Budworth Ch; **Underholts,** Wibtoft Lei; **Underleys,** Beer D; *Under Sike*, King's Norton Lei 1638; **Underwolds,** Wibtoft Lei; **Under Wood,** Wharton Ch: 'land lying below the named features'.

Underdale, Shrewsbury Sa (formerly *Hundredhale*), possibly 'nook of land where the hundred assembly was held' [OE *hundred, halh*].

Understanding, Halstock Do, one of the arbitrary names alluding to characteristic Puritan qualities, assigned in the eighteenth century by Thomas Hollis. See Lilburne Mead.

Ungains (Little), Hartlebury Wo, possibly a derogatory name of the same type as Small Gains (qv).

Union, Northenden Ch; **Union Field,** Eyam Woodlands Db: doubtless allusions to the Poor Law unions of parishes; the term came to be applied to the workhouse provided by such unions.

Unthank Bottom, Murton We, 'land occupied by squatters', *unthank* meaning 'without thanks or acknowledgment of ownership' [OE *unþanc*].

Up Croft, Hendon Mx; **Uphills,** Long Ditton Sr (*Upehyll* 1235): 'land above' [OE *upp*].

Upper Allotment, Pentrich Db; **Upper Cleaves,** Wellow So [OE *clif*]; **Upper Close,** Ilkeston Db, Pentrich Db, Ripley Db, Foston Lei, Isley Walton Lei, King's Norton Lei, Stoughton Lei, Welham Lei, Wardley R; **Upper Craft,** Freethorpe Nf [OE *croft*]; **Upper Croft,** Heanor Db, Pentrich Db, Scarcliffe Db, West Hallam Db; **Upper Lays,** Bengeo Hrt (*Laycroft* 1717); **Upper Leasow,** Minsterley Sa [OE *lǣs*]; **Upper Meadow,** Boxford Brk, Lubenham Lei; **Upper Pasture,** Newton Unthank Lei; **Uppersets,** Kingham O; **Upper Spital,** Oxted Sr [ME *spitel*]; **Upper Stubbs,** Merstham Sr (*The Stubbet* 1522) [OE *stubb*, 'tree-stump']; **Upper Temple,** Addington Sr [OE *tempel*]; **Upper Tye,** Betchworth Sr [OE *tēag*]; **Upper Wong,** Hoby Lei [ON *vangr*]: 'land above a named feature, or in a higher position than another piece of land bearing a similar name, or above or away from the village' [ME *upper*].

The Urchin, St Michaels Hrt; **Urchin Furlong,** Claydon O; **Urchinhill,** Killamarsh Db; **Urchin Hole,** Great Hucklow Db; **Urchin Park,** Northenden Ch; **Urchins Dumble,** Ansley Wa; *Urchins Mier*, Dersingham Nf 1560; **Urchins Moor,** Aston by Budworth Ch: 'land on which hedgehogs were found' [ME *urchen*].

Urn, Batcombe So; **Great & Little Urn,** Harpenden Hrt, '(secluded) nook of land' [OE *hyrne*].

V

Valley Close, Cantley Nf; Valley Field, Ashreigney D: self-explanatory.

Van Dieman's Land, Hucknall under Huthwaite Nt, Napton Wa; **Van Diemens,** Brinkworth W: transferred name for remote pieces of land. On 24 November 1642 Abel Janszoon Tasman discovered the island now named after him. He however gave it the name of Anthoony van Diemenslandt, in honour of the Governor-General of the Dutch East Indies. The name was changed to Tasmania in 1853. See Clark, *History of Australia*, i, 31.

Varendells, Broadwell Gl; **Varndell Copse,** Odiham Ha; **The Varndells,** Toddington Gl; **The Varundels,** Lower Slaughter Gl: 'quarter pieces of land' [OE *feorða-dǣl*].

Varneycombe, Shotteswell Wa (*Farnecumbe* 1261), 'fern valley' [OE *fearn*, *cumb*].

Vastly, Stebbing Ess (*Verselee* 1517), 'gorse clearing' [OE *fyrs*, *lēah*].

Venneyend Close, Hailey O, 'land at the marshy side' [OE *fennig*, *ende*].

Vent Field, Beckley & Stowood O, 'land by or containing a drain' [ME *vente*, 'outlet'].

(The) Vernal, Ellestone Gl, Chippenham W (*Vernhale* 1400); **Vernal Farm,** Tichborne Ha; **Vernalls,** Alveston Gl: 'fern nook' [OE *fearn*, *halh*].

Vestry Light, Bruern O, 'endowed land for the provision of a light in the vestry of the parish church'. Cf Lamplands.

Vetch Butts, Pownall Fee Ch; **Vetch Close,** Bucklebury Brk, Cubley Db, Whitchurch O; **Vetch Field,** Chorley Ch, Peover Superior Ch, Sutton Downes Ch; **Vetch Leaze,** Didmarton Gl: 'land on which vetches were grown'. The vetch (*Vicia sativa*) is a valuable fodder plant.

Vicar Ing, Owston WRY; **Vicar Leys,** Tuxford Nt; **Vicars Close,** Moss WRY; **Vicars Field,** Windsor Brk; **Vicars Hatchet,** Alton Pancras Do [OE **hæcc-geat*]; **Vicars Hern,** Bole Nt [OE *hyrne*]; **The Vicars Piece,** Caversfield O, Claydon O: 'land assigned to the vicar of the parish, glebe land'.

Vicarage Close, Caversfield O; **Vicarage Meadow,** Bushby Lei; **Vicarage Wood,** West Anstey D: 'land adjoining the vicarage'.

Vierny Field, East Anstey D, 'fern-covered land' [OE *fearnig*].

Vigo Farm, Dorking Sr, transferred name commemorating the naval victory of Admiral Parker in 1702, ending in the capture of Vigo in Spain.

The Vine(s), Hadlow K, Piddington O; **Vine Farm,** Langford Bd; **Vine Mead,** Cerne Abbas Do; **Viney Mead,** Burghfield Brk (*Vyneheye* 1294) [OE *(ge)hæg*]: 'land on or near which grapes were grown' [ME *vine*].

Vinegar, Widecombe D; **Vinegar Field,** Timperley Ch; **Vinegar Orchard,** Hallow Wo: names possibly alluding to the growing of cider apples.

The Vinegar Bottle, Fair Oak Ha, referring to the shape of the land.

The Vinery, Arrow Wa; **(The) Vineyard,** Hale Ch, Buckland D, Brailsford Db, Arne Do, Corfe Castle Do, Clifton Gl, Fairford Gl, Stoke Talmage O, Preston Montford Sa, Mytholmroyd WRY, Warmfield WRY; **Vineyard Field,** Great Waltham Ess (*Wynyerd* 1408); **Vineyard Hill,** Upper Slaughter Gl; **Vineyard Moor,** Eye & Dunsden O (*Wynyerd* 1603–4); **(The) Vineyards,** Ely C (*Le Vyneyerd* 1482), Hartpury Gl (*Wyneyard* 1542), Staunton Gl, Banbury O; **Lower Vineyards,** Hurstbourne Priors Ha: 'land on which grape vines were grown' [ME *vine, vinȝerd*]. The suggestion, reported by Barbara Kerr in 'Dorset fields and their names', 243, that Vineyard was commonly used in West Dorset for a home close, merits closer attention. Where vines were widely grown this connotation would obviously imply the primary sense of the word.

Vixendell, North Mimms Hrt, 'valley in which a vixen was seen' [ME *fixen*, OE *dell*].

Vox Hills, Durley Ha; **Vox Well,** Bishop's Cleeve Gl: 'land on which foxes were found' [OE *fox*].

W

Wad Barn, Berkswell Wa; **Wadberrow Hill,** Feckenham Wo [OE *beorg*]; **Wad Cabin,** Evington Lei, Weston Favell Nth; **Wad Close,** Lambley Nt; **Little Wad Close,** Little Kempsey Wo; **Wad Croft,** Wessington Db, Kettering Nth; **Waddon,** Fifehead Neville Do [OE *dūn*]; **Waddon Field,** Wychwood O (*Waddon*

1300); **Wad(d) Ground,** Banbury O, Wardlington O, Farnborough Wa; **Wad Houses,** Snaith WRY (*Wodehouses* 1326); **Wadland(s),** Barton Blount Db, Sutton on the Hill Db, Burton Overy Lei, Tilton Lei; **Wad Leaze,** Rencomb Gl [OE *lǣs*]; **Wad Orchard,** Blaston St Michael's Lei; *Wadeacre*, Walton Db 1312: 'land on which woad was grown or processed' [OE *wād*]. Woad (*Isatis tinctoria*) was cultivated largely as a cottage crop in the Middle Ages, extended to a field scale in Tudor times, and began to decline in the nineteenth century when aniline dyes were introduced. The famous blue colour was extracted from the leaves which were first fermented in sheds on or near the land where the crop was grown—hence the names including *Cabin* and *Houses*. The plant still grows wild in England, but is comparatively rare.

Waggon Hovel Close, Dadlington Lei, Peckleton Lei: 'land containing shed in which a waggon was housed'.

Waite Field, Sall Nf (*Tweit* 1347, *Thweit* 1356), 'land in or near a woodland clearing' [ON *þveit*].

Walk Close, Codnor & Loscoe Db, Babworth Nt; **Walk Field,** Havant Ha; **Walk Ground,** Charlcote Wa; **Walk Hill,** Egginton Db; **Walk Meadow,** Enbourne Brk, Beaford D, Hallow Wo; **Walkmile Croft,** Ashford Db (*Walkmylne Croft* 1529) [OE *myln*]; **Walk Mill Brow,** Barnacre La; **Walk Mill Close,** Taston Db; **Walk Wood,** Aldbury Hrt, St Paul's Walden Hrt: 'land on which the fulling of cloth took place' [OE *wealcan*].

Wall Bank, Matlock Bath Db, Elswick La; **Wall Close,** Chieveley Brk, Coventry Wa; **Wall Croft,** Freckleton La, Nailstone Lei; **Wall Ends,** Nursling Ha; **Wall Field,** Carleton La (*Redwalle* 1261), Holleth & Forton La; **Wall Furlong,** Tissington Db, Bryning La; **Wall Nook,** Houghton le Spring Du; **Walled Park,** Foston Lei; **(The) Walls,** Windsor Brk (*Le Walles* 1363), Charminster Do: 'land adjoining a wall, or containing a ruin', the exact sense being impossible to determine without local evidence [OE *weall*].

(The) Wallet(t), Pott Shrigley Ch, Newent Gl; **The Wallets,** Narborough Lei: '(land in) a hollow or pocket of a hill' [ME *walet*].

Walnut Crate, Stanton Fitzwarren W [OE *croft*]; **Walnut Croft,** White Notley Ess; **Walnut Garth,** Skelbrooke WRY; **Walnut**

Paddock, Stanton by Bridge Db; **Walnut Tree Close,** Peckleton Lei, Frayford O, Swerford O; **Walnut Tree Field,** East Anstey D; **Walnut Tree Ground,** Northmoor O; **Walnut Tree Hoppet,** High Easter Ess [OE **hoppet*]; **Walnut Tree Meadow,** Burghfield Brk; **Walnut Tree Pightle,** Hertingfordbury Hrt [ME *pightel*]; **Walnut Walk,** Swinford O: 'land containing or adjoining walnut trees'. Of eastern Mediterranean origin (the name means 'foreign nut'), the walnut has long been grown in Britain either for the nuts or for the timber, much prized in cabinet work. The presence of specimen trees in hedgerows or fields is usually due to rooks, which carry off large quantities of the nuts.

Wandale, Bempton ERY (*Wandelles* 13c), Folkton ERY (*Wandele* 1172), Hunmanby ERY (*Wandeiles* 13c), Warter ERY; **Wandales,** Hayton ERY (*Le Wandayles* 13c), Kirby Grindilythe ERY (*Wandayle* 12c), North Grimston ERY (*Wandail* 13c), Crackenthorpe We, Lowther We; **Wandels,** Nafferton ERY: 'share of the common field' [ME *wandel*].

Wantcatcher's Hook, Adderbury O, 'land assigned to the mole-catcher' [MnE dial. *want*].

War Close, Manston Do; **War Field,** Marston Montgomery Db, Drayton Sa; **War Meadow,** Burghfield Brk: possibly 'land adjacent to, or containing, an earthwork' [OE *weorc*].

Warden (Little, Middle & Great), Frolesworth Lei; **The Wardens,** Caynham Sa: 'enclosures' [OE *worðign*].

Ware Field, Sandhurst Brk; **Ware Hamm Close,** Oxford O [OE *hamm*]; **Ware Meadow,** Thame O: 'land near a weir' [OE *wer*].

Warlish (High & Low), Hylton Du, 'circular piece of land' [OE *hwerfel, ersc*].

Warrel Close, Wyke WRY; **Worrell Leas,** Coston Lei: 'land by a quarry' [ME *quarrelle*].

(The) Warren, Mappowder Do, Baggrave Lei, Rotherfield Greys O; **Warren Carr,** Wensley & Snitterton Db; **Warren Close,** Holt Lei, Lubenham Lei; **Warren Field,** Hadlow K; **Warren Heath,** Feltwell Nf; **Warren Wood,** Esher Sr (*Warren Grounde* 1642): 'land set apart for the breeding of rabbits' [ME *wareine*].

Warth, Eaton Ch, 'streamside land' [OE *waroð*].

Warthill, Little Ness Sa, 'land lying across a hill' [ON *þverr*].

Wash Lands, Melbourne Db; **Wash Pit Close,** Kings Norton Lei, Tooley Park Lei; **Wash Pit Dale,** Kirby Underdale ERY; **Wash Pit Meadow,** Ashby Folville Lei, Evington Lei, Scraptoft Lei; **Wash Pool Hill,** Enstone O: 'land near a cattle or sheep dipping place'.

Wasp Field, Tetton Ch, 'land infested by wasps'.

(The) Waste, Bradbourne Db, Eaton & Alsop Db: 'land enclosed from the manorial waste' [OE *wēste*].

Watchetts, Frimley Sr (*Whadeseyte*, *Whadeshate* 1418, *Wadeshete* 1548), 'woad furlong' [OE *wād, scēat*].

Water Close, Fenny Bentley Db; **Water Demesne,** Dorchester O; **Water Furlong,** Shirburn O; **Water Grip Furs,** Ebrington Gl [OE *grype*, 'ditch', *furh*]; **Water Hades,** Pillerton Wa [OE *hēafod*]; **Water Lands,** Enstone O; **Water Leys,** Hathersage Db [OE *lǣs*]; **Water Park,** Ashreigney D; **Water Rand,** Dorchester O [OE *rand*, 'edge, bank']; **Water Stitch,** Winsley W; **Watercourse Close,** Ellingham Nf; **Watery Close,** Foxton Lei, Frolesworth Lei (*The Watry Close* 1674); **Watery Ground,** Shipton under Wychwood O; *Watery Lande*, Dersingham Nf 1560; **Watery Meadow,** Scraptoft Lei; **Watery Piece,** Dorchester O: 'land by or containing a pool or stream'.

Waterfall Way, Moreton Pinkney Nth (*Waterfalmede* 1343), self-explanatory.

Water Furrows, Allestree Db, Houghton le Spring Du, Cirencester Gl, Aldbury Hrt (*Waterforrowes* 1638), Coston Lei, Willoughby Waterless Lei, Hendon Mx, Eakring Nt, Kneesall Nt, Daventry Nth (*Waterforowys* 14c), Churchill O, Sibford Gower O, Highworth W, Hullavington W, Stratford on Avon Wa Whitchurch Wa; **Water Furrows Close,** Owston Lei: 'land where water tends to lie in the furrows'.

Water Meadow, Enbourne Brk, Welford Brk, Hinton Parva Do, Hook Do, Harston Lei, Wonersh Sr: 'periodically flooded riverside pasture'.

Water Thorn Furlong, Sherington Bk 1740 (*Wartrou* c 1300), 'land by a gallows' [OE *wearg-trēow*].

Waterloo, Dalston Cu, Elwick Hall Du, Southam Gl; **Waterloo Barn,** Ansty W; **Waterloo Close,** Cookham Brk; **Waterloo Farm,** Wellesbourne Montford Wa; **Waterloo Wood,** Harthill Db: transferred name commemorating the battle near Brussels in 1815. Some of the examples may bear the sense of utter defeat which, paradoxically, has passed into the English proverbial expression 'to meet one's Waterloo'. But see also Duke.

Watt Croft, Aston Wa (*Watecroft* 13c, *Whatcroft* 1313), 'enclosure in which wheat was grown' [OE *hwǣte*, *croft*].

Wattledge, Biddestone W (*Wadlynch Close* 1650), 'ridged land on which woad was grown' [OE *wād*, *hlinc*].

Way Field, Abbotsham D, 'land beside a road' [OE *weg*].

Waypost Close, Bowden Magna Lei, 'land beside a signpost'.

Wear Field, Elstead Sr; **Wear Meadow,** Brimington Db, Eckington Db: 'land beside a weir' [OE *wer*].

Wearasome, Ovenden WRY; **Wearisome,** Hoff We: derogatory names for difficult land.

Week Farm, Ringwood Ha, 'dairy farm' [OE *wīc*].

Weighnought, Ham & Stone Gl, a derogatory name for unproductive land.

Weir Field, Clive Ch; **Weir Hill,** Minshull Vernin Ch; **Weir Leasow,** Yockleton Sa [OE *lǣs*]; **Weir Meadow,** Abbots Langley Hrt (*Weyers* 1583): 'land by a weir' [OE *wer*]. The Abbots Langley name may be 'land by a bathing place' [ME *weyour*].

Welcome Meadow, Fifield O, complimentary name for good land.

Well Acre, Longdon Wo; **Well Bank,** Sandbach Ch; **Well Breck,** Babworth Nc [OE *bræc*]; **Well Close,** Durley Ha, Knossington Lei; **Well Croats,** Bennington Hrt, Watton at Stone Hrt [OE *croft*]; **Well Croft,** Bosley Ch, Newbold Astbury Ch, Warmingham Ch, Great Gaddesden Hrt (*Wellecroft* 1432); **Well Cutts,** Flamstead Hrt (*Wellcroft* 1477) [OE *croft*]; **Well Field,** Bradwall Ch, Great Warford Ch, Henbury Ch, Newton Ch, Elwick Hall Du, Limpsfield Sr (*Wellefeldes* 1445); **Well Garth,** Shap Rural We [ON *garðr*]; **Well Hill,** Beechamwell Nf (*Wellehel* 1218); **Well**

Leasow, Church Pulverbatch Sa, Cound Sa, Brierley Hill St; **Well Meadow,** Enbourne Brk, Tytherington Ch, Alvington D, Beaford D, Lamberhurst K, Preston Patrick We; **Well Park,** East Allington D, West Alvington D; **Well Pightle,** Cantley Nf; **Well Yard,** Sall Nf (*Wellecroft* 1342): 'land by a well or spring' [OE *wella*].

Well Dale, Warter ERY (*Quelledale* 1197), 'circular valley' [OE *hwēol*, ON *dalr*].

Wellington, Elwick Hall Du, name commemorating Arthur, Duke of Wellington, the victor of Waterloo. See also Duke.

Werg Mill, Mildenhall W; **Wergs,** Stratfieldsaye Ha (*The Wirg* 17c); **Wergus,** Toot Baldon O; **Works Bed Furlong,** Toot Baldon O; **Wregs,** Brimpsfield Gl; **Wurgs Shaw,** Hartley Wespall Ha: probably 'land by, or containing, willow trees' [MnE dial. *werg*, 'willow'].

West Brecks, Cottam Nt [OE *bræc*]; **West Close,** Washington Du, Greetham R, Hook WRY, Snydale WRY; **West Croats,** Kirtling C [OE *croft*]; **West Croft,** Chobham Sr, Fockerby WRY, Stainforth WRY; **West Ellers,** Haltwhistle Nb [ON *elri*, 'alder']; **Westend,** Stainmore We; **West End Bottoms,** Hope Woodlands Db [OE *botm*]; **West Field,** Welford Brk (*Le Westfelde* 1557), Arrington C, Runcorn Ch, Melbourne Db (*Westfelde* 1415), Newbottle Du, Compton Abdale Gl, Eastington Gl, Siddington Gl, Kimpton Hrt, Shenley Hrt (*Westfeld* 1386), Welham Lei, Shepperton Mx, Haltwhistle Nb, Croxton Nf, Laxton Nt, Banstead Sr, Coulsdon Sr, Leigh Sr (*Westfeld* 1350), Woodmansterne Sr, Stoneleigh Wa, Fockerby WRY; **Great West Field,** Long Critchell Do; **West Field Close,** Tur Langton Lei; **Westgores,** Salperton Gl; **West Grove,** Boxford Brk; **West Halve,** Ogbourne St George W [OE *healf*]; **West Ham,** South Cerney Gl [OE *hamm*]; **West Haugh,** Haltwhistle Nb [OE *halh*]; **West Holme,** Beal WRY; **West Hook,** Ford Du; **West Ings,** Kellington WRY [ON *eng*]; **West Land(s),** Patrington ERY (*Westlands* 1533), Winestead ERY (*Westland* 1339), Henfield Sx (*Westlaund* 1373), Warmfield WRY; **West Leys,** Beeby Lei [OE *lǣs*]; **West Mead,** Harlestone Nth (*Westmede* c 1320); **West Meadow,** Clewer Brk (*Le Westmed* 1413), Repton Db, Stretton Db, Billesdon Lei; **West Park,** East Allington D; **West Wong,**

Stretton R [ON *vangr*]; **Western Down,** Arlington D; **Western Holmes,** Blaby Lei; **Western Meadow,** Ilsington D; **Westhow Field,** Thorganby ERY [ON *haugr*]: 'land to the western side of the parish, or to the west of some other piece of land' [OE *west*(*erne*)].

West Field, pre-enclosure great field name in Houghton Regis Bd, Souldrop Bd, Sundon Bd, Claydon Bk, Olney Bk, Shalstone Bk, Stewkley Bk, Chievely Brk, Stanford in the Vale Brk, Chippenham C, Harlton C, Shirebroke Db, Afflington Do, Bolam Du, Gainford Du, Shotton Du, Burton Agnes ERY, Garton on the Wolds ERY, Harpham ERY, Broxted Ess, Ablington Gl, Shipton Gl, Andover Ha, Charlton Ha, Gransden Hu, Weston Hu, Croxton L, Grimblethorp L, Kexby L, Legbourne L, Thurlby L, Upton L, Burton Lazars Lei, Kirkby Bellars Lei, Beechamwell Nf, Foston NRY, Marske NRY, Wheldrake NRY, Hucknall Torkard Nt, Knighton Nt, Walkeringham Nt, Adstone Nth, Evenley Nth, Flower Nth, Holdenby Nth, Pilsgate Nth, Barford O, Burford O, Cleveley O, Milcombe O, Westwell O, Wooton O, Tinwell R, Baltonsborough So, Bratton St Maur So, Curry Rivell So, Englishcombe So, Somerton So, Leek St, Angmering Sx, Atherington Sx, Worthing Sx, Marden W, West Overton W, Binley Wa, Long Lawford Wa, Kettlewell WRY, Kirk Deighton WRY, Mexborough WRY [OE *west*, *feld*].

Wet Acre, Cogshall Ch; **Wet Arse Gap,** Cleckheaton WRY; **Wet Butts,** Lower Whitley Ch; **Wet Close,** Duffield Db, Forncett St Peter Nf; **Wet Field,** Kettleshulme Ch, Siddington Ch, Somerford Booths Ch, Chinley Db; **Wet Foot,** Idbury O; **Wet Furrow,** Alstone Gl; **Wet Furrows,** Nether Seal Db, Spondon Db, Ashchurch Gl, Sheepy Magna Lei, Witherley Lei, Austrey Wa (*Wetforowes* 1585); **Wetlands,** Dorchester O, Cliburn We, Firbank We; **Wet Leaze Meadow,** Burghfield Brk; **Wet Meadow,** Alphington D, Aston Db, Bakewell Db, Pontesbury Sa; **Wet Reans,** Bispham La, Little Ness Sa [ON *rein*]; **Wet Rough,** Kenley Sa: self-explanatory names, some more vivid than others, referring to ill-drained land.

Wham, Goosnargh La, Inskip La, Woodplumpton La, Midgley WRY; **Whoms,** Stayley Ch: 'small valley, marshy hollow' [ON *hvammr*].

Wharf, Norton Ch (*The Warth* 1536), '(marshy) land beside a stream' [OE *waroð*].

Wharf, Heanor Db; **Wharf Close,** Pentrich Db, Shackerstone Lei; **Wharf Field,** Staveley Db; **Wharf Lane Field,** Chesterfield Db: 'land near a canal wharf' [OE *hwearf*].

Wharlicar, Newton with Scales La, 'land near or containing a circle of stones' [ON *hvirfill, akr*].

Wharrell Meadow, Strickland Roger We, 'grassland near a quarry' [ME *quarrelle*].

Wheat Acre Clough, Marple Ch; **Wheat Bank,** Bampton We; **Wheat Butts,** Bosley Ch, Normanton WRY (*Les Whetebuttes* 1408); **Wheat Close,** Bucklebury Brk, Alkmonton Db, Clowne Db, Rosliston Db, Hermitage Do, Ford Du, Chalford Gl, Hawkesbury Gl, Billesdon Lei, Burrough on the Hill Lei, Illston Lei, Knossington Lei, Stretton Parva Lei, Willoughby Waterless Lei, Chedlington O, Toot Baldon O; **Wheat Croft,** Adlington Ch, Faddiley Ch (*Quetecroft* 13c), Kettleshulme Ch, Dronfield Woodhouse Db, Eckington Db, Isleworth Mx, Pontesbury Sa, Kirk Bramwith WRY; **Wheat Crofts,** Weston Hrt; **Wheat Eyes,** Butley Ch [OE *ēg*]; **Wheat Fenny,** Bradford WRY; **Wheat Field,** Bollin Fee Ch, Chorley Ch, Handforth Ch, Yeardsley cum Whaley Ch, Barking Ess, Albury Hrt (*Whete Furlong* 1447), Idmiston W, Packwood Wa; **Wheat Hay,** Kingsley Ch, Aston Db; **Wheat Hill,** Billesdon Lei; **Wheat Holme,** Owston WRY; **Wheat Land,** Fritwell O; **Wheat Lands,** Scaftworth Nt; **Wheat Marsh,** Kellington WRY; **Wheat Parrock,** Crosthwaite We; **Wheat Piece,** Mollington O; **Wheat Reans,** Barrow Ch, Frodsham Lordship Ch; **Wheat Ridges,** Oulton Lowe Ch; **Wheat Waites,** Askham Nt [ON *þveit*]: 'land on which wheat grew well' [OE *hwǣte*].

Wheat Cake, Barnacre La, Greenhalgh La, Grimsargh La, Nateby La, Preston La, Woodplumpton La, Beetham We: a fanciful name for productive land.

Wheel Field, Eckington Db (*Wheele Filde* 1590), Goosnargh La; **Wheel Meadow,** Newton with Scales La: 'land near or containing a stone circle' [OE *hwēol*].

Wheel of Fortune, North Bradley W, 'unreliable land'.

Wheelbarrow Castle, Clun Sa, although it has all the appearance of an ironically derogatory name, this probably alludes to a circular tumulus [OE *hwēol*, *beorg*, ME *castel*].

Whin Close, Woodplumpton La, Little Strickland We; **Whin Field,** Dove Db, Ashton La, Goosnargh La; **Whin(n)s,** Woodthorpe Db, Barnacre La, Claughton La, Inskip La, Woodplumpton La, Hoff We, Ormside We, Stainmore We; **Whinny Bank,** Westby La, Crackenthorpe We, Newbiggin We; **Whinny Brow,** Claughton La, Hothersall La, Newbiggin We, Underbarrow We; **Whinny Close,** Beighton Db, Eckington Db, Killamarsh Db, Whitwell Db, Inskip La; **Whinny Field,** Pittington Du, Alston La, Bispham with Norbreck La, Brougham We; **Whinny Meadow,** Calow Db; **Winlow Field,** Eaton Ch [OE *hlāw*]; **Winney Hill,** Ilkeston Db; **Winns,** Westby with Plumpton La, Middleton We; **Wins Meadow,** Littleover Db: 'land on which gorse abounded' [ON *hvin*].

Whirl Piece, Wigginton O; **Whirl Pit(t)s,** Avening Gl, Dymock Gl; **Whirlstone,** Bagendon Gl; **Whirlimires,** Pittington Du: similar in meaning to Wheel Field (qv), though Whirlimires may allude to a circular boggy patch of land [OE *hwyrfel*, *hwerfel*].

White Acre, Ashmore Do; **White Cliff,** Sturston Db (*Le Whyteclif* c 1250); **White Close,** Welford Brk, Elwick Hall Du, Harpsden O, Yaxley Sf; **White Croft,** Bosley Ch, Hawkesbury Gl, Stoke Park Ha, Sturt & Urchfont W; **White Croft Meadow,** Albury Sr (*Wyhtecroft* 1492); **White Field,** Sawston C, Macclesfield Ch, Presbury Ch, Somerford Booths Ch, Houghton le Spring Du, Kenley Sa, Caterham Sr; **White Flat,** Clayworth Nt; **White Flatt,** Owston WRY; **White Hays,** Minety Gl [OE (*ge*)*hæg*]; **White Hill,** Rostherne Ch (*Quythul* 1307), Bibury Gl; **Whitelands,** Bibury Gl, Wellow So, Chiddingfold Sr; **White Leasow,** Church Pulverbatch Sa, Stony Stretton Sa, Feckenham Wo; **White Leazes,** Thorpe Thewles Du; **White Ley,** Ashreigney D, **White Lime Field,** Lamberhurst K [OE *līm*]; **White Meadow,** Boxford Brk, Butley Ch, Combebach Ch, Alkmonton Db, Green Fairfield Db; **White Moor,** West Alvington D, Mollington O, Sibford Gower O; **White Moor Closes,** Eggborough WRY; **White Park,**

West Alvington D; **White Wong,** East Drayton Nt: 'land with a white surface' [OE *hwīt*].

White Bread, Cheadle Ch, either a complimentary name suggesting the luxurious diet to be enjoyed by one who works the land, or 'white broad piece of land' [OE *hwīt*, *brǣdu*].

White Thorn Breck, Babworth Nt, 'sloe-tree thicket'. It is worth noting that both whitethorn and blackthorn are synonyms for the sloe (*Prunus spinosa*) [OE *bræc*].

Whitening Croft, Hurdsfield Ch; **Whitening Jacks,** Yockleton Sa; **Whittening Field,** Sound Ch: 'land on which cloth was bleached'.

Whitsundoles, Salford Bd; **Whitsun Leaze,** Iffley O; **Whitsun Meadow,** Kingsclere Ha; **Whitsunday Pasture,** Sysonby Lei: land changing use or tenancy at Whitsun.

Who'd Have Thought It, Thornton WRY, fanciful name for a secluded or inconsiderable piece of land.

Whore Comb, Hawkesbury Gl; **Whore's Quarter,** Burford O; **Whore's Slade,** Churchill O: 'foul or dirty land' [OE *horsc*].

Whorestone, Brimpsfield Gl; **Whorestone Furlong,** Desborough Nth (*Horestan* 1227): 'land by a boundary stone' [OE *hār*, *stān*].

Wich Field, Dunham Massey Ch, Sproston Ch, Timperley Ch; **Wick House Field,** Marbury Ch; **Wicks,** Little Leigh Ch; **Wychhouse Meadow,** Eaton Ch: 'land adjoining brinepits or salt-boiling houses' [OE *wīc*]. There is now no doubt that in Cheshire this term came to have the specialised meaning quoted, although elsewhere it bore the general sense of 'outlying farm devoted to a special agricultural activity'.

Wicken, Marton Ch; **Wicken Croft,** Bosley Ch; *The Wickenfield*, Wincle Ch 1611; **Wicken Meadow,** Over Alderley Ch; **Wickens Hay,** Newbold Astbury Ch [OE *(ge)hæg*]; **Wickin Stile,** Taxal Ch: 'land near or containing rowan trees' [OE *cwicen*].

Wicks, Lilley Hrt (*The Wick* 1538), 'outlying farm premises' [OE *wīc*].

Wide Dyke, Scarcliffe Db; **Wide Field,** Caddington Hrt, Rickmansworth Hrt (*Le Widefeld* t.Ric 2); **Widemoor Piece,** Englefield Brk (*La Wyde More* 1240); **Widgrave,** Frodsham Ch [OE *grǣfe*]; **Widmoor,** Corsham W (*Widemore* t.Hy 3): 'broad piece of land' or 'land by a broad topographical feature' [OE *wīd*].

Widow Heys, Over Alderley Ch; **Widow Pingle,** Clowne Db, Skegby Nt; **Widow's Allotment,** Carsington Db; **Widow's Close,** Killamarsh Db: 'dower land, land providing an income for a widow'.

The Wild Acre, Warburton Ch; **Wild Field,** Earls Colne Ess; **Wild Youth,** Bollington Ch [OE *eorðe*]: 'uncultivated land' [OE *wilde*].

(The) Wilderness, Walton Db, Buckminster Lei, Cadeby Lei, Rufford Nt, Kiddington O, Middleton Stoney O, Hinstock Sa, Ockley Sr: 'barren or uncultivated land'.

Willey Wood, Chedworth Gl; **Willow Bed,** Newton Ch, Alton Pancras Do, North Poorton Do, Weston Birt Gl, Barton We; **Willow Bed Close,** Scraptoft Lei; **Willow Bed Mead,** Welford Brk; **Willow Close,** Houghton on the Hill Lei, Knossington Lei; **Willow Croft,** Presbury Ch, Kings Norton Lei; **Willow Dikes,** Houghton le Spring Du, Ormside We; **Willow Field,** Landon Hills Ess, Bampton We; **Willow Garth(s),** Hemingbrough ERY, Rawcliffe WRY, Skelbrooke WRY; **Willow Hall,** Northenden Ch [OE *halh*]; **Willow Holt,** Lockington Lei, Clayworth Nt, Fledborough Nt, Tuxford Nt; **Willow Lands,** Wirksworth Db; **Willow Leasow,** Kenley Sa; **Willow Pit Close,** Wykin Lei; **Willow Sick,** Baggrave Lei; **Willow Sick Meadow,** Illston Lei; **Willow Tree Close,** Swadlincote Db, Burrough on the Hill Lei; **Willows,** Parwitch Db; **Willy Dike Brigg,** Long Marton We; **Willy Park,** Crosby Ravensworth We: 'land by, or containing, willow trees' [OE **wilig*]. This standard term for trees of the genus *Salix* may refer to the species elsewhere listed under specific names, eg Osier, Sallow and Withy. All willows require plenty of moisture, which explains references to streamside and poolside land.

Wimblebarrow, Horsley Gl, 'Winebald's mound' [OE *beorg*].

Wimblefield Clump, Herriard Ha; **Wimble Hill,** Childs Ercall Sa; **Wimblestraw Furlong,** Dorchester O; **Wimble Timble,** Coulsdon Sr (*Wimble Spindle Field* 1793); **Wimbol Field,** Stoke Ch; **Windlestraw Field,** Gawsworth Ch, Thelwall Ch; **Windlestrea Field,** Norland WRY; **Windles,** Westerleigh Gl: 'land on which dog's tail grass abounded' [OE *windel-strēaw*]. Crested dog's tail grass (*Cynosurus cristatus*) is a common plant of old grasslands; its low leaves make it of some value for sheep, and as it will resist drought and cold it is often planted on hill grasslands. Its stem is long and wiry like that of a rush.

Winch Dell, Abbots Langley Hrt; **Winch Mead,** Benson O, Whitchurch O: 'land beside a canal or river winch' [OE *wince*].

Windgates, Merrow Sr; **Winett Hill,** Sulgrave Nth; **Wingate Field,** Witley Sr: 'narrow gap in a hedge or between two hills' [OE **windgeat*].

Winding Carr, Tuxford Nt; **Winding Close,** East Dereham Nf; **Winding Lands,** Weston So; **Winding Piece,** South Warnborough Ha, Wellow So; **Winding Shott,** Harpenden Hrt, Stanwell Mx; **Big, Middle & Far Windings,** Odstone Lei: 'curving piece of land'.

Windmill Close, Ault Hucknall Db, Beighton Db, Calow Db, Huncote Lei, Market Bosworth Lei, Tur Langton Lei, Banbury O (*Wyndemylne Feilde* 1551–2), Austrey Wa, Clifton upon Dunsmore Wa, Warmfield WRY; **Windmill Croft,** Upper Rawcliffe La; **Windmill Field,** Goldington Bd, Higher Whitley Ch, Lymm Ch, Minshull Ch, Pownall Fee Ch, Rainow Ch, Upton Ch, Barlborough Db, Harlow Ess (*Wyndmylfeld* 1350), St Michaels Hrt (*Wyndemyl* 1482), Tring Hrt (*Mullefeld* 1367), Lamberhurst K, Goosnargh La, Deddington O, Bletchingley Sr, Cold Norton St, Sherston W, Wootton Wawen Wa, South Elmsall WRY; **Windmill Furlong,** Steeple Ashton W (*Wynmylfeld* t.Hy 8); **Windmill Ground,** Kintbury Brk, Wardington O; **Windmill Hill,** Blackwell Db, Chellaston Db, Repton Db, Heworth Du, Chapel Ess, Ruardean Gl, Aldbury Hrt (*Wyndmyllfeld* 1447), Catesby Nth (*Milnhill* 1272), Harleston Nth, Dawley Magna Sa, Solihull Wa (*Le Wynmulne Heth* 1325); **Windmill Meadow,** Goosnargh La; **Windmill Piece,** Alderwasley Db, Purton Hrt, Waterperry O, Wanborough W; **Windmill Post,** Barton in the Beans Lei, Nailstone Lei: 'land beside, or containing, a windmill'.

Windy Half Acre, Offerton Db; **Windy Harbour,** Stalmine with Staynall La, Upper Rawcliffe La [OE *here-beorg*, 'sheltered place']; **Windy Hills,** Durham Du; **Windy Oaks,** Hungry Bentley Db: 'land in an exposed position'; the paradox of Windy Harbour must remain unresolved for the present.

Windy Wednesday, Out Rawcliffe La, a fanciful name in which the name of the day of the week may have no special function apart from alliteration.

Wine Cellar, Albury Hrt, a complimentary name for profitable land, probably alluding also to the declivity in which the field is situated.

The Wineyards, Bisley Gl; *Le Wingherd,* Maids Morton Bk 1236; **The Winyard(s),** Upper Slaughter Gl, Over Norton O (*Wynyard* t.Hy 6): 'vineyards' [OE *wīn-geard*].

Winnowing Bank, Siddington Ch; **Winnowing Piece,** Kirk Ireton Db: 'land on which winnowing was carried out'. After the corn has been threshed (to separate the grain from the straw), it is next necessary to remove the chaff from the grain; a breeze blowing through a barn may sometimes be utilised, but machinery has been employed for the purpose since the mid-nineteenth century.

Winter Beck, Muston Lei, alludes to a stream which flows only in winter [ON *bekkr*].

Winter Beer, Spelsbury O (*Winter Beer Furlong* 1803), 'land on which barley was planted in winter' [OE *winter, bere*].

Winter Close, Ramsden O, Eggborough WRY; **Winter Croft,** Halton Ch; **Winterdole,** Aston Rowant O (*Wynt'dole* 1220); **Winter Edge,** Dyrham Gl [OE *ecg* or *edisc*]; **Winter Field,** Avening Gl (*Wynterfeld* 1381), Helsington We; **Big & Little Winter Foot,** Tilstone Fearnall Ch [OE *ford*]; **Winter Green,** Knebworth Hrt (*Wynterlase* 1433); **Winter Lears,** Widecombe D [OE *leger*]: 'land used in winter' [OE *winter*].

The Wire, Hallaton Lei; **Wire Banks,** Wingerworth Db; **Wirelands,** Woodthorpe Db: possibly 'land by a pond' [ME *weyour*].

Wiselack, Bampton We, Hillbeck We (*Wyes Flaskes* 1657): 'hollow, or boggy land growing with willows' [OE *wīðig*, ON *slakki, flask*].

Wish Mead, Hawkesbury Gl, Market Lavington W: 'marshy meadow' [OE *wisce*].

Witch Grass, Pownall Fee Ch; **Witches,** Holwell Do: 'land on which couch-grass flourished' [OE *cwice*]. See also Twitch Common.

Withens Field, Dunham on the Hill Ch; **Within,** Layton with Warbreck La; **Within Croft,** Clotton Hoofield Ch, Haughton Ch; **Within(s) Meadow,** Great Budworth Ch, Helsby Ch; **Within Platt,** Newton Ch; **Withins,** Brampton Db, Spondon Db: 'land on which willow trees grew' [OE **wīðign*].

Withers, Bakewell Db (*Le Wither* 1290) [ON *víðir*]; **Withey Bed Meadow,** Enbourne Brk; **Withey Gores,** Cheam Sr [OE *gāra*]; **Withish,** Cranleigh Sr (*Withiet* 1485) [OE *-et*, 'clump of trees']; **Withy Acre,** Daglingworth Gl; **Withy Bed(s),** Rosliston Db, Alton Pancras Do, Hillfield Do, Holwell Do, Bibury Gl, Mangotsfield Gl, Barford St John O, Eye & Dunsden O, Allesley Wa; **Withy Bed Nook,** Nether Seal Lei; **Withy Close,** Clewer Brk (*Wythy Crofte* 1558), Carlton Lei; **Withy Croft,** Great Warford Ch; **Withy Mead,** Holwell Do; **Withy Reams,** Little Ness Sa [ON *reinn*]; **Withy Reins,** Alderbury Sa; **Withy Sick,** Market Bosworth Lei; **Withy Sitch,** Water Orton Wa [OE *sīc*]: 'land on which willow trees grew' [OE *wīðig*, ON *víðir*].

Witness Close, Martley Wo, possibly 'land used by a cloth-bleacher' [MnE *whitener*].

Woad Ground, Aston Somerville Gl, Grest Rissington Gl, Hardingstone Nth 1752; **Woad Orchard,** Winchcombe Gl; **Wodells,** Spratton Nth (*Wadhill* 1717) [OE *hyll*]: 'land on which woad was grown' [OE *wād*]. See also Wad Barn.

Woe Furlong, Fairford Gl, Weedon Lois Nth, Malden Sr; **Woeful Long,** Newbold & Dunston Db: 'crooked division of the common field' [OE *wōh, furlang*].

Woeful Hill, Newent Gl (*Wlhameshull* c 1254), 'hill by Wulfham, ie the wolf enclosure', a name possibly recalling some encounter with a wolf in the locality [OE *wulf, hamm*].

Woefulls Field, Twyning Gl (*Woofalle* 1543); **Woofallys,** Ashover Db: 'crooked clearing' [OE *wōh, (ge)fall*].

Womans Croft, Partington Ch, Berkhamsted Hrt; **Womans Field,** Prestbury Ch, Somerford Booths Ch; **Womans Go,** Compton

Abdale Gl [OE *gāra*]: 'land owned or occupied by a woman' [OE *wifman*].

Womb Furlong, Great Longstone Db (*Womfurlong* 17c), 'land in a hollow' [OE *wamb*].

The Wong, Groby Lei, Harlestone Nth (*Le Wonge* 1320); **Wong Close,** Laxton Nt; **(The) Wongs,** Kings Norton Lei 1638, Farndon Nt, Sutton Bonington Nt; **Wung,** Harpole Nth: 'in-field, enclosed area within an open field' [ON *vangr*].

Woo Meadow, Cheswardine Sa, 'crooked grassland' [OE *wōh, mǣd*].

Wood Acre(s), Carrington Ch, Barnacre La, **Wood Bank,** Appleton Ch; **Wood Close,** Sherington Bk, Eyam Woodlands Db, Harthill Db, Morton Db, Tupton Db, Blaston St Giles Lei, Holt Lei, Medbourne Lei, Shangton Lei, Welham Lei, Cantley Nf, Sall Nf (*Wodecroft* 1331), Eakring Nt, Skellow WRY; **Wood Croft,** Lambourn Brk, Fenny Bentley Db, Fifehead Magdalen Do, Manuden Ess, Avening Gl (*Wodecroft* 1492), Croydon Sr; **Wood Edish,** Tabley Superior Ch [OE *edisc*]; **Wood End,** Kiddington O, Morland We; **(The) Wood Field,** Butley Ch, Crowley Ch, Pott Shrigley Ch, Ashreigney D, Hinton St Mary Do, South Weald Ess, Daglingworth Gl (*Le Wodefeld* c 1350), Croydon Sr, Weybridge Sr, Nuneaton Wa, Stoneleigh Wa, Dewsbury WRY; **Wood Fields,** Thorpe Thewles Du; **Wood Hays,** Dutton Ch; **Wood Holme,** Beal WRY [ON *holmr*]; **Wood Ing,** Crigglestone WRY [ON *eng*]; **Wood Lands,** Kingston Magna Do; **Wood Leasow,** Church Pulverbatch Sa; **Wood Leaze,** Bishop's Canning W; **Wood Mead,** Buckhorn Weston Do; **Wood Meadow,** Newton Unthank Lei, Corley Wa (*Wodefurlong* 1411); **Wood Nook,** Twycross Lei; **Wood Nook Close,** Wingerworth Db; **Wood Nooking,** Clayworth Nt; **Wood Park,** West Alvington D; **Wood Piece,** Pilsley Db, Wolstaston Sa; **Wood Pightle,** Soham C; **Wood Readings,** St Michaels Hrt; **Wood Ridding,** Stretton Db [OE **ryding*]; **Wood Slaight,** Bourton on the Hill Gl [OE *slæget*]: 'land adjoining a wood' [OE *wudu*].

Wood Field, pre-enclosure great field name in Breedon on the Hill Lei, Glenfield Lei, Nether Seal Lei, Stathern Lei.

Woodcock Field, Ingatestone Ess (*Wodcokesmade* 1490); **Woodcock Garth,** Bole Nt; **Woodcock Hiron,** Alderwasley Db [OE *hyrne*]; **Woodcock Hole,** Upton We; **Woodcock Mead,** Walkern Hrt; **Woodcock Paddock,** Manston Do: 'land frequented by woodcock'. The woodcock (*Scolopax rusticola*) is alluded to in numerous other names, eg Cock Crow, Cock Road, and Cockshoots [OE *cocc*].

Woodland, Stratford on Avon Wa (*Wodlond* 1339), 'land on which woad was grown' [OE *wād*].

Wooferdine Croft, Dymock Gl, 'wolf enclosure' [OE *wulf*, *worðign*].

Wool Dale, Holwell Lei; **Woolhangers,** Berrynarbor D [OE *hangra*]; **Wool Piece,** Abbotsham D; **Woolridges,** Henstridge So: 'land used for the production of wool'; these might have been fields in or near which shearing took place.

Woolhedge Garth, Holbeck WRY, 'land near a hedge used for drying or bleaching cloth'.

Woollery Croft, Bradwell Ch, 'land overgrown with alders' [OE *alor*, *ig*].

Woolmead, Farnham Sr (*Wolmed* 1346), 'wolf meadow' [OE *wulf*, *mǣd*].

Woolpack, Woodplumpton La, possibly 'wolf pit' [OE *wulf*, *pytt*].

Woolpit (Great & Little), Fordham Ess (*Wolpytgrave* 1390); **Woolpits,** Furneux Pelham Hrt, Bletchingley Sr; **Woolpits Common,** Cowley Gl (*Wolfputtes* 1287); **Woolspit,** Ashby St Ledgers Nth: '(land near) a wolf pit' [OE *wulf*, *pytt*]. It is interesting to note so many references to the trapping of wolves, and it is worth recording that these animals were numerous in England at the time of the Norman Conquest, quite rare by the end of the thirteenth century, but did not become extinct until Tudor times.

Woolrush, Everdon Nth (*Ulfriches* 1316), 'Wulfric's (land)'.

Wopses Castle, Puddletown Do, a derogatory reference to overgrown land, described by Barbara Keir as 'a scrubby plot' on the parish boundary ('Dorset fields', 148) [OE *wæps*].

Worden Piddle, Mortimer Brk (*Wordia* 12c), 'boggy land within an enclosure' [OE *worðign*, **pidele*].

Work Hards, Drayton St Leonard O, a self-explanatory derogatory name.

Workhouse Close, Black Bourton O, Chinnor O, Gomersal WRY (*The Workhous Croft* 1552); **Workhouse Croft,** Stenton by Dale Db, Whittington Db; **Workhouse Field,** Plumley Ch, Pownall Fee Ch, Doveridge Db, Codicote Hrt; **Workhouse Hill,** Hayfield Db; **Workhouse Meadow,** Cookham Brk: 'land by, or belonging to, a Poor Law institution'.

(The) World's End, Rushton Ch, Kimpton Hrt, Curbridge O, Netley Sa; **Little World's End & World's End Meadow,** Condover Sa; **Worlds End Piece,** Solihull Wa; **World's End Wood,** Clothall Hrt: 'land on or near the boundary of the parish'.

Worledge, Brackley Nth (*Hwerveldic* 1185); **Worley,** Overstone Nth (*Wherledyks* 13c): '(land by) a circular enclosure', possibly alluding to a prehistoric stone circle [OE *hwerfel*].

Worm Close, Eggborough WRY; **Worm Howes,** Kendal We (*Wormehowe* 1409) [ON *haugr*]; **Wormshill,** Todenham Gl; **Wormpath,** Towcester Nth (*Wormpath* 1437): 'land haunted by snakes': a reference to dragons is also possible, particularly perhaps in the Kendal example [OE *wyrm*].

Wormerscroft, Titsey Sr (*Wolmescroft* 1402), possibly 'Wulfmær's croft'.

Wormland, Oxted Sr (*Womblands* 1395), 'land in a hollow' [OE *wamb*].

Worm Stills, New Hutton We, probably '(land containing) shelters for cattle against flies in hot weather' [EMnE *wormstall*].

Worthy, Kington W; **Worthy Field,** Speen Brk (*Le Worthy* 1547); **Worthy Orchard,** Govewell Paddock So: 'enclosed land' [OE *worðign*].

Wortley, Bitton Gl, 'vegetable clearing' [OE *wyrt, lēah*].

Wot Ground, Hardingstone Nth (*Woad Ground* 1752), 'land on which woad was grown' [OE *wād*].

Wounds, Cransley Nth (*The Wonges* 17c), 'in-fields' [ON *vangr*].

Wrang, Ripley Db; **Wrangett,** Hardhorn with Newton La [*-et*]; **Wrang Hey,** Hambleton La [OE *(ge)hæg*]; **Wrangland Shoals,** Willingham C [OE *sceolh*]; **Wranglands Close,** Rampton Nt; **Wranglett,** Alston La; **The Wranglings,** Enderby Lei [OE *land*]: 'crooked piece of land' [ON *vrangr*]. Wrangland Shoals seems to be tautologous, since OE *sceolh* also means 'twisted, awry'.

Wray Field, Poulton La; **Hollow Wray,** Ribby La; **Wray Meadow,** Poulton La; **Wreay,** Shap Rural We: 'land in or by a nook' [ON *vrá*].

Wren Bridge, Sutton cum Duckmanton Db; **Wren Flat,** Mickleover Db; **Wren Leaze,** Daglingworth Gl; **Wren Shay,** Brackenfield Db [OE *sceaga*]: unless there is a similar meaning here to Wren Park (qv), these names must be taken as 'land where wrens were to be found' [OE *wrenna*].

Wren Park, Ashover Db, Ault Hucknall Db, Barlborough Db, Belper Db, Brackenfield Db, Edensor Db, Findern Db, Littleover Db, Normanton Db, Sawley & Wilsthorpe Db, Stony Middleton Db, Walton Db, Wessington Db, Birch Ess, Great Bradfield Ess (*Wren Park als Denge* 1484), Bulwell Nt, Piddington O; **Wren Park Shot,** Widdington Ess (*Wrenparke* 1480); **Little Wren,** Kirk Langley Db (*The Renn Park* 1655): fanciful name for a very small field. The distribution of the name may well be wider than the selection recorded, but its frequent occurrence in Derbyshire is noteworthy. The small size of the wren may be responsible for the name, but folklore references of an (at present) obscure kind may be involved.

Wrestling Piece, Brackenfield Db, 'land used for wrestling matches'.

The Wrong, Therfield Hrt (*Le Wrong* 1596); **Wrong Land(s),** Flintham Nt, Rampton Nt; **Wrong Roods,** Newton Solney Db; **Wrongway Field,** Wesham La; **(The) Wrongs,** Alphamstone Ess (*Wronge* 1504), East Dereham Nf, Forncett St Peter Nf: 'crooked piece of land' [ON *vrangr*].

Wry Flatt, Normanton WRY; **Wry Furlong,** Aldsworth Gl; **Wry Neck,** Hope Woodlands Db, Wykin Lei; **Wry Nooks,** Walworth Du: 'twisted piece of land' [OE **wrīo*].

Wry Furlong, Norton Hrt (*Rye Furlong* 1637), 'land on which rye was grown' [OE *rȳge*].

Wych Ground, Wroxton O, 'land on which wych elms grew'. The wych elm (*Ulmus montana*) is so called because of its pliant branches [OE *wice*].

Wych Hazel Copse, Church Oakley Ha, probably alludes to a plantation of either wych elms or hornbeams (*Carpinus betulus*).

Wye Mead, Chingford Ess (*Withimede* 1498); **Wye Meadow,** Arnside We; **Wythes,** Great Strickland We; **Wythwaite,** Beetham We [ON *þveit*]: 'land by, or containing, willow trees' [OE *wīðig*, ON *víðir*].

Wyer Meadow, Somerford Booths Ch; **Wyres Leasow,** Kenley Sa: either 'land by a pond' [ME *weyour*] or 'land on which rushes or rush-like grass grew' [OE *wīr*].

Wynehousecroft, Belper Db 1415, 'site of a building in which wine was made or stored' [OE *wīn-hūs*].

(*Le*) *Wyneyard*, Almondsbury Gl 1639, Beckford Gl 1470, Eastington Gl 1542; *Wynyarde*, Pershore Wo 1547; *Wynyearde*, Great Hampton Wo 1535; *Wynyȝard*, Leigh Wo 1338: 'vineyard'. These lost names are recorded because of the evidence they provide of the location of medieval wine production in England [ON *wīn-geard*].

X

Xenophon, Halstock Do, one of the numerous arbitrary names bestowed by Thomas Hollis in the eighteenth century. Xenophon (c 430–355 BC) was honoured probably as a follower and biographer of Socrates, but perhaps also as the reputed author of the *Constitution of the Athenians*, though this work was largely anti-democratic in spirit.

Y

Yain Croft, Peover Inferior Ch, 'lambing ground' [OE (*ge*)*ēane*].

Yanham, Grayrigg We; **Yannam,** Warcop We; **Yannams,** Brough Sowerby We; **Yannims,** Clifton We: 'detached piece of land' [ON *af-nám*].

Yard End Flatts, North Elmsall WRY; **Yard Furlong,** Wroxton O (*Yerdefurlong* 1242–3); **Yard Mead,** Egham Sr (*Yerdemede* 1333): 'land having an area of a quarter of a hide, or about thirty acres' [OE *gerd*].

Yaw Hills, Beer D; **Yea Mead,** Bradford on Avon W: 'land beside a stream' [OE *ēa*].

Yeanam, Nateby We, 'detached piece of land' [ON *af-nám*].

Yeaning Plot, Alton Pancras Do, 'lambing ground' [OE (*ge*)*ēane*].

(The) Yeald, Grimley Wo; **Yeald Close,** Idridgehay Db; **Yealds,** Witton cum Twambrook Ch; **Yeld,** Eaton Ch, Aston Db; **Yeld Close,** Brough & Shetton Db; **Yeld Meadow,** Dawley Magna Sa, Hinstock Sa; **The Yelds,** Berrington Sa, Condover Sa, Hinstock Sa; **Yield Field,** Aston by Budworth Ch; **Yield Rough,** Warburton Ch; **Yielding Field,** Norbury Db; **Yielding Mead,** Merstham Sr (*Yeldale Meade* 1522): 'sloping land' [OE *helde*].

The Yell, Pauntley Gl; **Yell Bank,** Gawsworth Ch; **Yell Brow,** Rainow Ch: either 'sloping land' or 'the L, ie L-shaped piece of land'.

Yellow Bank, Strickland Roger We; **Yellow Close,** Darrington WRY; **Yellow Croft,** Nether Alderley Ch; **Yellow Ham,** Doynton Gl [OE *hamm*]; **Yellow Piece,** Buxton Db: 'land with a yellow soil' [OE *geolu*].

Yem Croft, Prees Sa, either 'riverside land', from *ēam* (dative plural of *ēa*, 'river'), or 'M-shaped piece of land'.

The Yes Field, Swerford O, 'the S-shaped piece of land'.

Yesters, Baschurch Sa, 'land by or containing sheepfolds' [OE *eowestre*].

Yew Acre, Nether Alderley Ch; **Yew Close,** Canons Ashby Nth (*Le Owe Close* 1537); **Yew Croft,** Belper Db, Ovenden WRY; **Yew Tree Close,** Bucklebury Brk, Hammoon Do, Langley & Ruckley Sa; **Yew Tree Field,** Sutton Downes Ch; **Yew Tree Ground,** Whitchurch O; **Yew Tree Hassock,** Laverstoke Ha [OE *hassuc*]; **Yew Yaw,** Colesborne Gl [OE *ēa*]: 'land beside, or containing, yew trees'. The yew (*Taxus baccata*) is found in most parts of Britain, though it particularly favours chalk downs; its long life, strength, and frequently massive proportions make it a valuable wind-break and a shelter for cattle in upland areas [OE *īw*].

Le Ympeyerd, Brewood St c 1265; *Le Ympeyorth,* Macclesfield Ch 1323: 'nursery for Saplings' [OE *impa*]. See also Imp Yard.

Yolk of Egg, Kelsall Ch, Poulton cum Spital Ch, Rope Ch, Tranmere Ch; **Yolk of the Egg,** Thornton Hough Ch, Woodford Ch: a complimentary term for a choice piece of land. It has not so far been found outside Cheshire.

Yonder Mead, Bampton D; **Yonder Meadow,** Ilsington D; **Yonder Piece,** Ashmore Do: 'land on the far side' [ME *ȝonder*].

Yott Field, Hemel Hempstead Hrt (*Yeatfeild* 1623), 'land by or with a gate' [OE *gēat*].

Z

The Zetts, North Cerney Gl, 'parcels of meadow land'. Cf Setts.

Zidles, All Canning W (*Sidehills* c 1840), 'hilly land at the side'.

Zulu Land, Marlborough W, a transferred name alluding to land in a remote part of the parish. Now part of the province of Natal, in the Union of South Africa, Zululand was intermittently in the news from about 1838 onwards (about the time of the Marlborough Tithe Award), though it of course became most prominent in 1879–80, when Britain made war on the Zulu King, Cetewayo.

APPENDIX 1

GLOSSARY OF DENOMINATIVES COMMONLY FOUND IN ENGLISH FIELD-NAMES

Acre [OE *æcer*]: (1) arable strip, individual holding in a common field; (2) piece of arable land; (3) unit of area (particularly used with numbers in modern field names). Note that local acres (eg those of Cornwall and Cheshire) may differ considerably from the statute acre.

Allotment: land allocated to an individual, especially to a manorial or parish official in former times, but to any tenant at enclosure in exchange for holding and rights under the open-field system.

Assart [ME *assart*]: a piece of land, taken from waste or forest, cleared of trees, and converted into arable.

Balk, Baulk [OE *balca*]: unploughed piece of land in a common arable field, used as an access path or (occasionally) as a boundary between furlongs; tethered animals often grazed the balks.

Bank, Bong, Bonk [ME *banke*]: (1) slope in an otherwise level field; (2) long, low mound of earth serving as a boundary; (3) riverside land.

Barrow [OE *beorg*]: natural or artificial hillock; a tumulus.

Beck [ON *bekkr*]: a stream; land beside a stream.

Berry [OE *burh*]: fortified place; earthwork.

Bog(g) [ME *bog*]: marshy or badly drained piece of land.

Borough, Bury: alternative forms for either *barrow* or *berry*.

Bottom [OE *botm*]: land at the foot of a hill; land in a valley.

Brae [ON *brá*]: hillside; slope.

Brake [OE *bræc*]: waste land covered with brushwood.

Breach, Breech [OE *brǣc, brēc*]: land (newly) broken up.

Breck [OE *bræc*]: uncultivated land.

Broad [OE *brǣdu*]: wide strip of land in the common field.

Brook [OE *brōc*]: a stream; a streamside piece of land.

Brow [OE *brū*]: projecting edge of a hill or cliff.

Burn [OE *burna*]: a spring; a stream.

Bush [OE *busc*]: thicket; land overgrown with bushes.

Butt(s): (1) [ME *butte*] section of a common arable field which is shorter than other pieces in the same furlong, owing to the irregular shape of field boundaries, or owing to two furlongs meeting at an angle; (2) [OE *butt*] tree-stump, land covered with stumps of trees; (3) [ME *butt*] mound, site of archery targets.

Car(r)(s) [ON *kjarr*]: marshy land overgrown with brushwood.

Cleugh, Clough [OE **clōh*]: deep valley or ravine; a dell.

Cliff [OE *clif*]: steep slope of a hillside; an escarpment; the steep bank of a river.

Close [ME *clos(e)*]: enclosure; fenced or hedged piece of land.

Clump [OE *clympre*]: group of trees.

Co(o)mb [OE *cumb*]: a narrow valley; a hollow in the side of a hill.

Coppice [OF *copeiz*]: (1) young growth shooting from stumps of felled trees; (2) plantation of young trees.

Copse: alternative form of coppice.

Copy: alternative form of coppice; this form arose from the mistaken idea that *copeiz* was a plural, *copy* being the 'singular' adapted from it.

Co(a)t(e), Cut(t) [OE *cot*]: cottage, hut, animal house.

Cover(t) [ME *cover*]: land overgrown with shrubs and bushes, providing shelter for game.

Crat(e), Craught: see Croft.

Croat, Croft, Croud, Crowd: small piece of land, frequently attached to a house, and almost invariably enclosed [OE *croft*].

Dale: (1) [OE *dæl*] a hollow, a valley; (2) [ON *deill*] share of the common field.

Dalt [MnE dial. *dalt*]: share of common field.

Daymath, Demath: unit of area of meadow representing the amount of land that could be mown in a day by a single worker.

Daywork, Dark, Dork: unit of area of arable land representing the amount of land that could be ploughed in a day by a single worker.

Dean(e), De(e)n(e) [OE *denu*]: a valley; this element interchanges with *dell* (see Dell).

Dell [OE *dell*]: a valley, a (chalk) pit. This element interchanges with *denu* (see Dean, above), ie, modern names including *dell* have early forms with *denu* and vice versa.

Dike, Dyke [ME *dike*]: embankment; flood-bank.

Doat, Dote [MnE dial. *dalt*]: share of the common field.

Dole [OE *dāl*]: share of the common field.

Down [OE *dūn*]: a hill; an expanse of hilly country.

Dumble [OE **dumbel*]: a hollow; a shady dell; a wooded valley.

Ed(d)ish [OE *edisc*]: an enclosure; an enclosed park or pasture.

Edge: (1) possibly a form of Eddish (qv); (2) [OE *ecg*] an escarpment.

End [OE *ende*]: outlying part of an estate or farm.

Erg [ON *erg*]: a shieling, a hill-pasture, a pasture used only in summer.

Ersh [OE *ersc*]: a ploughed field.

-et [OE *-et*]: suffix indicating 'characterised by . . .'

Etch: alternative form of Ed(d)ish (qv).

Farm [ME *ferme*]: agricultural holding, consolidated group of enclosed pieces of land constituting an agrarian unit.

Farrow [OE *fær*]: a path.

Field: see Introduction, pp xi–xii.

Fit [ON *fit*]: grassland beside a river.

Flat(t): (1) piece of level ground; (2) [ON *flat*] division of the common field; a furlong or shott.

Fold [OE *fald*]: small enclosure; pen for animals.

Furlong [OE *furlang*]: main division of a common field; a shott. Originally meaning 'the length of the furrow', the word came to be applied to the block of strips which were all of the same length.

Furrow [OE *furh*]: piece of arable land.

Garston [OE *gærs-tūn*]: a grass enclosure; a paddock.

Garth [ON *garðr*]: an enclosure.

Go(ar), Gore [OE *gāra*]: triangular plot of ground; land in the angle where two furlongs adjoin.

Gr(e)ave, Greeve [OE *grǣfe*]: a grove, copse, thicket.

Green [OE *grēne*]: a grassy spot; a permanently green place.

Ground [OE *grund*]: large piece of grassland, especially lying at a distance from the village or farm.

Grove [OE *grāf*]: a copse.

Hale, Hall [OE *halh*]: a nook of land.

Half [OE *half*]: a part, a moiety; a half-acre.

Ham(m) [OE *hamm*]: an enclosure; a meadow, a riverside meadow.

Hanger [OE *hangra*]: a wooded hill.

Hatch [OE **hǣcce*]: an enclosing fence; a fenced piece of land.

Hatchet [OE **hǣcc-geat*]: a wicket gate; a piece of land access to which is gained by a wicket gate.

Haugh [OE *halh*]: a nook of land; (NCy) piece of riverside land.

Haw [OE *haga*]: a hedge; piece of land enclosed by a hedge.

Hay(s), Hey(s) [OE *(ge)hæg*]: fenced-in piece of land; part of a forest enclosed for preserving game.

Head(land) [OE *hēafod(land)*]: strip of land left unploughed for the plough to turn on. At the end of the ploughing, the headland was dug with the spade.

Heath [OE *hǣð*]: a tract of open uncultivated ground, covered with brushwood and heather.

Hern(e) Hirn [OE *hyrne*]: a nook or corner of land; land in the bend of a river.

Heugh [OE *hōh*]: see Hoe.

Hide, Hyde [OE *hīd*]: an amount of land for the support of one free family and its dependants; the area was estimated at 120 (statute) acres.

Hield [OE *helde*]: a slope.

Hoe, Hoo, Hough [OE *hōh*]: the end of a ridge where the ground begins to fall sharply; a bank.

Hold [ME *hold*]: (1) piece of property, a holding; (2) place of shelter.

Hole [OE *hol*]: a hollow; a pit.

Holm(e) [ON *holmr*]: piece of riverside land; a water-meadow.

Holt [OE *holt*]: a wood, a thicket.

Hop(e) [OE *hop*]: a piece of enclosed land, especially in marshes.

Hoppett [OE **hoppet*]: a small enclosure.

How(e) [ON *haugr*]: a natural or artificial mound; a tumulus.

Hurst, Hyrst [OE *hyrst*]: a copse, a wood; a wooded hill or slope.

Hyrn(e) [OE *hyrne*]: nook of land; land in the bend of a river.

Ing [ON *eng*]: meadow, pasture.

Inhams, Inhom(e)s [OE**innām*, ON *innám*]: land taken in.

Inhook [ME *inhoke*]: land temporarily enclosed during the fallow course of the open field.

Inland [ME *inland*]: land near a residence, land cultivated for the owner's use and not let to a tenant.

Inning [OE **inning*]: land taken in or enclosed.

Intack, Intak(e) [ON *Inntak*]: land taken in or enclosed.

Iron: see Hirn.

Jack: unused piece of land.

Knap(p) [OE *cnæpp*]: a short, sharp ascent; a hillock.

Knoll [OE *cnoll*]: a hill top; a hillock.

Lagger(s), Layer(s) [OE *leger*]: resting place; lair.

Lake: (1) [OE *lacu*] stream, water-course; (2) [ON *leikr*] (2) place where animals play.

Land [OE *land*]: a selion, a basic unit of ploughing in common arable fields.

Lane, Lea [OE *laning*]: track; right of way; lane.

Langate, Langet(t) [OE **langet*]: long strip of land.

Lawn [OF *launde*]: an open space in woodland; a forest glade; woodland pasture.

Lea, Lee [OE *lēah*]: a wood; woodland clearing; a meadow.

Leas(e), Leaze, Leys [OE *lӕs*]: pasture; meadow land.

Leasow [OE *lӕs*, dat. *lǣswe*]: pasture; enclosed land.

Ley: (1) [OE *lēah*] meadow; (2) [OE *lǣge*] untilled land.

Linch, Lynch [OE *hlinc*]: undulating sandy ground; a ledge of ploughland on a hillside; an unploughed strip between fields.

Loon(d), Loont: see Land.

Lound, Lownd [ON *lundr*]: a small wood; a grove.

Low [OE *hlāw*]: a mound, a hill; a tumulus.

Main(s), Mesne(s) [ME *main*, *mesne*]: demesne land; home farm.

Mar(r), Marsh [ON *marr*, OE *mersc*]: a fen; boggy land.

Mead(ow) [OE *mǣd*, dat. *mǣdwe*]: grassland (kept for mowing).

Mil(d)e, Myld [OE **mylde*]: soil, earth.

Mire, Myre [ON *myrr*]: bog; swampy ground.

Moor, More [OE *mōr*]: barren waste land; marshy land.

Moss [OE *mos*]: bog or swamp, characterised by a growth of moss.

Nap(p): see Knap(p).

Nook [ME *nok*]: small secluded patch of land; a small triangular patch.

Orchard [OE *ort-geard*]: fruit garden. Originally the sense was more general.

Over [OE **ofer*]: slope, hill, ridge; river-bank.

Paddock, Parrock [OE *pearroc*]: a small (grass) enclosure.

Park [ME *park*]: enclosed tract of land for beasts of the chase; a grass enclosure; a field of any kind (especially in SW counties).

Pasture [ME *pasture*]: grassland reserved for cattle or sheep to graze on (as opposed to meadow in the strict sense).

Patch [ME *pacche*]: small piece of ground.

Pen [OE *penn*]: temporary or permanent enclosure for animals.

Pickle, Pightle [ME *pightel, pichel*]: small enclosure; a croft.

Piece [ME *pece*]: allotment or portion of land.

Pike [OE *pīc*]: pointed piece of land.

Pilch [OE *pylece* 'triangular wrapper']: triangular field.

Pingle [ME *pingel*, nasalised form of *pightel*]: small enclosure; a croft.

Plank [ME *planke*]: narrow piece of land.

Plantation: land on which young trees are grown.

Plash(et) [OF *plaschiet*]: water-logged piece of land.

Plat, Plot [ME *plat*]: small piece of ground; portion or allotment.

Pleck [ME *plek*]: small piece of land.

Pot(t) [ME *potte*]: a deep hole; land covered in holes; a hollow in a hillside.

Pre [ME *pre, prey*]: a meadow.

Quarter [ME *quartier*]: portion, allotment.

Ray, Roe [ON *vrá*]: nook; outlying piece of land.

Reading, Reeding, Rid(d)ing [OE **ryding*]: clearing in woodland; assart; land taken into cultivation from waste.

Reans, Reins [ON *reinn*]: land on a boundary.

Ridge [OE *hrycg*]: a selion, a basic unit of ploughing in common arable fields.

Rigg [ON *hryggr*]: same as Ridge.

Rood [OE *rōd*]: piece of land about a quarter of an acre in extent.

Royd [OE **rod*]: a clearing in woodland.

Sarch, Sarts: see Assart.

Screed [ME *screed*]: narrow strip of land.

Several(s) [ME *several*]: land held individually in an area of common cultivation; enclosed land amid the furlongs of an open field.

Shaw, Shay [OE *sceaga*]: small wood, copse.

Sherd, Shord [OE *sceard*]: gap or cleft in a fence; clearing in a wood.

Shoot [OE **scīete*]: corner or nook; outlying strip of land; piece of land projecting beyond another.

Shot(t) [OE *scēat*]: a block of arable land, consisting of a number of selions or lands, all running in the same direction, and having at either end a headland on which the ploughteam could turn. Synonymous with furlong or flatt.

Sick, Sitch, Su(t)ch [OE *sīc*]: piece of land beside a stream.

Slade [OE *slǣd*]: a valley; a piece of low-lying marshy land.

Slai(gh)t, Sl(e)ight [OE **slǣget*]: a sheep pasture.

Slang [EMnE *slang*]: narrow piece of land; small, sinuous field.

Sling [ME *sling*]: loop; curving-field.

Slip(e) [ME *slipe*]: narrow strip of land.

Slough [OE *slōh*]: boggy piece of land.

Spinney [ME *spinei*]: plantation of young trees.

Spot [OE **spot*]: (very) small piece of land.

Start(s), Stert, Stort [OE *steort*]: tail of land, projecting piece of a field.

Sti(t)ch, Stu(t)ch [OE *stycce*]: a bit, a piece, portion or allotment of land.

Stubb(s), Stubbing [OE *stubb, stubbing*]: land covered in tree stumps; place from which many trees have been cleared.

Thwait(e) [ON *þveit*]: a clearing; a meadow or paddock.

Tye [OE *tēag*]: enclosure; pasture.

Tyning [OE *tȳning*]: land enclosed (with a fence).

Well [OE *wella*]: spring.

Wick [OE *wīc*]: dairy-farm; land used for a special purpose, whether agricultural or industrial.

Wong [ON *vangr*]: garden, in-field; piece of land near a house; enclosed land among open strips.

Wray, Wro(e) [ON *vrá*]: nook of land.

Yard [OE *geard*]: land by a house or other building; an enclosure.

Yardland: an area of land of indefinite area, but often taken to be a quarter of a hide (qv).

Yield [OE *helde*]: a slope.

APPENDIX 2

SELECT CLASSIFIED INDEX OF FIELD-NAMES

Names listed in the following categories are a small selection of those used as main head-words of the various articles in the dictionary section. Further examples will therefore be found within those articles, as well as in other places, in addition to those referred to.

1. Size of the field

(a) *General:* Big Acres, The Crate, Fardel, Farthing, Great Acre, The Hide, Little Acres, Little Pickle, Miccle Holme, Much Close, Peahill, Pickhill Bank, The Pingle, Pith Hill, The Pleck, The Plot, Small Beer Field

(b) *Acreage:* Acre Bit, Eight Acres, Eight Butts, Eighteen Acres, Eleven Acres, Elve Acre, The Fifteen Acres, Five Acres, Five and Four Acres, Five Butts, Five Days Math, The Forty Acres, Four Acres, Fourteen Acres, The Half Acre, Hundred Acres, Nine Acres, The Nineteen Acre, The One Acre, Senacre, Sim Butts, Six Acre Close, Three Ackers, Twentiaker

(c) *Fanciful names:* Forty Acres, Handkerchief, Hundred Acres, Huntitout, Little Breakfast, Million Roods, One Thousand Acres, Other Bit, Penny Cake, Seldom Seen, Thimble Hall, Thousand Acres

2. Distance from the village

Allege, Alma, America, Antigua, Babylon, Barbadoes, Barcelona, Blenheim, Bohemia, Botany Bay, Brittany, Bunker's Hill, Calais, Canaan Farm, Come By Chance, Discovery, Fan Demons, Far Close,

Goshen, Infield, Inkerman, Inlands, Newfoundland, Nineveh, Pennsylvania, Philadelphia, Port Mahon Garden, South Sea, Spioncop, Vigo Farm, Waterloo, World's End, Zululand

3. Direction

Above Dikes, Above Town, Austrian, Back Field, Bove Town, Buff Town Close, Corner Close, East Field, Fore Down, North Close, North East Close, Outrage Close, Overthwart, Side of the Hill, Southall, Tweenabrooks, Twixt Hedges, West Brecks, Yonder Field, Zidles

4. Order

(a) *Serial:* First Close, Mead Field, Middle Acres, Nigher Field, Second Close

(b) *Chronological:* Cae Hyn, New Berry Field, Old Bake

5. Shape

Awkward Croft, Boot Close, Bran Iron Piece, Carbut Whins, Cheesecake, Diamond, Elbow, The Ell, Em Furlong, Five Cornered Close, Forked Close, Garbage Furlong, The Goar, Half Kernal, The Harp, The Heart, Heater, The Hook, Horse Shoe Field, Hourglass, The Isle of Man, Jews Trump, The L Close, Langate, Leg of Mutton, The Letter L Field, Long Acre, Mans Leg, Nackerty, Neckcloth, Oval Close, Peak Field, Ranget, Roman T, Shelboard, Shewbread, Spectacles, The Spung, Square Close, Swallow Tail, T Acres, Tea Close, Triangle, Tyrant, Woe Furlong, The Yell, The Yes Field

6. Type, consistency, and colour of soil

Allam Field, Bald Ham, Bellandy Bit, Black Acre, Bomb Crater, Bone Dust Bit, Cacklemackle, Catbrain, Chalk Close, Checker Mead, Chintz Pattern, Clay Acre, Cobra, Featherbed, Granite Piece, Gravel Close, Greedy Guts, Hungary, Improved, Lamb Pitts, Malm, Marl Churl, Pebble Close, Pudding Acre, Soon Field, Treacle Nook, Turbary Croft

7. Fertility or profitability of the land

Bacon and Beans Meadow, Bare Arse, Bare Gains, Beggar Bank, Cains Ground, Carry Nothing, Dear Bolt, Dreadful, Empty Purse, Every Years Land, Famish Acre, Gomorrah Close, Hard Bargain, Labour in Vain, Long Friday, Make Me Rich, Mares Nest, Mount Folly, Muchado, Never Gains, No Mans Friend, Pickpocket, Pinchgut, Purgatory, Raw Bones, Small Gains, Sodom, Starvation Hill, Terrible, Troublesome, Twistgut, Wheat Cake

8. Natural features of topography etc

The Aytes, Bath Close, Beck Allans, Bosom Holme, Brook Close, Flit Furlong, The Forty, Heald, High Close, Knap, Mythe Close,

The Roundabout, Rumps and Buttocks, Wham, Yaw Hills, The Yeald

9. Type of cultivation, farming practices etc

The Acre, The Assart, August, The Bake, Beaten Flat, Burnbacked Meadow, Catch Crop Field, Dencher Field, Experiment Field, Garskin Bottom, The Himpey, Hinnox, Imp Yard, Ing Close, Inoculated Meadow, Jack Bank, The Lammas, The Meadow, Paring Field, Plough Close, Prae Wood, Purley, Push Ploughed Field, Riddance Meadow, Sart Field

10. Crops

Aniseed, Apley, Averhill, Balambs, Bannet Tree Hay, Barley Arrish, Barrack Field, Bear Close, Bigg Lands, Bullace Tree Close, Carrot Bank Field, Cherry Breck, Corn Close, Crab Close, Firmity, Lentil Close, Lincroft, Liquorice Close, Maize Acre, Mangold Field, Pellet Royd Wood, Potatoe Bed, Pyrcroft, Rape, Rioth, Royal Meadow, Slaughter, Turnep Croft, Wad Barn, Walnut Crate, Wheat Acre Clough

11. Wild plants, including trees

Acorn Bank, Alder Bungs, Apple Dumpling Butts, Birch Close, Bishop's Field, Bittersweet, Blackthorn, Blue Button, Burtree Bank, Cammack Field, Devils Bit, Dog Tails, Emmy Downs, Gods Knowl, Holligores, Keddle Dock Field, Nettlebed, Oak and Elm Piece, Oldery Field, The Orles, Pildash, Rye Grass, Sycamore Close, Vastly, Wimblefield Clump, Wye Mead, Wyer Meadow

12. Domestic and farm animals

Boar Close, Bull Acre, Calf Acre, Cat Furlong, Cattle Park, Edenbro, Foal Garth, Galloping Field, Oxall, Packhorse Close, Salgasson

13. Wild animals

Adder Field, Ant Banks, Asker Meadow, Badger Close, Cannery, Clapper, Cockadine, Cocks Crowed, Conegar, Crow Barrow, Cuckoo Alter, Cushy Bank, Doe Croft, Frog Hall, Glade Shade, Magpie Shaw, Mawkin, Midge Hole, Moths Croft, Nadder Hey, Stagwell, Starks Nest, The Urchin, Woodcock Field, Wooferdine Croft

14. Buildings

Armitage, Bacchus Close, Bark Mill, Barn Close, Bold Close, Brewery Close, Bungalow Close, Chancel Pightle, Church Acre(s), Cort Field, Dove Coat, Ducket, Easter Barton, Ewster Ham, Factory Close, Foundry Piece, Gaol Meadow, Gazebo Piece, Gin House Bank, Hall Close, Hermitage, House Close, Hovel Close, Hull Piece, Jail Bird, Kirk Acre, Laith Bank, Lewshill, Linhay Field, Loose Hay, Malthouse Close, Melon Ground, Mill Acre, Minster Field, The Pesthouse,

Pin Croft, Saltpie, Tanhouse Field, Vicarage Close, Windmill Close, Yesters

15. Roads, bridges etc
Brides Hall, The Carsie, Crouch Acre, Cuckstool Field, Cup and Saucer Field, Ducking Stool, Fingerpost Close, Footpath Field, Ford Mead, Gallantree Field, Gate Close, The Handpost, Highway Close, Milestone, Navigation Close, Pylons, Sign Board Piece, Turnpike Close, Waypost Close

16. Name of the owner
Bacon Close, Chesnut Heys, Dora's Field, Gilead Farm Pudenham, Silence

17. Trade or profession of the owner or occupier
Akerleys, Anchor Croft, Bailey Brow, Bishop Field, Blacksmith's Close, Doctor's Close, Millers Butts, Wantcatcher's Hook

18. Person or object maintained by the income from the land
Abbot Flat, Alms Close, Bell Acre(s), Candle Close, Chalice Field, Chantry Barn, Charity Close, Constable's Bank, Dagtail Piece, Friars Crofts, Glebe Close, Grammarian's Field, Hangman's Acre, The Hospital, Jillywoods, Kinch Holme, Ladies Close, Mince Croft, Monk Croft, Nun Ings, Pittance Close, The Prebend, Priest Acre, Purrance, Queen Anne's Bounty, The Quire, Reeve Close, Sub-Chanters Dole, Vestry Light, Vicar Ing, Widow Hays

19. Money value of the land
The Eight Pounds Close, Eighteenpennyworth, Five Penny, Forty Shilling Close, Halfpence, Penny Bank, Seven Shilling Worth, Sixteen Pound Meadow, Ten Groats Field, Twelve Pence, Twenty Shilling Field, Twopenneworth

20. Archaeological features
Arbour, Auberry Hill, Barrow Field, Castle Field, Elbrows, Gold Hord, Ivey Close, Pavement Field, Penny Pot Garth, Rampart Close, Roman Field, Street Acre, Wheel Field, Whirl Piece

21. The supernatural, folklore, and folk customs
Bear Park, Bogard Hall Close, Congellons, Devils Acre, Elflands, Fairy Croft, Hobgoblin, Holy Well, Konjohns Hole, May Acre, May Day Field, Midsummer Leys, Morris Ground, Oxhead Close, Pixie

22. Names of arbitrary application
Aristogyton, Bacon, Blucher, Duke, Lilburne Mead, Merciful, Nelson, Plato, Plutarch, Reasonableness, Understanding, Xenophon

23. Land on a boundary
Amen Corner, The Ball, Border Close, Bound Close, Burwandes, Epistle Field, The Gospel, Horestone Mear Common, Mark Field, Mear Oak Field, Paternoster, Procession Mere, Rain Close, The Reins, Rhyme Acre, Sheer Ash, Shire Field

24. Legal terms etc
Avenham Field, Battle Bank, Candlemas Croft, The Cangle, Challenge Moor, Chatter Holt, Cheat Meadow, Copyhold, Demesne, Enams, Encroachment, England, Flitlands, Franchise Croft, Freehold Close, Frith and Brith, Gist Head & Foot, How-so Meadow, Hundred, The Inake, Jointry, Lady Day Close, Main, Manchips Field, The Morrey, Parliament, Proxies, Tenantry Down

25. Industrial use of land
Bleach Field, Car Coal Field, Cinder Croft, Coal Pit Close, Cold Bakers, Cupids Close, Delfs, Dyer Lands, Frame Close, Gig Field, Kill Close, Limekiln Bottom, Oven Close, Pet Field, Quar Bush, Quisters Hey, Rack Close, Salt Acre, Sawpit Bank, Tanter Bank, Walk Close, Witness Close, Woolhedge Garth

26. Games
Bowlaway, Camping Close, Dancers Meadow, Football Butts, Plaistow, Play Cross, Playing Close, Prison Bar Field, Sport Field

APPENDIX 3

ARBITRARY FIELD-NAMES IN HALSTOCK, DORSET

The most numerous series of arbitrary, commemorative names is found among the field-names of Halstock, Dorset. The following survived to the early nineteenth century, and have been extracted from the Tithe Apportionment. It will be seen that most of these are simplex names, ie they have no denominative component; the only obvious exceptions are Lilburne Mead and Hiero Coppice. New England, though it fits the series if it is a transferred name from the North American place, may of course be a coincidental occurrence of a name possibly embodying ME *inland*.

Aristogyton
Aristotle
Bacon
Bastwick
Berne
Birch
Boston
Bradshaw
Brooke
Brutus
Burton
Care
Cicero
Commonwealth
Confusius
Constitution
Cook
Cotton
Education
Eliot
Freestate
Geneva
The Good Old Cause
Goodwin
Government
Hanover
Harmodius
Harris
Harrisons
Harvard
Hervey
Hiero Coppice
Holland
Hollis
Hutchinson
Ireton
January 30th
Kennett
Lampugnano
Lay Preacher
Leicester
Leslie
Liberty
Lilburne Mead
Locke
Ludlow
Lycurgus
Machiaval

Marvell	Peters	Socrates
Massachusetts	Plato	Solon
Menio	Plutarch	Sydney
Molineaux	Prynne	Temple
Mysala	Pythagoras	Thrasybulus
Nassaw	Reasonableness	Timoleon
Needham	Republic	Tindal
Neville	Revolution	Toleration
New England	Russell	Valtravers
Northumberland	Savile	Vane
Numa	Scot	Vevay
Olgiati	Secker	Webb
Pelopidas	Settlement	Xenophon

It will be seen that these names include those of political theorists of classical, medieval and more recent times; tyrannicides of all periods; places associated with the Puritans; other places famous for their democracy; the date of the execution of Charles I; politicians and generals of the Puritan revolution; and the virtues particularly revered by the men of the Commonwealth and by Thomas Hollis himself, whose name, it will be observed, is included in the list. Hollis was born in 1720 and early in life inherited extensive properties, from not only his father but also his great-uncle Thomas Hollis, benefactor of Harvard College. Hollis spent several hundred pounds yearly on books, many of which he presented to libraries, particularly those at Harvard, Berne and Zurich. He led the life of a recluse and abstained from alcohol, spices, salt, butter, milk and sugar. He was notorious for his extreme republican views, and was even reputed an atheist (though in fact he was a man of intense personal piety). He retired to a cottage on his Dorset estate in 1770 and died in 1774.

Hollis's interest in religious matters is illustrated by the names he gave to his land in Corscombe. These include **Calvin, Knox, Luther, Henry VIII,** and **Edward VI**. **Cromwell** refers to Thomas (c1485–1540), rather than to Oliver, the Protector. Less famous persons include **Coligny** and **Jerome of Prague**. The 1655 massacre of the Vaudois is recalled in **Waldenses** and **Piedmont Coppice**. Other names in this parish commemorate figures and features of legal history, such as **Bracton, Coke,** and **Selden,** together with **Magna Carta** and **Fleta,** the latter alluding to the summary of Bracton's *On the Laws and Customs of England*.. For further details see M. Lemmey: *The History of Halstock* (1985), pp. 31–3 and J. Field: *Compliment and Commemoration in English Field-Names*, 2nd edn. (1986), pp. 18–23.

BIBLIOGRAPHY

The dates cited are those of editions consulted

General historical works

Collingwood, R. G., and Myres, J. N. L., *Roman Britain and the English Settlements*, Oxford University Press, 1956

Darby, H. C., *Historical Geography of England*, Cambridge UP, 1951

Poole, A. L., *Medieval England*, OUP, 1958

Stenton, F. M., *Anglo-Saxon England*, OUP, 1947

Stenton, F. M., *The Danes in England* (British Academy Ralegh Lecture, 1927), OUP, 1957

General works on place-names and field-names

Cameron, K., *English Place-Names*, Batsford, 1963

Dickins, B. 'The progress of English place-names studies since 1901', *Antiquity*, XXXV (1961), 281–5

Ekwall, E., *Concise Oxford Dictionary of English Place-Names*, 3rd ed, OUP, 1951

Ekwall, E., *English River Names*, OUP, 1968

Ekwall, E., *Studies on English Place-Names*, Stockholm, 1936

Mawer, A., *Problems of Place-Name Study*, Cambridge UP, 1929

Mawer, A., 'The study of field-names in relation to place-names', in *Historical Essays in Honour of James Tait*, Manchester University Press, 1933

Mawer, A., and Stenton, F. M., *Introduction to the Survey of English Place-Names* (EPNS, I, Part i), CUP, 1933

Reaney, P. H., *The Origin of English Place Names*, Routledge, 1964

Smith, A. H., *English Place-Name Elements* (EPNS XXV, XXVI), Cambridge UP, 1956
Wainwright, F. T., *Archaeology and Place-Names and History*, Routledge, 1962
Wainwright, F. T., 'Field-names', *Antiquity*, XVII (1943), 57–66

Fields and field systems

Emmison, F. G., *Some Types of Common-Field Parish*, Standing Conference for Local History, 1965
Gray, H. L., *English Field Systems*, Merlin Press, 1959
Orwin, C. S. and C. S., *The Open Fields*, Oxford, 1967
Thirsk, J., 'The common fields', *Past & Present*, 29 (December, 1964), 3–25
Thirsk, J., 'The origin of the common fields', *Past & Present*, 33 (1966), 142–7
Titow, J. Z., 'Medieval England and the open-field system', *Past & Present*, 32 (December, 1965), 86–102

County and local surveys of place-names and field-names

Armstrong, A. M., and others, *The Place-Names of Cumberland* (EPNS, XX–XXII), CUP, 1950–2
Beresford, M. W., 'Glebe terriers and open field Leicestershire', *Transactions of the Leicestershire Archaeological Society*, XXV (1948), 77–126
Beresford, M. W., 'Glebe terriers and open field, Yorkshire', *Transactions of the Yorkshire Archaeological Society*, XXXVIII
Cameron, K., *The Place-Names of Derbyshire* (EPNS XXVII–XXIX), CUP, 1959
Dodgson, J. McN., *The Place-Names of Cheshire* (EPNS XLIV–XLVI: in progress), CUP 1970–1
Ekwall, E., *The Place-Names of Lancashire*, Manchester UP, 1922
Field, J., *Field-Names of the Gartree Hundred of Leicestershire* (unpublished MA thesis, University of Leicester), 1961
Fraser, W., *Field-Names in South Derbyshire*, Ipswich, 1947
Gelling, M., *The Place-Names of Oxfordshire* (EPNS XXIII, XXIV), CUP, 1953–4
Gover, J. E. B., and others, *The Place-Names of Devon* (EPNS VIII, IX) CUP, 1931–2
Gover, J. E. B., and others, *The Place-Names of Hertfordshire* (EPNS XV), CUP, 1938
Gover, J. E. B., and others, *The Place-Names of Middlesex* (EPNS XVIII), CUP, 1942
Gover, J. E. B., and others, *The Place-Names of Northamptonshire* (EPNS X), CUP, 1933

Gover, J. E. B., and others, *The Place-Names of Nottinghamshire* (EPNS XVII), CUP, 1940
Gover J. E. B., and others, *The Place-Names of Surrey* (EPNS XI), CUP, 1934
Gover, J. E. B., and others, *The Place-Names of Warwickshire* (EPNS XIII), CUP, 1936
Gover, J. E. B., and others, *The Place-Name of Wiltshire* (EPNS XVI), CUP, 1939
Grundy, G. B., *Saxon Charters and Field-Names of Somerset*, Bristol, 1935
Grundy, G. B., *Saxon Charters and Field-Names of Gloucestershire*, Bristol, 1935
Grundy, G. B., 'Saxon charters and field-names of Hampshire', *Archaeological Journal* 1921, 1924, 1926, 1927
Hoskins, W. G., 'The fields of Wigston Magna', *Transactions of the Leicestershire Archaeological Society*, XIX, 1943
Kerr, B., 'Dorset fields and their names', *Archaeology and History* (Dorset Nat Hist Soc Proceedings), 235–56, 1967
Kökeritz, H., *The Place-Names of the Isle of Wight*, Uppsala, 1940
Mawer, A., *The Place-Names of Northumberland and Durham*, CUP 1920
Mawer, A., and Stenton, F. M., *The Place-Names of Bedfordshire and Huntingdonshire* (EPNS III), CUP, 1926
Mawer, A., and Stenton, F. M., *The Place-Names of Buckinghamshire* (EPNS II), CUP, 1925
Mawer, A., and Stenton, F. M., *The Place-Names of Sussex* (EPNS VI, VII), CUP, 1929, 1930
Mawer, A., and Stenton, F. M., *The Place-Names of Worcestershire* (EPNS IV), CUP, 1927
O'Leary, J. G., *Dagenham Place-Names*, Dagenham Public Library, 1958
Reaney, P. H., *The Place-Names of Cambridgeshire and the Isle of Ely* (EPNS XIX), CUP, 1943
Reaney, P. H., *The Place-Names of Essex* (EPNS XII), CUP, 1935
Reaney, P. H., *The Place-Names of Walthamstow*, Walthamstow, 1930
Smith, A. H., *The Place-Names of the East Riding of Yorkshire* (EPNS XIV), CUP, 1964
Smith, A. H., *The Place-Names of Gloucestershire* (EPNS XXXVII–XLI), CUP, 1964
Smith, A. H., *The Place-Names of the North Riding of Yorkshire* (EPNS V), CUP, 1928
Smith, A. H., *The Place-Names of the West Riding of Yorkshire* (EPNS XXX–XXXVII), 1961–2

Smith, A. H., *The Place-Names of Westmorland* (EPNS XLII, XLIII), CUP, 1967
Wainwright, F. T., 'Field-names of Amounderness Hundred', *Transactions of the Historic Society of Lancashire and Cheshire*, XCIX, 181–222, 1945

Other local and general studies

Davies, J. C., *Bowden to Harborough*, Market Harborough, 1964
Finberg, H. P. R., *Gloucestershire*, Hodder & Stoughton, 1956
Fleure, H. J., *A Natural History of Man in Britain*, Collins, 1951
Gooder, A., *Plague and Enclosure: a Warwickshire Village in the Seventeenth Century*, Extra-Mural Department, University of Birmingham, 1965
Hoskins, W. G., *Leicestershire*, Hodder & Stoughton, 1957
Hoskins, W. G., *The Making of the English Landscape*, Penguin, 1970
Hoskins, W. G., *The Midland Peasant*, Macmillan, 1965
Jennings, P., *The Living Village*, Hodder & Stoughton, 1968
Millward, R., *Lancashire*, Hodder & Stoughton, 1955
Russell, Sir E. J., *The World of the Soil*, Collins, 1961
Stamp, L. D., *Britain's Structure and Scenery*, Collins, 1968
Stamp, L. D., *Man and the Land*, Collins, 1955
Trueman, A. E., *Geology and Scenery in England and Wales*, Penguin Books, 1949

Agricultural history

Ernle, Lord, *English Farming Past and Present*, Heinemann, 1961
Higgs, J., *The Land* (Visual History of Modern Britain series) Studio Vista, 1964
Orwin, C. S., *A History of English Farming*, Nelson, 1949
Seebohm, M. A., *The Evolution of the English Farm*, Allen & Unwin, 1952

Special topics

Brimble, L. J. F., *Flowers in Britain*, Macmillan, 1944
Butlin, R. A., 'Some terms used in agrarian history', AHR, IX, 98–104, 1961
Clark, C. M. H., *A History of Australia* (2 vols), Melbourne, 1968
Dodgson, J. McN., 'Cheshire field-name elements' [*day-math*, *day-work*, and *slang*], *Notes & Queries*, NS 15 (1968), 123–4
Earle, J., *English Plant Names from the Tenth to the Fifteenth Century*, Oxford, Clarendon Press, 1890
Edlin, H. L., *British Woodland Trees*, Batsford, 1944
Edlin, H. L., *Trees, Woods, and Man*, Collins, 1956
Field, J. E., *The Myth of the Pent Cuckoo*, 1913

Fisher, J., *Bird Recognition* (3 volumes), Penguin Books, 1947
Hubbard, C. E., *Grasses*, Penguin Books, 1954
Hurry, J. B., *The Woad Plant and its Dye*, OUP, 1930
Hutchinson, J., *Common Wild Flowers*, Penguin Books, 1946
Pitt, F., *Birds in Britain*, Macmillan, 1948
Ranson, F., *British Herbs*, Penguin Books, 1949
Stokoe, W. J., *The Observer's Book of British Grasses, Sedges, and Rushes*, Warne, 1942

ADDITIONAL BIBLIOGRAPHY

Adams, I. H., *Agrarian Landscape Terms: a Glossary for Historical Geography*, Inst. of British Geographers, 1976
Beckensall, S., *Northumberland Field Names*, Newcastle, Graham, 1977
Bond, J., 'Oxfordshire field-names', *Oxfordshire Local History*, 1 (1982), 2–15
Cameron, K., 'Early field-names in an English-named Lincolnshire village', in Sandgren, F. (ed.), *Otium & Negotium*, Stockholm, Kungl. Backtryckeriet, 1973, 38–43
Fellows-Jensen, 6., 'English field-names and the Danish settlement', *Festskrift til Kristian Hald*, Copenhagen, 1974, 43–5
Field, J., *Compliment & Commemoration in English Field-Names*, Edinburgh, Council for Name Studies, 1973; 2nd edn. 1986
—, 'Crops for man and beast', *Leeds Studies in English* XVIII (1987), 157–71
—, 'Derogatory field-names', *EPNS Journal* 9 (1976–77), 19–25
—, 'Land, people and field-names', *Bedfordshire Family Hist. Soc. Jnl.* 6 (1987–88), 25–30
—, 'Progress in field-name studies', *Local Historian* 13 (1978–79), 388–96
—, 'Rutland field names: some comparisons and contrasts', *Rutland Record* 1 (1980), 19–24
—, 'Size and shape in English field nomenclature', *Names* 23 (1975), 6–25
Foxall, H. D. G., *Shropshire Field Names*, Shrewsbury, Shropshire Archaeological Society, 1980
Insley, J., 'Field-names and the Scandinavian settlement of England', *Beiträge zur Namenforschung* 23 (1985), 113–28
—, 'Personal names in field and minor names', *EPNS Journal* 10 (1977–78), 41–72
Keene, C. H., *The Field-Names of the London Borough of Ealing*, (Field-Name Studies No. 1), Nottingham, EPNS 1976

Mills, A. D., 'Some alternative analyses of medieval field-names', *Leeds Studies in English* XVIII (1987), 201–8
Standing, R., *The Field-Names of Angmering, Ferring, East Preston, Kingston* (Field-Name Studies No. 2), Nottingham, EPNS 1986

ACKNOWLEDGEMENTS

I am grateful to Professor Kenneth Cameron, Honorary Director of the Survey of English Place-Names, for much helpful advice and for his courtesy in allowing me to make abundant use of the publications of the English Place-Name Society. My thanks are also due to a number of other friends in the Society. Dr Margaret Gelling and Mr David Mills kindly provided lists of field-names from collections they are assembling for their respective volumes of the Survey, on Berkshire and Dorset. Through the kind offices of Messrs J. McN. Dodgson and A. R. Rumble I have been able to make use of other unpublished lists in the possession of the English Place-Name Society.

Dr V. G. Watts very generously provided lists from his County Durham collection. I must also thank Mr David Tew for supplying Rutland names, and Dr Barrie Cox for filling gaps in my Leicestershire lists. Mr H. D. G. Foxall not only sent me lists of Shropshire names, but also replied very fully to many supplementary enquiries. Tribute must be paid to his careful mapping of the field-names of numerous Shropshire townships; these copies of the tithe maps have been most valuable, and it is to be hoped that Mr Foxall's example will be followed by local historians and cartographers in other counties. I am glad and grateful to be able to reproduce one of these excellent maps.

Miss Barbara Kerr's article, 'Dorset fields and their names', is widely admired, and I am grateful to her for permission to quote from it.

I acknowledge with thanks permission to make use of lists of modern field-names collected by the Devon Federation of Women's Institutes and the Leicestershire and Rutland Federation of Women's Institutes.

I am grateful to Mr Leslie Dunkling, president of the Names Society, for his friendly interest and his kindness in enabling me to make contact with a number of correspondents, among whom Messrs C. V. Appleton, G. A. Coulson, D. W. Hamley, and H. B. Sharp have provided some useful lists of names.

The prompt and courteous assistance of librarians and archivists must also be acknowledged. Thanks are due to Dr Leslie Parker, county archivist of Leicestershire, for his help, and to Mr G. A. Chinnery, archivist of the City of Leicester, whose assistance was most valuable to me when I was making my collection of Leicestershire names. It must also be placed on record that the collection of names in the Sparkenhoe and Guthlaxton Hundreds of Leicestershire was made possible by a generous grant by the Leverhulme Trustees, to whom I offer my sincere thanks.

Mr John Parfitt, librarian of Dacorum College, and his staff, are cordially thanked for their unfailing help. I am grateful also to my colleagues, Mr Ralph Ison and Mr Derek Bloxham, for many valuable suggestions during the progress of this work.

Though I leave until last my thanks to my wife, it is not because her help has been any less than that of others or that my gratitude is less real.

INDEX

This general index refers to material contained in the Introduction and Appendices, and to selected topics not readily found in the alphabetical entries in the Dictionary.